John Donne
An Annotated Bibliography of Modern Criticism
1912–1967

University of Missouri Studies LX

JOHN DONNE

An Annotated Bibliography of Modern Criticism

1912–1967

John R. Roberts

University of Missouri Press
Columbia, 1973

Copyright © 1973 by
The Curators of the University of Missouri
University of Missouri Press, Columbia, Missouri 65201
ISBN 0–8262–0136–9
Library of Congress Catalog Number 72–93760
Printed and bound in the United States of America

To the Memory
of
Helen C. White

Contents

Preface

The aim of this bibliography is to provide students of John Donne with a much needed research tool. This study is the first to collect and annotate the extensive criticism and scholarship on Donne written in this century. In part, however, the present effort is an extension of and elaboration on portions of earlier bibliographical studies: *Studies in Metaphysical Poetry: Two Essays and a Bibliography* by Theodore Spencer and Mark Van Doren (New York: Columbia University Press, 1939) and A *Bibliography of Studies in Metaphysical Poetry* 1939–1960, compiled by Lloyd E. Berry (Madison: University of Wisconsin Press, 1964). As their titles indicate, both works include not only Donne but the other metaphysical poets as well; however, neither is annotated. Spencer and Van Doren list items from 1912 to 1938; Berry continues from 1939 to 1960. My study begins at 1912, the date of H. J. C. Grierson's monumental edition of Donne's poetry. Although all scholars are aware that the modern interest in Donne did not suddenly burst forth on the scene in that year, Grierson's edition was the first major effort in this century to deal with Donne in a thoroughly scholarly and serious way. The present bibliography ends at 1967, a purely arbitrary point, since more recent studies were not always available and bibliographical aids were incomplete.

In 1931, the tercentenary anniversary of Donne's death, T. S. Eliot, one of the critics most responsible for Donne's enormous popularity in the twentieth century, announced that "Donne's poetry is a concern of the present and the recent past, rather than of the future" ("Donne in Our Time" in A *Garland for John Donne 1631–1931*, ed. Theodore Spencer [Cambridge, Mass.: Harvard University Press], p. 5). Berry's work and this bibliography prove that that prophetic utterance was mistaken. Donne continues to engage some of the best minds of the scholarly world, and nearly all serious students of literature recognize that he occupies a permanent and significant position in our understanding of the development of English poetry.

Some of the items in this bibliography are admittedly minor efforts, but others represent major contributions to our understanding and knowledge not only of Donne but of the seventeenth century, of metaphysical poets as a whole, and even of the nature of poetry. Although my own critical biases and preferences may at times show, the annotations are not evaluative, because what is important and/or useful to one scholar or critic, I find, may not be equally so for another. In referring to Donne's poems, I have followed H. J. C. Grierson's text (1929).

I have tried to make the bibliography as complete and comprehensive as possible, but from the first it was clear that certain limitations had to be imposed. The basic guideline has been to include all articles and books specifically about Donne written from 1912 to 1967. I have also attempted to include extended discussions of Donne that appear in books not centrally concerned with him. Nearly every book or article concerning metaphysical poetry or individual metaphysical poets contains some discussion of Donne, but the inclusion of all items that mention Donne in relation to Herbert, Crashaw, Vaughan, Marvell, Carew, Traherne, *et al.* would have extended the present bibliography far beyond manageable bounds. Since my primary aim is to list and annotate Donne criticism, I have not included all editions of the poetry and prose that have appeared in this century. I have included, however, the ones that contain significant critical discussion, such as the California edition of the sermons. Publications are listed according to the date of the edition I used in preparing my bibliographic entry; reprints, revisions, and new editions have not, in all instances, been recorded. Book reviews have been excluded, for the most part, and brief mentions in books and articles as well as references in encyclopedias and literary histories have been omitted. Dissertations have been eliminated. The reader is encouraged, however, to check *Dissertation Abstracts* and *Dissertation Abstracts International* for the more recent ones. Many items written in foreign languages have been included, but no full, systematic attempt has been made to find them all.

It is a pleasure to acknowledge and thank those who have generously assisted in this project. First of all, I am most indebted to the efforts of my two research assistants, Marcia and Douglas Collins, who painstakingly gathered materials and did much of the preliminary work that made this study possible. I wish to thank Professor Lloyd E. Berry and Professor Burton A. Milligan, both of the University of Illinois, who, at different times, encouraged me and suggested several improvements. Mrs. Ann-Todd Rubey, Humanities Librarian at the University of Missouri—Columbia, was always helpful in locating books and articles unavailable in the University of Missouri library. Several members of the faculty and students of the University of Missouri—Columbia, helped me with items in foreign languages, particularly M. Bonner Mitchell, Dennis M. Mueller, Anthony DeBellis, Maarten Nieuwenhuizen, Karen Nickell, Norimasa Oshiro, and Alvaro Bueno. I owe much to my colleagues in the Department of English at the University of Missouri for their helpful suggestions. My wife, Lorraine, not only proofread the final draft but, like all good wives, supported me by listening and encouraging. I wish also to acknowledge the assistance of the Faculty Research Council of the University of Missouri, which supported the project by awarding to me two Summer Research Fellowships and other smaller grants. I wish to thank the Marquis of Lothian and the National Portrait Gallery, London, for allowing me to use the Lothian portrait of Donne.

This bibliography is dedicated to the memory of the late Professor Helen C. White of the University of Wisconsin. Years ago, when I was beginning my academic career, Professor White inspired me to center my scholarly interests on Donne and the metaphysical poets. I have always felt grateful for her advice and example.

J. R. R.
Columbia, Missouri
September 1, 1972

Abbreviations of Titles
of Journals

ABR • American Benedictine Review

AION-SG • Annali Istituto Universitario Orientale, Napoli, Sezione Germanica

AL • American Literature

AN&Q • American Notes and Queries (New Haven, Conn.)

Archiv • Archiv für das Studium der Neueren Sprachen und Literaturen

BB • Bulletin of Bibliography

BJRL • Bulletin of the John Rylands Library

BLR • Bodleian Library Record

BNYPL • Bulletin of the New York Public Library

BuR • Bucknell Review

C&M • Classica et Mediaevalia

CathW • Catholic World

CE • College English

CL • Comparative Literature

CLAJ • College Language Association Journal (Morgan State Coll., Baltimore)

CLS • Comparative Literature Studies (U. of Ill.)

CR • The Critical Review (Melbourne)

CritQ • Critical Quarterly

DownR • Downside Review

DUJ • Durham University Journal

EA • Etudes Anglaises

E&S • Essays and Studies by Members of the English Association

EIC • Essays in Criticism (Oxford)

ELH • Journal of English Literary History

ELN • English Language Notes (U. of Colo.)

EM • English Miscellany

ES • English Studies

ESPSL • O Estado de São Paulo, Suplemento Literário

Expl • Explicator

GR • Germanic Review

GRM • Germanisch-romanische Monatsschrift, Neue Folge

HLQ • Huntington Library Quarterly

HudR • Hudson Review

JAAC • Journal of Aesthetics and Art Criticism

JEGP • Journal of English and Germanic Philology

JHI • Journal of the History of Ideas

KR • Kenyon Review

L&P • Literature and Psychology (U. of Hartford)

LHR • Lock Haven Review (Lock Haven State Coll., Pa.)

McNR • McNeese Review (McNeese State Coll., La.)

MissQ • Mississippi Quarterly

ML • Modern Languages (London)

MLN • Modern Language Notes

MLQ • Modern Language Quarterly

MLR • Modern Language Review

MP • Modern Philology

MR • Massachusetts Review (U. of Mass.)

MSpr • Moderna Språk (Stockholm)

N&Q • Notes and Queries

Neophil • Neophilologus (Groningen)

NRF • Nouvelle Revue Française

NS • Die Neueren Sprachen

PBA • Proceedings of the British Academy

PBSA • Papers of the Bibliographical Society of America

Person • The Personalist

PLPLS • Proc. Leeds Philosoph. and Lit. Soc.

PMASAL • Papers of the Mich. Acad. of Science, Arts, and Letters

PMLA • Publications of the Mod. Lang. Assn. of America

PoetryR • Poetry Review (London)

PQ • Philological Quarterly (Iowa City)

PR • Partisan Review

PSA • Papeles de Son Armadans (Mallorca)

QJS • Quarterly Journal of Speech

QQ • Queen's Quarterly

REL • Review of English Literature (Leeds)

RenP • Renaissance Papers

RES • Review of English Studies

RFE • Revista de Filología Española

RHT • Revue d'Histoire du Théâtre

RLV • Revue des Langues Vivantes (Bruxelles)

RN • Renaissance News

RSH • Revue des Sciences Humaines

RusR • Russian Review

SAB • South Atlantic Bulletin

SAQ • South Atlantic Quarterly

SB • Studies in Bibliography: Papers of the Bibliographical Society of the University of Virginia

SCN • Seventeenth-Century News

SEL • Studies in English Literature, 1500–1900

SN • Studia Neophilologica

SoR • Southern Review (Louisiana State U.)

SP • Studies in Philology

SR • Sewanee Review

SRen • Studies in the Renaissance

SUSFL • Studi Urbinati di Storia, Filosofia e Letteratura

TCBS • Transactions of the Cambridge Biblio. Soc.

TLS • [London] Times Literary Supplement

TNTL • Tijdschr. voor Ned. Taal- en Letterkunde (Leiden)

TSE • Tulane Studies in English

TSL • Tennessee Studies in Literature

TSLL • Texas Studies in Literature and Language

URev • University Review (Dublin)

UTQ • University of Toronto Quarterly

UWR • University of Windsor Review (Windsor, Ontario)

XUS • Xavier University Studies

1912

᪐§ 1. DONNE, JOHN. *The Poems of John Donne*. Edited from old editions and numerous manuscripts, with introductions and commentary, by Herbert J. C. Grierson. Vol. I, The text of the poems, with appendices; Vol. II, Introduction and commentary. Oxford: The Clarendon Press. xxiv, 474 p.; cliii, 276 p.

Reprinted, 1953.

One-volume ed. with a revision of the critical introduction, 1929.

Pages xxxiv–xlix of Volume II are reprinted with slight alterations in *John Donne: A Collection of Critical Essays*, ed. Helen Gardner (1962), pp. 23–35.

Pages xlv–xlvii are reprinted in *Discussions of John Donne*, ed. Frank Kermode (1962), pp. 39–40.

Volume I contains the complete poems in the order of the 1633 edition. For those poems that do not appear in this edition, the first edition in which they do appear (1635, 1649, 1650, 1669) is the authority. Earlier editions and most of the extant manuscripts were consulted and taken into account. Three appendices: (1) Donne's Latin poems and translations; (2) poems wrongly attributed to Donne in the old editions (1633–1669) and the principal manuscript collections, arranged according to their probable authors; (3) a selection of poems that frequently accompany poems by Donne in manuscript collections or have been ascribed to him by modern editors. Index of first lines. Volume II contains a critical introduction to Donne's poems (pp. v–lv), a discussion of the text and canon of the poems (pp. lvi–cliii), and an extensive commentary on individual poems (pp. 1–275).

᪐§ 2. LANG, ANDREW. "Late Elizabethan and Jacobean Poets," in *History of English Literature from "Beowulf" to Swinburne*, pp. 283–302. London: Longmans, Green and Co., Ltd.

Short, generally unfavorable account of Donne's poetry (pp. 284–88). "He is a poet by flashes, which are very brilliant with strange coloured fires. . . . His poetry . . . exercised an influence not wholly favourable on his successors; happily it did not affect Lovelace and Herrick" (p. 288).

᪐§ 3. REED, EDWARD BLISS. "The Jacobean and Caroline Lyric," in *Elizabethan Lyrical Poetry from Its Origins to the Present Time*, pp. 233–301. New Haven: Yale University Press; London: Humphrey Milford and Oxford University Press.

Surveys works of twenty seventeenth-century poets. The comments on Donne are a curious blend of praise and disapproval. Donne "wrote verses crabbed and unmusical in their movement and disconcerting, to say the least, in their rhymes" (p. 235). These "unmusical moments" are attributed to at least three factors: (1) Donne's poems were "struck off at white heat, and were never revised" (p. 237); (2) "instead of deliberately and searching painfully for the well-made phrase, he was content with the first imperfect utterance" (p. 237); (3) "he flouted the ideas of the day" and with a "morbid strain" deliberately challenged the sweetness of Spenser and others. Suggests that Donne's reputation has fallen into neglect in part because of his shocking subject matter and tone: "To-day Donne's poems are never imitated; they are not even widely read, for though he has his circle of devoted admirers, their number is small" (p. 233).

⋙ 4. SAINTSBURY, GEORGE. A *History of English Prose Rhythms*. London: Macmillan and Co., Ltd. 489 p.
Donne is mentioned in passing but always approvingly. A short passage from one of the sermons is briefly analyzed for its rhythmical effects (pp. 162–63). Concludes that the passage has "never been surpassed" for its wedding of "Shakespearian diction" with "absolute perfection of rhythmical—never metrical—movement" (p. 163).

⋙ 5. SPEARING, EVELYN M. "Donne's Sermons, and Their Relation to His Poetry." *MLR*, 7:40–53.
Regrets that no modern edition of Donne's prose works exists and that insufficient critical attention has been given to them. Argues that Donne exhibits the "same agility of intellect and same intensity of imagination" (p. 40) in his prose that can be found in his poetry and examines briefly this relationship. Maintains that "It is the 'quintessenced, passionate, melancholy imagination' of Donne, which pervades both his poetry and prose, and finds in both its chief delight in the contemplation of Love and Death, that forms the real link between the two modes of expression" (p. 48).

⋙ 6. THOMAS, [PHILIP] EDWARD. *The Tenth Muse*. London: Martin Secker. vii, 141 p.
Survey of twenty-four love poets from Chaucer to Shelley. Considers Donne briefly (pp. 21–28). Mostly a cataloguing of several of Donne's attitudes toward women and love as reflected in a number of his love poems.

1913

⋙ 7. BROOKE, RUPERT. "John Donne." *Poetry and Drama*, 1:185–88.
Approximately half of this article is a review of Grierson's edition of the poems; the remainder is Brooke's own thoughts on Donne's poetry, especially its intellectuality and nonvisual aspects. "He never visualizes,

or suggests that he has any pleasure in looking at things. His poems might all have been written by a blind man in a world of blind men" (pp. 186–87). Praises Donne for his ability to "curiously wed fantastic imagination with the most grave and lofty music of poetry" (p. 188).

≈§ 8. Moore-Smith, G. C. "Donniana." *MLR*, 8:47–52.
Lists some forty corrections, queries, and suggestions concerning relatively minor points in Sir Edmund Gosse's *Life and Letters of John Donne* (1899). Had submitted a similar list earlier to *MLR*, 4 (1908–1909). Withdraws two objections listed in the earlier article.

≈§ 9. Rhys, Ernest. "Metaphysical Lyrics—The 'Sons of Ben'—The Puritan Repression—Herrick," in *Lyric Poetry*, pp. 195–209. London and Toronto: J. M. Dent & Sons, Ltd.; New York: E. P. Dutton & Co., Inc.
Brief, uncomplimentary evaluation of Donne's poetry. "In his cycle of love-poems, he moves from verses that seize the ear and hold it with intense melody to others that fall dull as schoolmaster's jests" (pp. 195–96). Sees Donne as an overly ingenious juggler of words and ideas.

≈§ 10. Schelling, Felix E. "Lyrical Poetry in the England of the Tudors," in *The English Lyric*, pp. 31–72. Boston: Houghton Mifflin Co.
Points out some general characteristics of the poems, especially Donne's originality in his uses of the metaphor.

≈§ 11. Spearing, E. M. "A Chronological Arrangement of Donne's Sermons." *MLR*, 8:468–83.
Reprinted in *A Study of the Prose Works of John Donne*, ed. Evelyn Simpson (1924), pp. 340–55; 2d ed. (1948), pp. 339–56.
Gives three lists: (1) the sermons that have a date clearly given in the heading; (2) those for which conjectural or approximate dates can be given; (3) those for which no date can be assigned. Of the 154 sermons considered, only 30 are relegated to the last category.

≈§ 12. Spurgeon, Caroline F. E. "Philosophical Mystics," in *Mysticism in English Literature*, pp. 72–110. Cambridge: Cambridge University Press.
Argues that in Donne's treatment of love, his mystical attitude is most obviously presented. "He holds the Platonic conception, that love concerns the soul only, and is independent of the body, or bodily presence; and he is the poet, who, at his best, expresses this idea in a most dignified and refined way" (p. 75). Considers none of Donne's specifically religious poems. Maintains that Donne was "so richly endowed with intellectual gifts, yet failed to reach the highest rank as a poet" (p. 73).

1914

⫷§ 13. EATON, HORACE AINSWORTH. "The *Songs and Sonnets* of John Donne." *SR*, 22:50–72.

Appreciative essay on general characteristics of the poetic style, temperament, and range of ideas in the *Songs and Sonets*. Calls them "records of the struggles and visions of youth" (p. 71). Praises their spontaneity, sincerity, and intimate quality: "They lie, indeed, too close to intense emotions for perfect expression, but in that gain splendor of momentary effects" (p. 71).

⫷§ 14. GOSSE, EDMUND. *Gossip in a Library*. New York: Charles Scribner's Sons. vi, 277 p.

Reminiscences about various books in the author's library, one of which is *Deaths Duell*. Calls it "one of the most 'creepy' fragments of theological literature" (p. 44). Comments on the portrait of Donne in his winding sheet, which appears as a frontispiece to the volume, and calls it "one of the grimmest freaks that ever entered into a pious mind" (p. 41). Brief synopsis of the sermon. Praises Donne as "one of the greatest Churchmen of the seventeenth century, and one of the greatest, if the most eccentric, of its lyrical poets" (p. 43).

⫷§ 15. GRIERSON, H. J. C. "Donniana." *MLR*, 9:237–39.

Several corrections and additions to the notes of *The Poems of John Donne* (1912).

⫷§ 16. KEYNES, GEOFFREY. *Bibliography of the Works of Dr. John Donne. Dean of St. Paul's*. Cambridge: Printed for the Baskerville Club and sold by Bernard Quaritch, London, W. xii, 167 p.

2d ed., 1932.

3d ed., 1958.

First edition of the major Donne bibliography (limited to 300 copies). Descriptive bibliography composed of five major sections: (1) prose works, (2) poetical works, (3) Walton's Life of Donne, (4) biography and criticism (39 items listed), and (5) five appendices: Works of Donne's son, John Donne, D.C.L.; Works by John Done, *Polydoron* and *The Ancient History of the Septuagint*; Works persistently but wrongly attributed to Donne; Books from Donne's library (13 items listed); a book dedicated to Donne by Roger Tisdale entitled *The Lawyers Philosophy: or, Law Brought to Light. Poetized in a Diuine Rhapsodie or Contemplatiue Poem* (London, 1622); and iconography (paintings, stone effigies, engravings of Donne). List of printers and publishers, 1607–1719. Index.

1915

◆§ 17. Brett-Smith, H. F. B. "A Crux in the Text of Donne." *MLR*,
      10:86–88.
Believes that the word "towring" in "Elegie XII" (l. 42) is a form of
"twire," which means "to peep" or "ogle."

◆§ 18. Colvin, Sir Sidney. "On Concentration and Suggestion in Poet-
      ry." *English Association Pamphlet*, No. 32:17–19.
Considers Donne among "the minority who by principle or instinct
pack and condense and concentrate and compress habitually and all the
time" (p. 17). Calls him an intellectual athlete who "went beyond all
his contemporaries in his love of acrobatic thought-play and of forcing
together into strained imaginative relation ideas that naturally had
none" (p. 17).

◆§ 19. Krapp, George Philip. "The Pulpit," in *The Rise of English
      Literary Prose*, pp. 153–217. New York: Oxford University Press,
      Inc.
General critical comment on Donne's prose style and religious attitudes in the sermons. Maintains that "the ideal which Donne and the
conservative thinkers of his time were striving to realize was to enunciate
truth in such terms as appealed to the common judgment of reasonable
men and as would save the quest for truth from sinking into the expression of personal and individual extravagances of opinion" (p. 209). Views
the sermons as Donne's best literary efforts: "In his poems Donne seems
to have found difficulty in making language . . . supple enough to gird
about his giant fancy. No such difficulty appears in the sermons. They
are written, not in a swift or facile style, but in a long, full rhythm, often
complicated but perfectly mastered" (p. 211).

◆§ 20. MacLeane, Douglas. "Donne." *The Saturday Review* (Lon-
      don), 21 August, pp. 178–79.
Takes notice of Keynes's bibliography published in 1914 and questions whether Donne deserves such attention. Mostly an unsympathetic
survey of Donne's poetry and prose: "If one compares Donne with an
epigrammatic poet of the nineteenth century, Coventry Patmore, the
advantage is wholly with the latter in respect of a tender sweetness and
charm of style, as well as elevation and gracefulness of thought, and
though the older writer has more flame it is often a murky one, and not
seldom a make-believe" (p. 178). Condemns *An Anatomie of the World*
but finds the *Divine Poems* to have "pregnant and happy expressions"
(p. 179).

1916

✑§ 21. ARONSTEIN, PH. "John Donne und Francis Bacon: Eine Beitrag zum Kampf der Weltanschauungen im Zeitalter der Renaissance in England." *Englische Studien*, 49:360–76.

Biographical data about the writers and discussion of the development of their respective philosophies. Their differences are illustrated in their reactions to the death of the Earl of Essex. Compares the fortunes of the two men after Essex's death. Bacon advanced, while Donne was initially beset with misfortunes. The turning point for Donne came when he wrote the *Anniversaries*. Discusses *The Progresse of the Soule* and relates it to Essex and Elizabeth. Brief discussion of both of the *Anniversaries*. Bacon is described as an advocate of inductive learning, Donne as an advocate of intuitive learning.

✑§ 22. SYMONS, ARTHUR. "John Donne," in *Figures of Several Centuries*, pp. 80–108. London: Constable and Company, Ltd.

Appreciative essay. A survey of Donne's life and works that relies heavily on Gosse. Concerning Donne's use of language, the author notes: "The words themselves rarely count for much, as they do in Crashaw, for instance, where words turn giddy at the height of their ascension. The words mean things, and it is things that matter" (p. 97). Praises Donne's intellectual perception and his ability to represent the wide range of human emotions. Argues that Donne lacks the great poet's control of form and that beauty in Donne breaks through only rarely and then in spite of the poet.

1917

✑§ 23. ALDEN, RAYMOND MACDONALD. "The Lyrical Conceit of the Elizabethans." *SP*, 14:129–52.

Donne mentioned only in passing. Defines and classifies the conceit, using Sidney and Shakespeare for illustration. Challenges the notion that the conceit nullifies emotional sincerity. Classifies and discusses conceits under three major categories: (1) verbal conceits; (2) imaginative conceits—the metaphor–simile type, the personification type, and the myth type; and (3) the logical conceit—the paradox type and the logical-metaphysical type.

✑§ 24. BRADFORD, GAMALIEL. "The Poetry of Donne," in *A Naturalist of Souls: Studies in Psychography*, pp. 63–96. New York: Dodd, Mead, & Co.

Revised ed., Boston and New York: Houghton Mifflin Co., 1926.

A collection of previously published essays. Defines *psychography* as "the condensed, essential, artistic presentation of character" (p. 9). A biographical sketch and a general survey of the poetry. Donne has "the moral dignity and grandeur of a soul which, not ignorant of the wretchedness of this world, is yet forever ravished with the love and worship of the eternal" (p. 96).

⮬§ 25. BRIGGS, WILLIAM DINSMORE. "Source-Material for Jonson's 'Underwoods.'" *MP*, 15:85–120.
Argues that "Elegie XV: The Expostulation" is probably Jonson's, not Donne's. Especially lines 39ff. are echoed in several of Jonson's works.

⮬§ 26. JACKSON, GEORGE. "The Bookshelf by the Fire: V. John Donne." *Expository Times*, 28:216–20.
Donne is dismissed as an artist: "It must be freely admitted that neither as poet, preacher, nor letter-writer is Donne ever likely to gain the suffrage of more than the few" (p. 217). Characterizes much of his secular poetry as "fit only for the dunghill" (p. 218). States that the only interest one can possibly have in Donne today is "in the strange fascination of his complex and mysterious personality" (p. 218). Biographical sketch, mostly of Donne's later life.

⮬§ 27. PICAVET, FRANÇOIS. "The Mediaeval Doctrines in the Work of Donne and Locke." *Mind*, n.s., 26:385–92.
Review of works that resulted from the author's classes and lectures on medieval philosophy. Surveys the study by Mary Paton Ramsey entitled *Les Doctrines Médiévales Chez Donne* (1917). The author's conclusion, based on Miss Ramsey's research, is that "Donne transmitted the philosophy and theology of the Middle Ages to his followers.... It is as moralist, as mystic and as poet, that his individuality reveals itself. He may thus be considered as an interpreter of his epoch. As a poet of real genius he is greater than his time; as priest he spoke a language and expressed a thought which must be understood by his contemporaries. And that thought is above all mediaeval and Plotinian" (p. 392).

⮬§ 28. RAMSEY, MARY PATON. *Les Doctrines Médiévales Chez Donne, Le Poète Métaphysicien de l'Angleterre* (1573–1631). London: Oxford University Press. xi, 338 p.
2d ed., 1924.
A study of Donne's verse and prose to determine his relation to medieval thought. Concludes that, although Donne was unique in many ways as moralist, mystic, and poet, he was not original in his metaphysics and theology: "Tout enfant de la Renaissance que soit Donne par certains côtés, le caractère général de son esprit est médiéval" (p. 322). Maintains that Donne accepted the basic doctrines, the point of view, and the vocabulary of Plotinism. The book is divided into four major sections: (1) general introduction (pp. 1–33); (2) survey of the life and

intellectual formation of Donne (pp. 34–127); (3) Donne's "doctrines" (pp. 128–280); (4) conclusion. Section 3 has chapters on the following subjects: "De l'Univers ou de l'Etre," "De Dieu," "Des Anges ou Substances Séparées," "De l'Homme," "De l'Union avec Dieu ou de l'Extase," and "Des Sciences." Five appendices list authors that Donne cites in his prose works.

1918

≪§ 29. QUILLER-COUCH, ARTHUR. "Some Seventeenth Century Poets," in *Studies in Literature*, pp. 96–117. New York: G. P. Putnam's Sons; Cambridge, England: University Press.

Biographical sketch. Argues that "the great Donne, the real Donne," is to be found "not in his verses, into which posterity is constantly betrayed, but in his *Sermons*" (p. 107). Severely critical of Donne as a poet: "He has no architectonic gift in poetry: in poetry the skill that articulated, knit, compacted his *Sermons* and marched his arguments as warriors in battalion, completely forsook him" (p. 110). Concludes that Donne is an "imperfect mystic" and an "imperfect poet." "I suppose his poem *The Flea* to be about the most merely disgusting in our language. He will ruin an exquisite poem (for us) by comparing two lovers' souls with a pair of compasses" (p. 130).

1919

≪§ 30. ARONSTEIN, PHIL. "John Donnes Liebeslyrik." GRM, 7:354–69.

General characteristics of the love poems. Points out that Donne differs from Petrarch and the troubadours, because at the center of his poems is not the beloved but his own feelings. Discusses Donne's use of language, hyperbole, and wit. Maintains that Donne's influence on the following generation was not always good, because his imitators used his techniques but lacked his capacity for feeling. His poetry seems modern because of its outspoken subjectivism.

≪§ 31. DONNE, JOHN. *Donne's Sermons: Selected Passages*. With an essay by Logan Pearsall Smith. Oxford: Clarendon Press. lii, 263 p.

Introduction (slightly revised) reprinted in *Reperusals and Recollections* (1936), pp. 222–55.

Consists of a critical introduction (pp. xiii–liii), 155 selections from the sermons (pp. 1–241), and explanatory notes (pp. 243–63). States that the underlying purpose of the selections is not theological, didactic, or historical but rather to present Donne as a man, an artist, and a writer. Selections arranged according to various subjects: (1) autobiographical passages; (2) passages that deal with contemporary events or allusions; (3) passages that illustrate the more secular aspects of Donne's thought;

(4) passages that deal with religious faith; (5) passages of the greatest eloquence, in which Donne discusses such matters as man's knowledge of God, the Fall, man's moral nature, death, judgment, and heaven; (6) an extract from *Deaths Duell*.

⊷§ 32. HUXLEY, ALDOUS. "Ben Jonson." *London Mercury*, 1:184–91.
  Reprinted in *On the Margin: Notes and Essays by Aldous Huxley* (1923).
  Review of *Ben Jonson*, G. Gregory Smith (1919). Compares Jonson and Donne: "Like Donne he was a realist. He had no use for claptrap, or rant, or romanticism" (p. 187). Concerning Donne's influence: "His followers took from him all that was relatively unimportant—the harshness, itself a protest against Spenserian facility, the conceits, the sensuality tempered by mysticism—but the important and original quality of Donne's work, the psychological realism, they could not, through sheer incapacity transfer into their own poetry. Donne's immediate influence was on the whole bad. Any influence for good he may have had has been on poets of a much later date" (p. 186).

⊷§ 33. LOWES, JOHN LIVINGSTON. *Convention and Revolt in Poetry*.
  Boston and New York: Houghton Mifflin Co. 346 p.
  Singles out Donne as the most "salient instance in English poetry of this revolution from the conventional to an unchartered individuality of expression" (p. 152).

⊷§ 34. OSMOND, PERCY H. *The Mystical Poets of the English Church*.
  London: Society for Promoting Christian Knowledge; New York: The Macmillan Co. xi, 436 p.
  Anthology of mystical poets of the English Church, with a few extracts from those outside that communion, in which Donne is included only reluctantly (pp. 46–54). Argues that, although Donne is generally considered a mystical poet, the designation is a misnomer, for the most part. Reproduces part of *Of the Progresse of the Soule*, maintaining that Donne's claim to the title of mystical poet is based largely on this poem. Mentions the other religious poems but concludes that Donne's religious poetry never clearly strikes a mystical note.

⊷§ 35. W., E. W. "Donne's Puns." *TLS*, 11 December, p. 750.
  Comments on the "sun–son" pun in "A Hymne to God the Father" and "To Christ." Points out similar pun in Herbert's "The Sonne" and Vaughan's "The Night."

1920

❧ 36. ANON. "Donne's Sermons." *The Nation* (London), 27:247–48.

General appreciative essay. Laments that the sermons have been too exclusively treated as literature, theology, or the reflections of an interesting personality and not as religion: "To think of Donne as a human battlefield of conflicting and distracting emotions is a false notion; the story of his moral, intellectual, and artistic pilgrimage is that he left women for God and took over with him from the one absorbing loyalty to the other his whole fleet of ideas, knowledge, and language. His fleet was for winning battles, not literary regattas" (p. 248).

❧ 37. ALDEN, RAYMOND MacDONALD. "The Lyrical Conceits of the 'Metaphysical Poets.'" *SP*, 17:183–98.

Sequel to Alden's "The Lyrical Conceit of the Elizabethans," *SP*, 14 (1917):129–52. Catalogues some of the major conceits of Donne, Carew, and Cowley under the categories of Imaginative Conceits (image play) and Logical Conceits (play of reasoning). Second category is subdivided between the "paradox type" and the "logical–metaphysical type" of conceit. Does not see a definite split between the Petrarchan lyricists and the metaphysical poets. Maintains that the metaphysical poets developed the "logical–metaphysical" conceit to its utmost while relying less on the other types.

❧ 38. ARONSTEIN, PHILIPP. *John Donne als Dichter: Ein Beitrag zur Kenntnis der Englischen Renaissance.* Halle: Neimeyer. 101 p.

Published as "John Donne" in *Anglia*, 44 (1920):115–213.

Divided into three major parts: (1) general study of Donne's life and personality; (2) broad survey of the poetry; (3) study of Donne's craftsmanship. Based essentially on Gosse and Grierson. Although there is nothing essentially new in this essay, it served to introduce Donne to a German audience. Challenges the idea that Donne is artificial and attempts to demonstrate that there is a close relationship between Donne's life and poetry. Calls Donne an "Ich-Künstler."

❧ 39. BAILEY, JOHN. "The Sermons of a Poet." *Quarterly Review*, 233:317–28.

Ostensibly a review of *Donne's Sermons*, ed. L. P. Smith (1919), but the book is mentioned only in passing. Attributes the revival of interest in Donne to the fact that he is "the most self-willed individualist of all our older poets" (p. 317) and sees in El Greco "many of the qualities that form the great modern attraction of Donne" (p. 320). Rather critical of Donne as a poet, he remarks that, although "he ranks among the great geniuses who have written English poetry, he does not quite rank among the great English poets" (p. 320). Praises the sermons, suggesting that the demands of the pulpit restrained Donne's "colloquial realism" and his "subtle intellectual fugues" (p. 321).

◄§ 40. CLOUGH, BENJAMIN C. "Notes on the Metaphysical Poets." *MLN*, 35:115–17.
Possible allusion to *The Progresse of the Soule* (ll. 511–12) in Butler's *Hudibras* (Part I, Canto 1, ll. 649–50). Possible allusion to the epigram "Antiquary" (Grierson's edition, I, p. 77) in Dryden's *Upon the Death of Lord Hastings* (ll. 83–84).

◄§ 41. ELIOT, THOMAS STEARNS. "Imperfect Critics," in *The Sacred Wood: Essays on Poetry and Criticism*, pp. 15–41. London: Methuen & Co., Ltd.
1st American ed., New York: Alfred A. Knopf, Inc., 1921.
2d English ed., with a new preface, 1928.
Suggests the kinship of Chapman and Donne: "In common with the greatest—Marlowe, Webster, Tourneur, and Shakespeare—they had a quality of sensuous thought, or of thinking through the senses, or of the senses thinking, of which the exact formula remains to be defined. If you look for it in Shelley or Beddoes, both of whom in very different ways recaptured something of the Elizabethan inspiration, you will not find it, though you may find other qualities instead. There is a trace of it only in Keats, and, derived from a different source, in Rossetti. You will not find it in the *Duke of Gandia*" (pp. 20–21).

◄§ 42. GRAY, M. MURIEL. "Drummond and Donne." *TLS*, 8 April, p. 225.
Possible borrowings by Drummond in *Cypresse Grove* and "It autumn was and on our hemisphere" from the *Anniversaries*.

◄§ 43. GUINEY, LOUISE I. "Donne as a Lost Catholic Poet." *The Month*, 136:13–19.
Maintains that "Donne's Catholicism, as a creed and a code of action, can have gone not very far beyond his majority; but as an influence, it wrought upon him to the end of his life" (p. 13). Suggests that the religious poems may have been written before 1598. Outlines Donne's Catholic connections, especially the members of his family.

◄§ 44. LYND, ROBERT. "John Donne." *London Mercury*, 1:435–47. Reprinted in *The Art of Letters* (1920), pp. 29–48.
General critical survey of the poetry and prose within a biographical framework. Commenting on the *Elegies*, the author states: "He was a virile neurotic comparable in some points to Baudelaire, who was a sensualist of the mind even more than of the body. His sensibilities were

different as well as less of a piece, but he had something of Baudelaire's taste for hideous and shocking aspects of lust" (p. 437).

⋙ 45. MOORE-SMITH, G. C. "Izaak Walton and John Donne." *MLR*, 15:303.
A possible allusion in Walton's *Life* to Donne's "Sermon XVIII" in the *XXVI Sermons* (1660).

⋙ 46. [SQUIRE, SIR JOHN COLLINGS.] "Dr. Donne's Tomb," in *Books in General by Solomon Eagle*, pp. 115–18. 2d series. New York: Alfred A. Knopf, Inc.
Selections from a series contributed weekly to the *New Statesman* beginning in 1913 under the pseudonym of Solomon Eagle. A narrative essay about the author's visit to the tomb of Donne in St. Paul's.

1921

⋙ 47. DUNN, S. G. "The Authorship of 'Polydoron.'" *TLS*, 7 July, p. 436.
Attributes *Polydoron* and *The History of the Septuagint* to Donne's son, John Donne.

⋙ 48. ELIOT, THOMAS STEARNS. "The Metaphysical Poets." *TLS*, 20 October, pp. 669–70.
Reprinted in *Homage to John Dryden: Three Essays on Poetry of the Seventeenth Century* (1924); the contents of *Homage* were reprinted in *The Hogarth Essays* (1928) and in *Selected Essays, 1917–1932* (1932; 2d English ed., 1934; 2d American ed., 1950; 3d English ed., 1951).
Reprinted in *Criticism: the Major Texts*, ed. Walter Jackson Bate (1952), pp. 529–34; and in *Discussions of John Donne*, ed. Frank Kermode (1962), pp. 42–47.
Trans. into French by Henri Fluchère in *Cahiers du Sud*, 28 (1948): 487–98.
Eliot maintains, "The poets of the seventeenth century, the successors of the dramatists of the sixteenth century, possessed a mechanism of sensibility which could devour any kind of experience. . . . In the seventeenth century a dissociation of sensibility set in, from which we have never recovered; and this dissociation, as is natural, was due to the influence of the two most powerful poets of the century, Milton and Dryden" (p. 669). The metaphysical poets were "engaged in the task of trying to find the verbal equivalent for states of mind and feeling" (p. 670). Eliot illustrates his point by saying: "The difference is not a simple difference of degree between poets. It is something which had happened to the mind of England between the time of Donne or Lord Herbert of Cherbury and the time of Tennyson and Browning; it is the difference

between the intellectual poet and the reflective poet. Tennyson and Browning are poets, and they think; but they do not feel their thought as immediately as the odour of a rose. A thought to Donne was an experience; it modified his sensibility" (p. 669). For a reply by George Saintsbury, see *TLS*, 27 October, p. 698.

ᴥᔥ 49. [―――]. "The Metaphysical Poets." *TLS*, 3 November, p. 716.
Reply to George Saintsbury, *TLS*, 27 October, p. 698. "Mr. Saintsbury appears to believe that these poets represent not merely a generation, but almost a particular theory of poetry. The 'second thoughts' to which he alludes are, I think, and as I tried to point out, frequent in the work of many other poets besides, of other times and other languages. I have mentioned Chapman, and the contemporaries of Dante. I do not believe that the author of *Hamlet* and *Measure for Measure* was invariably satisfied with 'the first simple, obvious, natural thought and expression of thought.'" For a reply by Saintsbury, see *TLS*, 10 November, p. 734.

ᴥᔥ 50. GOSSE, EDMUND. "The Sepulchral Dean," in *Books on the Table*, pp. 185–89. London: William Heinemann, Ltd.
Partly a review of *Donne's Sermons*, ed. L. P. Smith (1919). Briefly comments on the revival of interest in Donne's poetry and maintains that "the verse of Donne has now become assured of a foremost place in all intelligent study of our literature" (p. 186). Calls the sermons a "howling wilderness" (p. 188). First appeared in the *Sunday Times* (London), 12 October 1919.

ᴥᔥ 51. GRIERSON, HERBERT J. C., ED. *Metaphysical Lyrics & Poems of The Seventeenth Century: Donne to Butler.* Selected and edited, with an essay by Herbert J. C. Grierson. Oxford: The Clarendon Press. lviii, 244 p.
Reprinted, 1925, 1928, 1936, 1942, 1947, 1950, 1958, 1962. First issued in Oxford Paperbacks 1965. Galaxy 1959.
Introduction reprinted in *The Background of English Literature* (1925), pp. 115–66.
Pages xiii–xxxviii reprinted in *Seventeenth Century English Poetry: Modern Essays in Criticism*, ed. William Keast (1962), pp. 3–21.
Contains a major critical introduction (pp. xiii–lviii); selections from twenty-six poets divided into three categories: love poems, divine poems, and miscellanies (pp. 1–215); notes (pp. 217–40); an index of first lines (pp. 241–44). By the introduction and the choice of poems included, Grierson, in effect, defines the metaphysical school, although he is cautious with the term itself. Yet he maintains that the term *metaphysical* "lays stress on the right things—the survival, one might say the reaccentuation, of the metaphysical strain, the *concetti metafisici ed ideali* as Testi calls them in contrast to the imagery of classical poetry, of medi-

aeval Italian poetry; the more intellectual, less verbal, character of their wit compared with the conceits of the Elizabethans; the finer psychology of which their conceits are often the expression; their learned imagery; the argumentative, subtle evolution of their lyrics; above all the peculiar blend of passion and thought, feeling and ratiocination which is their greatest achievement. Passionate thinking is always apt to become metaphysical, probing and investigating the experience from which it takes its rise. All these qualities are in the poetry of Donne, and Donne is the great master of English poetry in the seventeenth century" (pp. xv–xvi). The other poets considered in the introduction are primarily contrasted with or compared to Donne. Yet Grierson cautions, "To call these poets the 'school of Donne' or 'metaphysical' poets may easily mislead if one takes either phrase in too full a sense" (p. xxx).

◄§ 52. MAIS, S. P. B. "John Donne" in *Why We Should Read*, pp. 51–57. London: Richards.

General appreciative essay. Concludes that one should read Donne "for his fiery imagination, for his deep and subtle analysis, for his humanity, for his passion, for his anti-sentimentalism, for his eager search 'to find a northwest passage of his own' in intellect and morals, for the richness and rarity of the gems with which all his work, both prose and poetry, is studded, for his modernity and freshness" (p. 57).

◄§ 53. MATHEWS, C. ELKIN. "Elegiac Lines on Dr. Donne." *TLS*, 6 October, p. 644.

Reproduces a short elegiac poem about Donne found on the flyleaf of a copy of the 1635 edition of the poems. The volume has the autograph of George Dubourg (1790–1882).

◄§ 54. SAINTSBURY, GEORGE. "The Metaphysical Poets." *TLS*, 27 October, p. 698.

Reply to T. S. Eliot, *TLS*, 20 October, pp. 669–70. Points out that when Dryden used the term *metaphysics* in connection with Donne's poetry, he did not equate it with philosophy but rather opposed it to nature. The word in Greek means "second thoughts, things that come *after* the natural first." Maintains that "this definition would ... fit all the poetry commonly called 'metaphysical,' whether it be amatory, religious, satirical, panegyric, or merely trifling; while 'philosophical,' though of course not seldom suitable enough, sometimes has no relevance whatever [for] these poets always 'go behind' the first, simple, obvious, natural thought and expression of thought." For a reply by Eliot, see *TLS*, 3 November, p. 716.

◄§ 55. ———. "The Metaphysical Poets." *TLS*, 10 November, p. 734.

A reply to T. S. Eliot, *TLS*, 3 November, p. 716. "I fully agree with him that, in the great examples he quotes, and perhaps in all similar things, there *is* 'second thought.' I might even go so far as to say—indeed I meant to hint this in my last sentence—that all true poetry must be in a way second thought, though much second thought is not in any way poetry. What I was endeavouring to point out was that, *in this period* [the seventeenth century], the quest of the second thought became direct, deliberate, a business, almost itself a *first* thought."

◄§ 56. SAMPSON, JOHN. "A Contemporary Light upon John Donne."
    E&S, 7:82–107.

Discusses the marginalia and comments apparently written by the royal divine, Giles Oldisworth (1619–1678), contained in a 1639 edition of *Poems, by J. D. With Elegies On the Authors Death*.

◄§ 57. SITWELL, SACHEVERELL. *Doctor Donne and Gargantua. The First*
    Three Cantos. London: Favil Press, 1921–26. 14 p.

Three cantos of a long, symbolic poem in which Gargantua is representative of man's physical nature and Donne of man's spiritual nature. A narrative in rhymed, irregular meter with passages of free verse. Three more cantos were added in 1930, and the whole was published as *Doctor Donne & Gargantua: The First Six Cantos* (London: Gerald Duckworth & Co., Ltd.; New York: Houghton Mifflin Co., 1930. 80 p.).

◄§ 58. THOMPSON, ELBERT N. S. "Mysticism in Seventeenth-Century
    English Literature." *SP*, 18:170–231.

Mentions Donne only in passing. Argues that, in spite of the fact that Donne's "habits of thought, like certain aspects of his temperament, were alien to mysticism" (p. 193), he evidences, a fascination for the mystic's way of knowing, especially in the sermons. Says that in the love poems, Donne celebrates love as a passion that will "raise man above the limiting conditions of physical existence into the freedom of the spiritual world" (p. 193). Concludes, "Deeply versed as he was in theology, Donne might have given, in either prose or verse, a full statement of the mystic's faith" (p. 194), but such a statement is not to be found.

1922

◄§ 59. DUCKETT, ELEANOR S. "Some English Echoes of Catullus." *The*
    Classical Weekly, 15:177–80.

Cites four instances of Catullian echoes: "The Baite" (ll. 1–4), "A Valediction: forbidding mourning" (ll. 5–8), "Lovers infinitenesse" (ll. 1–6), "A Feaver" (ll. 1–4).

&§ 60. Hodgson, Geraldine E. "Anglo-Catholic Mystics and Others,"
in *English Mystics,* pp. 208–72. London: A. R. Mowbray & Co.;
Milwaukee: Morehouse Publishing Co.

Very general consideration of Donne as a mystic (pp. 242–46). Several quotations from the religious poems to support the position with little or no explanation.

&§ 61. Nethercot, Arthur H. "The Term 'Metaphysical Poets' before
Johnson." *MLN,* 37:11–17.

Points out that "the use of the term 'metaphysical' in connection with certain poets or with certain types and styles of poetry was far from uncommon in the seventeenth and eighteenth centuries, and that therefore there were various sources from which Johnson might have got the suggestion for his phrase, altho probably the responsibility was mainly Dryden's" (pp. 12–13).

&§ 62. ———. "The Reputation of John Donne as Metrist." *SR,*
30:463–74.

Traces the critical attitude toward Donne as a metrist from the seventeenth to the twentieth century. Attributes the neoclassical dislike of Donne's metrics to the fact that only the satires were seriously considered. The change came about gradually in the nineteenth century, although many dissenting voices are still heard in the twentieth century, when Donne was more generally admired and considered a major lyric poet. The metrical roughness came to be seen as an effort on Donne's part to reform English verse, not merely the result of slovenly craftsmanship or a poor ear.

1923

&§ 63. Affable Hawk [pseud. for Desmond MacCarthy]. "Books in
General." *The New Statesman,* 20:660.

Familiar essay in which the author indicates the popularity of Donne among the young poets of the 1920s. Questions whether Eliot is a likely successor of Donne and proposes Browning as the "nearest approximation." Lists some of Donne's major characteristics as a poet.

&§ 64. Beresford, John. "A Seventeenth-Century Jester: John Donne
the Younger," in *Gossip of the Seventeenth and Eighteenth Centuries,* pp. 59–91. London: Richard Cobden-Sanderson.

Presents Donne's son "not as a mere contemptible debauchee, but rather as an ingenuous and incorrigible jester, which such of his published works as exist unquestionably prove him to be" (pp. 60–61). A reaction to Augustus Jessopp's severe appraisal of him in the *Dictionary of Na-*

tional Biography. Donne the younger's editorship of his father's works is outlined and his own writings are briefly surveyed.

◄§ 65. BREDVOLD, LOUIS I. "The Naturalism of Donne in Relation to Some Renaissance Traditions." *JEGP*, 22:471–502.
Reprinted in abridged form in *Discussions of John Donne,* ed. Frank Kermode (1962), pp. 48–55.

While recognizing the many inconsistencies in Donne, the author maintains that "there must be some principle of continuity in the intellectual and spiritual history of Donne" (p. 47). Limits his study to the "young Donne as a 'revolutionist in love', to a more thorough analysis than has yet been presented of his audacious and singularly modern philosophy of that subject, and a discussion of some similar development of thought in the Renaissance with which Donne may have been acquainted" (p. 472). Concerning the love poems that are devoted to the witty notion that inconstancy is the only constant element in love, the author points out that Donne's "appeal is ever to Nature for the justification of a frankly sexual conception of love" (p. 474). Yet, he maintains that "Donne's Naturalism cannot be understood apart from his Scepticism, which made it possible" (p. 474). Surveys the basic notions of Stoicism, Epicureanism, and Skepticism and traces them through the early Christian era to the medieval period and finally to the Renaissance. Especially important are the various notions concerning Natural Law. Concludes, "Montaigne had, before Donne, brought together the two philosophies, Scepticism and Naturalism, which characterized the 'Libertine' tradition. To this tradition or school, John Donne for a long time belonged, and Montaigne seems ... most likely to have been his master" (p. 498).

◄§ 66. DONNE, JOHN. *Devotions Upon Emergent Occasions by John Donne.* Edited by John Sparrow, with a bibliographical note by Geoffrey Keynes. Cambridge: University Press. xxx, 160 p.

Contains an introduction by Sparrow (pp. vii–xxiv), a bibliographical note on the text and its history by Keynes (pp. xxv–xxx), the text of the *Devotions* (pp. 1–147) preceded by a facsimile of the title page of the 1624 edition, Donne's dedicatory epistle to Prince Charles, a Latin index to the subject of each meditation, and notes (pp. 151–60). Sparrow writes: "The *Devotions* are no model for a handbook of piety, no collection of prayers such as their title implies.... The book is not a model of Donne's prose style, though it does contain glorious examples of his work; its value is not its philosophy, its theology, or any reasoning or argument that it contains, but it is extraordinarily interesting as a unique revelation of a unique mind. It shows us the intensity and the complexity of Donne's feelings; it shows us his personal philosophy—

not his studied opinions on intellectual or theological problems, but his secret thoughts on what concerned him most. It does not explain, it reveals; it makes clear that 'natural, unnatural' perversity in Donne's nature which made him at once the most human and the most incomprehensible of beings" (pp. xxii–xxiii).

⊷§ 67. ELIOT, THOMAS STEARNS. "John Donne." *Nation and Athenaeum*. 30:331–32.
Essentially a review of the *Love Poems of John Donne* (Nonesuch Press, 1923), but Eliot's own critical evaluation of Donne predominates. "One of the characteristics of Donne which wins him, I fancy, his interest for the present age, is his fidelity to emotion as he finds it; his recognition of the complexity of feeling and its rapid alterations and antitheses" (p. 332). Praises Donne for his honesty of feeling and ranks him with the early Italians, Heine, and Baudelaire as "a poet of the world's literature." Concludes, "Our appreciation of Donne must be an appreciation of what we lack, as well as of what we have in common with him ... we cannot have any order but our own, but from Donne and his contemporaries we can draw instruction and encouragement" (p. 332).

⊷§ 68. FAUSSET, HUGH I'ANSON. "Idealism and Puritanism," in *Studies in Idealism*, pp. 87–116. London and Toronto: J. M. Dent & Sons, Ltd.; New York: E. P. Dutton & Co., Inc.
Presents Donne as a poet who had difficulty reconciling the material and spiritual: "Donne loved the physical with all the healthy relish of Elizabethan youth, but as his Puritan conscience forbade him to rest satisfied with the rewards of the body, so his love of life assured him of a reality beyond the bounds of logic. He combined the lust of the brute, the curiosity of the scientist and the aspirations of the saint, and as the heat of youth cooled, the latter two qualities predominated over the former, upon the memory of which, however, they drew for experience" (p. 97).

⊷§ 69. FORREST, HENRY T. S. *The Five Authors of "Shake-speares Sonnets."* London: Chapman & Dodd, Ltd. 271 p.
Purports to demonstrate, "Of the one hundred and fifty-four sonnets published in 1609 under the title of 'Shake-speares Sonnets,' Shakespeare was responsible for rather less than a quarter, while nine-tenths of the remainder were contributed in varying proportions by four other poets (who may be identified with more or less certainty as Barnes, Warner, Donne, and Daniel) writing in competition with him and each other in a series of private sonnet-tournaments, which were fought out some time between 1594 and 1599, under the auspices of the Earl of Southampton" (p. 7). Refers to Donne as the "Humorist" throughout.

◄§ 70. Gosse, Edmund. "Metaphysical Poetry," in *More Books on the Table*, pp. 307–13. London: William Heinemann, Ltd.

Essentially a review of *Metaphysical Lyrics & Poems*, ed. H. J. C. Grierson (1921). Commenting on Donne's influence, the author suggests that the "great gift which Donne passed down to his disciples was an intellectual intensity of expression. He taught the poets to regard mellifluousness with suspicion, if it concealed poverty of thought, and to be more anxious to find words, even stumbling and harsh words, for their personal emotions, than to slip over the surface of language in a conventional sweetness" (pp. 311–12). First appeared in the *Sunday Times* (London).

◄§ 71. Jenkins, Raymond. "Drayton's Relation to the School of Donne, as Revealed in the *Shepheards Sirena.*" *PMLA*, 38:557–87.

An allegorical reading of Drayton's poem, which maintains that the poem is about Drayton's hostile attitudes toward the "new poetry," and especially toward the person and poetry of Donne, and his bemoaning the state of poetry in general in 1627. Drayton's adverse attitudes toward Donne are attributed to several reasons: (1) Donne's satirizing of the Spenserian poets; (2) Donne's rejection of the established ideals, conventions, poetic materials, and verse forms of the time; (3) Drayton's jealousy over the Countess of Bedford's rejection of him and her patronage of Donne; (4) Donne's early life, his association with the court; (5) Donne's challenging of the notion of poetry as the handmaiden of virtue; (6) Donne's dislike and parodying of the pastoral; (7) Donne's circulating his poetry in manuscript rather than having it openly published. For a reply by J. William Hebel, see *PMLA*, 39 (1924):814–36.

◄§ 72. Read, Herbert. "The Nature of Metaphysical Poetry." *The Criterion* (London), 1:246–66.

Reprinted in *Reason and Romanticism: Essays in Literary Criticism* (1926), pp. 31–58; in *Collected Essays in Literary Criticism* (1938), pp. 69–88, in *The Nature of Literature* (1956), pp. 69–88.

Defines the nature of metaphysical poetry: "I will define it as the emotional apprehension of thought—or, to use words suggested by Dante, as thought transmuted into vision" (p. 249). Uses Donne to illustrate the definition: "In Donne we do as a matter of fact find the first consciousness of felt thought, and his compasses and mandrakes are small matters in comparison to this" (p. 253). Much is an elaboration on Eliot's concept of "unified sensibility." Milton is singled out as having done more than any other poet to destroy the metaphysical tradition.

◆§ 73. SIMPSON, EVELYN M. "John Donne and Sir Thomas Overbury's 'Characters.'" *MLR*, 18:410–15.

A bibliographical study of the three "characters"—"The True Character of a Dunce," "An Essay of Valour," and "Newes from the very Countrey"—which Donne contributed to Overbury's collection. "Newes" first appeared in the second edition entitled *A Wife Now the Widow of Sir Thomas Overbury* (1614) and the others first appeared in the eleventh edition entitled *Sir Thomas Overbury His Wife* (1622).

◆§ 74. TAYLOR, RACHEL ANNAND. "The Renaissance Ferment," in *Aspects of the Italian Renaissance*, pp. 251–301. London: G. Richards; Boston and New York: Houghton Mifflin Co.

Revised and enlarged ed. entitled *Invitation to Renaissance Italy* (1930).

Donne is mentioned only briefly. Especially emphasized is his "Renaissance dualism": "He was medieval and modern, he was schoolman and scholar, he was lover and hater, he was mystic and materialist, he was the apologist for suicide, and died Dean of St. Paul's" (p. 287). Calls Donne "the greatest love-poet in the language, except perhaps the Shakespeare of the Sonnets" (p. 288).

◆§ 75. WHITBY, CHARLES. "The Genius of Donne." *PoetryR* (London), March:67–81.

General appreciative essay on Donne's life and poetry. States "Donne's reputation as a poet stands to-day as high, perhaps higher, than it has ever done, but he is comparatively little read" (p. 71), because "while women probably form the majority of habitual readers of verse, the critics and connoisseurs who determine poetic repute are mostly men" (p. 71), and they are not offended by Donne's frankness and obscenity. Concludes, "Only the most alert and athletic mind can follow without fatigue the flight of Donne's nimble fancy, in its quest of new images and bizarre similitudes" (p. 81).

◆§ 76. WYLD, HENRY CECIL. *Studies in English Rhymes from Surrey to Pope*. London: John Murray (Publishers), Ltd. xiii, 140 p.

Surveys rhymes during the sixteenth and seventeenth centuries as a way to establish pronunciation patterns of the period. Donne is mentioned throughout and used to illustrate how words that in our more current English do not appear to rhyme were exact rhymes at an earlier time.

1924

◄§ 77. BENSLY, EDWARD. "Dr. Andrews and Bacon's Apophthegms."
  N&Q, 146:85–86.

In the 1635 edition of the poems, there are some Latin lines with the heading, "De Libro, cum mutuaretur impresso, domi a pueris frustratim lacerato, et post reddito manuscripto. Doctissimo amicissimoque v. D. D. Andrews." Chambers and Grierson identify Andrews as a certain Francis Andrews. Bensly argues that he is in fact Richard Andrews, one of Donne's close friends.

◄§ 78. BREDVOLD, LOUIS I. "Sir T. Egerton and Donne." *TLS*, 13 March,
  p. 160.

Reproduces a passage from Francis Osborne's *Advice to a Son* (1656), which suggests that Egerton was harsh with Donne at the time of his marriage, because he was jealous of Donne's ability and was eager to hire someone of less efficiency and self-confidence.

◄§ 79. FAUSSET, HUGH I'ANSON. *John Donne: A Study in Discord*.
  London: Jonathan Cape, Ltd. 318 p.

A study of Donne's personality in which biography, criticism, and pyschology are mingled. Donne is described as "a genius physically and intellectually 'possessed,' one who ranged almost every scale of experience, and upon each struck some note, harsh, cunning, arrogant or poignant, which lingers down the roof of time; a poet who was at times near a monster, full-blooded, cynical and gross, a thinker, curious, ingenious and mathematical, a seer brooding morbidly over the dark flux of things, a saint aspiring to the celestial harmony" (p. 20). Includes four major chapters entitled "The Pagan," "The Penitent," "The Pensioner," and "The Preacher," preceded by a prologue and followed by an epilogue. Sets out to show that Donne "enjoyed neither a physical nor a spiritual harmony, but was torn in the strife between his intelligence and his impulses" (pp. 314–15), and yet "It was Donne's great and tragic destiny to experience the worst agonies of that inconclusive battle, and to bequeath to literature the tale of it" (p. 315). Concludes, "Like some distracted microcosm, Donne reflects and condenses the long labour of the man to outgrow the beast and approach the divine" (p. 318).

◄§ 80. GASELEE, STEPHEN. "The Soul in the Kiss." *The Criterion*, 2:349–
  59.

Traces references in ancient and modern literature to the conceit of souls mingling in the kiss or the transference of souls by means of the kiss found in *The Greek Anthology* and sometimes attributed to Plato. Mentions Donne as using the conceit in "To Sr Henry Wotton: Sir, more then kisses, letters mingle Soules;/For, thus friends speake" (l. 1).

۶§ 81. HEBEL, J. WILLIAM. "Drayton's 'Sirena.'" *PMLA*, 39:814–36.

Reply to Raymond Jenkins, *PMLA*, 38 (1923):557–87. Argues that Drayton is referring to Ben Jonson, not Donne, in his description of Olcon in the *Shepheards Sirena*. For a reply by Jenkins, see *PMLA*, 42 (1927): 130–39.

۶§ 82. HUTTON, W. H. "John Donne, Poet and Preacher." *Theology* (London), 9:149–65.

Appreciative biographical and critical survey of Donne's life and works. "Donne will always be remembered as a poet; not quite a great poet—a poet's poet perhaps; unequal, not often reaching the very highest, yet often of passionate intensity; hardly ever quite simple, yet on a rare occasion exquisitely so; almost always profound and heart-searching, full all through of unfamiliar, unexpected felicities" (p. 152). Praises Donne as an eloquent preacher and sensitive theologian: "Donne belongs to the company of S. Paul and S. Bernard and S. Francis, and Hooker and Wesley and Pusey and Newman" (p. 165).

۶§ 83. NETHERCOT, ARTHUR H. "The Reputation of the 'Metaphysical Poets' during the Seventeenth Century." *JEGP*, 23:173–98.

Considers separately the reputations of Donne, Cowley, Cleveland, Carew, Herbert, Crashaw, Vaughan, and Quarles during the seventeenth century. Lists references and critical comment on Donne as a poet before 1700, including such well-known names as Jonson, Drummond of Hawthornden, Carew, Walton, Fuller, Aubrey, Edward Phillips, and Anthony à Wood, as well as William Winstanley, Langbaine, William Walsh. Concludes that "the tradition of Donne's reputation as a poet with great wit and learning, but with much harshness, was continued thruout the seventeenth century. Few ... perceived much intensity of poetic feeling. Donne was also widely (perhaps more widely) known as a conspicuous figure in the church. But on the whole his influence and popularity were both constantly diminishing" (p. 177). Cowley, Cleveland, and Herbert were much more popular. Discusses Dryden's critical comments on the metaphysicals and gives a brief account of the shifting literary tastes of the Restoration, which account for the decline of interest in and appreciation for Donne and the metaphysicals.

۶§ 84. SIMPSON, EVELYN M. *A Study of the Prose Works of John Donne*. Oxford: The Clarendon Press. vi, 367 p.

2d ed., 1948.

"The present volume is an attempt to give a clear and detailed account of the prose works of John Donne, and to show that a knowledge of these is essential to the right understanding of his life and character" (p. iii). Divided into twelve chapters: (1) Introduction, in which the relation of the poetry to the prose is emphasized (pp. 1–12); (2) Sketch of Donne's Life (pp. 13–44); (3) Donne as a Man of Letters, a survey of the general characteristics of his artistic sensibility and the workings of his mind (pp. 45–64); (4) Donne as a Theologian (pp. 65–87); (5) The Medieval and Mystical Elements in Donne's Thought (pp. 88–131); (6) Juvenalia (pp. 132–143); (7) Biathanatos (pp. 144–64); (8) Pseudo-Martyr and Ignatius his Conclave (pp. 165–90); (9) The Essays in Divinity (pp. 191–221); (10) Devotions upon Emergent Occasions (pp. 222–33); (11) The Sermons (pp. 234–70); (12) The Letters (pp. 271–320). Three appendices: (A) Unpublished Sermon by Donne (pp. 321–39), (B) A Chronological Arrangement of Donne's Sermons which originally appeared in *MLR*, 8 (1913):468–83 (pp. 340–55), (C) Prose Works attributed to Donne (pp. 356–59). The last seven chapters give a survey of the textual history of the individual prose works, a critical evaluation of each, and extensive summaries.

◄§ 85. SPARROW, JOHN. "On the Date of Donne's 'Hymne to God my God, in my Sicknesse.'" *MLR*, 19:462–66.

Argues for 1623 as the probable date of composition. For a reply by Evelyn Simpson, see *MLR*, 41 (1946):9–15.

◄§ 86. THOMPSON, ELBERT N. S. "Familiar Letters," in *Literary Bypaths of the Renaissance*, pp. 91–126. New Haven: Yale University Press; London: Oxford University Press.

Brief comment on Donne's letters. "In the main, Donne indulged in a tissue of involved compliment and adulation. Like his poetry, the letters overflow with strange mystical conceits and dialectic" (p. 112). Discusses Donne's theory of letter writing.

◄§ 87. WELLS, HENRY W. *Poetic Imagery: Illustrated from Elizabethan Literature*. New York: Columbia University Press. vii, 231 p.

Reprinted, New York: Columbia University Press (1924, 1951); New York: Russell & Russell, Inc. (1961).

The primary purpose of this study is "to disclose some of the bases of poetic imagery by a review of Elizabethan metaphor," and the secondary purpose is "to disclose some of the chief tendencies in the imagery of English poetry during the lifetime of Shakespeare" (p. 20). Donne, although mentioned throughout, is the principal subject of Chapter V, "The Radical Image" (pp. 121–37). The *radical image* occurs "when two terms of a metaphor meet on a limited ground, and are otherwise definitely incongruent. It makes daring excursions into the seemingly commonplace. The minor term promises little imaginative value. In a coldness to apparently incongruent suggestion this figure approaches the neutral comparison, while in ingenuity it approaches the conceit" (p. 31). Points out that not all of Donne's metaphors can be called radical but concludes, "In Donne and his followers and in the plays of Webster,

Marston, Chapman, Tourneur and Shakespeare, Radical metaphor reached its crest" (p. 136).

1925

◄§ 88. AFFABLE HAWK [PSEUD. FOR DESMOND MacCARTHY]. "Books in General." *The New Statesman*, 26:80.

In a review of *Elizabethan Lyrics*, Norman Ault, the author agrees with Ault that "Absence, hear thou my protestation" should be considered Donne's: "I have always resented its banishment to the appendix in Professor Grierson's edition of Donne's poems." Also suggests several other emendations that he would like to see in Grierson's edition. For a reply by H. J. C. Grierson, see *The New Statesman*, 26:108.

◄§ 89. BREDVOLD, LOUIS I. "The Religious Thought of Donne in Relation to Medieval and Later Traditions," in *Studies in Shakespeare, Milton and Donne*, pp. 191–232. University of Michigan Publications, Language and Literature, I. New York: The Macmillan Co.; London: Macmillan and Co., Ltd.

Studies Donne's "intellectual and religious experience, his mingled scepticism and mysticism, with the double purpose of tracing his religious development and re-stating, with special emphasis on some hitherto neglected phases, his relation to medieval thought" (pp. 196–97). States that in his early life Donne was a skeptic, that he welcomed the concept of mutability, and that he was strongly anti-Stoic. Donne was always aware of both Copernicus and the New Philosophy, and was greatly influenced in his work and his thinking by both. Maintains that, although Donne was well-disposed toward Aquinas and Scholastic thinking, he treated everything ultimately in the light of his own experience, thus coming to believe that reason is subordinate to faith. Discusses Donne in relation to the philosophy of Saint Augustine: "He belonged to the anti-intellectual tradition of Augustine" (p. 224). Concludes by studying Donne's metaphysical style: "If the term 'metaphysical' be understood to signify a poet expounding medieval philosophy, or indeed any philosophy, it is not applicable to Donne; he expounded no system, he was not a philosophical poet in the sense that Lucretius was, or Sir John Davies, his contemporary. If by the epithet we mean only that Donne used, in his 'conceits,' some of the terms and distinctions of medieval thought, it may be admitted to be partially applicable, though misleading in its emphasis. Donne took his imagery wherever he found it—from Renaissance science, from daily life, or from the Church Fathers or the disquisitions of the Schools. He used the imagery understood by the educated men of his time. But his purpose was to express his inner self, his moods, whims, emotions, aspirations, in their infinite complexity and subtlety" (p. 232).

◄§ 90. DE HAVILLAND, M. "Two Unpublished Manuscripts of John Donne." *London Mercury*, 13:159–62.

A letter addressed to George More and a fragment of a pious meditation discovered among the manuscripts at Loseley House. Suggests that the letter is Donne's but is uncertain about the second item.

◄§ 91. DUCKETT, ELEANOR SHIPLEY. *Catullus in English Poetry*. Smith College Classical Studies, No. 6. Northampton, Mass.: Smith College. 199 p.

Suggests that three of Donne's poems echo Catullus' *Carmina*: "The Baite" (*Carmina* 5), "Elegie XV: The Expostulation" (*Carmina* 70), and "Lovers infinitenesse" (*Carmina* 87).

◄§ 92. FORSYTHE, R. S. "The Passionate Shepherd; and English Poetry." *PMLA*, 40:692–742.

Points out the probable source of Marlowe's "The Passionate Shepherd to His Love" and traces the influence of the poem down to the present time. Attempts to show that a new literary device, "the invitation to love," became established in English poetry and has persisted. "The Baite" is mentioned several times; no satiric intent is seen in the poem. Notices a likeness between Donne's poem and a passage in Chapman's *The Blind Beggar of Alexandria*.

◄§ 93. [GEORGE, ROBERT ESMONDE GORDON]. *Outflying Philosophy*. London: Simpkin, Marshall & Co. 356 p.

A literary study of the religious element in the poems and letters of John Donne and in the works of Sir Thomas Browne and of Henry Vaughan the Silurist. Includes an account of the interest of these writers in Scholastic philosophy, in Platonism and in hermetic physic, and some notes on witchcraft by Robert Sencourt (pseud.). A study of Donne, Browne, and Vaughan, "especially in their relation to the supernatural and to the religion they absorbed from their environment, to ascertain how far their writing is tinctured with religion, and to discuss the actual nature of their religion from the literary point of view" (p. 26). Calls Donne a "mystifying human character" who even in his love poetry evinces the signs of the mystic. Surveys Donne's theological and metaphysical attitudes, as deduced from his writings. Sees Donne's attitude on friendship as having transcendental meaning. In Appendix IV (pp. 333–40) conjectures about Donne's relationship with Marlowe.

◄§ 94. GREENLAW, EDWIN. "The New Science and English Literature in the Seventeenth Century." *The Johns Hopkins Alumni Magazine*, 13:331–59.

Surveys the impact of the New Science on seventeenth-century consciousness and on the literature of the period, which reflects that consciousness. Notes that Donne reflects "the conflict between theories of disintegration and of comprehensive harmony, a clash between the older metaphysics and the tenets of Copernicus and Galileo" (p. 345).

◄§ 95. GRIERSON, H. J. C. "Donne's Poems." *The New Statesman,* 26:108.

Reply to "Affable Hawk," *The New Statesman,* 26:80. Argues that he excluded "Absence, hear thou my protestation" from Donne's canon not merely on internal evidence but rather on convincing external evidence as well. Suggests that John Hoskins is the probable author of the poem. Challenges the several textual emendations recommended by "Affable Hawk." The last five paragraphs are a reply by "Affable Hawk," partly apologetic and partly maintaining his original suggestions.

◄§ 96. LEA, KATHLEEN M. "Conceits." *MLR,* 20:389–406.

Discusses the differences between the Elizabethan and metaphysical conceit: "For the most part we may say that the besetting sin of the Elizabethans was the over-emphasis of the simile, the tendency to digress upon the comparison. This fault was to be corrected by the next generation. The 'metaphysical' poets regarded the simile as useful, not as an ornamental device: and the conceits of their poetry were due to under-emphasis" (p. 398). Concerning Donne, the author says: "While his work cuts directly across the facile love-poetry of his age, it is generally said that Donne revolted against Petrarchanism. He left no word to this effect. The change which he made was radical because it was unconscious. He was not externally minded: and he was inspired with a desire not to reform, but to explore ... he turned inwards to discover the labyrinths of his own mind. He was not read in the Italian sonneteers, but in the schoolmen, the physicians and metaphysicians quoted in the *Anatomy of Melancholy*" (p. 399). Contrasts Donne and Herbert: "Herbert was arguing from the physical to the spiritual: Donne, certain of the spiritual experience, was searching for the clearest illustration by which he could communicate it. Where Donne found poetry too difficult, Herbert found it too easy" (p. 401).

◄§ 97. NETHERCOT, ARTHUR H. "The Reputation of the 'Metaphysical Poets' during the Age of Johnson and the 'Romantic Revival.'" *SP,* 22:81–132.

Surveys critical attitudes toward the metaphysical poets during the eighteenth and early nineteenth centuries. Maintains that during the whole of the eighteenth century, it was the common opinion that "Donne was greatest as a satirist (practically the first in England), that he was inferior as a lyricist, and that he knew nothing about 'numbers.' He was also still remembered as a preacher and prose writer" (p. 83). The notion of a "school of metaphysical poetry" was not generally recognized before Johnson. Surveys Johnson's unfavorable comments and his importance in shaping critical opinion during the remainder of the eighteenth century. Treats the interest of the romantics in the metaphysical poets in the last few pages of the article.

⋙§ 98. ———. "The Reputation of the 'Metaphysical Poets' during the Age of Pope." *PQ*, 4:161–79.

Maintains in this brief summary of early eighteenth-century attitudes toward the metaphysical poets that "in spite of the wide and continued diffusion of the Metaphysical taste through the early decades of the eighteenth century, readers and critics soon developed the reaction which had been indicated by the later seventeenth century, so that before many years scarcely any one dared admit himself an unswerving admirer of the Metaphysical writers. Many of these were becoming neglected or else forgotten, although the more important ones still retained a reputation for certain qualities or types of work" (p. 176). For instance, "Donne was still known for his wit and learning, his preaching, his satires, and his rhythmical imperfections—when he was known at all —but his fame was already assuming the low estate which it was to hold until the nineteenth century" (p. 176). Cowley was best known; Quarles fared reasonably well, "thus showing that the populace does not always follow the verdict of the professional critics" (p. 177).

⋙§ 99. POTTLE, FREDERICK A. "Two Notes on Ben Jonson's *Staple of News.*" *MLN*, 40:223–26.

Suggests that the line "Look to me, wit, and look to my wit, Land" (*Staple of News*, I, i, 3) is a close parody of the first line of Donne's "Elegy upon the untimely death of the incomparable Prince Henry."

⋙§ 100. PRAZ, MARIO. *Secentismo e Marinismo in Inghilterra: John Donne—Richard Crashaw*. Firenze: La Voce. xii, 294 p.

Revised form of the Donne section plus two new chapters, *La Poesia Metafisica Inglese del Seicento: John Donne* (Roma: Edizione italiani, 1945), 173 p.

Later revised form, *John Donne* (Torino: S.A.I.E., 1958), 277 p.

Two separate studies in one volume: John Donne (pp. 3–141) and Richard Crashaw (pp. 145–283), with a bibliography of primary and secondary sources (pp. 287–94). Intended primarily for the Italian reader unfamiliar with either poet. Traces the "spiritual biography" of each poet ("the poems as lived"); analyzes and translates many of the chief poems ("the poems as works of art"); shows how each poet is related to the general European movement that is variously known as Marinism, Gongorism, or secentismo. Analyzes the lyrics of Donne and Campion in order to distinguish Donne's particular qualities (pp. 95–106). Discusses how Donne as a metaphysical poet differs from Dante (pp. 99–101, 107ff.). Donne, unlike Dante, does not present as fact a system of ideas but uses ideas as courtly expedients, not so much a search for essential truth as an exercise of the mind. Donne remains basically a figure independent of the general movement of secentismo, but he reflcts its intellectual and artistic concerns.

₰§ 101. WALKER, HUGH. "Elizabethan and Jacobean Verse Satire," in *English Satire and Satirists*, pp. 57–90. London: J. M. Dent & Sons Ltd.; New York: E. P. Dutton & Co.
Calls the satires "weighty in thought and rich in wit, but almost intolerable in style" (p. 69). Discusses Elizabethan concepts of satirical harshness. Summary of themes and influences in Donne's satires. Praises Lodge for his superior metres.

₰§ 102. WHIPPLE, T. K. "The English Epigram: 1590–1600," in *Martial and the English Epigram from Sir Thomas Wyatt to Ben Jonson.* University of California Publications in Modern Philology, Vol. 10, No. 4:327–66. Berkeley: University of California Press.
Several references to Donne's satires. Concludes, "In compression, in paradox and satire, they are as close an equivalent to Martial as we shall find, though none is derived from him" (p. 368).

1926

₰§ 103. BROWN, CHARLES R. "Donne and Shakespeare." *N&Q*, 151:421–22.
Requests information on whether or not a letter and poem printed in *Plays of Shakespeare*, Vol. I, eds. Charles and Mary Cowden Clarke (Cassell and Co.) are Donne's. The editor indicates that Basse, not Donne, is the author.

₰§ 104. ELIOT, T. S. "Lancelot Andrewes." *TLS*, 23 September, pp. 621– 22.
Reprinted in *For Lancelot Andrewes* (1928); *Selected Essays, 1917–1932* (1932, 1934, 1950, 1951); *Essays, Ancient and Modern* (1936).
Trans. into German by Ursula Clemen in *Ausgewahlte Essays 1917–1947* (1950).
A contrast of the sermons of Donne and Andrewes: "Donne is much less the mystic; he is primarily interested in man. He is much less traditional. In his thought Donne has, on the one hand, much more in common with the Jesuits, and, on the other hand, much more in common with the Calvinists than Andrewes.... Donne will certainly have always more readers than Andrewes, for the reason that his sermons can be read in detached passages and for the same reason that they can be

read by those who have no interest in the subject" (p. 622). Donne is "the religious spellbinder, the Reverend Billy Sunday of his time, the flesh-creeper, the sorcerer of emotional orgy" (p. 621).

◆§ 105. ———. "Note sur Mallarmé et Poe," trans. Ramon Fernandez. *NRF*, 27:524–26.

Distinguishes between the philosophical and metaphysical poet. Donne, Poe, and Mallarmé are discussed as representative of the latter: "Donne, Poe et Mallarmé ont la passion de la spéculation métaphysique, mais il est évident qu'ils ne *croient* pas aux théories auxquelles ils s'intéressent ou qu'ils inventent à la façon dont Dante et Lucrèce affirmaient les leurs. Ils se servaient de leurs théories pour atteindre un but plus limité et plus exclusif: pour raffiner et pour développer leur puissance de sensibilité et d'émotion. Leur oeuvre était une expression de leur sensibilité *au-delà des limites du monde normal*, un découverte de nouveaux objets propres à susciter de nouvelles émotions" (p. 525).

◆§ 106. HAMILTON, GEORGE ROSTREVOR. "Wit and Beauty: A Study of Metaphysical Poetry." *London Mercury*, 14:606–20.

Attempts to point out that "conditions were in some ways more favourable to metaphysical poetry in the last decades of the Victorian age than in the early seventeenth century" (p. 620). Discusses Francis Thompson as a more perfect realization of metaphysical poetry than Donne or Crashaw.

◆§ 107. MÉGROZ, R. L. "The Wit and Fantasy of Donne." *Dublin Magazine*, n.s., 1:47–51.

Attributes Donne's present popularity to his "combination of intellectual dissatisfaction and emotional fervour" (p. 47). Donne's ability to fuse intellect and emotion, to apply wit to experience, and to write with "overpowering emotional conviction" (p. 49) are pointed out in select passages from the poems and from the sermons.

◆§ 108. MITCHELL, F. L. "Jack Donne, the Pagan; John Donne, the Divine." *Bookmans Journal*, 14:15–18.

Appreciative essay on Donne's personality. Points out that "there were not two Donnes but one Donne, and the apparently contradictory elements in his character might be reconciled if one could only discover his secret. It is the fascination of this secret that draws so many people again and again to study the life and works of this singular man" (p. 15).

◆§ 109. MORLEY, CHRISTOPHER D. "Every Tuesday," in *The Romany Stain*, pp. 205–10. Garden City, N. Y.: Doubleday, Page & Co.

Reprinted in *Essays* (New York: Doubleday, Doran & Co., 1928), pp. 1060–65.

General familiar essay. Most of the comments are reactions to *John Donne: A Study in Discord*, H. I'A. Fausset (1924): "though I have not traversed it all, I found suggestions that led me toward private analogies valuable to myself" (p. 206).

👉 110. PAYNE, FRANK WALTER. *John Donne and His Poetry*. Poetry and Life Series, No. 35. London: George G. Harrap & Co., Ltd. 167 p.

The series attempts "to interest the reader in the lives and personalities of the poets dealt with, and at the same time to use biography as an introduction and key to their writings" (p. 6). Views Donne as "the tortured battle-stead of the great forces of his time, and his poetry is the record of the struggle" (p. 14). A personality study in which the poems are used to support certain assumptions about Donne's mental attitudes and moods. A veritable anthology of the poems with running commentary.

👉 111. SIMPSON, EVELYN M. "Donne's Essays in Divinity." *TLS*, 21 January, p. 44.

A cancelled dedication to Sir Henry Vane, Jr. by John Donne the younger. A minor correction to this article is made in *TLS*, 4 February, p. 80.

👉 112. THOMPSON, ELBERT N. S. *The Seventeenth-Century English Essay*. University of Iowa Humanistic Studies, 3, No. 3. Iowa City: University Press. 149 p.

A general critical study of the essay with brief comments on *Essayes in Divinity*, *Devotions upon Emergent Occasions*, and *Paradoxes and Problemes*.

👉 113. WILDER, MALCOLM L. "Did Jonson Write 'The Expostulation' Attributed to Donne?" *MLR*, 21:431–35.

Argues that Jonson, not Donne, is the author of the elegy.

1927

👉 114. ANON. "Memorabilia." *N&Q*, 153:56.

A reply to F. P. Wilson, *RES*, 3:272–79. On the basis of the deposition of William Scudamore and Robert Chambers, it is suggested that Donne was born before June of 1572.

👉 115. DEBACKER, FRANZ. "De zoogezedge Invloed van John Donne op Constantijn Huygens: Een Aanvulling van Eymael's Bewijsvoering op Grond van Donne-vertalingen van Huygens," in *Album opgedragen aan Prof. Dr. J. Vercoullie*, Vol. II, pp. 93–105. Brussels: Pagina.

It is commonly thought among Dutch scholars that Donne had a strong influence on Huygens, his Dutch translator. H. J. Eymael's study of this influence is based on external evidence—Huygens's acquaintance with Donne and his translation of nineteen poems—and on internal evidence—a similarity in tone and philosophy of life in their poetry. Questions how much this represents a true influence on Huygens, because there is some doubt about how well Huygens knew Donne, and there is a good deal of evidence that the similarity in tone and philosophy of life was a reflection more of the times than of a direct influence. Detailed comparison of Huygens's translations with the original poems. Finds so many mistranslations and distortions in Huygens's work that it must be evaluated more as his own poetry rather than as Donne's. Believes that the reason so many Dutch scholars find similarities between the two poets is that they know Donne primarily through the translations. Compares Donne to Baudelaire, Swinburne, and Yeats as an original poet and asks to what extent an interest in Donne can be awakened by the translations of Huygens.

◄§ 116. ELIOT, T. S. "Deux Attitudes Mystiques: Dante et Donne," trans. Jean de Menasce, in *Le Roseau d'Or, Oeuvres et Chroniques,* 14(3):149–73.

For reprints, see Donald Gallup, *T. S. Eliot: A Bibliography* (New York: Harcourt, Brace & Co., 1969), D143.

Unpublished Clark lecture; not published in English. Eliot maintains that from the time of Dante to the time of Donne, there was a difference in the notion of the body and the soul, which is reflective of the difference between the basic philosophies of the two periods. The Italian love poets (in particular Dante, Guinizelli, Cavalcanti, and Cino) stress the notion of contemplation of beauty and the dignity of the love object, whereas Donne argues for union and possession of the beloved in his poetry. An extended analysis of "The Extasie" is used to show Donne's fundamental attitude of dualism between the body and soul, a notion that Eliot calls modern, and thus one that was essentially foreign to the Italian writers of the fourteenth century.

◄§ 117. JENKINS, RAYMOND. "Drayton's 'Sirena' Again." *PMLA,* 42: 130–39.

A reply to J. William Hebel, *PMLA,* 39 (1924):814–36, which was an attack on Jenkins's earlier article in *PMLA,* 38 (1923): 557–87. Jenkins identified "Angry Olcon" as Donne; Hebel had argued that Jonson is a more likely possibility. The author attacks Hebel's position and supplies more evidence to support his original position.

⊷§ 118. Keeble, Samuel E. "The Musings of a Memorable Dean."
London Quarterly Review, 147:221–32.
By means of numerous quotations and slight critical comment, the
author wishes "to give but a faint conception of the richness, variety,
originality, piety, and beauty of Donne's little known and less read Devotions" (p. 230). Several notes about Donne's illness in 1623 and a
discussion of his preoccupation with and preparation for death.

⊷§ 119. Mégroz, Rodolphe Louis. "Donne and St. Augustine," in
Francis Thompson: The Poet of Earth in Heaven: A Study in
Poetic Mysticism and the Evolution of Love-Poetry, pp. 145–60.
London: Faber & Gwycr.
Influence of Donne on Thompson and a discussion of the ways in
which the two poets differ as well as share similar mystical attitudes.
Sees Saint Augustine as the link between the two, since both were in-
fluenced by Augustine.

⊷§ 120. Potter, George Reuben. "Milton's Early Poems, The School
of Donne, and the Elizabethan Sonneteers." PQ, 6:396–400.
Maintains that "since so many of Milton's conceits echo distinctly the
earlier Elizabethans, the conclusion seems inevitable that the reflection
in them of Donne's school is considerably less, and that of the Elizabethan sonneteers considerably greater, than is usually assumed" (p.
400).

⊷§ 121. Robbie, H. J. L. "An Undescribed MS. of Donne's Poems."
RES, 3:415–19.
Bibliographical description and discussion of a manuscript of Donne's
poems in University Library, Cambridge (Additional 5778), called "one
of the largest extant MS. collections of Donne's poems" (p. 416).

⊷§ 122. Schelling, Felix E. "Ben Jonson and the Classical School," in
Shakespeare and Demi-Science: Papers on Elizabethan Topics, pp.
59–84. Philadelphia: University of Pennsylvania Press.
Brief discussion of Jonson's relation to Donne and the contrast between them: "Between Jonson and Donne there is the kinship of intellectuality; between Spenser and Donne the kinship of romanticism; between Spenser and Jonson the kinship of the poet's joy in beauty. Spenser
is the most objective and therefore allegorical and mystical; Donne is
the most subjective and the most spiritual; Jonson, the most artistic and
therefore the most logical" (p. 67). References throughout to Donne.

⊷§ 123. Simpson, Evelyn M. "Two Manuscripts of Donne's Paradoxes
and Problems." RES, 3:129–45.
Detailed account of the paradoxes and problems in the Wyburd MS.
and the O'Flaherty MS.

124. TATE, ALLEN. "Poetry and the Absolute." SR, 35:41–52.

Maintains, "A serious poet is preoccupied with the writing of poems that fuse an intensely felt ordinary experience, and intense moral situation, into an intensely realized art" (p. 45). States that "John Donne, a mystical poet too intelligent to be deluded into moral exhortation, into 'the easy gospels bruited hither and yon', found the ultimate value of experience to be its ordered intensification; and this is the sole value and meaning of poetry" (p. 45). Uses "The Funerall" as an example for his argument: "It is great art because its absolute quality is created out of the perceptions not of an easy, imaginable world, but of the accepted, common-sense world" (p. 42).

125. WILLIAMSON, GEORGE. "The Talent of T. S. Eliot." SR, 35: 284–95.

Revised and reprinted in the University of Washington Chapbooks, No. 32, ed. Glenn Hughes (Seattle, 1929).

Describes Eliot as "a true metaphysical poet in the line of John Donne" (p. 284). Discusses Eliot's debts to Donne and their similarities, "Undoubtedly there is a kinship of mind between Eliot and Donne, but this kinship has served to make Eliot more conscious that the virtue of the metaphysical poets was, in his own words, 'something permanently valuable, which subsequently disappeared, but ought not to have disappeared'. This virtue he attempts to recover in his literary analysis and in his poetic practice" (p. 292).

126. WILSON, F. P. "Notes on the Early Life of John Donne." RES, 3:272–79.

Four notes on Donne's early life, primarily from the records at London Guildhall: (1) a discussion of his patrimony (estimated at 750 pounds) and the history of his father's will; (2) a note on his birth (probably between the end of 1571 and June 19, 1572); (3) a sketch of Donne's stepfather, John Symmings, a London physician; (4) a note on the date of Donne's early travels abroad. For a reply by an anonymous author, see N&Q, 153:56.

1928

127. BOLTON, JOSEPH S. G. "Introduction" to *Melanthe: A Latin Pastoral Play of the Early Seventeenth Century* by Samuel Brooke. Edited, with biographical introduction, by Joseph S. G. Bolton. Yale Studies in English 79:1–37. New Haven: Yale University Press; London: Humphrey Milford and Oxford University Press.

A summary statement of Samuel Brooke's lifelong friendship with Donne, especially his role in the circumstances surrounding Donne's marriage.

128. DARK, SIDNEY. *Five Deans: John Colet, John Donne, Jonathan Swift, Arthur Penrhyn Stanley, William Ralph Inge.* New York: Harcourt, Brace & Co. 255 p.

Unfavorable biographical sketch of Donne as a churchman (pp. 54–108). Maintains that "It is indeed as an artist, and as an artist alone, that Donne is worthy of remembrance" (p. 107). Describes Donne's conversion to Anglicanism as being "entirely in accord with self-interest" (p. 57). Maintains that Donne entered the Anglican Church "to gain a livelihood, and the Church saved him from the penury that had been the curse of his life" (p. 106). Compares Swift and Donne, "That they were ordained is much less a reflection on their characters than a criticism of the Church and a demonstration of its character in the times in which they lived" (p. 7).

129. EMPEROR, JOHN BERNARD. *The Catullian Influence in English Lyric Poetry, Circa 1600–1650.* University of Missouri Studies, Vol. 3, No. 3. Columbia: University of Missouri. 133 p.

Finds likeness to Catullus in the following of Donne's poems: "The Message" (*Carmina* viii, 12–19), "A nocturnall upon S. Lucies day" (*Carmina* v), "Elegie VIII: The Comparison" (*Carmina* xliii), "Elegie XII: His parting from her" (*Carmina* lxviii, 75–77, 79–80 and *Carmina* lxi, 106–9), "Upon Mr. Thomas Coryats Crudities" (*Carmina* xcv, 7–8), "Epithalamion made at Lincolnes Inne" (*Carmina* lxi, 146–48 and *Carmina* lxviii, 81–83), "Loves Dietie" (*Carmina* lxxxv). No direct borrowings are suggested, except for "Elegie XV: The Expostulation," which "shows very clear evidences of a fairly intimate acquaintance with the Latin poet" (p. 41).

130. JOHNSON, BEATRICE. "Classical Allusions in the Poetry of Donne." *PMLA*, 43:1098–109.

Maintains that "an examination of the allusion to Greek mythology in the poetry of Donne makes it clear that he had part in the all-but-universal interest of the Elizabethans in classical material, and that he uses this material with characteristic independence and originality" (p. 1098). Points out forty-two allusions to mythology in the *Songs and Sonets.* "Always, Donne uses terms of Greek mythology with a skill or adeptness which is amazing. His use shows both an analysis of the meaning of the myth and a synthetic conclusion as to its significance, in his application of it to the particular matter at hand" (p. 1107).

131. LEGOUIS, PIERRE. *Donne the Craftsman: An Essay upon the Structure of the Songs and Sonnets.* Paris: Henri Didier; London: Humphrey Milford and Oxford University Press. 98 p.

Reprinted, New York: Russell & Russell, Inc., 1962.

Pages 71–79 are reprinted in *John Donne: A Collection of Critical Essays*, ed. Helen Gardner (1962), pp. 36–51.

Emphasis on Donne as a highly conscious artist in reaction to those who make him "a sort of romantic genius, uncouth and unkempt, who cared nothing for the form of poetry so long as he could unlock his heart with the key, not of the regular sonnet, but of the irregular lyric" (p. 11). Discusses Donne's use of various stanzaic forms and gives critical attention to the dramatic elements in the love poetry. Concludes that "biographers should fight shy of interpreting the *Songs and Sonets* as a record of Donne's love-affairs, except in the most general terms" (p. 80). Supports his points by extensive analyses of individual poems and passages from poems. Especially important are his comments on "The Extasie," which he considers to be a seduction poem. Appendix A deals with irregularity in Donne's verse; Appendix B challenges Grierson's point that "The Primrose," "The Blossome," "The Dampe," "The Funerall," and "The Relique" are addressed to Mrs. Herbert. For a reply by George Reuben Potter, see *PQ*, 15 (1936):247–53.

∾§ 132. MacCarthy, Desmond. "Reader's Bibliography of John Donne." *Life and Letters*, 1:156–60, 433.

Annotated checklist of twenty-six items, mostly nineteenth- and early twentieth-century editions and critical studies.

∾§ 133. Praz, Mario. "Machiavelli and the Elizabethans." *PBA*, 14: 49–97.

Surveys Elizabethan attitudes towards Machiavelli and the uses of Machiavellianism in the literature of the time. Discusses *Ignatius his Conclave* and Donne's treatment of Machiavelli in that work (pp. 87–92).

∾§ 134. Read, Sir Herbert. *Phases of English Poetry*. London: Hogarth Press. 158 p.

General appreciative comments about Donne's poetry (pp. 62–68). States that "Donne's greatest poetry is his love poetry: there passion and wit are united in a poetic idiom as original and fascinating as any in the range of English literature" (p. 63). Donne "showed conclusively that the material of philosophy was also the material of poetry" and this was "in the nature of a discovery for English poetry, though it was not a new thing in itself, for Greek and Latin and Italian poetry had shown Donne the way" (p. 67).

∾§ 135. Robbie, H. J. L. "Two More Undescribed MSS. of John Donne's Poems." *RES*, 4:214–16.

Description of the Donne items in British Museum Collection 3998 and the Dobell MS.

☙§ 136. Roberts, R[ichard] Ellis. "The Prisoner of God," in *Readings for Pleasure and Other Essays,* pp. 101–9. London: Methuen & Co., Ltd.

2d ed., 1931.

Much expanded version of a review of *A Study of the Prose Works of John Donne,* by Evelyn Simpson (1924), which appeared in the *Observer,* 4 January 1925, p. 5. Characterizes Donne as a person who was always a prisoner, first to the senses and to the intellect, then to the circumstances of life, and at last to God. Claims that Donne discovered "the natural prison for the aspiring soul was the supernatural; that man is so made that bondage alone is the true condition of his longings and desires, which, in a vacant licence or a meaner prison, can never be satisfied or fulfilled" (p. 109).

☙§ 137. Simpson, Evelyn M. "A Note on Donne's Punctuation." *RES,* 4:295–300.

Challenges McKerrow's assertion in *Introduction to Bibliography* (1927) that Elizabethan authors were careless about punctuation and that the printers supplied most of the punctuation and dictated usage. Argues that "A careful examination of the extant manuscripts of Donne leads inevitably to the conclusion that punctuation, far from being left entirely to the printer, was a matter of concern to the author, and also to some extent to his copyists, except to those who cared nothing about his meaning" (p. 296). Examples given to show that Donne was careful and consistent in his use of punctuation.

☙§ 138. Sparrow, John. "Donne's Table-Talk." *London Mercury,* 18: 39–46.

Discusses the relation between a collection of epigrams and witty sayings entitled "Newes from the very Countrey," first printed in the second edition of Thomas Overbury's *Wife* (1614) and a series of 145 sayings found in a MS. in the collection at Burley-on-the-Hill, printed in Appendix IV of L. Pearsall Smith's *Life and Letters of Sir Henry Wotton* (1907), and described as notes of *Table-talk.*

☙§ 139. Terrill, T. Edward. "A Note on John Donne's Early Reading." *MLN,* 43:318–19.

The source of Donne's motto, "Antes muerta que mudada," is identified as Montemayor's *Diana.* Donne refers to Montemayor as late as 1616 in a letter. See also Ernst G. Mathews, *MLN,* 56 (1941): 607–9.

☙§ 140. Williamson, George. "The Nature of the Donne Tradition." *SP,* 25:416–38.

Maintains that Donne "belongs in the direct current of English poetry and not in one of the eccentric eddies" (p. 416). Challenges Dr. Johnson's comments on metaphysical poetry. An analysis of the general characteristics of Donne's verse, in particular the unified sensibility of the poems, their wit, the brilliant uses of the conceit, the uses of analytic and argumentative thought, the skillful uses of language and prosody, the range of the themes, and the problem of obscurity. Defines the Donne tradition as "complex, sensuous, and intellectual as opposed to the simple, sensuous, and passionate tradition" (p. 438).

≈§ 141. WRIGHTSON, RODGER. "A Note on the Poetry of John Donne." *Bookmans Journal*, 16:373–79.
Calls Donne fascinating and yet alternately repulsive and attractive. Lists some of the characteristics that account for his appeal in the twentieth century, especially "his embracement of life" (p. 374), the fact that Donne was a modernist, and also that he was a mystic (p. 378). "When all due importance, in holding the reader's interest, is given to his nervous vitality, his energy and learning, and to the way in which his complex personality shows itself in all his poems, it must be owned that the more or less frequent outcrops of extraordinary poetic power and outbursts of passion are the cement which holds him in his exalted position" (p. 376).

1929

≈§ 142. ANON. "The Gloomiest Dean. Donne Manuscript Found in Edinburgh." *The Scotsman* (Edinburgh), 29 October.
Unavailable.

≈§ 143. COGAN, ISABEL. "John Donne: Poet and Metaphysician." *PoetryR*, 20:183–94.
Primarily a review of *John Donne: Complete Poetry and Selected Prose*, ed. John Hayward (1929). Surveys the general characteristics of Donne's thought and style. "He gathered together with amazing erudition a heterogeneous mass of material, but failed to present a systematic body of philosophy. It was not until later that the fluctuating trend of his thought was welded together into a definite system by his successors. As a metaphysician, therefore, Donne is somewhat disappointing; he opens the door but a crack into the realms of mysticism, and closes it all too hastily, leaving the reader doubtful whether the poet himself has passed over the threshold, or is still beating at the door" (p. 192).

≈§ 144. DRAPER, JOHN W. *The Funeral Elegy and the Rise of English Romanticism*. New York: New York University Press. xv, 358 p.
References throughout to Donne's treatment of death. Comments briefly on his funeral elegies and asserts that Donne was the first to use the term *funeral elegy* as a title.

৳§ 145. ELIOT, T. S. "The Prose of the Preacher: The Sermons of Donne." *The Listener*, 2 (July 3):22–23.

Calls the sermons "reasoning in emotion" (p. 22). Praises Donne as being more readable than Andrewes or Taylor. Two qualities are singled out for praise: "a curious knowledge of the human heart, and a stateliness of phrase and image hitherto possible only in verse" (p. 22). Concludes, "with Donne the sensibility of the poet and dramatist is infused into a prose which is that of the man of thought" (p. 23).

৳§ 146. FROST, A. C. "John Donne and a Modern Poet." *Cambridge Review*, 50:449–50.

Discusses imagination and wit in Donne's verse. Suggests that Donne maintains in his poetry the Petrarchan ideal of love. "At his heart he was always hopefully certain of the ideal love of soul and soul, but he could never persuade his morbidly active mind that this was so except by actually willing himself into an agonized balance of thought and intuition" (p. 449). Compares Donne and Eliot. Praises Donne's "urgency" and finds Eliot lacking in this quality.

৳§ 147. GARROD, H. W. "Cowley, Johnson, and the 'Metaphysicals,'" in *The Profession of Poetry and Other Lectures*, pp. 110–30. Oxford: The Clarendon Press.

Attempts to resurrect Cowley as a poet and to answer some of Dr. Johnson's criticism. Donne is mentioned throughout, mostly to show that Cowley is less successful than Donne: "That he has thus risen, Donne owes, partly, I do not doubt, to qualities in him greater far than any which time will discover in Cowley—to his far deeper spirituality, and, at the same time, richer sensuosity."

৳§ 148. GRIERSON, SIR HERBERT J. C. "Love-Poetry," in *Cross Currents in English Literature of the XVIIth Century*, pp. 130–65. London: Chatto & Windus Ltd.

Reprinted, New York: Harper Torchbooks, 1959; Gloucester, Mass.: Peter Smith, 1965.

Mentions Donne in this survey of love poetry. Discusses the sensual in Donne. Denying that Donne is a voluptuary, the author states, "Donne is almost an ascetic in his disregard of physical beauty.... He was a sensualist as Tolstoi was, one for whom woman was a curious and perpetual interest at once attracting and repelling, but never to be regarded with indifference.... This poetry is a more complete mirror than any other one can recall of love as a complex passion in which sense and soul are inextricably blended" (p. 145).

≈§ 149. ———. "Donne and Lucretius." *TLS*, 5 December, p. 1032.

Discusses whether "turne" or "tune" is the preferable reading in "Goodfriday, 1613. Riding Westward" (l. 22). Prefers "turne" and cites Lucretius as a possible source for Donne's concept.

≈§ 150. HEBEL, JOHN WILLIAM, AND F. A. PATTERSON, ASSISTED BY C. M. COFFIN. *English Seventeenth Century Literature: A Brief Working Bibliography*. New York: Columbia University Press. 10 p.

Lists twenty-two primary and secondary works on Donne.

≈§ 151. HOLMES, ELIZABETH. *Aspects of Elizabethan Imagery*. Oxford: Blackwell. x, 134 p.

Reprinted, Ann Arbor, Mich.: University Microfilms, Inc., 1962; New York: Russell and Russell, Inc., 1966.

Argues that "Intensity, curiosity, subtlety, wit serving passion or almost passionate in itself, are not the characteristics of the religious, fastidious, precious seventeenth century alone. These qualities, though the seventeenth century accentuates and isolates them, are found as well in the more broadly-thinking, more humanistic and secular age that went before; and there is no discontinuity between the age of Shakespeare and that of the metaphysical poets" (p. 2). Calls Donne the "link between the Elizabethan dramatists and the Caroline poets" (p. 2). Maintains, "It was largely due to him that the metaphysical element in the drama was drawn into the lyric, finding a home there, and leaving the drama to become—apart from Ford's best work—more secular, commonplace, and superficial" (pp. 2 3). Lyly, Sidney, Peele, Greene, Marlowe, Nash, Dekker, Chapman, Marston, Tourneur, Webster, and especially Shakespeare are discussed. Comparisons and contrasts with Donne throughout.

≈§ 152. HOUSMAN, LAURENCE. "The Mortuary," in *Cornered Poets: A Book of Dramatic Dialogues*, pp. 237–56. New York: Jonathan Cape & Harrison Smith, Inc.

An imaginary dialogue between Donne, Donne's housekeeper, and Nicholas Stone, the craftsman who carved his effigy.

≈§ 153. PLOWMAN, MAX. "An Appreciation of the Poems of John Donne." *Everyman*, (February 14):9–10.

General appreciative statements about Donne's art and sensibility. A list of editions of Donne's poems.

≈§ 154. QUILLER-COUCH, SIR ARTHUR. "The English Elegy (II)," in *Studies in Literature: Third Series*, pp. 25–53. Cambridge: University Press; New York: G. P. Putnam's Sons.

Brief mention of Donne in this survey of the classical elegy in English.

"Such conceits as he evokes from his grisly meditations, or spins around them, came to him naturally and therefore pardonably. But when his successors imitate him in these as in other of his peculiarities, lacking his inspiration, they are apt merely to offend us" (p. 32).

◄§ 155. RICHARDS, I. A. *Practical Criticism: A Study of Literary Judgment*. New York: Harcourt, Brace & Co. 375 p.

Records and comments on various student reactions to "Holy Sonnet VII: At the round earths imagin'd corners, blow" (pp. 42–50). Attempts to show primarily the inadequacy of the responses. The remainder of the book does not discuss Donne directly but rather sets up some guidelines for reading and understanding poetry.

◄§ 156. SAITO, TAKESHI. "John Donne, his later life and works." *Studies in English Literature* (Tokyo), 9:79–106.

General survey of Donne's later life (from 1610) and works as an introduction for Japanese readers. Reads the poems and prose as autobiographical statements.

◄§ 157. TAGGARD, GENEVIEVE, ED. *Circumference: Varieties of Metaphysical Verse 1456–1928*. New York: Covici Friede, Inc. xiii, 236 p.

An anthology of metaphysical poetry which includes twenty-five poems by Donne. In Part I (pp. 3–13), the editor broadly defines metaphysical poetry as reflective of a "state of mind." Considers Donne and Emily Dickinson as the most genuine metaphysical poets and regards Keats as the best example of what a metaphysical poet is not. Limited to 1,050 copies.

◄§ 158. Z[ABEL], M[ORTON] D. "The Mechanism of Sensibility." *Poetry: A Magazine of Verse* (Chicago), 34:150–55.

Points out that in modern poetry "Poetry again becomes (in Mr. Eliot's phrase) an elaborate 'mechanism of sensibility.' In this respect it wins the designation 'metaphysical,' and with it a comparison with the art of the writers who lived in the early decades of the seventeenth century" (p. 151). Suggests the influence of Donne on Alice Meynell, Francis Thompson, Gerard Manley Hopkins, T. S. Eliot, Edith Sitwell, Sherard Vines, Allen Tate, Archibald MacLeish, Yvor Winters, Louise Bogan, Hart Crane, and especially Elinor Wylie. Maintains that the metaphysical sensibility is not always successful. "The fusion all great art requires is absent in its attempts to analyze and detail the complex existences of the poets. Their poems are significant of a salient factor in present-day art and at times they achieve great beauty, but they also make clear why the lyric poet still wins a faithful admiration for his simpler and more appealing art" (p. 155).

1930

❧ 159. Butt, J. E. "John Donne and Lincoln's Inn." *TLS*, 10 April, p. 318.

Two references to Donne found in W. P. Baildon's text of the "Black Books of Lincoln's Inn." Maintains that it is impossible that Donne made his foreign travels between 1594 and 1596. For a reply by I. A. Shapiro, see *TLS*, 16 October, p. 833, and 23 October, p. 861.

❧ 160. Donne, John. *The Courtier's Library, or Catalogus Librorum Aulicorum incomparabilium et non vendibilium by John Donne*. Edited by Evelyn Mary Simpson with a translation. London: The Nonesuch Press. 93 p.

Reprint of the *Catalogus Librorum*, "an elaborate jest in the manner of Rabelais, who had given a mock catalogue of books in the Library of Saint-Victor" (p. 1). First added by Donne the younger to the 1650 edition of the poems and "reprinted in the editions of 1654, 1669, and 1719 but not afterwards" (Keynes, 3d ed., p. 179). Translation from the Latin by Percy Simpson. Contains an introduction (pp. 1–26), the Latin text (pp. 27–38), the translation (pp. 39–53), explanatory notes (pp. 54–78), and textual notes (pp. 79–93).

❧ 161. Eliot, T. S. "Thinking in Verse: A Survey of Early Seventeenth-Century Poetry." *The Listener*, 3:441–43.

Points out that Donne thinks in verse in contrast to the Elizabethans who sing in verse. His poetry is that "which suggests music, but which, so to speak, contains in itself all its possible music; for if set to music, the play of ideas could not be followed. . . . The complications of thought and feeling which in the Elizabethan time are found chiefly in dramatic blank verse pass over, with Donne, into the shorter and semi-lyrical poem" (p. 442). Suggests that Donne was influenced by Saint Ignatius.

❧ 162. ———. "Rhyme and Reason: The Poetry of John Donne." *The Listener*, 3:502–3.

Challenges five widely accepted beliefs about Donne: (1) that he was a philosopher and thus a philosophical poet; (2) that he had a medieval mind; (3) that he is a mystical poet; (4) that the poems are autobiographical and thus reflect his immediate personal experiences; (5) that the verse is unmetrical, rough, unpolished, and generally lacking in metrical skill. Discusses the nature of metaphysical poetry: "Of metaphysical poetry in general we may say that it gets its effects by suddenly producing an emotional equivalent for what seemed merely a dry idea, and by finding the idea of a vivid emotion. It moves between abstract thought and concrete feeling; and strikes us largely by contrast and continuity, by the curious ways in which it shows thought and feeling as different aspects of one reality" (p. 502).

🔊§ 163. ————. "The Devotional Poets of the Seventeenth Century: Donne, Herbert, Crashaw." *The Listener*, 3:552–53.

Discusses the conversational quality of Donne's verse and the problem of sincerity. Concludes that the two greatest creative acts of Donne are "his introduction of a new vocabulary in verse, and his introduction of new metres" (p. 552). Distinguishes between religious verse and devotional verse: "I call 'religious' what is inspired by religious feeling of some kind; and 'devotional' that which is directly about some subject connected with revealed religion" (p. 552). Compares and contrasts Donne with Herbert, Crashaw, and Vaughan.

🔊§ 164. EMPSON, WILLIAM. *Seven Types of Ambiguity*. London: Chatto & Windus Ltd. 325 p.

Reprinted, New York: Harcourt, Brace & Co., 1937.

2d ed., London: Chatto & Windus Ltd., 1947; New York: New Directions, 1949.

3d ed., London: Chatto & Windus Ltd., 1953; Norfolk, Conn.: J. Laughlin (New Directions), 1953; New York: The Noonday Press, 1955.

Pages 139–48 of 3d ed. are reprinted in *John Donne: A Collection of Critical Essays*, ed. Helen Gardner (1962), pp. 52–60.

A close reading of "A Valediction: of weeping" (pp. 175–83) in which the author uses Donne's poem to illustrate the fourth type of ambiguity. States that Donne's poem is ambiguous "because his feelings were painfully mixed, and because he felt that at such a time it would be ungenerous to spread them out clearly in his mind; to express sorrow at the obvious fact of parting gave an adequate relief to his disturbance, and the variety of irrelevant, incompatible ways of feeling about the affair that were lying about in his mind were able so to modify, enrich, leave their mark upon, this plain lyrical relief as to make it something more memorable" (p. 183). Comments briefly on "Holy Sonnet XIII: What if this present were the worlds last night?" (pp. 183–84) and "The Apparition" (pp. 184–86) to illustrate further his central point.

🔊§ 165. GRIERSON, H. J. C. "The Oxford 'Donne.'" *TLS*, 20 February, p. 142.

Comments on the 1929 edition of Donne's poems. Promises a description of a new manuscript that contains several items by Donne. Comments on Baxter.

🔊§ 166. ————. "Donne's Satyres, II., ll. 71–73." *TLS*, 6 March, p. 190.

Reply to Charles Sisson, *TLS*, 20 February, p. 142. Rejects the suggestion that line 71 of *Satyre II* should read "Braying like Asses." For a reply by Sisson, see *TLS*, 13 March, p. 214.

◄§ 167. HAMER, ENID. *The Metres of English Poetry.* London: Methuen & Co., Ltd.; New York: The Macmillan Co. xi, 340 p.

Brief comments on Donne's metrics (pp. 50, 237, 199–202). Particularly singled out for comment are the religious poems: "Nothing in all sonnet literature approaches the blend, or swift alternations, of exquisite tenderness and amazing energy, reverent simplicity and subtle philosophy which characterise these poems of Donne" (p. 200).

◄§ 168. NETHERCOT, ARTHUR H. "The Reputation of Native Versus Foreign 'Metaphysical Poets.'" *MLR*, 25:152–64.

Studies the English reputation of Marino, du Bartas, and Góngora. Concludes, "In the early seventeenth century all three continental poets had considerable weight and authority. They were read, translated, and imitated. By the Restoration all were being severely attacked for excesses of style—whereas the English metaphysicals were yet fairly well entrenched in popular regard. During the age of Pope the foreigners were held in even more contempt than the English, for whom some readers and critics still had a good word to say. During the age of Johnson that dictator's criticisms of the English would seem fulsome encomiums compared to what was being generally said about the foreigners. There was a revival of interest in the English Metaphysicals as a minor aspect of the Romantic Revival. But there was no such revival for Marino, Du Bartas, and Góngora" (p. 164). Donne is not mentioned specifically.

◄§ 169. SHAPIRO, I. A. "John Donne and Lincoln's Inn, 1591–1594—I." *TLS*, 16 October, p. 833; "John Donne and Lincoln's Inn, 1591–1594—II." *TLS*, 23 October, p. 861.

In part a reply to J. E. Butt, *TLS*, 10 April, p. 318. Examines the complete text of the "Black Books of Lincoln's Inn," which contains several references to Donne during the years 1591–1594. Maintains that Donne's foreign travels must have occurred some time between July 1593 and the spring of 1598.

◄§ 170. SIMPSON, EVELYN M. "William Strachey." *TLS*, 31 July, p. 628.

Reply to Charles Strachey, *TLS*, 24 July, p. 611. Points out that the letter described as previously unpublished appears on p. 317 of *A Study of the Prose Works of John Donne* (1924).

◄§ 171. SISSON, CHARLES. "The Oxford 'Donne.'" *TLS*, 20 February, p. 142.

Suggests that line 71 of *Satyre II* should be emended to read "Braying like Asses" rather than "Bearing like Asses." For a reply by H. J. C. Grierson, see *TLS*, 6 March, p. 190. See also Sisson, *TLS*, 13 March, p. 214.

✎§ 172. ———. "Donne's Satyres, II., ll. 71–73." *TLS*, 13 March, p. 214.

Reply to H. J. C. Grierson, *TLS*, 6 March, p. 190. Supports his contention that line 71 of *Satyre II* should read "Braying like Asses." See also Sisson, *TLS*, 20 February, p. 142.

✎§ 173. STRACHEY, CHARLES. "William Strachey." *TLS*, 24 July, p. 611.

Publication of a Donne letter discovered in 1905 by Logan Pearsall Smith. Identifies the Sir T. G. referred to in the letter as Sir Thomas Glover. For a reply by Evelyn M. Simpson, see *TLS*, 31 July, p. 628.

✎§ 174. TOLLES, CATHERINE. "The Fire and Dew of Emily Dickinson." *The Mount Holyoke Monthly*, 37:209–22.

Discusses Emily Dickinson as a metaphysicist, which the author defines as one who "stirs up the world, looks at it through psychological eyes, plays with it, turns it inside out, analyzes it; then he synthesizes it into one systematic principle through the multiplicity of his observations" (p. 210). Makes a series of comparisons between Emily Dickinson and Donne: their lives are seen as somewhat analogous, as well as their poetic sensibilities and vision. Concludes, "Emily Dickinson, then, is like John Donne, a psychological metaphysicist—introspective, with a curious coldness and ability to probe the mind; but she is also like Ralph Waldo Emerson, the philosophical metaphysicist" (p. 216).

✎§ 175. WILLIAMSON, GEORGE. *The Donne Tradition: A Study in English Poetry from Donne to the Death of Cowley*. Cambridge: Harvard University Press; Oxford: University Press. x, 264 p.

Reprinted, New York: The Noonday Press, 1958 (paperback) and 1961; New York: The Noonday Press, ed. bound by Peter Smith, 1958.

While recognizing that the metaphysical poets were unaware of belonging to a particular school of poetry, the author holds that there was a Donne tradition, although perhaps not sharply defined. Argues that, although "there was no sealed tribe of Donne," nevertheless, "his influence was the most profound and pervasive of any in the first half of his century" (p. 229). Traces Donne's influence to the death of Cowley. Chapter I contains a general biographical sketch of Donne. Chapter II, "The Nature of the Tradition," presents the main features of the poetry of the Donne tradition, especially intellectual intensity, unified sensibility, wit, the conceit, analysis, technical features, particular uses of language, erudition, and difficulty. "The nature of this tradition may be concisely defined as complex, sensuous, and intellectual as opposed to the simple, sensuous, and passionate tradition" (p. 57). Chapter III offers a comparison of Chapman and Donne. In Chapter IV, "Prologue to the Succession," the author writes: "The line of Metaphysicals in the seventeenth century becomes distinct in the influence of poet upon poet, deriving more or less directly from Donne, but remaining a thing of individuals rather than a school, till it attains something like critical consciousness in the mind of Dryden" (p. 75). Two major aspects of the Donne tradition are discussed—the conceit and *metaphysical shudder*, the term the author applies to the emotional quality of the poems. Chapter V traces the sacred line of the tradition in Herbert, Crashaw, and Vaughan, while Chapter VI traces the profane line in Lord Herbert of Cherbury, Henry King, Marvell, and Aurelian Townshend. Chapter VII presents a critical survey of "The Chief Offenders"—namely Cleveland, Benlowes, and Cowley. Chapter VIII discusses the similarities and dissimilarities between Donne and Jonson and maintains that Donne was the chief influence on the Cavalier poets: "Donne was their inspiration" (p. 200). Chapter IX surveys Dryden's attitudes toward the Donne Tradition and accounts briefly for the reaction that set in during the Restoration. The final chapter is entitled "A Short View of the Tradition." Appendix A (pp. 251–52) is "A Chronology of Inheritance." Appendix B (p. 253) is a list of seventeenth-century editions of Donne's poems. Appendix C (pp. 254–57) is a collection of conceits from Chapman's poems. Appendix D (pp. 258–64) is a selective bibliography of 61 items.

◄§ 176. WILLMORE, M. O. "John Donne." *London Quarterly Review*, 153–54:109–11.
Finds two strains combined in Donne's poetry, "the learned and erudite, and the passionate and real" (pp. 109–10). Maintains that, although Donne was a man of learning, he is not the same as Lucretius and Dante, poets who found their poetic inspiration in their philosophical conceptions of the universe.

1931

◄§ 177. ANON. "Dr. John Donne." *The Manchester Guardian Weekly*, 24, No. 14 (April 3):273.
Commemorative biographical sketch on the occasion of Donne's tercentenary celebration.

◄§ 178. ANON. "John Donne." *TLS*, 26 March, pp. 241–42.
General appreciative essay stressing in particular Donne's paradoxical and ambivalent mind. Resists a strictly autobiographical approach. "All that we can know is that Donne was attempting to lay bare certain moods and feelings and to tell the truth about them" (p. 241).

◄§ 179. ANON. "John Donne: Preacher and Bencher of Lincoln's Inn." *The Times* (London), 31 March, p. 16.
Note commemorating the 300th anniversary of Donne's death. A presentation of his connection with Lincoln's Inn, not only as a student but

also as the Divinity Reader of the House, from October 24, 1616, to February 11, 1622, a position considered "in those days as one of the most important clerical positions in London." After his resignation, Donne was appointed Bencher of the House and allowed to keep his chambers.

❧ 180. ADDLESHAW, S. "A Famous Dean: Dr John Donne of St. Paul's." *Church Quarterly Review*, 113:38–54.
General survey of Donne's modern revival, of his biography, and particularly of his religious attitudes. Claims that "Donne's permanent claim to our interest, consists in the fact, that in his best work, he reveals his own vivid personality, lays bare his own soul and mind, so that we can know him as we know few writers" (p. 54).

❧ 181. BEACHCROFT, T. O. "Quarles—and the Emblem Habit." *Dublin Review*, 188:80–96.
Consideration of the operation of the emblem and the symbolic habit of mind that it produced and reflected. States that "Donne's poems abound in good emblem thought, forming sometimes complete poems, sometimes less complete emblem passages in longer poems" (p. 92). Comments particularly on "The Primrose" and "The Flea," though other emblematic passages are mentioned. Concludes, "It is in Donne . . . who makes most striking use of the emblem habit among the metaphysical poets in general" (p. 93).

❧ 182. BENNETT, R. E. "John Manningham and Donne's Paradoxes." *MLN*, 46:309–13.
Announces the discovery of selections from four paradoxes in the *Diary of John Manningham*, edited by John Bruce for the Camden Society in 1868. Two are definitely Donne's, and two are tentatively attributed to Donne. Concludes, "the Manningham material constitutes our earliest dated reference to any of the paradoxes, and shows that a manuscript, containing material which has not been found, was in circulation early in 1603" (pp. 312–13).

❧ 183. BENSLY, EDWARD. "A Query on Donne's Sermon XXX." *N&Q*, 161:230.
In part a reply to a query made by A. C. Howell, *N&Q*, 161:156–57. Notes that Thomas Brooks (1608–1680) gives the number of "God's Books" as six, one of which is "the book of man's conscience" found in Donne's sermon.

❧ 184. CHAMBERS, E. K. "An Elegy by John Donne." *RES*, 7:69–71.
Transcript of a hitherto unpublished elegy by Donne found in the Holgate MS. in the Pierpont Morgan Library. First line: "When my heart was mine owne, and not by vows."

⊷§ 185. CRUM, RALPH B. "Poetry and the New Science," in *Scientific Thought in Poetry*, pp. 40–60. New York: Columbia University Press.

Argues that Donne resisted the new thought but utilized the new imagery that science made available. "It is to be noted that Donne does not champion the new science, nor can it be said that his many ingenious images are drawn primarily from that source. The influence that science had upon him can best be seen, I believe, in his questioning attitude of mind, and in his tendency to experiment with poetic imagery. Much of his imagery is drawn from scientific analogies, and he pointed the way in this respect to many other English poets of this time" (p. 47).

⊷§ 186. DEAS, M. C. "A Note on Rowland Woodward, the Friend of Donne." *RES*, 7:454–57.

Summarizes the known facts about Rowland Woodward and presents several new pieces of information gathered from the registers of St. Mary-le-Bowe, the letters of Wotton, and the Public Record Office.

⊷§ 187. ELIOT, THOMAS STEARNS. "Donne in Our Time," in *A Garland for John Donne, 1631–1931*, ed. Theodore Spencer, pp. 3–19. Cambridge, Mass.: Harvard University Press; London: Humphrey Milford, Oxford University Press.

States that "Donne's poetry is a concern of the present and the recent past, rather than of the future" (p. 5) and suggests that "it is impossible for us or for anyone else ever to disentangle how much [of Donne's modern popularity] was genuine affinity, genuine appreciation, and how much was just a *reading into* poets like Donne our own sensibility, how much was subjective" (p. 6). Qualifies his earlier estimates of Donne by pointing out that in Donne's poetry "there is a manifest fissure between thought and sensibility, a chasm which in his poetry he bridged in his own way, which was not the way of medieval poetry. His learning is just information suffused with emotion, or combined with emotion not essentially relevant to it" (p. 8). Recognizes both Donne and Dryden as great reformers of English verse and maintains that the popularity of any poet is greatly conditioned by shifting literary perspectives and tastes. "Donne and Dryden were *equally* reformers of the language; both brought in a vital and energetic simplicity, and natural conversational speech in verse" (p. 17). Says that Donne's sermons "will disappear as suddenly as they have appeared" (p. 19), but, "It is hardly too much to say that Donne enlarged the possibilities of lyric verse as no other English poet has done" (p. 14).

⋅≈§ 188. ELLIOTT, G. R. "John Donne: The Middle Phase." *The Book-man* (New York), 73:337–46.

Rejects the *psycho-romantic* views of Donne. In Donne's own century "His violent contrasts were accepted, apparently, as quite natural. No one was trying to fuse them in the pale heat of psychologic theory. No modern biographer was trying to fit all his parts into a single smart picture" (p. 338). Surveys Donne's middle phase briefly and concludes, "When an adequate critical biography of him comes to be written, it will interpret his whole life and work in the light of his middle phase, for this . . . was not *merely* a phase, much less a negligible phase. It represents the groundtone of the whole man. This fact was of course not at all clear to Donne himself. In his late years, he liked to disparage his middle years, and to damn his early years. But the truth is, he was not nearly so damned at twenty, nor so saved at fifty, as he wished to believe; or as romantic critics would like to believe with certain changes in terminology" (p. 346).

⋅≈§ 189. EVANS, E. W. PRICE. "John Donne—The Poet-Preacher of St. Paul's." *The Welsh Outlook* (Cardiff), August:208–10.

General character sketch in commemoration of Donne's tercentenary celebration. Points to Donne's Welsh lineage. Singles out the sermons as Donne's most impressive literary efforts.

⋅≈§ 190. FAUSSET, HUGH I'A. "The Poet and His Vision." *The Bookman* (London), 79:341–42.

Suggests that Donne's unified sensibility is the main reason for his modern revival. "It is because his poetry is such an intricate composite of living thought and sensuous experience that it appeals so strongly to a generation which is struggling to free itself from a mental consciousness that has brought spiritual death in its train" (p. 342). First article in a series of four entitled "In Memory of John Donne" in *The Bookman* (London), 79:341–47. For the other three articles, see Christopher Saltmarshe, "John Donne: The Man and His Life"; Cyril Tomkinson, "A Note on the Personal Religion of Dr. Donne"; F. R. Leavis, "The Influence of Donne on Modern Poetry."

⋅≈§ 191. FOSTER, THOMAS. "The Tragedy of John Donne." *The Month* (London), 157:404–9.

Discusses Donne's abandonment of Catholicism. Says he is "inclined to doubt whether his change of faith was prompted by the conscientious convictions that some of his biographers assume" (p. 406). Sees Donne as a cynic, an immoral youth, a place seeker who was willing to abandon his Catholic faith for temporal gains. Concludes that Donne "did not die a Catholic; but it is certain that he did not die a Protestant. He died an enquirer, and one who had already moved far on the way to that place whither all roads lead" (p. 409).

ᴥᴥ 192. Grierson, H. J. C. "Donne and the Roman Poets." *TLS*, 26 February, p. 154.
A reply to Jack Lindsay, *TLS*, 19 February, p. 135. States that only in "The Expostulation" are Donne's borrowings from Ovid obvious and that the poem did not appear in the first edition of Donne's verse, but it did appear in Jonson's *Underwoods*. Nevertheless argues that the poem is Donne's, but points out that the Ovidian echoes are part of the argument for attributing it to Jonson. Notes that the borrowing from *The Greek Anthology* that appears in "A Tale of a Citizen and his Wife" (ll. 64 65) had been pointed out previously.

ᴥᴥ 193. Hacker, Mary. "To John Donne." *The Bookman* (London), 80:140.
An original sonnet on Donne for which the author was awarded one guinea.

ᴥᴥ 194. Hayward, John. "A Note on Donne the Preacher," in *A Garland for John Donne, 1631–1931*, ed. Theodore Spencer, pp. 73–97. Cambridge, Mass.: Harvard University Press; London: Humphrey Milford and Oxford University Press.
Points out that Donne's sermons were "the only works which he designed for posterity, and which he left revised and corrected by his own hand with the wish that his son should print them after his death" (p. 76). Discusses the relationship between the sermons as delivered and the printed texts, and concludes, "Generally speaking, his practice appears to have been that of the lecturer, who, in introducing a collection of his printed lectures, announces in his preface that his words, though substantially the same as those uttered before an audience, have been altered in places to conform to the permanent requirements of a book" (pp. 85–86). Discusses in some detail six of the sermons that exist in two versions to illustrate his conclusion.

ᴥᴥ 195. Howell, A. C. "A Query on Donne's Sermon XXX, Folio of 1640." *N&Q*, 161:156–57.
In addition to the conventional references to "the Book of God's Word" and "the Book of God's Works," the author finds a reference to "the Book of Man's Conscience" in "Sermon XXX." Points out that the same triad appears in Felltham's "Resolves," No. clxviii, and suggests a possible borrowing either way. For a reply by Edward Bensly, see *N&Q*, 161:230.

✍§ 196. HUTCHINSON, F. E. "Donne the Preacher." *Theology* (London), March:155–63.

Discusses the continuity between Jack and John Donne. Surveys the career of Donne as a preacher, comments briefly on the style and techniques of the sermons, and makes several observations on the subject matter of the sermons.

✍§ 197. JOHNSON, STANLEY. "Donne's 'Autumnall Elegy.'" *TLS*, 30 April, p. 347.

A reply to Jack Lindsay, *TLS*, 19 March, p. 234. Suggests that the source for the reference to Xerxes and the plane-tree is most probably Aelian's *Variae Historiae*, not William Browne's *Britannia Pastorals*. Agrees with Grierson that "The Autumnall" was most likely written at some time between 1607 and 1609.

✍§ 198. KITCHIN, GEORGE. "Jacobean and Later Seventeenth Century Parody and Burlesque," in *A Survey of Burlesque and Parody in English*, pp. 68–98. Edinburgh, London: Oliver and Boyd.

Comments briefly on Donne's uses of parody (pp. 70–73) and calls them "some remnants of mediaeval burlesque." Discusses "The Baite" as a parody of Marlowe's "Come Live with Me," "The Sunne Rising" as a parody of the aubade, "The Will" as a parody of the medieval will-and-testament poem, and "An Epithalamion, Or mariage Song on the Lady Elizabeth, and Count Palatine" as employing the use of the play of the birds in the burlesque Court of Love poem.

✍§ 199. LEAVIS, F. R. "The Influence of Donne on Modern Poetry." *The Bookman* (London), 79:346–47.

"In the tradition established by Donne it was assumed that a poet should be a man of distinguished intelligence, and that he should bring into his poetry the varied interests of his life. This, to put it briefly, is the importance of Donne to modern poetry" (p. 346). General attack on nineteenth-century poetry, which was "characteristically preoccupied with the creation of a dream-world" (p. 346). Praises Eliot's poetry and criticism for restoring "the seventeenth century to its proper place in the English tradition" (p. 347). Modern poets owe much to Eliot, because "what they will learn from him will be, as much as anything, how to learn from Donne" (p. 347). The fourth article in a series of four entitled "In Memory of John Donne" in *The Bookman* (London), 79: 341–47. For the other three articles, see Hugh I'A. Fausset, "The Poet and His Vision"; Christopher Saltmarshe, "John Donne: The Man and His Life"; Cyril Tomkinson, "A Note on the Personal Religion of Dr. Donne."

✒§ 200. LINDSAY, JACK. "Donne and the Roman Poets." *TLS*, 19 February, p. 135.

Points out several of Donne's borrowings from Roman poets: Catullus, Propertius, Petronius, Martial, Juvenal, and an epigram in the *Palatine Anthology*. "The Expostulation" is called "a mosaic of borrowings from Catullus." For a reply by H. J. C. Grierson, see *TLS*, 26 February, p. 154.

✒§ 201. ———. "The Date of Donne's 'Autumnall' Elegy." *TLS*, 19 March, p. 234.

Suggests 1613 as the most probable date for the composition of the poem. This conclusion is based primarily on a reference to Xerxes and the plane-tree, which occurs in William Browne's *Britannia's Pastorals*, Book II, Song IV. For a reply by Stanley Johnson, see *TLS*, 30 April, p. 347. See also E. E. Duncan-Jones, *N&Q*, n.s., 7(1960):53.

✒§ 202. MACAULAY, ROSE. "Anglican and Puritan," in *Some Religious Elements in English Literature*, pp. 84–126. London: Hogarth Press.

Brief sketch of Donne's religious temperament. Praises his intensity and intellectualism in particular.

✒§ 203. NICHOLLS, NORAH. "The Early Editions of John Donne." *The Bookman* (London), 79:370–71.

Very general survey of the early editions.

✒§ 204. PORTER, ALAN. "Dean Donne." *Spectator*, 146:539–40.

Appreciative essay on Donne as an "original" in his personality as well as his works. Comments on his preoccupation with the theme of death. Briefly traces Donne's reputation and concludes that "in our own day . . . there is probably no poet more seriously studied and more admired. . . . Perhaps what wins him most admiration is that he found a means to express passion without sentiment" (p. 540).

✒§ 205. PRAZ, MARIO. "Donne and the Poetry of His Time," in *A Garland for John Donne, 1631–1931*, ed. Theodore Spencer, pp. 51–72. Cambridge, Mass.: Harvard University Press; London: Humphrey Milford, Oxford University Press.

Reprinted in revised form in *John Donne: A Collection of Critical Essays*, ed. Helen Gardner (1962), pp. 61–76.

In a much revised form, this essay appears in *The Flaming Heart: Essays on Crashaw, Machiavelli, and Other Studies in the Relations between Italian and English Literature from Chaucer to T. S. Eliot*, Mario Praz (Garden City, N. Y.: Doubleday & Co., Inc., 1958), pp. 186–203.

Using "The Dreame" as a point of departure, the author stresses the originality of Donne's verse, in particular, "its dramatic character, its metrical originality, its crabbed and prosaic imagery" (p. 56) and emphasizes Donne's concern with the total effect of the poem: "His sole preoccupation is with the whole effect" (p. 57). Suggests that "the 'argumentative, subtle evolution' of the lyric strain is the thing Donne shares only with such mediaeval poets as Guido Guinizelli, Guido Cavalcanti, and Dante in his minor mood; the other metaphysical characteristic, the 'peculiar blend of passion and thought, feeling and ratiocination,' of which 'learned imagery' is the consequence, is by no means such a rare thing in poetry that traces of it may not be found in many Elizabethan writers, chiefly in the dramatists" (p. 58). Points out that Donne's "cultural equipment was in many ways that of a Scholastic thinker; hence the curious affinity some of his poetry shows to that of Dante's circle. With the difference that, whereas those mediaeval poets believed in the scientific and philosophical theories they accepted as the background of their verse, Donne, living in an age of scientific revolution, could not help surveying with a sceptic's eye the state of confusion presented by a changing world" (p. 61). Compares Donne's religious verse to that of Michelangelo and comments on several similarities, yet concludes, "Donne, of course, could not know Michelangelo's sonnets which were posthumously published in 1623. But for his peculiar mixture of realism and platonism, for the dramatic turn of his genius as well as for his laborious yearnings for beauty and religion, for that double character of half-baffled, half-triumphant struggle, for his power of depicting the horrors of sin and death, and the terrible effects of the wrath of God, Donne is perhaps nearer to Michelangelo than to anyone else" (p. 72). Places Donne in his own time but suggests his originality and his appeal to modern sensibility.

⋙§ 206. RAMSAY, MARY PATON. "Donne's Relation to Philosophy," in *A Garland for John Donne, 1631–1931*, ed. Theodore Spencer, pp. 99–120. Cambridge, Mass.: Harvard University Press; London: Humphrey Milford, Oxford University Press.

States that "Donne and his successors are by no means the only Metaphysicals, and of Donne himself it cannot be said that he originated the metaphysical element in poetry" (p. 102). However, she admits that "there is in Donne what we may call a particular metaphysical quality, over and above that which is common to his generation" (p. 104). The two main sources that impart to Donne's writings their own essential quality are: (1) his personality, "the individual quality of his genius, intangible and undefinable" (p. 102); and (2) "the material in which he works, the selection which his genius makes from the elements presented to it on which he exerts its action to combine them into a work of art" (p. 104). The essay is primarily concerned with the latter, particularly the ways in which certain aspects of scholastic philosophy affected

Donne's vision of reality and thus his poetry. Argues that Donne's poetry is conditioned by the disintegration of the scholastic system under attack from the New Philosophy. Donne stands as the great amphibian, in a sense, between the two conflicting worlds. Although Donne utilized elements from the scholastic system and continued to think in terms of the older system, "something irreplaceable has been lost; the unifying principle, the conception of completeness, the certainty return no more" (pp. 113–14).

⊷§ 207. RYLANDS, GEORGE. "English Poets and the Abstract Word." *E&S* of 1930, 16:53–84.
Discusses different ways in which concrete and abstract words are combined and used in English poetry. Considers Donne to be more emotional than Eliot, more concrete than Shelley. "Donne calls absence a thing; Shelley calls desolation a thing; it is significant. In Donne, however, abstract words nearly always define states of mind or of being: the abstractions of Shelley are spiritual; he peoples the universe with influences and spirits" (p. 60).

⊷§ 208. SALOMON, LOUIS B. *The Rebellious Lover in English Poetry.* Philadelphia: University of Pennsylvania Press. 359 p.
Brief comments throughout on Donne's rebellious and cynical expression of love toward women in his poetry in this study devoted to tracing "the progress of amorous insubordination through English poetry: that is, to observe the poetical expression of attitudes opposed to the usual devoted submissiveness of love verses" (p. 1).

⊷§ 209. SALTMARSHE, CHRISTOPHER. "John Donne: The Man and His Life." *The Bookman* (London), 79:343–44.
Biographical sketch that challenges the myth of Jack and John Donne. Describes Donne as being "wholly out of sympathy with the various romantic reactions, religious, political and literary, from the Renascence" (p. 343). Second article in a series of four entitled "In Memory of John Donne" in *The Bookman* (London), 79:341–47. For the other three articles, see Hugh I'A. Fausset, "A Poet and His Vision"; Cyril Tomkinson, "A Note on the Religion of Dr. Donne"; F. R. Leavis, "The Influence of Donne on Modern Poetry."

⊷§ 210. SCHIRMER, WALTER F. "Die geistesgeschichtlichen Grundlagen der englischen Barockliteratur." *GRM*, 19:273–84.
Discusses the philosophical background of the English baroque. Donne is placed with Herbert, Vaughan, and Crashaw in the mystic current as opposed to the Puritan stream. Donne's poetry is characterized by its dominating subjectivity. He translates emotion into intellectual terms rather than into conventional metaphorical terms. Donne is direct, be-

cause he wants something other than Petrarchan idealism, and, like Milton, he tries to justify love as passion. His *discordia concors* reflects the split in the age. The divine poems founded the school of the personal, intellectually satiated, religious lyric in England.

◄§ 211. SHAPIRO, I. A. "The Text of Donne's *Letters to Severall Persons*." *RES*, 7:291–301.

Attempts "to discover from internal evidence how the text of 1651 was obtained, and how far it may be trusted" (p. 292).

◄§ 212. SIMPSON, EVELYN M. "Donne's 'Paradoxes and Problems,'" in *A Garland for John Donne, 1631–1931*, ed. Theodore Spencer, pp. 21–49. Cambridge, Mass.: Harvard University Press; London: Humphrey Milford, Oxford University Press.

Surveys the textual and critical history of the *Paradoxes and Problemes* and emphasizes the pervasive influence of Martial. Recognizes these exercises as "the earliest, and also the slightest, of his prose works" (p. 23) and warns against taking the morality of these pieces at face value. "Donne is writing as the clever young man who wishes to be thought more unscrupulous than he is. He writes to amuse, to startle, and to shock. He has no thought of publication, but he sends copies of his paradoxes with strict injunctions of secrecy to certain chosen friends, young, fashionable, and discontented like himself" (p. 30). Concludes, "It was fitting that his first literary attempts at literary prose should take this particular form. For what was Donne's work, all through his life, but the asking of the questions and the statement of paradoxes? Paradox is at the heart of all his theology; problem is the essence of his poetry. To find the One behind the Many, to trace the permanent throughout the ever-changing, to ask the riddle of the universe, this was the quest on which Donne set forth early, and continued late till death overtook him" (pp. 42–43). Appendix on Donne's reading of Martial (pp. 44–49).

◄§ 213. SPARROW, JOHN. "The Date of Donne's Travels," in *A Garland for John Donne, 1631–1931*, ed. Theodore Spencer, pp. 121–51. Cambridge, Mass.: Harvard University Press; London: Humphrey Milford, Oxford University Press.

Reviews a number of problems concerning Donne's biography, especially during the period of his young manhood. Argues that the most convincing date for Donne's early travels on the Continent is 1595–1596.

◄§ 214. ———. "A Book from Donne's Library." *London Mercury*, 25:171–80.

Description of a volume of Latin poems in the Bodleian, entitled *Epigrammata et Poematia Vetera*, ed. P. Pithou (Paris, 1590), which contains marginal notes by Donne.

❧§ 215. ———. "The Earlier Owners of Books in John Selden's Library." *Bodleian Quarterly Record*, 6:263–71.

Lists eighteen volumes bearing Donne's signature and motto, which are found among the books from the Selden Library now housed in the Selden End.

❧§ 216. ———. "John Donne and Contemporary Preachers: Their Preparation of Sermons for Delivery and for Publication." *E&S of 1930*, 16:144–178.

Discusses the "normal history of the text of a seventeenth-century sermon from its delivery to its publication, illustrating the account with a few examples from well-known and easily accessible material" (p. 144). Recounts the textual history of Donne's sermons.

❧§ 217. ———. "Donne's Religious Development." *Theology* (London), March:144–54.

Traces Donne's religious development and maintains that there was no "moment of a single great change making a sanctified out of an unregenerated character" (p. 154). Judging from Donne's writings, "there is no trace of a conversion from scepticism to a belief in God" (p. 148) nor was his break with Catholicism sudden and violent. "His decision not to adhere to the faith of his parents was made gradually, it was made on purely intellectual grounds, and it was made when Donne's religious life was at its lowest degree of intensity; he never was—he was only born a Roman Catholic; he was not converted to Anglicanism, he simply discovered himself to be an Anglican" (p. 149). The change from layman to priest is viewed not as a significant moment in his religious development but simply as a 'fresh impulse to the practical expression of his devotion" (p. 153).

❧§ 218. SPENCER, THEODORE, ED. *A Garland for John Donne, 1631–1931*. Cambridge, Mass.: Harvard University Press; London: Humphrey Milford, Oxford University Press. 202 p.

Reprinted, Gloucester, Mass.: Peter Smith, 1958.

A collection of eight essays in honor of the tercentenary of the death of Donne. Each of these essays has been entered separately in the bibliography. Contains the following items: T. S. Eliot, "Donne in Our Time" (pp. 1–19); Evelyn M. Simpson, "Donne's 'Paradoxes and Problems' " (pp. 21–49); Mario Praz, "Donne and the Poetry of His Time" (pp. 51–71); John Hayward, "A Note on Donne the Preacher" (pp. 73–97); Mary Paton Ramsey, "Donne's Relation to Philosophy" (pp. 99–120); John Sparrow, "The Date of Donne's Travels" (pp. 121–51); George Williamson, "Donne and the Poetry of Today" (pp. 153–76); and Theodore Spencer, "Donne in His Age" (pp. 177–202).

⌐§ 219. ————. "Donne and His Age," in *A Garland for John Donne,*
1631–1931, ed. Theodore Spencer, pp. 177–202. Cambridge, Mass.:
Harvard University Press; London: Humphrey Milford, Oxford
University Press.

Maintains that Donne's style "is merely the form of his thought, and
his thought reflects more completely than any of his contemporaries, the
varying states of mind which England, from 1590 to 1620, experienced
with such bewildering rapidity" (p. 180). To illustrate his central premise, the author divides Donne's creative life into three periods: "the
first, from 1590 to 1601, is a time of action crossed by conflicting currents
of passion and cynicism; the second, from his marriage to his ordination
(1601–1614), is a time of unhappy meditation; the third, from his ordination to his death (1614–1631), is a time of acceptance, achieved
through union of action and meditation" (p. 180).

⌐§ 220. STEWART, JEAN. "The Late Renaissance," in *Poetry in France
and England,* pp. 45–65. London: Leonard and Virginia Woolf at
the Hogarth Press.

Attempts "to trace, simultaneously, the evolution of poetry in France
and in England, and to show how, at certain periods, the guiding principles of art were alike in both countries, although the application of those
principles was characteristically different; and how, at other times, each
country follows an entirely independent line of development" (p. 8).
Elementary survey of the basic characteristics of Donne's poetry (pp.
57–61) with the suggestion that nothing paralleling the metaphysical
sprang up in France at the same period.

⌐§ 221. SUNNE, RICHARD. "Books in General." *The New Statesman and
Nation,* n.s., 1:222.

General tribute to Donne—"the most remarkable instance outside
Spain of a man of high imagination and great intellectual gifts deciding
that, after all, the Renaissance had not brought the age of faith to an
end" (p. 222). Discusses briefly Donne's popularity, his skepticism, and
his interest in metaphysical speculation and death.

⌐§ 222. TOMKINSON, CYRIL. "A Note on the Personal Religion of Dr.
Donne." *The Bookman* (London), 79:345–46.

Brief survey of Donne's religious attitudes and development. Comments on his consciousness of sin, his horror of hell, his humility, and
the genuinely spiritual nature of his vocation to holy orders. Sees the
death of Anne More in 1617 as a turning point in Donne's religious development, "something like a conversion" (p. 346). Concludes, "Inconsistency must never be confused with hypocrisy; and Donne was utterly
sincere" (p. 346). Third article in a series of four entitled "In Memory
of John Donne" in *The Bookman* (London), 79:341–47. For the other

three articles, see Hugh I'A. Fausset, "The Poet and His Vision"; Christopher Saltmarshe, "John Donne: The Man and His Life"; F. R. Leavis, "The Influence of Donne on Modern Poetry."

◄§ 223. WHITE, HELEN C. *English Devotional Literature [Prose] 1600–1640*. University of Wisconsin Studies in Language and Literature, No. 29. Madison, Wisconsin: University of Wisconsin Press. 307 p.

Critical survey of Catholic and Protestant books of devotion published between 1600 and 1640 and of the historical circumstances from which they arose and were shaped. Refers to Donne throughout. Contrasts Donne's *Devotions* with those of Lancelot Andrewes (pp. 252–57). "It is from first to last as a book of devotion, that we value Andrewes' work; it is as a book of religious psychology, a book of deep and intimate self-revelation, that we treasure Donne's" (p. 253). Discusses the *Devotions* in the light of the devotional revival of the period.

◄§ 224. WILLIAMSON, GEORGE. "Donne and the Poetry of Today," in *A Garland for John Donne, 1631–1931*, ed. Theodore Spencer, pp. 153–76. Cambridge, Mass.: Harvard University Press; London: Humphrey Milford, Oxford University Press.

Discusses the nature and extent of Donne's influence on modern poets, particularly T. S. Eliot, Herbert Read, John Crowe Ransom, and Elinor Wylie. Proposes "to deal above all with the Donne who exists for the contemporary poet" (p. 155) and to make clear that "Most of the contemporary poets who have been influenced by Donne have been influenced by those aspects of him which T. S. Eliot has made accessible in our time" (p. 155). States that "The greatest hold of Donne and the Elizabethans on Eliot and other contemporary poets lies in this: they provide the greatest instance in our literature of poets moulding language to new developments of sensibility" (pp. 161–62). Comparing Donne and Eliot, the author notes: "In nothing are Donne and Eliot more akin than in the fact that each has taught his fellow poets what it means to be 'contemporary.' The immediate result in both cases has been that their idioms have become extremely contagious and their attitudes the attitude of a generation. To be contemporary in the right sense means to find the peculiar emotional tension of the time and to mould language to its expression" (p. 165).

◄§ 225. WOOD, H. HARVEY. "Donne's 'Mr. Tilman': A Postscript." *TLS*, 9 July, p. 547.

Postscript to Wood's article "A Seventeenth-Century Manuscript of Poems by Donne and Others," in *E&S* of 1930, 16:179–90. Identifies Mr. Tilman as Edward Tilman of Pembroke.

⮾§ 226. ————. "A Seventeenth-Century Manuscript of Poems by Donne and Others." *E&S* of 1930, 16:179–90.

Describes a manuscript discovered at Taverham Hall near Norwich, which contains seventeen items attributed to Donne. Contains a poem by Mr. Tilman entitled "Mr. Tilman of Pembroke Hall in Cambridge his motives not to take orders," a poem that apparently occasioned Donne's "To Mr. Tilman after he had taken orders." Tilman's poem is reproduced for the first time (pp. 184–86). A postscript appears in *TLS*, 9 July, p. 547. See also John Butt, *TLS*, 15 December 1932, p. 963, and 29 December, p. 989.

1932

⮾§ 227. AIKEN, PAULINE. *The Influence of the Latin Elegists on English Lyric Poetry, 1600–1650, with Particular Reference to the Works of Robert Herrick.* University of Maine Studies, Second Series, No. 22. Orono: University of Maine Press. 115 p.

Maintains that Donne and his followers were much less influenced by the Latin elegists than were other poets of the period. "Donne, himself, holds rather consistently to the standards he set for poetry, and only rare echoes of the Augustans appear in his verse. *The Indifferent*, however, undoubtedly owes much to Ovid. In Donne's other poems only a few scattered phrases suggest the Elegist" (p. 35). Suggests that the first stanza of "The Sunne Rising" echoes Ovid, *Amores* (I, xiii).

⮾§ 228. BALD, R. C. *Donne's Influence in English Literature.* Morpeth: St. John's College Press. 62 p.

Reprinted, Gloucester, Mass.: Peter Smith, 1965.

Traces the influence of Donne from his own time to the present. Concludes, "The metaphysical poets of the seventeenth century turned to Donne as their Master. They reproduced his gestures and his mannerisms freely, even if they did not always catch his spirit; certain of them, perhaps, missed altogether some of the things that seem most vital to us. But the poets of the present, viewing him across a gap of three centuries, can see more clearly the enduring qualities of his mind, a mind subtle and sensitive, blown on by gusts of passion and beset by cross-currents of doubt and feeling. For the time being, Donne is the most modern of the great English poets of the past" (p. 62). Discusses Donne's influence on Carew, Lovelace, Suckling, Herbert, Vaughan, Crashaw, Traherne, Cowley, and Marvell. Suggests that Dryden and the lyricists of the Restoration are much indebted to Donne. Traces briefly the fortune of Donne during the eighteenth and nineteenth centuries. Concerning the modern revival, the author comments: "To understand Donne's appeal at the present day, it is necessary to indicate the qualities of mind revealed in his work which are akin to the mind of our times" (p. 52). Points out these similarities. Mentions the Donnean quality of much modern poetry, especially that found in the work of Rupert Brooke, Sacheverell Sitwell, Edith Sitwell, W. J. Turner, and T. S. Eliot.

◄§ 229. BUSH, DOUGLAS. *Mythology and the Renaissance Tradition in English Poetry.* Minneapolis: University of Minnesota Press; London: Humphrey Milford, Oxford University Press. viii, 360 p.
Revised ed., New York: W. W. Norton & Co., Inc., 1963.
Compares Donne and Chapman: "Donne's work, though circulating privately, had more influence than Chapman's, but Chapman's published poems were the first open revolt against orthodox or conventional canons of Elizabethan taste" (p. 199). Brief comments on Donne's uses of mythology: "The whole body of Donne's work contains much more mythological allusion than one remembers at first, yet his best-known pieces have hardly any. . . . Instead of diffuse Italianate word-painting, we have in Donne's mythology the stamp of his special qualities, wit, realism, ratiocination, learning, concentration of feeling and expression, sometimes deliberate harshness and ugliness. What his contemporaries would spread over a page he puts into a line and a half" (p. 224). Suggests that many of Donne's poems "in their intensity are closer to Catullus and some other ancients than are those of his fellow lyricists with their more obvious classicism" (p. 224). Recognizing that some of Donne's poems echo Ovid, the author points out that they differ from the conventional Renaissance Ovidian love poem primary, because "his mind rather than his eye is at work" (p. 225).

◄§ 230. BUTT, JOHN. "John Donne's 'Mr. Tilman.'" *TLS,* 15 December p. 963 and 29 December p. 989.
In reference to H. Harvey Wood, *E&S* of 1930, 16 (1931):179–90. Identifies Mr. Tilman as Edward Tilman of Pembroke College, who was ordained priest on March 12, 1619–20. Second note indicates that Butt was, in fact, anticipated by Wood, *TLS,* 9 July 1931, p. 547.

◄§ 231. ——. "Walton's Copy of Donne's *Letters* (1651)." *RES,* 8:72–74.
Description of several textual alterations and emendations made by Izaak Walton in his copy of the *Letters to Severall Personages* (1651) now in Salisbury Cathedral Library.

◄§ 232. ELTON, OLIVER. "Poetry, 1600–1660," in *The English Muse: A Sketch,* pp. 202–31. London: G. Bell and Sons, Ltd.
Reprinted, 1937.
Brief survey of Donne's poetry and prose and of his influence on other

poets of the period. "Many of Donne's longer works are shapeless; but his lyrics and sonnets, whether sacred or profane, have one master-quality: strength and economy of design. The mixture of 'false' wit with the true, the rapid zigzags of the thought, and the general strangeness of the style, easily make us overlook this virtue, which was Donne's most valuable lesson to the poets" (p. 212).

⮢§ 233. FICKE, ARTHUR DAVISON. "Soul in Torment." *Forum*, 88:151.
Nine-stanza original poem on Donne.

⮢§ 234. FRIEDERICH, WERNER P. *Spiritualismus und Sensualismus in der Englischen Barocklyrik*. Weiner Beitrage zur Englischen Philologie, v. 57. Vienna and Leipzig: Wilhelm Braumüller. 303 p.
Attempts to show that the term *baroque* can be applied to the English lyric of the seventeenth century. The age was one of polarization, of disharmony, of contrasts. Donne, together with Herrick and Vaughan, best embodies the polarity of the age in his poetry. Donne helped to overcome the Petrarchanism of the age. In his poetry one finds very little Platonic love or desireless adoration of the beloved. Yet there is a metaphysical sublimation of his own feelings in his poems that is strongly under the influence of the religious–philosophical counterstream of the century. Comments on the sensuality and spirituality of the age. Discusses Donne's religious poetry. Comments on the effects of inner conflict on the content and style of the poetry. Numerous examples of Donne's poetic techniques are given.

⮢§ 235. GREENE, GUY SHEPHARD. "Drummond's Borrowing from Donne." *PQ*, 11:26–38.
Surveys briefly the literary and personal relationship between the two poets and points out that in his prose essay *A Cypresse Grove* Drummond borrowed from Donne's two *Anniversaries*.

⮢§ 236. HUGHES, MERRITT Y. "The Lineage of 'The Extasie.'" *MLR*, 27:1–5.
Supports Grierson's reading of the poem and opposes Fausset's "minor heresy that 'The Extasie' was felt by its author as a revolt against 'Platonism'" (p. 2). Maintains, in contrast to Legouis, that the poem belongs to "the stream of tradition rather than to an original dramatic impulse on Donne's part" (p. 2). Gives several examples of Italian and French Neoplatonic poets who use the theme of "The Extasie," especially Antoine Héroët and Benedetto Varchi. Concludes that Donne "must have realized that he was dramatising a great commonplace of the casuistic idealism of the Italians" (p. 5).

◆§ 237. JOHNSON, ELEANOR ANGLIN. "John Donne, 1572–1631." *Congregational Quarterly*, 10:41–49.

General, appreciative essay. Argues against the myth of Jack and John Donne and stresses that his works, both poetry and prose, must be considered as a whole. Emphasizes Donne's passion and wit.

◆§ 238. KEYNES, GEOFFREY. A *Bibliography of Dr. John Donne, Dean of St. Pauls*. 2d ed. Cambridge: The University Press. xiv, 195 p. 3d ed., 1958.

Much expanded and revised version of the first edition of 1914. Contains twelve new illustrations; 151 items in the "Biography and Criticism" section (in contrast to only 40 in the first edition); many new entries, especially in the sections on the poems, the letters, and the sermons; Appendix I, "Works by John Donne, D.C.L." is expanded from 3 items to 6; and Appendix III, "Books from Donne's Library," contains 61 entries (in contrast to only 14 in the first edition). The first edition contained 169 main entries; the second edition contains 339.

◆§ 239. LEGOUIS, PIERRE. "Sur un vers de Donne." *Revue Anglo-Américaine*, 10:49–50, 228–30.

Comments on lines 197–198 of *The second Anniversarie*. Discusses the dual naming of Venus as both Hesper and Vesper and points out the significance of the duality in the lines. For a reply by Merritt Y. Hughes, see *University of California Publications in English*, 4(1934):61–89.

◆§ 240. MCCOLLEY, GRANT. "The Theory of a Plurality of Worlds." *MLN*, 47:319–25.

Points out that in the seventeenth century the acceptance of the Copernican system frequently included acceptance of the notion of the plurality of inhabited worlds. Illustrates the point by referring to several seventeenth-century thinkers, among whom Donne is included. "Among the earliest of these associations are those made by Donne in An *Anatomie of the World* and *Ignatius His Conclave*. In the latter work he refers to Galileo's observations, and suggests that the Jesuits are the proper persons to colonize the moon. In the *Anatomie*, he links the hypothesis with the doctrine of a plurality of worlds of systems, and attacks it, at least indirectly, as a part of the new philosophy then disrupting the universe" (pp. 320–21).

◆§ 241. MITCHELL, W. FRASER. *English Pulpit Oratory from Andrewes to Tillotson: A Study of Its Literary Aspects*. London: The Society for Promoting Christian Knowledge; New York and Toronto: The Macmillan Co. xii, 516 p.

Although Donne is mentioned throughout, he is considered primarily in Section II of Chapter V entitled "Andrewes, the 'Witty' Preachers, and Donne" (pp. 148–94). Compares and contrasts Donne with Andrewes, Henry King, Mark Frank, and other "witty preachers" of an Anglo-Catholic persuasion. Critical commentary on the style, techniques, and subject matter of Donne's sermons.

◄§ 242. SHAPIRO, I. A. "John Donne and Parliament." *TLS*, 10 March, p. 172.
Indicates that Donne was a member of Parliament on two separate occasions—in 1601 and again in 1614.

◄§ 243. TATE, ALLEN. "A Note on Donne." *The New Republic*, 70: 212–13.
Reprinted in *Reactionary Essays on Poetry and Ideas* (1936), pp. 64–72; *On the Limits of Poetry* (1948), pp. 325–32; *Collected Essays* (1959), pp. 547–52.
Essentially a review of *A Garland for John Donne, 1631–1931*, ed. Theodore Spencer (1931), in which the author not only surveys the several essays but contributes his reflections on Donne.

◄§ 244. TILLOTSON, GEOFFREY. "The Commonplace Book of Arthur Capell." *MLR*, 27:381–91.
Description of Harleian MS. 3511, a commonplace book presumably the work of Arthur Capell the younger (1631–1683) in which thirteen of Donne's poems appear.

◄§ 245. WILLIAMSON, GEORGE. "The Donne Canon." *TLS*, 18 August, p. 581.
Description of an annotated 1639 edition of Donne's poems, perhaps the work of George Thomason. Indicates that four of the poems are marked "nt licensed nor Dr. Donns." The poems are, according to the numbering of the 1639 edition, "Elegie XV: Julia," "Elegie XVI: A Tale of a Citizen and his Wife," *Satyre VI*, and "A Dialogue between Sr Henry Wotton and Mr. Donne." None of these appeared in the 1633 edition; all were in the 1635 edition. Grierson eliminated the last two from the canon of his edition, and Williamson argues for excluding the first two also.

◄§ 246. WOOLF, VIRGINIA. "Donne after Three Centuries," in *The Second Common Reader*, pp. 22–37. London: Leonard and Virginia Woolf at the Hogarth Press; New York: Harcourt, Brace & Co.

Attempts to account for Donne's popularity in the twentieth century. Praises the "explosion with which he bursts into speech" (p. 20) and his "power to suddenly surprising and subjugating the reader" (p. 21) and his "psychological intensity and complexity" (p. 29) among other qualities. "Not only did he see each spot and wrinkle which defaced the fair outline; but he noted with the utmost curiosity his own reaction to such contrasts and was eager to lay side by side the two conflicting views and to let them make their own dissonance" (p. 25).

1933

❧ 247. BENNETT, R. E. "The Addition to Donne's *Catalogus Librorum.*" *MLN*, 48:167–68.

Comments on three lines found in the Trinity MS. at the end of Donne's list of imaginary books, not printed in *Poems* (1650). Agrees with Evelyn Simpson that they refer to real works and suggests that they represent "the beginning of a list of encomiums and paradoxes, or treatments of unworthy subjects" (p. 167). "At least, if we accept, with Mrs. Simpson, the addition in the Trinity MS. as Donne's, we know some of the paradoxical material which he had uppermost in his mind; and this knowledge is of value with reference to his own paradoxes" (p. 168).

❧ 248. BROWN, ALEC. "Some Notes on Scientific Criticism in Connection with the Clarendon Edition of Donne." *Dublin Magazine*, 8:20–31.

Proposes "to indicate, through examples from a classic edition of one poet, that in the editing of a text no factor other than the application of scientific method can be allowed" (p. 20). Takes examples "for the illustration of the inadequacy of the traditional method from one of the best and most monumental editions of a poet ever made under that method: that is, Professor Grierson's edition of Donne's poems, done by the Clarendon Press" (p. 22).

❧ 249. BUCHAN, HANNAH A. "Thomas Pestell's Poems in MS. Malone 14." *Bodleian Quarterly Record*, 8:329–32.

Description of Pestell's poems in MS. Malone 14, written near the end of the first half of the seventeenth century. Contains two elegies in which Donne is praised. Donne is called "Black prince of witts, ye most illustrious Dunn" and "The late Copernicus in Poetrie." Suggests that possibly Pestell was acquainted with Donne through their mutual friendship with the Countess of Huntingdon.

⋙ 250. CHAMBERS, E. K. "The Disenchantment of the Elizabethans," in *Sir Thomas Wyatt and Some Collected Studies*, pp. 181–204. London: Sidgwick & Jackson.

In his comments on Donne (pp. 202–4), the author remarks, "They are contradictory and often perverse moods that Donne will express, full of the self-torturings of a philosophic amorist, caught in the obvious shames of his own body. But they bring a new note of sincerity into English song, a note which, it need hardly be said, Donne's own disciples were in their turn, quick to lose" (p. 203).

⋙ 251. DREW, ELIZABETH. *Discovering Poetry*. New York: W. W. Norton & Co. 224 p.

Reprinted, 1962.

Donne is mentioned throughout and used to illustrate certain concepts of the nature of poetry. The obscurity of Blake and Eliot, who speak in a "symbolic private language," is contrasted with that of Donne, Shakespeare, and Hopkins. Donne's obscurity "is the difficulty of abnormal compression and richness in the use of language, by which it is weighted with a supernormal significance" (p. 83). Comments on the compass image in "A Valediction: forbidding mourning": "What the poet is concerned with is the *feel* of a pair of compasses, that sense of leaning and firmness and the 'pull' between the two feet, and the translation of those sensations into emotional terms" (p. 156). Speaks of Donne's bringing "all he has learnt and read and thought into direct kinship with his emotional experience" (p. 188).

⋙ 252. HADDOW, G. C. "Donne's Prose." QQ, 40:87–98.

Brief survey of the prose works with the controlling thesis that "behind the flawed and strained character of his style, one feels the force of intense individuality" (p. 98). Views the prose pieces as the "expression of a personality so complex that any attempt to describe it in a phrase or to classify Donne is like attempting to force all nature to submit to a particular philosophy" (p. 87).

⋙ 253. PEARSON, LU EMILY. "John Donne's Love Lyrics," in *Elizabethan Love Conventions*, pp. 223–30. Berkeley: University of California Press; London: Cambridge University Press.

Argues that Donne is "independent of the revolt against Petrarchism, that he simply reflects another phase of the Renaissance attitude toward love" (p. 224). Points out that Donne did not "discard conceits or satirize them because they were shallow or ridiculous. Rather he sought to go beyond their conventional ideas, beyond the usual portrayal of love in order to find what is lurking in the shadows" (p. 228). Concludes, "Donne has merely succeeded in going beyond the idealizing of passion.

He has pierced the veil of illusion and has found in actual experience the joy which others before him could only long for" (p. 229).

❧ 254. SMITH, JAMES. "On Metaphysical Poetry." *Scrutiny*, 2:222–39. Reprinted in *Determinations*, ed. F. R. Leavis (1934).

Extended definition of metaphysical poetry in an attempt to show precisely how it differs from other kinds of poetry that are sometimes closely associated with it. The author asserts, "It is, that verse properly called metaphysical is that to which the impulse is given by an overwhelming concern with metaphysical problems; with problems either deriving from, or closely resembling in the nature of their difficulty, the problem of the Many and the One" (p. 228). Contrasts Donne with Dante, Lucretius, Chapman, and others. Points out that these poets "wrote metaphysics in poetry, rather than metaphysical poetry" (p. 237). "Whereas Dante and Lucretius take seriously the propositions they quote, Donne does not do so: he quotes them, not as themselves true, but as possibly useful for inducing a belief in something else, which he believes is true" (p. 223). A distinguishing mark of metaphysical poetry is its particular use of the conceit; in the the metaphysical conceit "tension between the elements continues" (p. 234). The two elements "can enter into a solid union and, at the same time maintain their separate and warring identity" (p. 234), a union "of things that, though hostile, in reality cry out for association with each other" (p. 235).

❧ 255. TATE, ALLEN. "A Note on Elizabethan Satire." *The New Republic*, 74:128–30.

Essentially a review of *The Oxford Book of Sixteenth Century Verse*, ed. E. K. Chambers. Discusses Hall, Marston, Tourneur, and Donne as forming a school of satire, which as a group has been variously ignored or misjudged in the past.

1934

❧ 256. ANON. "Seventeenth-Century Verse." *TLS*, 1 November, pp. 741–42.

A lead article that is ostensibly a review of *The Oxford Book of Seventeenth Century Verse*, eds. Grierson and Bullough, *Four Metaphysical Poets*, Joan Bennett and *The Metaphysical Poets*, J. B. Leishman; however, these books serve only as a basis for the reviewer's own comments on metaphysical poets. Suggests that the early seventeenth century was fortunate to be a period between "fashionable" poetry and "professional" poetry: "Poetry had stepped down from Court and out into a wider world" (p. 741), yet it had not become a profession as it would after the Restoration. Praises Donne's uniqueness and influence, and yet points out that the reader of the *Oxford Book of Seventeenth Century Verse* "will be surprised to find not how much, but how little, of the best verse of the seventeenth century recalls Donne to their minds" (p. 742).

◄§ 257. ATKINS, SIDNEY H. "Mr. Banks and His Horse." *N&Q*, 167: 39–41.

Lists sixteenth- and seventeenth-century references to the famous showman and his performing horse. Reference found in *Satyre I* (ll. 79–82). See also Atkins, *TLS*, 22 May 1937, p. 396.

◄§ 258. BATESON, F. W. "Elizabethans, Metaphysicals, Augustans," in *English Poetry and the English Language: An Experiment in Literary History*, pp. 26–64. Oxford: The Clarendon Press.

2d ed., New York: Russell & Russell, Inc., 1961.

Contends that "the age's imprint in a poem is not to be traced to the poet but to the language. The real history of poetry is . . . the history of the changes in the kind of language in which successive poems have been written. *And it is these changes of language only that are due to the pressure of social and intellectual tendencies*" (p. vi). Discusses Donne's obscurity and ambiguity, "The phrases of Shakespeare and Donne, in particular, often seem to be on the point of sloughing their original meanings and vanishing, bright winged things, in the aura of suggestion they irradiate" (p. 44).

◄§ 259. BENNETT, JOAN. *Four Metaphysical Poets: Donne, Herbert, Vaughan, Crashaw*. Cambridge: University Press. 135 p.

2d ed., 1953; 2d ed. reprinted with corrections, 1957.

3d ed., with a new chapter on Marvell and title changed to *Five Metaphysical Poets*, 1964; 3d ed. reprinted, 1966.

Consists of seven chapters: (1) Introduction, (2) John Donne, 1573–1631, (3) Donne's Technical Originality, (4) George Herbert, 1593–1633, (5) Henry Vaughan, 1622–1695, (6) Richard Crashaw, 1613?–1649, and (7) Religious Poetry, a Postscript. Short bibliography. Summarizes in the introduction the basic characteristics of metaphysical style. Maintains, "The word 'metaphysical' refers to style, not to subject-matter; but style reflects an attitude to experience" (p. 3). Suggests, "The peculiarity of the metaphysical poets is not that they relate, but that the relations they perceive are more often logical than sensuous or emotional, and that they constantly connect the abstract with the concrete, the remote with the near, and the sublime with the commonplace" (p. 4). Surveys in Chapter 2 the variety of tone and intention in Donne's poetry as a preliminary to the study of his poetic method in Chapter 3. Stresses in particular that "Donne recognized the unity of his experience" (p. 16) and that "A robust delight in dialectic is the most constant feature of Donne's poetry as of his prose" (p. 20). Shows the close relation between his secular poetry and his specifically religious verses. Discusses how Donne utilizes his intellectual interests in the poetry. Considers the technical matters of Donne's verse, especially its varied rhythms. Suggests, "His principal innovation was to make cadences of speech the staple of his rhythm; contemporary dramatists had done this in blank verse, but no one had so far attempted it in lyrical poetry" (p. 44). Discusses Donne's influence on the religious poetry that followed him. Concludes with a critical discussion of the nature of religious poetry.

◄§ 260. BROOKS, CLEANTH. "A Note on Symbol and Conceit." *American Review*, 3:201–11.
In response to Edmund Wilson's comments in *Axel's Castle*, the author sets out "to inquire just what the relation of symbolism to metaphysical poetry is; and, furthermore, to examine more closely the charge that metaphysical poetry is itself romantic and escapist" (p. 202). Concludes, "With the acquisition of these qualities—irony, realistic diction, wit, the ability to fuse heterogeneous materials and to synthesize opposed impulses—symbolist poetry coalesces with metaphysical. The faults to be censured may be many: lack of taste, strained images, et cetera. What is important to observe, however, is that they will not be the faults characteristic of romanticism: sentimentality, vulnerability to irony, and escapism" (p. 208). Sees Yeats's "Sailing to Byzantium" as very close to the metaphysical tradition: "It is not over-literal perhaps, to interpret the voyage to Byzantium as one which has carried the poet, if not over to the metaphysicals, at least very close to them" (p. 211). Passing references to Donne.

◄§ 261. BROOKS, HAROLD. "Donne and Drant." *TLS*, 16 August, p. 565.
Points out a possible parallel between the metaphor of the huge hill (*Satyre III*, ll. 77–82) in Thomas Drant's *Horace His arte of Poetrie, Epistles and Satyrs Englished* (1567). For a reply by Jack Lindsay, see *TLS*, 23 August, p. 577 and by V. Scholderer, see *TLS*, 30 August, p. 589.

◄§ 262. BUTT, JOHN. "Izaak Walton's Methods in Biography." *E&S* of 1933, 19:67–84.
Surveys Walton's methods and varying aims in the *Lives*. Suggests that Henry King may have asssisted Walton with his *Life of Donne*. "It is worth noticing that of Walton's narrative of the early life of Donne, the part which needed least alteration in subsequent editions was the account of Donne's courtship and marriage, of which Henry King would have special knowledge from his father" (p. 80).

⊷§ 263. CLINE, JAMES M. "The Poetry of the Mind." *University of California Publications in English*, 4:27–47.

"Poetry of the mind" is defined as that particular kind of poetry that communicates "not *what the poet has perceived*, but *how he is perceiving it*" (p. 27). In contrast to Pope's proverbialism, "Donne's poetry does not record the result of his meditation merely, but reveals the very act of a mind in possession of intellectual passion" (p. 28). Discusses briefly Donne's metrics and prose style. Concludes, "To establish a relationship between the mind and the accepted truths of religion was perhaps Donne's greatest service to the world, and that for which his genius was best suited" (p. 52).

⊷§ 264. COFFIN, CHARLES M. "Bibliography of Donne." *TLS*, 2 August, p. 541.

Lists two items found in the Bodleian Library overlooked by Keynes in his second edition of the Donne bibliography (1932): (1) a copy of *Six Sermons Upon Severall Occasions* and (2) an isolated copy of the sixth of these sermons entitled *A Sermon Upon the xv. verse of the viii. Chapter of John.*

⊷§ 265. DOGGETT, FRANK A. "Donne's Platonism." *SR*, 42:274–92.

Maintains that thinking is a part of Donne's style and yet "Donne is not a philosophic poet in the likeness of Spenser, not a poet with a system like Lucretius or Blake, nor an ethical poet like Wordsworth. He is concerned with mental experience and worldly affairs, human contacts and rationalized imagination: in general these are the subjects of his poems" (p. 274). Summarizes some of the basic tenets of Platonism as reflected in English poetry from Spenser to Milton. Points out some isolated examples of Neoplatonic doctrines in Donne's poetry but concludes that "these are non-essential to the central doctrines of the aesthetic morality from which Donne separated himself; or they are concessions to the courtly fashions of the day that Donne allowed himself to make in some instances" (pp. 280–81). Brief analysis of "The Extasie," which refutes much previous criticism. Concludes that Donne differed from the English Neoplatonists "in the absence of an aesthetic basis for his ethics and in the high position he gives the body in love as well as in theology. There are Platonic elements in his poetry, but they seem to derive from his study of the Scholastic writers rather than from Hoby, or Ficino, or the other sources of Neo-Platonic thought among Englishmen of his age. If he did study those works he rejected their conclusions, and retained only those elements that he could have gotten from medieval sources" (pp. 291–92).

266. GRØNBECH, VILHELM. "Donne," in Mystikere i Europa og Indien, pp. 3–53. Vol. IV. Copenhagen: Branner.

Discusses Donne's changing attitudes towards sex and women throughout his life as reflected in the poetry and prose. Examines various conflicts in Donne's work, which reflect the tensions in his soul.

267. HAGEDORN, MARIA. Reformation und spanische Andachsliteratur, Luis de Granada in England. Leipzig: Tauchnitz. 165 p.

Traces the influence of Luis de Granada, Spanish poet and devotional writer, on Donne (pp. 140–43). Finds a number of similarities between Donne and Granada in Donne's religious poetry and sermons. Comments on Donne's interest in Spanish literature and points out similarities between the metaphors employed by the two poets.

268. HARRISON, CHARLES TRAWICK. "The Ancient Atomists and English Literature of the Seventeenth Century." Harvard Studies in Classical Philology, 45:1–79.

Argues that Donne was acquainted with Lucretius, since he speaks of the firmament's being "crumbled out again to his atomies" (p. 19).

269. HUGHES, MERRITT Y. "Kidnapping Donne." University of California Publications in English, 4:61–89.

Objects to "the critical self-consciousness in our admiration for Donne" (p. 61). States, "We kidnap him from the past and make him a 'philosopher' and 'poet-hero' . . . by insisting on (a) his intellectuality, which is our term for his wit, and on (b) his skepticism, which is our term for his attitude toward the natural sciences and metaphysics" (p. 62). Concerning Donne's wit, the author concludes, "Whatever ground there may be for making Donne's wit a touchstone for contemporary poetry, there is none for making it a master key to literary history. The more absolute we make our estimate of Donne's wit in general, the less historically revealing becomes our appreciation of Donne" (p. 67). Concerning Donne's skepticism, the author states, "All the evidence shows that from his first literary experiments until he wrote Death's Duell, Donne thought of the universe as the Ptolemaic machine pictured by St. Thomas and Dante, and that for him time began and ended with creation" (p. 74). Rejects Legouis's reading of "The Extasie" as an example of reading a modern meaning into the poem. Suggests that "To try to see him as he was, is like removing fourteenth-century gilding from a Russian icon of the tenth century. Every audience makes its own experience of an artist's work, and when the artist is removed from his public by three hundred years, and when the modern conception of him has been interlaced with original and fructifying theories of poetry by at least one great poet, the recovery of the historic reality is an ungrateful task" (pp. 86–87).

270. LEISHMAN, J. B. *The Metaphysical Poets: Donne, Herbert, Vaughan, Traherne.* Oxford: The Clarendon Press. 232 p.

Reprinted, Ann Arbor, Mich.: University Microfilms Inc., 1962; New York: Russell & Russell, Inc., 1963.

General introduction to the four poets for the general reader. Virtually an anthology with a running critical commentary. Each study is contained within a biographical framework. The section on Donne (pp. 1–98) is nearly twice as long as any of the other three sections. Although the author warns against seeing Donne's poetry as strictly autobiographical, he discusses it primarily as reflections of Donne's various stages and moods: "On the whole it seems wiser to assume as a matter of course that great poets mean what they say" (p. 13).

271. LEWIS, E. GLYN. "Donne's Third Satyre." *TLS*, 6 September, p. 604.

Reply to Jack Lindsay, *TLS*, 23 August, p. 577. Challenges Lindsay's comment that the argument of *Satyre III* is that of the humanist. Minimizes the Horatian influence. For a reply by Lindsay, see *TLS*, 20 September, p. 636.

272. ———. "Donne's Third Satyre." *TLS*, 27 September, p. 655.

Reply to Jack Lindsay, *TLS*, 20 September, p. 636. Agrees with Lindsay that there is a humanist influence in Donne's early poetry, but maintains that Donne "retains a clear understanding of metaphysical values" and that "these metaphysical principles assume paramount importance and serve to modify, if they do not determine, the attitude of the poet."

273. ———. "An Interpretation of Donne's 'Elegie—The Dream.'" *MLR*, 29:436–40.

Suggests that the "image" referred to in the poem is not a portrait but rather a mental picture and an abstract, metaphysical idea. Maintains dual meanings for "image" and "heart." States that Donne's "manipulation of the two meanings included in the word 'heart'—reason and affection—and the two meanings included in the term 'image,' together with his opposition of 'phantasy' and 'reason,' suggests that Donne delights more in the analysis and construction of patterns rather than in the contemplation of simple, unique moments of experience" (p. 439). Also discusses the dramatic and technical aspects of the poem.

274. LINDSAY, JACK. "Donne and Drant." *TLS*, 23 August, p. 577.

In part, a reply to Harold Brooks, *TLS*, 16 August, p. 565. Suggests that when Donne composed the hill metaphor in *Satyre III* (ll. 77–82), he had in mind Saint Augustine's *Confessions* (X, xxvi, l. 37) and merged it with Drant's figure. Also considers Martial as a possible source and postulates that lines 74–77 of the satire may have been suggested by some lines from the *Phaedrus*. "This is all meagre enough; and the only definite influences seem Horace and Montaigne." For a reply by E. Glyn Lewis, see *TLS*, 6 September, p. 604.

◆§ 275. ———. "Donne's Third Satyre." *TLS*, 20 September, p. 636.
Reply to E. Glyn Lewis, *TLS*, 6 September, p. 604. Qualifies his comment that Donne argues as a humanist in the satire and maintains his position that the Horatian element is strong. For a reply by Lewis, see *TLS*, 27 September, p. 655.

◆§ 276. POTTER, GEORGE REUBEN. "John Donne's Discovery of Himself." *University of California Publications in English*, 4:3–23.
Attempts to expose "those complicated emotions which lie at the background of his poetic experiences" (p. 4) and in particular Donne's passionate interest in his own personality. "Behind nearly all his verse lies a constant, restless, dominating, and insatiable longing to solve the riddle of his own personality" (p. 8) and "even his most passionate mood as lover, or his most exalted moods as a preacher, Donne never ceased to be impelled by his passion to know himself" (p. 9). Numerous examples are presented to demonstrate that "self-knowledge is an undercurrent through all his verse" (p. 9).

◆§ 277. SCHOLDERER, V. "Donne and Drant." *TLS*, 30 August, p. 589.
In part a reply to Harold Brooks, *TLS*, 16 August, p. 565. Points out an illustration of an Italian medal of 1504, which depicts a man circling a hill as a parallel to the hill metaphor in *Satyre III* (ll. 77–82). The legend on the medal consists of a line from Ovid (somewhat altered), which describes the failure of Phaeton.

◆§ 278. SHARP, ROBERT LATHROP. "The Pejorative Use of *Metaphysical*." *MLN*, 49:503–5.
Traces the changing etymology of the word from simply meaning "above the material world, supersensible, and hence above 'nature'" (p. 504) to its pejorative meaning of "non-sensical." Concludes, "Both Dryden and Dr. Johnson were . . . aware of this pejorative sense and took advantage of it, thereby suggesting to their readers not only that Donne, Cowley, and the rest were thoughtful, speculative, and abstract, but that they dealt in notions which, to a neo-classical mind, were incomprehensible, vague, and repugnant to common sense" (p. 505).

◆§ 279. ———. "Some Light on Metaphysical Obscurity and Roughness." *SP*, 31:497–518.
Presents evidence to show: (1) that obscurity and roughness "aroused contemporary comment; (2) that they were thought of in connection with metaphysical poetry; and (3) that they played a purposeful part in

it" (p. 497). While maintaining that many of the metaphysical poets simply consciously "imitated Donne because he had vitalized a poetry that had been in danger of becoming effete" (p. 498), the author nevertheless points out, "This change from sweetness and melodiousness to obscurity and roughness was more than the private affair of one poet" (p. 499). Argues, "It reflected a broader change in the consciousness of the nation" (p. 499). Considers Donne, Lord Herbert, Benlowes, and the Duchess of Newcastle in this light. Asserts that "Donne's obscurity, rising from his thought and his images, is the result of a poetic ambition which sought expression not for the inexpressible but for the untraditional. One of his means of enlarging the field of communicable experience was the conceit. As opposed to what it became in the hands of some of the later metaphysicals—that is, a mere matter of imagery, therefore external and more an end than a means—it was for him both intellectual and emotive" (p. 503).

◄§ 280. SIMPSON, EVELYN M. "More Manuscripts of Donne's *Paradoxes and Problems." RES*, 10:288–300, 412–16.

Discovers that "portions of the *Paradoxes and Problems* are extant in no less than seventeen manuscripts belonging to the first half of the seventeenth century" (p. 288), all of which are independent of the printed text. Detailed bibliographical description of the following manuscripts: Dobell MS., Ashmole MS. 826, Burley and Westmoreland MSS., Bridgewater MS., Phillipps MS., Stephens MS. (S), British Museum MSS., and Trinity College MSS.

◄§ 281. SMITH, W. BRADFORD. "What is Metaphysical Poetry?" SR, 42:261–72.

"Metaphysical Poetry is a paradoxical inquiry, imaginative and intellectual, which exhausts, by its use of antithesis and contradiction and unusual imagery, all the possibilities in a given idea. This idea will predominantly be a psychological probing of love, death, or religion as the more important matters of experience in the life of the poet, and will be embodied in striking metaphorical utterance or in the use of the common (familiar) or the scientific word" (p. 263). Reviews other definitions from Drummond to Williamson. Uses Donne throughout to illustrate his definition. Calls Marvell's "To His Coy Mistress" the perfect metaphysical poem.

◄§ 282. TAGGARD, GENEVIEVE. "John Donne: A Link Between the 17th and 20th Centuries." *Scholastic*, 24:11–12.

Points out the merits of reading Donne. Outlines some of the more obvious general characteristics of the love poetry and includes a few comments on Donne's biography.

283. WILLIAMSON, GEORGE. "The Libertine Donne." *PQ*, 13:276–91.

Reprinted in *Seventeenth Century Contexts* (London: Faber and Faber, Ltd.; Chicago: University of Chicago Press, 1960), pp. 42–62.

Comments on the philosophical position of *Biathanatos* and reviews John Adams's *Essay concerning Self-Murther* (1700), which attacks Donne's position "to make sure that it be stamped for what it was in his day, a libertine document, in which he attempted to nullify the insinuation of its learning" (p. 285). Reviews libertinism. Concludes, "*Biathanatos* is crucial in Donne's thought because it illuminates the intermediate ground between his earlier scepticism and naturalism and his later scepticism and mysticism" (p. 291). Describes the work as "the paradox of paradoxes; it is Donne's putting off the old life that he may put on the new, but not so completely as to deceive the libertine eyes of the Restoration. Adams did not so much correct the portrait left by Walton as cut a new silhouette of Donne to hang in another wing of the gallery beside Hobbes and Montaigne" (p. 291).

1935

284. ALEXANDER, HENRY. "John Donne, Poet and Divine." *QQ*, 42: 471–81.

General survey of Donne's life with general comments on the poetry and prose: "Truly a perplexing and mysterious human personality, a motley figure in a motley age" (p. 481).

285. BENNETT, R. E. "Donne and Sir Thomas Roe." *TLS*, 31 January, p. 62.

Identifies Sir Thomas Roe as the addressee of a letter written by Donne from Chelsea, November 25, 1625 (Gosse, *Life and Letters of John Donne*, II, 222–25).

286. BROOKS, CLEANTH. "Three Revolutions in Poetry: I. Metaphor and the Tradition." *SoR*, 1:151–63.

First in a series of three articles on modern poetry by Cleanth Brooks; see also *SoR*, 1:328–38, 568–83. Challenges conservative critics who maintain "the division of the world into poetic and nonpoetic, and the segregation of the intellect from the emotions" (p. 152). Views the modern conceit in historical perspective. Points out that modern poets are "the restorers of orthodoxy, attempting to bring back into poetry some of the virtues of the School of Donne" (p. 162). Stresses the importance of the functional nature of the radical metaphor and shows that Donne's compass image in "A Valediction: forbidden mourning" is functional, whereas Milton's metaphors and similes are primarily decorative. Donne used as illustration throughout.

👉§ 287. ———. "Three Revolutions in Poetry: II. Wit and High Seriousness." *SoR*, 1:328–38.

Second in a series of three articles on modern poetry by Cleanth Brooks; see also *SoR*, 1:151–63, 568–83. Argues that "the play of the intellect and the play of wit are not intrinsically incompatible with the poet's seriousness, or with his sincerity in implying to the reader that he means to be taken seriously" (p. 329). Points out that much metaphysical poetry "occupies this shadowy borderland between frankly playful vers de société and deeply serious lyric poetry. It is most important to notice that the deepening seriousness, when it occurs, is not accompanied by a correspondent lessening of the play of wit" (p. 330). Mentions in particular "Batter my heart" and "To Christ."

👉§ 288. ———. "Three Revolutions in Poetry: III. Metaphysical Poetry and the Ivory Tower." *SoR*, 1:568–83.

Third in a series of three articles on modern poetry by Cleanth Brooks; see also *SoR*, 1:151–63, 328–38. Defines metaphysical poetry as "a poetry in which the heterogeneity of the materials and the opposition of the impulses united are extreme. Or if one prefers to base himself directly on Coleridge: it is a poetry in which the poet attempts the reconciliation of opposite or discordant qualities" (p. 570). Challenges those who insist on the didactic function of poetry or on the scientific validity of the poetic statement. Agrees with I. A. Richards that "It is never what a poem says that matters, but what it is" (p. 573). Sees modern poets returning to the orthodoxy of the past, specifically the seventeenth century, in an attempt to repair the damage caused by the Age of Reason and the Romantic Movement. Considers Eliot, Tate, Ransom, Crane, Warren, and even Hardy and Yeats in this light. Compares Donne and Yeats. Donne is mentioned throughout.

👉§ 289. EMPSON, WILLIAM. *Some Versions of Pastoral*. London: Chatto & Windus Ltd. 298 p.

First published in U. S. as *English Pastoral Poetry* (New York: W. W. Norton & Co., 1938). Several reprints.

Uses Donne's *Holy Sonnets*, especially "I am a little world" as poems that show the Renaissance desire to make the individual more independent than Christianity allowed (pp. 74–77). Discusses "The Crosse" in the light of the idea that Christ is diffused throughout nature (pp. 78–80). States that all of Donne's best poems are built on the central idea of the One and the Many. Discusses *The first Anniversary* briefly and sees Elizabeth Drury as the Logos (pp. 80, 139). Discusses "The Extasie" and the idea that love is the source of knowledge of oneself and the world (pp. 82, 133–35).

◆§ 290. GARVIN, KATHARINE. "Looking Babies." TLS, 23 November, p. 770.

Comments on lines 11–12 of "The Extasie." "Probably the meaning was that by looking into each other's eyes lovers could see small reflections of themselves." Suggests that Donne's metaphor is perhaps the earliest instance of the idea. For a reply by Geoffrey Tillotson, see TLS, 7 December, p. 838. See also three entries under one title by Jack Lindsay, F. P. Wilson, and R. D. Waller, TLS, 14 December, p. 859.

◆§ 291. J. "All Tincture." N&Q, 168:62.

Asks what "All tincture" means in the poem beginning "Sleep, sleep old Sun." For a reply by Herbert Maxwell and R. S. B., see N&Q, 168:104. Both suggest that the word refers to color, not alchemy.

◆§ 292. KEYNES, GEOFFREY. "The Earliest Compositions of Sir Thomas Browne." TLS, 25 February, p. 134.

Identifies the "Tho. Browne" who contributed elegiac lines to the 1633 edition of the poems (thereafter eliminated) not as the great doctor of Norwich, as he been assumed, but rather as a Thomas Browne (1604–1673), a student at Christ Church in 1620 and later domestic chaplain to Archbishop Laud in 1637. Signed the imprimatur of the LXXX Sermons in 1640.

◆§ 293. LEAVIS, F. R. "English Poetry in the Seventeenth Century." Scrutiny, 4:236–56.

Reprinted with the addition of Note A, "Carew and the Line of Wit," and Note B, "Cowley," as "The Line of Wit" in Revaluation: Tradition & Development in English Poetry (London: Chatto & Windus Ltd., 1936; New York: George W. Stewart, Publisher, Inc., 1947; New York: W. W. Norton & Co. by arrangement with George W. Stewart Publisher, Inc., 1963), pp. 10–41.

Comments on Donne's originality, control of a stanzaic forms, mastery of tone, and highly dramatic qualities. Praises Donne as a "living poet": "It is not any eccentricity or defiant audacity that makes the effect here so immediate, but rather an irresistible rightness" (p. 237).

◆§ 294. LINDSAY, JACK, F. P. WILSON, AND R. D. WALLER. "Looking Babies." TLS, 14 December, p. 859.

A reply to Katharine Garvin, TLS, 23 November, p. 770. Three entries under one title. Finds earlier uses of the metaphor of "looking babies" than Donne's "The Extasie." See also Geoffrey Tillotson, TLS, 7 December, p. 838.

◄§ 295. MATSUURA, KAICHI. "Lyrical Poems of John Donne." *Studies in English Literature* (Tokyo), 15:58–67.

General introduction to the secular and sacred lyrics for the Japanese reader. Surveys Donne's philosophy of love and comments on his preoccupation with the problems of the relationship of the body and the soul, the erotic and the sacred.

◄§ 296. MAXWELL, HERBERT AND R. S. B. "John Donne's 'All Tincture.'" *N&Q*, 168:62, 104.

Reply to J., *N&Q*, 168:62, who asks what "All tincture" means in the poem beginning "Sleep, sleep old Sun." Suggests that the word refers to color, not alchemy.

◄§ 297. MAXWELL, IAN R. "John Donne's Library." *TLS*, 11 July, p. 448.

Addition to Keynes's list of books in Donne's library—*Dialogue du fou et du sage*. A copy in the British Museum bears Donne's signature and motto and is dated in the museum's catalogue conjecturally as 1510. Suggests that the copy may have belonged to John Heywood, Donne's grandfather, who perhaps used the *Dialogue* as a model.

◄§ 298. MORE, PAUL ELMER, AND FRANK LESLIE CROSS. *Anglicanism: The Thought and Practice of the Church of England, Illustrated from the Religious Literature of the Seventeenth Century.* Milwaukee: Morehouse Publishing Co. lxxvi, 811 p.

Brief comments on Donne's poetry. Praises Donne's wit, use of language, imagery, etc. Suggests, "Just as Leonardo and Raphael were the culmination of their schools of Italian art, and stumbling-blocks to their slavish imitators, so was Donne to his poetical heirs" (p. lxv). Reproduces "The Crosse" and selections from the sermons. Brief biographical sketch.

◄§ 299. NICOLSON, MARJORIE. "The 'New Astronomy' and English Literary Imagination." *SP*, 32:428–62.

Reprinted with slight alterations in *Science and Imagination* (Ithaca, N. Y.: Great Seal Books, Division of Cornell University Press; London: Oxford University Press, 1956), pp. 30–57.

Suggests that the discovery of Kepler's "new star" in 1604 and in particular the publication of Galileo's *Sidereus Nuncius* in 1610 "marked a turning-point in thought, and occasioned a response on the part of men of letters much more pronounced and much more important than that produced by the *De Revolutionibus Orbium Coelestium* of Copernicus" (p. 429). States that "Of all the English poets, there was none who showed a more immediate response to the new discoveries than John Donne, nor is there in English literature a more remarkable example of the immediate effect of the *Sidereus Nuncius*" (p. 449). Donne's interest seems keenest in those works written between 1604 and 1614; thereafter it apparently waned. Discusses in particular *Letters to Severall Personages*, *The first Anniversary*, and *Ignatius his Conclave*. In his later writings Donne still refers to astronomy, but these references are rare in the sermons and the divine poems.

◄§ 300. SHAPIRO, I. A. "Donne and Sir Thomas Roe." *TLS*, 7 February, p. 76.

Supports the position of R. E. Bennett, *TLS*, 31 January, p. 62, that Sir Thomas Roe is the addressee of a letter written by Donne from Chelsea, November 25, 1625 (Gosse, *Life and Letters of John Donne*, II, 222–25).

◄§ 301. SHARP, ROBERT LATHROP. "Observations on Metaphysical Imagery." *SR*, 43:464–78.

Stresses the "organic growth of figurative language and the capacity of poets to adjust their imaginations to the resultant new levels of the poetic idiom" (p. 464) and cautions that "the delights of poetry for Donne and the metaphysicals were not wholly what they are for us" (p. 465). States that "No other metaphysical possessed Donne's genius, but they all agreed with Donne that a faster, more efficient rhetoric should be used and that the rhetoric merely of periphrasis and adornment was exhausted. If they were led into obscurity and roughness, these faults, like the inevitable extravagance, became apparent only to the next generation of poets, the neo-classicists" (p. 478). Maintains that Donne's metaphors "are two steps removed from the plain statement of prose; they require a double instead of a single mental jump. To few readers is a double jump of this kind natural" (p. 469). Points out, "Because the poetic idiom of the Elizabethans was already a welter of metaphors, with countless variations of the same notion, the poetic necessity of being new and different led the metaphysicals to sensitize their perceptions. . . . Whereas the Elizabethans began with an idiom on a lower figurative level the metaphysicals begun with the figures of Shakespeare" (p. 470).

◄§ 302. SMALLEY, DONALD A. "Browning and Donne." *TLS*, 10 October, p. 631.

Requests information on any of the volumes of Donne's poetry once owned by Browning or by his father. Notes that by his sixteenth birthday Browning had set Donne's "Goe, and catche a falling starre" to music and that by 1842 he had a thorough knowledge of Donne's poetry.

303. THOMPSON, W. MEREDITH. *Der Tod in der englischen Lyrik des siebzehnten Jahrhunderts*. Sprache und kultur der germanischen und romanischen völker . . . A. Anglistische reihe . . . Bd. xx. Breslau: Priebatsch. viii, 97 p.

Discusses attitudes toward death in the seventeenth century. Analyzes the problem of death in the works of prominent poets. Donne's position is that of the teaching of the Anglican Church of the period. Donne makes contradictory statements about predestination and original sin in his poems. Apparently he held two different views about the physical–spiritual aspects of death; at one point he says that the soul leaves the body immediately upon death while elsewhere he says that souls will creep from the grave on Judgment Day. Donne had the typical Elizabethan love of life and exaggerated fear of death, yet he viewed death as a means by which he could be freed from the ever-increasing burden of sin.

304. TILLOTSON, GEOFFREY. "Looking Babies." *TLS*, 7 December, p. 838.

In part a reply to Katharine Garvin, *TLS*, 23 November, p. 770. Discusses the metaphor possibly implied by "looking babies" in lines 11–12 of "The Extasie." Points out that in Greek as well as in Latin the words for pupil of the eyes, doll, and girl are similar. See also Jack Lindsay, F. P. Wilson, and R. D. Waller, *TLS*, 14 December, p. 859.

305. WHITE, HAROLD OGDEN. "The Theory of Imitation from Jonson Onward," in *Plagiarism and Imitation During the English Renaissance: A Study in Critical Distinctions*, pp. 120–202. Cambridge: Harvard University Press.

Brief discussion of Donne's attitude toward imitative practice (pp. 126–28). Donne believed that "literature is a mine, from which all writers may dig treasure; the writer who transforms what he takes from his predecessors into 'as much and as good' is not in debt to his sources, for he has added to the treasure which posterity will have at its disposal in turn; borrowed matter is to be thankfully acknowledged, not ungratefully purloined by stealth" (pp. 127–28). Donne's most explicit statement on the matter is found in the preface to *The Progresse of the Soule*. His condemnation of simple plagiarism is found in *Satyre II* (ll. 25–30).

306. WILD, FRIEDRICH. "Zum Problem des Barocks in der englischen Dichtung." *Anglia*, 59:414–22.

Defines the concept of the baroque for English literature and gives examples of poets and aspects that might be called baroque. Presents a list of poets whose work contains baroque elements, one of which is Donne. Discusses Donne's conceits.

ᵉᵍ 307. WILLIAMSON, GEORGE. "Mutability, Decay, and Seventeenth-Century Melancholy." *ELH*, 2:121–50.
Reprinted in *Seventeenth Century Contexts*, ed. William Keast (London: Faber and Faber, Ltd.; Chicago: University of Chicago Press, 1960, 1961), pp. 9–41.
Surveys theories of mutability and decay in the sixteenth and seventeenth centuries. Notes, "Perhaps no writer in the early seventeenth century reminds us of the changing astronomical views more often than Donne. Copernicus, Tycho Brahe, Galileo, and Kepler, or the 'new philosophy,' are never very far from his thoughts when he turns from the microcosm to the macrocosm" (p. 140). Brief comments on *Biathanatos*, several sermons, the *Anniversaries*, and the *Devotions*.

1936

ᵉᵍ 308. BENNETT, R. E. "Donne and 'The Queen.'" *TLS*, 29 August, p. 697.
Identifies the correspondent to whom Donne addressed a letter (Gosse, *Life and Letters of John Donne*, II, pp. 16–17) as Sir Henry Goodere. Letter contains a pun on the name of Bishop John King.

ᵉᵍ 309. BOTTING, ROLAND B. "A Donne Poem?" *TLS*, 14 March, p. 224.
Rejects as Donne's the poem "To his friende Captaine Iohn Smith, and his Workc" in Smith's *The Generall Histoire of Virginia* (1624) on the grounds that it does not reflect Donne's habitual poetic usage. See also Beach Langston, *TLS*, 18 January, p. 55; B. H. Newdigate and John Hayward, *TLS*, 25 January, p. 75; Newdigate, *TLS*, 8 February, p. 116 and *London Mercury*, 33:424–25; I. A. Shapiro and E. K. Chambers, *TLS*, 1 February, p. 96.

ᵉᵍ 310. BRITTIN, NORMAN A. "Emerson and the Metaphysical Poets." *AL*, 8:1–21.
Discusses the influence of the metaphysicals on Emerson and Emerson's appreciation of these poets. "It is when he attempts to find imagery to express his Heraclitan idea of the universe that Emerson approaches nearest Donne" (p. 15). Concludes, "Emerson's poetry, not in general, but in numerous individual passages, resembles slightly that of Donne and Cowley, and strongly, that of Herbert and Marvell" (pp. 20–21).

ᵉᵍ 311. BROOKS, CLEANTH, JOHN THIBAUT PURSER, AND ROBERT PENN WARREN. *An Approach to Literature: A Collection of Prose and Verse with Analyses and Discussions*. Baton Rouge: Louisiana State University Press. 578 p.
Revised ed., New York: Appleton-Century-Crofts, Inc., 1939; 3d ed.,

New York: Appleton-Century-Crofts, Inc., 1952; 4th ed., New York: Appleton-Century-Crofts, Inc., 1964; alternate 4th ed., New York: Appleton-Century-Crofts, Inc., 1967.

First and second editions contain "The Funerall" with no explication. Third edition contains an explication of "The good-morrow" (pp. 373–76) and "The Funerall" with an exercise (pp. 396–97) and "Valediction: forbidding mourning" with no commentary. Fourth edition contains a reprint of the explication of "The good-morrow" from the third edition (pp. 366–68) with the addition of one new sentence, reproduces "Valediction: forbidding mourning" with no comment, and includes "The Funerall" with the same exercise found in the third edition (pp. 395–96). The fourth alternate edition contains all the Donne items exactly as they appear in the fourth edition.

✑§ 312. CHAMBERS, E. K. "A Donne Poem?" *TLS*, 1 February, p. 96.
Rejects "To his friende Captaine Iohn Smith, and his Worke" in Smith's *Generall Historie of Virginia* (1624) as being Donne's. See also Beach Langston, *TLS*, 18 January, p. 55; B. H. Newdigate and John Hayward, *TLS*, 25 January, p. 75; I. A. Shapiro, *TLS*, 1 February, p. 96; Newdigate, *TLS*, 8 February, p. 116; Roland B. Botting, *TLS*, 14 March, p. 224; and Newdigate, *London Mercury*, 33:424–25.

✑§ 313. COLERIDGE, SAMUEL TAYLOR. "Lecture X. Donne. I. Marginalia from 'Literary Remains' and II. Marginalia from 'Literary World,' " in *Coleridge's Miscellaneous Criticism*, ed. Thomas Middleton Raysor, pp. 131–45. Cambridge: Harvard University Press.
Collection of Coleridge's various critical comments on Donne.

✑§ 314. DUNN, ESTHER CLOUDMAN. "A Note on John Donne," in *The Literature of Shakespeare's England*, pp. 158–63. New York: Charles Scribner's Sons.
Maintains, "Donne articulates a new quality which was tentative and fugitive in Ralegh and some other Elizabethan poets. The Elizabethan term, 'conceit,' so often warped from its essential meaning, holds in itself the simple interpretation of this quality. It is a new or revived emphasis upon the thought and perception of individual man and an immediate and untrammelled use of figures to transfer this material to poetry" (p. 163).

✑§ 315. FRENCH, J. MILTON. "Bowman v. Donne." *TLS*, 12 December, p. 1035.
Traces several lawsuits between John Donne the younger and Francis Bowman, stationer of Oxford and London, concerning the publication of Donne's sermons.

◄§ 316. GRETTON, GEORGE. "John Donne: The Spiritual Background."
Britannica (Hamburg), 13:53–65.
Studies some of the formative influences on Donne's poetry, particularly the Catholic religion, Scholasticism, the religious mood of the times, and the temper of the Renaissance.

◄§ 317. GROS, LÉON-GABRIEL. "Présentation de John Donne." *Cahiers du Sud*, 15:785–93; "Poèmes." *Cahiers du Sud*, 15:794–802.
The first item is a general introduction to Donne's love poetry for the French reader. Comments on Donne's basic attitudes towards love as reflected in the poetry and outlines the more obvious stylistic features. Compares Donne to the surrealists, to Baudelaire, and to other French poets. The second item contains nine translations of poems from the *Songs and Sonets* into French.

◄§ 318. HAYWARD, JOHN. "A Donne Poem?" *TLS*, 25 January, p. 75.
Maintains that "To his friende Captaine Iohn Smith, and his Worke" discovered in Smith's *Generall Historie of Virginia* (1624) and attributed to Donne by Beach Langston (*TLS*, 18 January, p. 55) and B. H. Newdigate (*TLS*, 25 January, p. 75) is more likely the work of John Donne the younger or perhaps John Done, author of *Polydoron*. See also I. A. Shapiro and E. K. Chambers, *TLS*, 1 February, p. 96; Newdigate, *TLS*, 8 February, p. 116; Roland B. Botting, *TLS*, 14 March, p. 224; and Newdigate, *London Mercury*, 33:424–25.

◄§ 319. HUSAIN, I[TRAT]. "John Donne, on Conversion." *Theology* (London), 299–301.
Reprinted as an appendix to *The Dogmatic and Mystical Theology of John Donne* (London: The Society for the Promoting of Christian Knowledge; New York: The Macmillan Co., 1938), pp. 144–47.
Comments on several passages from the sermons in which Donne "definitely declared himself against changing one's religion, and fully explained the meaning and significance of his conception of the Catholic Church" (p. 299).

◄§ 320. INCE, RICHARD. "Donne and Giordano Bruno." *TLS*, 27 June, p. 544.
Agrees with Jack Lindsay (*TLS*, 20 June, p. 523) that Donne was influenced by Bruno. Suggests that Donne perhaps was introduced to the work of Bruno by Henry Percy, 9th Earl of Northumberland. See also Frances A. Yates, *TLS*, 4 July, p. 564 and Lindsay, *TLS*, 11 July, p. 580 and 24 July 1937, p. 544.

◈§ 321. JORDAN, WILLIAM K. "The Dominant Groups, 1603–1625. Development of Governmental and Anglican Thought with Respect to Religious Dissent," in *The Development of Religious Toleration in England from the Accession of James I to the Convention of the Long Parliament (1603–1640)*. Vol. II, pp. 17–114. Cambridge: Harvard University Press.

Brief consideration of Donne's attitudes toward religious toleration and ecumenism (pp. 41–43). "With Donne, a tolerant and moderate definition was given to the Anglican position, but the great preacher remained isolated. His thought is to be linked with that of the moderates who subscribed to no party rather than with the main stream of Anglican theory" (p. 43).

◈§ 322. LANGSTON, BEACH. "A Donne Poem Overlooked." *TLS*, 18 January, p. 55.

Argues that a poem entitled "To his friende Captaine Iohn Smith, and his Worke" in Smith's *Generall Historie of Virginia* (1624) was written by Donne. See also B. H. Newdigate and John Hayward, *TLS*, 25 January, p. 75; I. A. Shapiro and E. K. Chambers, *TLS*, 1 February, p. 96; Newdigate, *TLS*, 8 February, p. 116; Roland B. Botting, *TLS*, 14 March, p. 224; and Newdigate, *London Mercury*, 33:424–25.

◈§ 323. LEAVIS, F. R. "The Line of Wit," in *Revaluation: Tradition & Development in English Poetry*, pp. 10–41. London: Chatto & Windus Ltd.

Reprinted, New York: George W. Stewart Publishers, Inc., 1947; New York: W. W. Norton & Co., 1963.

Explores the line of wit that runs from Donne to Pope. Comments on the "irresistible rightness" of Donne's verse, "The extraordinary force of originality that made Donne so potent an influence in the seventeenth century makes him at once for us, without his being the less felt as of his period, contemporary—obviously a living poet in the most important sense" (p. 11). Stresses Donne's control of intonation, rhythm, and movement through careful manipulation of stanza form, his uses of the speaking voice, the range of his dramatic qualities. Comments on the combined influence of Donne and Jonson on the poets who follow them, especially Carew and Marvell. Supports Eliot's notion of "dissociation of sensibility." Three notes appended to the essay: (1) "Carew and the Line of Wit" (pp. 37–38); (2) "Cowley" (pp. 38–39); and (3) "Herrick" (pp. 39–41).

◈§ 324. LINDSAY, JACK. "Donne and Giordano Bruno." *TLS*, 20 June, p. 523.

Suggests that the circle metaphor as well as lines 7–10 in "Loves Alchymie" were suggested by Bruno. See also Richard Ince, *TLS*, 27 June,

p. 544; Frances A. Yates, *TLS*, 4 July, p. 564; and Jack Lindsay, *TLS*, 11 July, p. 580 and 24 July 1937, p. 544.

❧ 325. ————. "Donne and Giordano Bruno." *TLS*, 11 July, p. 580.
Re-enforces his earlier claim that Bruno influenced Donne (*TLS*, 20 June, p. 523). Cites several examples of similarities and concludes, "It is not too much to claim that it was the impact of Bruno's work on Donne that created Donne's 'originality'." See also Richard Ince, *TLS*, 27 June, p. 544; Frances A. Yates, *TLS*, 4 July, p. 564; and Lindsay, *TLS*, 24 July 1937, p. 544.

❧ 326. MATHEWS, ERNST G. "A Spanish Proverb." *TLS*, 12 September, p. 729.
Suggests that a Spanish proverb used in Donne's letter to Sir Henry Goodere in *Letters to Severall Personages* (1651, pp. 103–4) was taken from Melchor de Santa Cruz's *Floresta Española* (printed 18 times between 1594 and 1674). Suggests that the book should be added to Donne's library of Spanish works.

❧ 327. MOORE, JOHN F. "Scholasticism, Donne and the Metaphysical Conceit." *Revue Anglo-Américaine*, 13:289–96.
Maintains that Scholasticism "absorbed and transformed, became Donne's natural idiom, characteristic of both his poetry and prose" (p. 289). Emphasizes, however, that Donne utilized Scholasticism for literary ends. "It seems accurate, if lurid, to say that scepticism debauched Scholasticism, and that the offspring of this unnatural union, the metaphysical conceit, looks somewhat like its mother, but has its father's wild and irresponsible ways" (p. 296).

❧ 328. NEWDIGATE, B. H. "A Donne Poem?" *TLS*, 25 January, p. 75.
Announces that he discovered independently the poem signed "IO: DONE" in Smith's *Generall Historie of Virginia* (1624). Agrees with Beach Langston (*TLS*, 18 January, p. 55) that the poem should be attributed to Donne. See also John Hayward, *TLS*, 25 January, p. 75; I. A. Shapiro and E. K. Chambers, *TLS*, 1 February, p. 96; B. H. Newdigate, *TLS*, 8 February, p. 116; Roland B. Botting, *TLS*, 14 March, p. 224; and Newdigate, *London Mercury*, 33:424–25.

❧ 329. ————. "A Donne Poem?" *TLS*, 8 February, p. 116.
Defends his attribution to Donne of "To his friende Captaine Iohn Smith, and his Worke" in Smith's *Generall Historie of Virginia* (1624). See also Beach Langston, *TLS*, 18 January, p. 55; B. H. Newdigate and John Hayward, *TLS*, 25 January, p. 75; I. A. Shapiro and E. K. Chambers, *TLS*, 1 February, p. 96; Roland B. Botting, *TLS*, 14 March, p. 224; and Newdigate, *London Mercury*, 33:424–25.

◀§ 330. ————. "An Overlooked Poem by John Donne?" *London Mercury*, 33:424–25.

Argues that "To his friende Captaine Iohn Smith, and his Worke" discovered in Smith's *Generall Historie of Virginia* (1624) was written by Donne. Points out that after he had submitted his find to the *London Mercury*, Beach Langston simultaneously made the same announcement in *TLS*, 18 January, p. 55. See also Newdigate and John Hayward, *TLS*, 25 January, p. 75; I. A. Shapiro and E. K. Chambers, *TLS*, 1 February, p. 96; Newdigate, *TLS*, 8 February, p. 116; and Roland B. Botting, *TLS*, 14 March, p. 224.

◀§ 331. POTTER, GEORGE REUBEN. "Donne's *Extasie*, Contra Legouis." *PQ*, 15:247–53.

A reply to Pierre Legouis's reading of "The Extasie," in *Donne the Craftsman* (1928), in which Legouis views the poem essentially as a seduction poem. Maintains that in "The Extasie" Donne "came as close as he ever did to putting in words those subtle relations between the body and the mind of which he was conscious continually, and most keenly when he was passionate in love" (p. 247). Supports this position primarily by citing passages in other of Donne's works where Donne is apparently serious about the problems of body and soul. "Only the strongest evidence would warrant the assumption that Donne used cynically in one poem ideas which so profoundly moved him wherever else he wrote about them. And there is . . . no such evidence" (p. 252). Expresses the fear that Legouis's position opens up the larger possibility that much of Donne's poetry is merely a kind of posturing.

◀§ 332. SAMPSON, ASHLEY. "The Resurrection of Donne." *London Mercury*, 33:307–14.

Maintains that Donne's popularity in the twentieth century "owes less to his intrinsic virtues as a poet than to the fact that this generation has endured the pangs which brought Donne to maturity as an individual" (p. 308). Brief summary of the likenesses between Donne and the consciousness of poets of the 1920s and 1930s.

◀§ 333. SHAPIRO, I. A. "A Donne Poem?" *TLS*, 1 February, p. 96.

Rejects as Donne's "To his friende Captaine Iohn Smith, and his Worke" discovered in Smith's *Generall Historie of Virginia* (1624). See also Beach Langston, *TLS*, 18 January, p. 55; B. H. Newdigate and John Hayward, *TLS*, 25 January, p. 75; E. K. Chambers, *TLS*, 1 February, p. 96; Newdigate, *TLS*, 8 February, p. 116; Roland B. Botting, *TLS*, 14 March, p. 224; and Newdigate, *London Mercury*, 33:424–25.

◄§ 334. SMITH, LOGAN PEARSALL. "Donne's Sermons," in *Reperusals and Recollections*, pp. 222–55. London: Constable and Company, Ltd.; Toronto: Macmillan Co. of Canada Ltd.; New York: Harcourt, Brace & Co.

Slightly revised version of Smith's introduction to *Donne's Sermons: Selected Passages* (1919).

◄§ 335. TEAGER, FLORENCE S. "Patronage of Joseph Hall and John Donne." *PQ*, 15:408–13.

Accounts for the disparity of treatment given Hall and Donne by Sir Robert Drury. Argues from contemporary records that in 1605, when Sir Robert denied Hall an annual ten-pound stipend, he was apparently in some financial difficulty but that by 1610, when he leased Drury House to Donne, he had attained financial security.

◄§ 336. TREDEGAR, VISCOUNT. "John Donne—Lover and Priest." *Essays by Divers Hands* (Royal Society of Literature), 15:161–202.

Sees all of Donne's work as "the pure fire of a soul's honest and intensive self-expression" (p. 11). Biographical sketch that stresses the continuity between Jack and John. General appreciative survey of the poetry and sermons, with numerous selections from both.

◄§ 337. WATKINS, W. B. C. "Spenser to the Restoration (1579–1660)," in *Johnson and English Poetry Before 1660*, pp. 58–84. Princeton: Princeton University Press.

Comments on Dr. Johnson's evaluation of Donne as a poet and on his extensive familiarity with the Donne canon. "Johnson knew Donne's poetry thoroughly—how thoroughly one does not realize until searching through the *Dictionary*, where he quotes Donne steadily from the beginning to the end" (p. 80). Lists the Donne sources used by Johnson for the *Dictionary* (pp. 96–97).

◄§ 338. WHITE, HELEN C. *The Metaphysical Poets: A Study in Religious Experience*. New York: The Macmillan Co. ix, 444 p.

Reprinted, 1962 (Collier Books).

A study of five poets—Donne, Herbert, Crashaw, Vaughan, and Traherne. Discusses in the introduction (pp. 1–27) how mysticism and poetry are alike and how they differ. Concludes that none of the five poets considered are genuine mystics in the strict sense of the word, but that all, to varying degrees, evidence elements of mysticism in their verse. Chapter I, "The Intellectual Climate" (pp. 28–48), Chapter II, "The Religious Climate" (pp. 49–69), and Chapter III, "Metaphysical Poetry" (pp. 70–94) set up the necessary background and generalities as a framework for the discussion of the individual poets (two chapters to each of the poets). Chapter IV, "The Conversions of John Donne" (pp.

95–120) is a sketch of Donne's life and his religious and philosophical temperament. Chapter V, "The Divine Poetry of John Donne" (pp. 121–49) is devoted to a study of Donne's religious sensibility and attitudes as these are reflected in his sacred verse. Considers the poems as reflections of Donne's personal tensions and of his complex religious sensibility. In the conclusion, the author presents a series of comparisons and contrasts among the five poets.

⋖§ 339. WILLIAMSON, GEORGE. "Senecan Style in the Seventeenth Century." *PQ*, 15:321–51.

Traces the development of Senecan prose style during the seventeenth century and mentions Donne as an adopter of Senecan style.

⋖§ 340. ———. "Strong Lines." *ES*, 18:152–59.

Reprinted in *Seventeenth Century Contexts*, ed. William Keast (London: Faber and Faber, Ltd.; Chicago: University of Chicago Press, 1960, 1961), pp. 120–31.

Reprinted in *Discussions of John Donne*, ed. Frank Kermode (Boston: D. C. Heath & Co., 1962), pp. 58–63.

Discusses the term *strong lines*. Regrets that "the term 'metaphysical' has obscured the more inclusive epithet 'strong-lined.' For the early seventeenth-century poets no term but 'strong lines' seems to have abstracted the peculiar essence of their kind of poetry" (p. 158). Comments briefly on Donne to show that his contemporaries saw him primarily as a strong-lined poet, not as a metaphysical.

⋖§ 341. YATES, FRANCES A. "Donne and Giordano Bruno." *TLS*, 4 July, p. 564.

Agrees with Jack Lindsay (*TLS*, 20 June, p. 523) and Richard Ince (*TLS*, 27 June, p. 544) that Donne was influenced by Bruno. See also Lindsay, *TLS*, 11 July, p. 580 and 24 July 1937, p. 544.

1937

⋖§ 342. ASHLEY-MONTAGU, M. F. "Donne the Astronomer." *TLS*, 7 August, p. 576.

Reply to I. A. Shapiro, *TLS*, 3 July, p. 492. Challenges Shapiro's statement that "the earliest datable work in which Donne displays any knowledge of the 'new astronomy' is 'Ignatius his Conclave'." Maintains that Donne's first allusion to the New Science is in the second part of *Biathanatos*. See also W. Fraser Mitchell, *TLS*, 10 July, p. 512 and 7 August, p. 576; I. A. Shapiro, *TLS*, 17 July, p. 528 and 14 August, p. 592; and Pierre Legouis, *TLS*, 31 July, p. 560.

⋘§ 343. ATKINS, SIDNEY H. "Donne's Satires." *TLS*, 22 May, p. 396.

Dates the *Satyres* as 1596–1597. In *Satyre IV* there is a reference to the loss of Amiens, an event that occurred in March of 1597. In *Satyre I* there is a reference to Banks's horse (ll. 79–82); a great interest was shown in the horse in 1595–1597. See Atkins's note on Banks's horse in *N&Q*, 167 (1934):39–41. See also G. B. Harrison, *TLS*, 29 May, p. 412.

⋘§ 344. BALD, R. C. "Three Metaphysical Epigrams." *PQ*, 16:402–5.

Argues that the epigram "Fall of a wall" does not refer to an event during Donne's Cadiz expedition in 1596, as Grierson suggests in his edition, but rather to an event that occurred in 1589 and recorded by Sir George Buc and Stow. Suggests that perhaps this is Donne's earliest poem.

⋘§ 345. BENNETT, R. E. "Tracts from John Donne's Library." *RES*, 13:333–35.

Note on a group of nine tracts, now at Harvard (self-mark Nor 5200), of which only the second and seventh, both bearing Donne's signature, can be identified as belonging to him. Both Gosse and Keynes suggest that all nine were in Donne's possession.

⋘§ 346. ————. "Walton's Use of Donne's Letters." *PQ*, 16:30–34.

Shows that Walton in the 1670 edition of the *Life* freely adapted the letters to his own artistic ends, sometimes making a composite of several letters, adding place and date to suit the context, and adding to Donne's statements. Argues that Walton's sketch of Donne is essentially correct, even though the documents have been altered.

⋘§ 347. COFFIN, CHARLES MONROE. *John Donne and the New Philosophy*. Morningside Heights, N. Y.: Columbia University Press. viii, 311 p.

Reprinted, 1958.

Suggests that by exploring in detail Donne's familiarity with the New Science one can find, in part, "an explanation of the compelling interest he has had for the twentieth century" (p. vii). Donne "represents the effort of the late Renaissance mind to make an adjustment to its world of changing values without sacrificing its regard for the equal claims of emotion and reason" (p. 6). Summarizes the main elements of the old cosmology and describes the New Science. Shows Donne's interest in and knowledge of the main discoveries and scientific questions of the day (Kepler, Gilbert, Galileo, etc.). Discusses the problems of the relation of faith and reason in a rapidly changing world. Points out the influence of the New Philosophy on Donne's thought and imagination and in the process illuminates many passages from Donne's works.

◄§ 348. ————. "Donne's Astronomy." *TLS*, 18 September, p. 675.

Reply to I. A. Shapiro, *TLS*, 3 July, p. 492. Argues that "if an allusion to the shadow of Venus is to become involved in an attempt to date the eighth Problem, it is well to conjecture that sometime shortly after the publication of Kepler's book on the new star, September 1606, is a more plausible date for its composition than 1611."

◄§ 349. CROFTS, J. E. V. "John Donne." *E&S* of 1936, 22:128–43.

Reprinted as "John Donne: A Reconsideration" in *John Donne: A Collection of Critical Essays*, ed. Helen Gardner (1962), pp. 77–89.

Stresses the personal quality of Donne's writings, which distinguish them from those of the classicists. Suggests that the technique and imagery of a Donne poem reflects the mind of "a man who felt that in the last resort the structures of the intellect were useless, and that contact with ultimate reality could be found only in passion: the passion of love, or the passion of faith" (p. 143). Challenges Eliot's concept of "unified sensibility." "He was never really interested enough in his own thought to take it as seriously as his critics. . . . It was Donne's sensibility that modified his thought, mammocked it, made a guy of it in poem after poem" (p. 142). Points out that a principle of opposition governs the imagery and technique of a Donne poem, not unification.

◄§ 350. DOUDS, JOHN BOAL. "Donne's Technique of Dissonance." *PMLA*, 52:1051–61.

Discusses the varieties of *discordia concors* in Donne's poetry to illustrate what is distinctive in his style and vision of the world. Tonal dissonance, metrical dissonance, as well as various rhetorical and imagistic dissonances are illustrated. Concludes that dissonance is "a most serviceable instrument—in fact, a prime necessity—for expressing Donne's multiple sensibility, his complex moods, and the discords of his temperament. In short, the dissonance of style reflects a dissonance inwardly experienced" (p. 1061).

◄§ 351. HARRISON, G. B. "Donne's Satires." *TLS*, 29 May, p. 412.

Supports Atkins (*TLS*, 22 May, p. 396) that the *Satyres* should be dated 1596–1597. An allusion in *Satyre II* (ll. 56–60) to the "Sclavonian scolding," an event that occurred on July 23, 1597.

◄§ 352. HENDERSON, FLETCHER ORPIN. "Traditions of *Précieux* and *Libertin* in Suckling's Poetry." *ELH*, 4:274–98.

Shows that Suckling either ridiculed or ignored the cult of the *précieuse* and the new doctrines of Platonic love, which were popular in court circles during the reign of Charles I. "His usual expression in love poetry was guided by a 'libertin' naturalism which he derived directly from Donne, whose poetic disciple he was, and from the minor *libertin* poets

in France, of whom he had first-hand knowledge" (p. 298). Comments
on Suckling's borrowings from Donne (pp. 280–81). Discusses the *Songs
and Sonets* in the light of the *libertin* tradition.

◄§ 353. JOHNSON, FRANCIS R. "The Quest for Physical Confirmation of
the Earth's Motion," in *Astronomical Thought in Renaissance
England: A Study of the English Scientific Writings from 1500 to
1645*, pp. 211–47. Baltimore: The Johns Hopkins Press; London:
Humphrey Milford, Oxford University Press.
Maintains that Donne's "allusions and images drawn from science are
generally precise, rather than vague, and based now upon the old, and
now upon the new, theories, depending on his poetic purposes" (p. 243).
Stresses Donne's interest in and knowledge of contemporary developments in astronomy and suggests that Donne's most significant work
dealing with the new astronomy is *Ignatius his Conclave*. Appendix A,
"Chronological List of Books Dealing with Astronomy Printed in England to 1640," lists the seventeenth-century editions of *Ignatius his Conclave*.

◄§ 354. LEGOUIS, PIERRE. "John Donne." *TLS*, 31 July, p. 560.
Reply to I. A. Shapiro, *TLS*, 3 July, p. 492 and 17 July, p. 528. Points
out Donne's carelessness in astronomical references in "Probleme IX" of
Paradoxes and Problemes. See also W. Fraser Mitchell, *TLS*, 10 July,
p. 512 and 7 August, p. 576; M. F. Ashley-Montagu, *TLS*, 7 August, p.
576, and I. A. Shapiro, *TLS*, 14 August, p. 592.

◄§ 355. LINDSAY, JACK. "Donne and Blake." *TLS*, 24 July, p. 544.
A note on Donne; another on Blake. Maintains his earlier position
(*TLS*, 20 June 1936, p. 523 and 11 July 1936, p. 580) that Donne was
greatly influenced by Giordano Bruno, especially by his *Spaccio* and his
Heroici. Points out that Donne was not, however, greatly influenced by
Bruno's scientific thinking. Suggests that Donne read Charles Esti-
enne's *Paradoxes*. See also Richard Ince, *TLS*, 27 June 1936, p. 544 and
and Frances A. Yates, *TLS*, 4 July 1936, p. 564.

◄§ 356. LYON, T[HOMAS]. *The Theory of Religious Liberty in England
1603–39*. Cambridge: University Press. viii, 241 p.
Discusses Donne's position on religious toleration, which is marked by
"a liberalism which is rare in early seventeenth-century theologians" (p.
57). Although Donne was not a believer in exclusive salvation, he, like
Hooker, holds to the orthodox theory of theological persecution when
the errors promulgated are those in the will rather than those in the
understanding. "As to Hooker, Church and State to Donne are two aspects of one body, and he is theoretically at the other extreme of separa-

tism" (p. 59). Donne believed in the theory of the divine right of the King in civil and ecclesiastical affairs "though the power of the King extended not to making new articles of faith but simply to enforcing the truth of God's word" (p. 60).

357. MITCHELL, W. FRASER. "John Donne the Astronomer." *TLS*, 10 July, p. 512.

Reply to I. A. Shapiro, *TLS*, 3 July, p. 492. Maintains that Donne's references to astronomy are not necessarily statements of what he believed but are used as illustrations and as elements of his wit. Nevertheless, the sermons abound in references to astronomy. "The passages cited leave us in doubt as to Donne's personal attitude to the astronomical questions of his time. We find him holding fast to at least the Tychonian, probably even to the Copernican, system of the geocentric universe; he avoids enumerating the planets when to do so would involve his taking sides in a purely scientific controversy; and he 'sounds' faintly satirical in his reference to Galileo's discovery." See also I. A. Shapiro, *TLS*, 17 July, p. 528 and 14 August, p. 592; Pierre Legouis, *TLS*, 31 July, p. 560; W. Fraser Mitchell, *TLS*, 7 August, p. 576; and M. F. Ashley-Montagu, *TLS*, 7 August, p. 576.

358. ———. "Donne the Astronomer." *TLS*, 7 August, p. 576.

Reply to I. A. Shapiro, *TLS*, 17 July, p. 528. Maintains his earlier position (*TLS*, 10 July, p. 512) that "on the evidence of the Sermons nothing definite can be inferred as to Donne's astronomical beliefs, except that, like many in his time, he found himself puzzled." See also I. A. Shapiro, *TLS*, 3 July, p. 492 and 14 August, p. 592; Pierre Legouis, *TLS*, 31 July, p. 560; M. F. Ashley-Montagu, *TLS*, 7 August, p. 576.

359. MORLEY, CHRISTOPHER. "Courting John Donne." *Saturday Review of Literature*, 16:10, 16.

Reprinted with slight revisions in *Letters of Askance* (Philadelphia: J. B. Lippincott Co., 1939), pp. 152–61.

Appreciative comments on the love poems, with several attacks on Jessopp, who was "not able to feel much enthusiasm for Donne as a poet."

360. ROBERTS, MICHAEL. "The Seventeenth Century: Metaphysical Poets and the Cambridge Platonists," in *The Modern Mind*, pp. 88–117. New York: The Macmillan Co.

General treatment of Donne's uses of science and his ability to "leap from one world-view to another, confident that the certainties of religion were of a kind different from those which could be said in scientific sentences, one word to each thing, and yet not altogether incommunicable" (p. 90).

◄§ 361. RUGOFF, MILTON A. "Drummond's Debt to Donne." *PQ*, 16: 85–88.

A list of eight parallel passages to show that in A *Cypresse Grove* Drummond borrowed phrases and images, and in one case the essential idea, from Donne, especially from the *Anniversaries*.

◄§ 362. SHAPIRO, I. A. "John Donne the Astronomer: The Date of the Eighth Problem." *TLS*, 3 July, p. 492.

Argues that "Probleme VIII" of *Paradoxes and Problemes* was written sometime between January 1611 and March 1612. Suggests that Donne accepted the Tychonian system of the universe. See also Charles Monroe Coffin, *TLS*, 18 September, p. 675; I. A. Shapiro, *TLS*, 17 July, p. 528 and 14 August, p. 592; Pierre Legouis, *TLS*, 31 July, p. 560; and M. F. Ashley-Montagu, *TLS*, 7 August, p. 576; and W. Fraser Mitchell, *TLS*, 10 July, p. 512 and 7 August, p. 576.

◄§ 363. ———. "Donne a Tychonian?" *TLS*, 17 July, p. 528.

Reply to W. Fraser Mitchell, *TLS*, 10 July, p. 512. Points out that "an understanding of the Tychonic system and of the very important position it held in seventeenth-century science and thought is essential to a just appreciation of the literature of the period." See also Shapiro, *TLS*, 3 July, p. 492 and 14 August, p. 592; Pierre Legouis, *TLS*, 31 July, p. 560; Mitchell, *TLS*, 7 August, p. 576; and M. F. Ashley-Montagu, *TLS*, 7 August, p. 576.

◄§ 364. ———. "John Donne." *TLS*, 14 August, p. 592.

Reply to Pierre Legouis, *TLS*, 31 July, p. 560; W. Fraser Mitchell, *TLS*, 7 August, p. 576; and M. F. Ashley-Montagu, *TLS*, 7 August, p. 576. Discusses Donne's theories of astronomy. Defends his earlier position in *TLS*, 3 July, p. 492 and 17 July, p. 528. See also W. Fraser Mitchell, *TLS*, 10 July, p. 512.

◄§ 365. UMBACH, HERBERT H. "The Rhetoric of Donne's Sermons." *PMLA*, 52:354–58.

Brief description of Donne's manner of composing the sermons, pointing out the differences between written sermons and spoken sermons. General appreciative comment on the artistic merits of the sermons and a description of the main characteristics of Donne's prose style.

1938

◄§ 366. ANON. "Devotional Poetry: Donne to Wesley: The Search for an Unknown Eden." *TLS*, 24 December, pp. 814, 816.

Maintains that "Religious verse is seldom the statement of assured belief but more often the passionate protestation of a mind that wishes to believe and believes and doubts again. [Therefore,] the periods most prolific of devotional masterpieces are those in which a certain body of religious faith is counterbalanced by a definite strain of inquietude" (p. 814). Characterizes Donne and the metaphysical poets as fitting this description. Donne emerges as "a master of religious eloquence" and yet he "is the least literary of devotional poets, but the most fascinating, the most complicated and the most persuasive" (p. 814), because Donne represents less stylized and less conventional attitudes and postures toward the experience of doubt and faith.

❧ 367. BENNETT, JOAN. "The Love Poetry of John Donne. A Reply to Mr. C. S. Lewis," in *Seventeenth Century Studies Presented to Sir Herbert Grierson*, pp. 85–104. Oxford: The Clarendon Press.

Reprinted in *Seventeenth Century English Poetry: Modern Essays in Criticism*, ed. William R. Keast (New York: Oxford University Press, 1962), pp. 111–13; *John Donne's Poetry*, ed. A. L. Clements (New York: W. W. Norton & Co., 1966), pp. 160–77.

In part a reply to C. S. Lewis in "Donne and Love Poetry in the Seventeenth Century" in *Seventeenth Century Studies Presented to Sir Herbert Grierson*, pp. 64–84. Argues that Donne is one of the great love poets in English. Analyzes several poems in order to define the range and variety of amorous postures and attitudes prevalent, thereby suggesting that there is more substance in Donne's love philosophy than Lewis allows. Shows that Donne "did not think sex sinful, and that contempt for women is not a general characteristic of his love poetry" (p. 102). Maintains that in the poems Donne expresses "almost everything a man can feel about a woman, scorn, self-contempt, anguish, sensual delight, and the peace and security of mutual love" (p. 104).

❧ 368. BISHOP, JOHN PEALE. "John Donne's Statue." *New Republic*, 97:198.

An original poem on Donne's effigy.

❧ 369. BROOKS, CLEANTH, AND ROBERT PENN WARREN. *Understanding Poetry: An Anthology for College Students*. New York: Henry Holt & Co. xxiv, 680 p.

Various editions.

Compares the tone of Herrick's "To Blossoms" and Donne's "The Blossome" (pp. 367–74). Explication of "If poysonous mineralls" (pp. 520–24).

❧ 370. FEDDEN, HENRY ROMILLY. *Suicide: A Social and Historical Study*. London: Peter Davies Limited. 351 p.

Comments on Donne's attitude toward suicide (pp. 135–36, 142, 181–83). "Donne's conclusion is that the Canon law against suicide is ac-

corded a very exaggerated respect and that it is the expression of a preju-
dice rather than an accepted orthodox dogma" (p. 136). Brief comments
on *Biathanatos* (pp. 181–83).

◄§ 371. FLOWER, ROBIN. "A Poet's Love Story." *Times* (London), 2
November, pp. 15–16.
Announcement of fifteen Donne letters (autographs) for sale, which
until recently had been in private collections. Urges that these letters,
which are called "the largest and certainly the most important body of
such material in existence," be purchased for the British Museum. In
particular, these letters concern the occasion of Donne's marriage. Recounts the known facts about the courtship, marriage, and immediate
aftermath.

◄§ 372. GRETTON, GEORGE H. *John Donne. Seine Beziehung zu seiner
zeit und sein Einfluss auf seine „nicht-metaphysischen"* Nachfol-
ger: *Carew, Suckling, Marvell und Rochester*. Düsseldorf: G. H.
Nolte. 53 p.
Considers Donne not so much as the founder of the metaphysical
school but rather as a representative of a certain world view and as representative of the spiritual attitude of the English Renaissance. Traces
Donne's influence on Carew, Suckling, Marvell, and Rochester, who are
considered not directly associated with the school. Suggests that these
poets are a connecting link between the Renaissance and the Restoration
and thus represent the last phase of a continuing developing tradition
rather than a sudden break.

◄§ 373. HELTZEL, VIRGIL B. "An Early Use of Donne's Fourth Satire."
MLN, 53:421–22.
Points out that lines 18–23 (slightly altered) of *Satyre IV* are quoted
in Joseph Wybarne's *New Age of Old Names* (1609).

◄§ 374. HENNECKE, HANS. "John Donne und die 'metaphysische Lyrik'
Englands." *Die Literatur*, 41:21–24.
Summarizes critical opinion on Donne from the seventeenth to the
twentieth century. Suggests that it is time for Donne to be discovered in
Germany. Comments on the learned aspects of Donne's poetry and on
his ability to transform abstract concepts into speech. Suggests that one's
attitude toward Donne depends on one's estimate of the conceit. Presents a biographical sketch and points out that there are similarities between Donne and the practices of German poets that were Hennecke's
contemporaries.

⊷§ 375. Heuer, Hermann. "Browning und Donne (Hintergründe einer
       Wortentlehnung)." *Englische Studien*, 72:227–44.
Discusses the influences of Donne on Browning and the similarities between the two poets. Uses the word *hydroptic* from Browning's "A Gram-
marian's Funeral" to show that Browning found the word in Donne.
Shows that Donne was one of Browning's favorite poets.

⊷§ 376. Husain, Itrat. *The Dogmatic and Mystical Theology of John
       Donne*. With a preface by Sir Herbert J. C. Grierson. Published
       for the Church Historical Society. London: The Society for Pro-
       moting Christian Knowledge; New York: The Macmillan Co. xv,
       149 p.
From a close study of the sermons, the author purports to show Donne's
defence of Anglican doctrine and ritual. The first chapter considers
Donne's orthodox defense of the Anglican Establishment against both
the Puritans and the Catholics. The second chapter treats Donne as a
theologian and discusses his views on the articles of faith, the sacraments,
saints, prayer for the dead, and various religious practices. The third
chapter discusses Donne's treatment of revealed theology. The fourth
outlines his views on the Fall and on sin. The fifth reviews Donne's attitudes on soteriology, while the sixth surveys his views on eschatology. The
seventh chapter summarizes Donne's mystical theology. The author
writes, "This book is the first attempt which has so far been made to
study in a systematic manner the dogmatic and mystical theology of
John Donne, and if I have succeeded, in however small a measure, in
establishing Donne's position as a faithful and sincere son of the Anglican Church, and as one of those who like Hooker, Parker and Andrewes,
defended her against the attack of Puritans and Papists alike, I shall not
have laboured in vain" (p. xv). Reproduces as an appendix "John Donne,
On Conversion," *Theology* (London), May 1936, pp. 299–301. Short
bibliography.

⊷§ 377. James, Philip. "Death's Duell." *TLS*, 8 October, p. 652 and 15
       October, p. 668.
Supplements Geoffrey Keynes, *TLS*, 24 September, p. 620, by pointing out that a copy of Walter Colman's poem from which the title
Deaths Duell was plagiarized by Roger Muchill exists in the Victoria
and Albert Museum. Makes additional notes on the copy in the Victoria
and Albert Museum in the second article.

⊷§ 378. Keynes, Geoffrey. "Death's Duell." *TLS*, 24 September, p.
       620.
States that the title *Death's Duell* was conferred on Donne's last ser-
mon by a certain Roger Muchill, a bookseller at Bull's Head, St. Paul's
Churchyard. Apparently Muchill plagiarized the title from a poem by

Walter Colman entitled "La Dance Machabre or Death's Duell," printed by William Stanby and entered at Stationer's Hall on June 13, 1631. Donne's sermon was entered on September 30 of the same year. See also Philip James, *TLS*, 8 October, p. 652 and 15 October, p. 668.

⌇§ 379. Lewis, C. S. "Donne and Love Poetry in the Seventeenth Century," in *Seventeenth Century Studies Presented to Sir Herbert Grierson*, pp. 64–84. Oxford: Clarendon Press.

Reprinted in *Seventeenth Century English Poetry: Modern Essays in Criticism*, ed. William Keast (New York: Oxford University Press, Inc., 1962), pp. 92–110.

Pages 73–84 reprinted in *John Donne: A Collection of Critical Essays*, ed. Helen Gardner (Englewood Cliffs, N. J.: Prentice-Hall, Inc., 1962), pp. 90–99.

Reprinted in *John Donne's Poetry*, ed. A. L. Clements (New York: W. W. Norton & Co., 1966), pp. 144–60.

An essentially iconoclastic evaluation of Donne and of the critical attitudes of Donne critics in the 1930s. "It is not impossible to see why Donne's poetry should be overrated in the twentieth and underrated in the eighteenth century; and so far as we detect these temporary disturbing factors explain the varying appearances of the object by the varying positions of the observers, we shall come appreciably nearer to a glimpse of Donne *simpliciter*" (p. 64). Rejects the idea that Donne is a liberator, who substituted the real, the live, or the sincere for the merely artificial and conventional in love poetry. Links Donne with the plain style poets that preceded him, especially Wyatt, and sees Donne as reinforcing and developing those elements. "What gives their peculiar character to most of the *Songs and Sonets* is that they are dramatic in the sense of being addresses to an imagined hearer in the heat of an imagined conversation, and usually addresses to a violently argumentative character" (p. 68) Discusses the seriousness of the love poems and concludes, "Seldom profound in thought, not always passionate in feeling, they are none the less the very opposite of gay" (p. 70). Considers the various attitudes toward love and sexuality in the poems and contrasts Catholic and Protestant sensibilities toward sex and woman to show the influence of Donne's Catholic heritage. The author's final judgement of Donne is that his "poetry is too simple to satisfy. Its complexity is all on the surface—an intellectual and fully conscious complexity that we soon come to the end of" (p. 80). Minimizes the influence of Donne on later seventeenth-century poets and states that "When we have once mastered a poem by Donne there is nothing more to do with it" (p. 81). For a reply, see Joan Bennett, "The Love Poetry of John Donne. A Reply to Mr. C. S. Lewis" in *Seventeenth Century Studies Presented to Sir Herbert Grierson*, pp. 85–104.

◆§ 380. Lewis, E. G. "The Question of Toleration in the Works of
    John Donne." *MLR*, 33:255–58.
Challenges the traditional view that Donne was unusually tolerant in
matters of religious conformity. Maintains that "an analysis of Donne's
political theory, as it is expressed, somewhat unsystematically, in his
works, will reveal that Donne advocated adherence to authoritative opinion upon important points of fundamental doctrine, and developed an
attitude, also, which demanded strict compliance to the King's wishes
in the less important matters of ritual and discipline" (p. 255). Argues
that "while Donne was willing to tolerate other national Churches, and
even the Roman Catholic Church, within liberally defined bounds of
essential doctrine, he was averse from granting any measure of liberty
with the English Church" (p. 257). Essentially a study of Donne's views
on the relationship of the Church and state.

◆§ 381. Ransom, John Crowe. "Shakespeare at Sonnets." *SoR*, 3:531–
    53.
Reprinted with revisions in *The World's Body* (New York: Charles
Scribner's Sons, 1938), pp. 270–303.
An iconoclastic attack on Shakespeare's sonnets in which Donne's
lyrics are considered generally superior. Maintains that occasionally
Shakespeare is a metaphysical poet in the sonnets. Shakespeare's usual
art in the sonnets is called "associationist poetry, a half-way action pro-
viding many charming resting-places for the feelings to agitate themselves; . . . on the other hand, there is a metaphysical poetry, which elects
its line of action and goes straight through to the completion of the
cycle and extinction of the feelings" (p. 545).

◆§ 382. Silk, C. E. B. "To John Donne." *Cornhill Magazine*, 157:218.
An original poem in honor of Donne.

◆§ 383. Tate, Allen. "Tension in Poetry." *SoR*, 4:101–15.
Reprinted with revisions in *Reason in Madness: Critical Essays* (New
York: G. P. Putnam's Sons, 1941), pp. 62–81; *Collected Essays* (Denver:
Alan Swallow Publisher, 1959), pp. 83–85.
An explication of lines 21–24 of "A Valediction: forbidding mourning"
(pp. 109–11) as illustration of the concept that "the best poetry's mean-
ing is its 'tension,' the full body of all the extension and intension that
we can find in it" (p. 109).

◆§ 384. Turnell, Martin. *Poetry and Crisis*. London: Sands, The
    Paladin Press.
Brief discussion of Donne (pp. 22–30) in which he is described as
presenting for the first time in its most radical form "that divided self
which is characteristic of modern poetry" (p. 27). Donne expresses the
"poet's awareness of living in an age of spiritual crisis" (p. 27).

◄§ 385. UNTERMEYER, LOUIS. "Wit and Sensibility: Metaphor into Metaphysics," in *Play in Poetry*, pp. 3–24. New York: Harcourt, Brace & Co.

Examines the serious element of play in Donne and others. Discusses in particular "The Flea" and "Batter my heart."

1939

◄§ 386. BELL, CHARLES. "Donne's 'Farewell to Love.'" *TLS*, 1 July, p. 389.

Argues against Grierson's and Hayward's emendation of lines 28–30 of the poem and gives his own reading. See also Arthur Coon, *TLS*, 12 August, p. 479.

◄§ 387. BENNETT, R. E. "John Donne and Everard Gilpin." *RES*, 15: 66–72.

Identifies E. G. of the verse epistle that begins "Even as lame things thirst perfection" as Everard Gilpin. Gives more positive reasons for the identification than does Gosse, who originally suggested the possibility. Gives a short sketch of Gilpin's life and Donne's possible friendship with him. Suggests that 1593 is a good conjecture for the date of composition of the epistle. Indicates Gilpin's knowledge and use of Donne's satires. For a reply by P. J. Finkelpearl, see *RES*, n.s., 14 (1963):164–67.

◄§ 388. BOWERS, FREDSON. "An Interpretation of Donne's Tenth Elegy." *MLN*, 54:280–82.

"Elegie X" has been variously entitled "The Dreame" and "The Picture," based on the editors' understanding of the word *Image* in the first line of the poem. Rejects both notions and argues that *Image* means "the Platonic 'fairer forme.'" Interprets the poem in this light. For a reply by Elias Schwartz, see *Expl*, 19 (1961):Item 67.

◄§ 389. BROOKS, CLEANTH. *Modern Poetry and the Tradition*. Chapel Hill: University of North Carolina Press. xi, 253 p.

A defense of modern poetry, in which the metaphysicals are seen as not only an influence but also as forefathers of the moderns. "The most important resemblance between the modern poet and the poets of the sixteenth and seventeenth centuries lies not in the borrowing of a few 'metaphysical' adjectives or images, or the cultivation of a few clever 'conceits.' That is why the 'metaphysical' quality of the best of the moderns is not the result of a revival, or the aping of a period style. The fundamental resemblance is in the attitude which the poets of both periods take toward their materials and in the method which both, at their best, employ" (p. 53). Detailed discussion of metaphor, irony, and wit to show the affinities of certain moderns and the metaphysicals. Donne is mentioned throughout by way of illustration, as a kind of touchstone to what is valuable in poetry. Proposes a revised history of English poetry, beginning with Donne and Jonson, a rather clear application of Eliot's notion of "dissociation of sensibility" to the history of poetry.

❧ 390. Coon, Arthur M. "Farewell to Love." *TLS*, 12 August, p. 479.
 Explicates lines 28–30 of the poem. See also Charles Bell, *TLS*, 1 July, p. 389.

❧ 391. De Selincourt, Ernest. "The Interplay of Literature and Science During the Last Three Centuries." *Hibbert Journal*, 37: 225–45.
A broad historical sketch of the relation between science and literature in which Donne is very briefly mentioned as "a disciple of the old scholasticism." Maintains that "the new science impressed him less as an intellectual triumph than with the uncertainty of all human knowledge" (p. 228).

❧ 392. Ince, Richard. *Angel from a Cloud*. London: Massie Publishing Co. Ltd. ix, 452 p.
A fictionalized biography of Donne.

❧ 393. McPeek, J. A. S. *Catullus in Strange and Distant Britain*. Harvard Studies in Comparative Literature, xv. Cambridge: Harvard University Press. xvii, 411 p.
Traces the influence of Catullus on English poetry. Concludes that in general Donne "has obliterated his traces behind him, so that one cannot easily determine whence he has derived the great part of his ideas. In studying his poetry, we have to deal with tenuous hints of his reading, not with passages lifted bodily from the French, Spanish, Italian, and Latin" (pp. 51–52). Maintains that in spite of his independence of thought, Donne "appears to have been directly acquainted with at least a few of the carmina" (p. 52). Comments throughout on Donne, especially on "An Epithalamion, Or mariage Song on the Lady Elizabeth, and Count Palatine" (pp. 207–11).

❧ 394. Rugoff, Milton Allan. *Donne's Imagery: A Study in Creative Sources*. New York: Corporate. 270 p.
Reprinted, New York: Russell & Russell, Inc., 1962.
Chapter I discusses what an image is and its significance as a key to the creative imagination of the writer. Chapter II outlines the method used in classifying and collecting some 2,261 of Donne's images. Part I (Chapters III–IX) presents images drawn from books, science, and the arts—the world of learning in general. Part II (Chapters X–XVI) discusses domestic images or everyday images. Part III (Chapters XVII–

XX) discusses images from the world of nature—the heavens, the sea, and animals. Points out that "in turning to learning and science, to the mechanical and technical, and to the esoteric or the inobvious—for these, as we have seen again and again, are the larger tendencies of his imagery— Donne sought above all analogies which were precise, original, and uniquely illuminating" (p. 239). Shows that there is little difference between the imagery of the prose and that of the poetry. Challenges Dr. Johnson's attack on metaphysical poetry: Donne's imagery "was the result not of whim and perversity but of an extremely analytical mind seeking to illuminate the most intense feeling" (p. 242). Characterizes Donne as "a writer who forsook for the most part the accepted poetic beauties and the romantic overtones of traditional imagery—particularly those of classical mythology and the world of nature; who forsook the charm of both the simple and the sensuous, leaving the first for poets like Herrick and the second for those like Keats . . . who forsook, though much less completely, the warmth and humanity of the familiar and the common, finding more attractive that which lay hidden beneath them; and who gave up, finally, loveliness in general, because above all he worshipped sense and intellectual meaning—those same gods to whom he had sacrificed smooth metre and liquid rhythm" (p. 244). Appendix, a table of sources, divided according to the various titles and subtitles of the chapters of the book.

≈§ 395. SIMPSON, EVELYN. "Jonson and Donne: A Problem in Authorship." *RES*, 15:274–82.

Argues on the basis of the manuscript tradition and the early editions that "The Expostulation" is Donne's, but that the three elegies that are closely associated with the poem are Jonson's, perhaps in imitation of Donne.

≈§ 396. SPENCER, THEODORE, AND MARK VAN DOREN. *Studies in Metaphysical Poetry: Two Essays and a Bibliography*. New York: Columbia University Press. 88 p.

Reprinted, Port Washington, N. Y.: Kennikat Press Inc., 1964.

Part I contains two essays. (1) "Recent Scholarship in Metaphysical Poetry" (pp. 3–18) by Spencer, in which some of the major developments in metaphysical criticism are briefly outlined, especially Donne scholarship, which is called "a kind of microcosm of scholarship relating to metaphysical poetry in general" (p. 14). (2) "Seventeenth-Century Poets and Twentieth-Century Critics" (pp. 21–29) by Van Doren, in which various notions of metaphysical poetry are reviewed, especially Eliot's concept of "unified sensibility." Maintains, however, that the outstanding feature of metaphysical poetry is its humor: "Humor is the life of their poetry; wit is its language" (p. 28). Part II presents a bibliography of studies in metaphysical poetry from 1912 to 1938 (pp. 33–83).

Items are arranged chronologically by author with an additional section entitled "General Studies." There are 199 items listed under Donne.

⋙ 397. WILLIAMSON, GEORGE. "Donne's 'Farewell to Love.'" *MP*, 36:301–3.

Argues against both Grierson's and Hayward's emendation of lines 28–30 of the poem. Presents his own reading of the lines. See also Charles Bell, *TLS*, 1 July, p. 389 and Arthur Coon, *TLS*, 12 August, p. 479.

⋙ 398. WINTERS, YVOR. "The Sixteenth Century Lyric in England: A Critical and Historical Reinterpretation." *Poetry*, 53:258–72, 320–25; 54:35–51.

Reprinted in *Elizabethan Poetry: Modern Essays in Criticism*, ed. Paul J. Alpers (New York: Oxford University Press, Inc., 1967), pp. 93–125.

Attempts "to define certain major talents of the century who have been neglected, along with certain related minor talents equally neglected; to revaluate certain established reputations; to offer a new historical outline and a new set of critical emphases for the century; and to base my conclusions in every case on poems specifically named" (p. 260). Concludes, "the Petrarchans represent a tendency of secondary importance in the century, not of primary. The great lyrics of the 16th century are intellectually both profound and complex, are with few exceptions restrained and direct in style, and are sombre and disillusioned in tone. If we regard as the major tradition of the century the great poems of Gascoigne and Raleigh, and those most closely resembling them by Greville, Jonson, Donne, and Shakespeare, we shall obtain a very different view of the century from that which we shall obtain by regarding as primary Sidney, Spenser and the song-books; we shall bring much great poetry to light; and we shall find the transition to the next century far less obscure" (p. 51). Compares Donne to Gascoigne, Jonson, Sidney, and Shakespeare.

1940

⋙ 399. ANON. "A Book from Donne's Library." *BLR*, 1:147–48.

Acquisition of a copy of *Histoire remarquable et veritable de ce qui s'est passé par chacun iour au siege de la ville d'Ostende . . . A Paris, Chez Adrian Beyes, rue sainct Iaques ioignant la Rose blanche. M.DC.IV.* Signed by Donne and contains his motto.

⋙ 400. ANON. "Desiderata Bodleiana." *BLR*, 1:205.

Short list of Donne editions that the library is eager to purchase.

❧§ 401. ANON. "John Donne: Desiderata." *Yale University Library Gazette*, 15:47–48.
Lists 36 Donne items that Yale would like to acquire.

❧§ 402. BENNETT, R. E. "Donne's Letters from the Continent in 1611–1612." *PQ*, 19:66–78.
Chronological ordering of 19 letters that Donne wrote just before, during, and immediately after his travels with Sir Robert Drury on the Continent in 1611–1612. Discredits Walton's story about Donne's vision of his wife during the travels.

❧§ 403. BROWN, MARY. "Verses on Donne's Burial." *N&Q*, 178:12.
Asks if anyone has identified the "unknown friend" who, according to Walton, wrote the epitaph "Reader! I am to let thee know." See also Arthur Coon, *N&Q*, 178:251.

❧§ 404. COMBS, HOMER CARROLL, AND ZAY RUSK SULLENS. A *Concordance to the English Poems of John Donne*. Chicago: Packard & Co. ix, 418 p.
Based on Grierson's one-volume edition of the poems (1929). Excludes Latin poems and translations included in Grierson's Appendix A and the doubtful poems in Appendix B.

❧§ 405. COON, ARTHUR M. "Verses on Donne's Burial." *N&Q*, 178:251.
Reply to Mary Brown, *N&Q*, 178:12. States that the "unknown friend" who, according to Walton, wrote the epitaph "Reader! I am to let thee know" has not been identified.

❧§ 406. ESCOTT, H. "The Modern Relevance of John Donne." *Congregational Quarterly* (London), 28:57–64.
Biographical sketch with the intention of illustrating how Donne's life and conflicts have relevance to the spiritual needs of our time.

❧§ 407. EVANS, B. IFOR. "Donne to Milton," in *Tradition and Romanticism: Studies in English Poetry from Chaucer to W. B. Yeats*, pp. 44–60. London: Methuen & Co., Ltd.; New York: Longmans, Green & Co., Ltd.
Attacks Donne for a lack of seriousness. "His learning, medieval and contemporary, was used at times captiously as if he consoled himself for some incapacity to integrate his knowledge by playing with it in complicated patterns as he exploited his troubled passion" (p. 46). Prefers the *Anniversaries*.

✎§ 408. GRIERSON, SIR HERBERT. "Bacon's Poem 'The World': Its Date
and Relation to Certain Other Poems," in *Essays and Addresses
by Sir Herbert Grierson*, pp. 221–37. London: Chatto & Windus
Ltd.

Reprint of an article which originally appeared in *MLR*, 6 (1911):145–
56. Maintains that Donne's verse letter to Sir Henry Wotton that begins "Sir, more then kisses, letters mingle Soules" is in part a comment
on Bacon's poem, which Wotton had possibly shown to him. Presents
evidence to show the close relationship among Bacon, Wotton, and
Donne before the Essex affair.

✎§ 409. HIJIKATA, TATSUZO. "John Donne's 'Songs and Sonets.'" *Studies in English Literature* (Tokyo), 20:336–47.

General introduction for the Japanese reader. Selects several of the
poems and analyzes them, to determine the general characteristics of
Donne's love poetry. Stresses the idea that, although Donne uses philosophy in his poetry, he is not a philosophical poet. Maintains that even
if the ideas used to convey Donne's lyrical statements are no longer of
immediate interest to the modern reader, he is still attracted by Donne's
wit and poetic artistry.

✎§ 410. JONAS, LEAH. "John Donne," in *The Divine Science: The
Aesthetic of Some Representative Seventeenth-Century English
Poets.* New York: Columbia University Press. Columbia University
Studies in English and Comparative Literature, 151:273–79.

Notes that Donne has almost nothing to say directly about the aesthetics of his poetry. Pieces together scattered comments by Donne in the
poems that tend to illustrate some aspects of his poetic theory and de-
duces from these the basic principles that informed his art. Maintains
that Donne changed the course of English poetry by example, not
precept. Mentions throughout Donne's influence on other poets and
their attitudes toward his art.

✎§ 411. M. M. "Satires and Sermons by John Donne." *More Books: The
Bulletin of the Boston Public Library*, 15:251–52.

Briefly describes the following Donne acquisitions: two sermons—
Encaenia, the Feast of Dedication (1623) and *A Sermon, preached
to the Kings Majestie at Whitehall* (1626); a calf-bound volume containing *Paradoxes* (1651), *Ignatius his Conclave* (1653), and *Essayes in
Divinity* (1651).

✎§ 412. NICOLSON, MARJORIE. "Kepler, the *Somnium*, and John Donne."
JHI, 1:259–80.

Reprinted in part in *Voyages to the Moon* (New York: The Macmillan Co., 1948), pp. 49f.

Reprinted with slight revision in *Science and Imagination* (Ithaca, N. Y.: Cornell University Press; London: Oxford University Press, 1956), pp. 58–79.

Suggests that Donne had seen a manuscript copy of Kepler's *Somnium* and utilized it in composing *Ignatius his Conclave*, "the first modern cosmic voyage in England" (p. 251). Maintains that Donne "deliberately adopted the double device of dream and cosmic voyage used by Kepler in the *Somnium*, with the result that the *Conclave of Ignatius* has continued to puzzle critics who have recognized the inconsistency of the two different forms employed by Donne, but who have found no satisfactory explanation for the lack of artistic unity in the finished work" (p. 274).

⋙ 413. POTTER, GEORGE REUBEN. "Donne's Paradoxes in 1707." *MLN*, 55:53.

John Dunton, founder of the Athenian Society, published in 1707 *Athenian Sport: or, Two Thousand Paradoxes Merrily Argued To Amuse and Divert the Age*. Without acknowledgement, he includes all of Donne's *Paradoxes* except "Paradox XII." Concludes, "Donne's *Paradoxes* could not have been at all commonly known to Englishmen in 1707, or Dunton would hardly have dared risk the charge of plagiarism by printing them as his own."

⋙ 414. SHARP, ROBERT LATHROP. *From Donne to Dryden: The Revolt Against Metaphysical Poetry*. Chapel Hill: University of North Carolina Press. xiii, 221 p.

Traces the change in taste in the seventeenth century from poetry that the author calls extravagant, obscure, and harsh (the three elements of metaphysical poetry he chooses to emphasize) to the kind of poetry that exalts the standards and practice of propriety, clarity, and harmony. Examines both the literary and nonliterary forces that set up a reaction against Donne and the metaphysical poets. "The revolt was not a silent one; it was articulate in criticism as well as in poetry. Thoroughgoing, it reached to the root of poetry and affected the experience underlying literary creation. By following it, the reader should get a clearer notion of what happened to English poetry between 1600 and 1700" (p. xii). In addition to a general preface and an introduction, there are seven main chapters: (1) Donne and the Elizabethan Poets, (2) The Course of Metaphysical Poetry, (3) The Faith of the Critics, (4) The Protest of the Poets, (5) The Return to Nature, (6) New Standards, (7) John Dryden.

⋙ 415. SHUSTER, GEORGE N. "Milton and the Metaphysical Poets," in *The English Ode from Milton to Keats*. Columbia University Studies in English and Comparative Literature, 150:64–92. New York: Columbia University Press.

Brief mention of Donne. Concludes that Donne's "temper as a creative artist is that of Rabelais and Villon, inseparable from the late
medieval university with its fondness for speculation and sensualism
alike; and his forms are not those of Greece and Rome, despite everything
he owed to the Jesuit humanists" (p. 83). Suggests that "the irregular
stanzas he employs have more in common with the lyric interludes of
drama and masque than with the melic patterns of the Greeks or their
English imitators" (p. 83).

⋙ 416. [VAN DE WATER, CHARLOTTE]. "The First of the Moderns."
       Scholastic, 37:20.
General introduction to Donne's poetry for high school students.

⋙ 417. WELLS, HENRY W. *New Poets from Old: A Study of Literary
       Genetics*. New York: Columbia University Press. x, 356 p.
Studies the indebtedness of modern poets to earlier poets. Refers to
Donne throughout and discusses in particular Donne's influence on
Elinor Wylie and W. B. Yeats (pp. 249–61).

⋙ 418. WILLIAMSON, GEORGE. "Textual Difficulties in the Interpreta-
       tion of Donne's Poetry." *MP*, 38:37–72.
Reprinted in *Seventeenth Century Contexts*, ed. William Keast (Chicago: University of Chicago Press, 1960, 1961), pp. 78–119.
A vindication of the 1633 text of the poems (and occasionally the
1635 text). Challenges several of Grierson's emendations and interpretations and attempts to demonstrate that the readings of the 1633 and
1635 editions can be justified and that the suggested changes are not
necessary.

1941

⋙ 419. ANON. "Hemingway's Title." *Wilson Library Bulletin*, 15:515.
Points out that the title for *For Whom the Bell Tolls* is from the
seventeenth meditation of the *Devotions*.

⋙ 420. ANON. "John Donne, O. P." *Time*, 13 January, p. 76.
Reprinted in *Essay Annual*, ed. E. A. Walter (Chicago: Scott, Fores-
man & Co., 1941), p. 153.
Suggests that Hemingway's *For Whom the Bell Tolls* has made Donne
a best-seller and announces that the works of Donne are out-of-print
in the U. S.

◀§ 421. ALLEN, DON CAMERON. "Some Aspects of the Dispute About
Astrology Among Elizabethan and Jacobean Men of Letters," in
*The Star-Crossed Renaissance: The Quarrel About Astrology and
Its Influence in England*, pp. 147–89. Durham, N. C.: Duke Uni-
versity Press.
Reprinted, New York: Octagon Books, Inc., 1966.
Several references to Donne's attitude concerning astrology (pp. 154,
188–89). Maintains that while there is no open denial of astrology in
Donne's works, his personal attitude about it is not clear.

◀§ 422. ———. "Donne's Suicides." *MLN*, 56:129–33.
Speculates on Donne's reading and his method of taking notes, illustrated by his use of examples of suicides in *Biathanatos* and the *Devotions*. Concludes that Donne "was not particularly discriminating
about the origin of these illustrations and derived them from the classics
and from contemporary sources without bothering to check the cor-
rectness of the contemporary accounts by the classical originals. He
seems to have kept some type of notes from which he wrote and which
like so many notes became in time 'too cold' to be trustworthy. Our
final conclusion is that Donne was probably not so great a classical student as some modern scholars would have him be" (pp. 132–33).

◀§ 423. ———. "Donne and the Bezoar." *MLN*, 56:609–11.
In the seventh meditation of the *Devotions*, Donne writes that "the
refuse of our servants (would be) bezoar enough." Points out that both
Andreas Bassius' *De Gemmis et Lapidibus Pretiosis, eorumque viribus*
(Italian 1581 or 1587, Latin 1603) and Anselmus Boetius de Boot's
Gemmarum et Lapidum Historia (1609) contain extensive commentaries
on the curative effects of bezoar and suggest that it is a panacea. Suggests
that Donne "had these contemporary definitions in mind" (p. 611), a
point that illustrates his up-to-date knowledge of contemporary medicine.

◀§ 424. BABB, LAWRENCE. "Melancholy and the Elizabethan Man of
Letters." *HLQ*, 4:247–61.
General survey "to determine just what the Elizabethans meant when
they called the man of letters melancholy, to explain in terms of Renaissance medical theory how he became melancholy, and to present illustrations of intellectual melancholy drawn from the drama and from the
ranks of actual Elizabethan writers" (p. 247). Points out that Donne
complains of the disease in his *Devotions* and that Walton calls it his
"constant infirmity" (pp. 259–60).

܆§ 425. BENHAM, ALLEN R. "The Myth of John Donne the Rake," in
Renaissance Studies in Honor of Hardin Craig, ed. Baldwin Max-
well *et al.*, pp. 273–81. Stanford: Stanford University Press.
Reprinted in *PQ*, 20 (1941): 465–73.
Challenges the notion that Donne's love poems reflect his dissolute life,
while the later religious poems illustrate his conversion and repentance.
Examines the evidence that led Gosse and others to this conclusion.
"Gosse's theory . . . in view of the facts and considerations herein set
forth, unless more and better evidence for it is forthcoming, is properly
denominated *The Myth of John Donne the Rake*" (p. 281).

܆§ 426. BENNETT, JOAN. "An Aspect of the Evolution of Seventeenth-
Century Prose." *RES*, 17:281–97.
Uses Donne's sermons to illustrate the kind of language increasingly
distrusted and objected to by the reformers of seventeenth-century prose
style, a style that reflected changing attitudes and perceptions. Contrasts
Donne and Tillotson.

܆§ 427. BENNETT, ROGER E. "Donne's 'Letters to Severall Persons of
Honour.'" *PMLA*, 56:120–40.
Proposes "to formulate working hypotheses about the editorial processes which determined the *Letters to Severall Persons*, first by discovering what the most probable sources of the letters were, and second by
examining the motives and methods which governed their arrangement
and the headings which were given to them" (p. 120). Concludes that
Donne the younger falsified many of the headings in order to create
the impression that many people of varying importance were addressed.
Finds that 120 of the letters were written to four recipients (the greater
part addressed to Sir Henry Goodere). Suggests that Donne the younger
had access to the correspondence of their recipients and not to his
father's originals. For a summary of Bennett's conclusions, see B. H.
Newdigate, *N&Q*, 180:441.

܆§ 428. BOTTING, ROLAND B. "The Reputation of John Donne During
the Nineteenth Century." *Research Studies of the State College of
Washington*, 9:139–88.
Surveys critical comment on Donne during the nineteenth century to
show that Donne became increasingly appreciated during the period
and to suggest that the basis for this attitude had its roots in the shifts in
sensibility and critical perspective at work during that time. Quotes
eminent poets and critics of the period.

܆§ 429. CARLETON, PHILLIPS D. "John Donne's 'Bracelet of Bright Hair
About the Bone.'" *MLN*, 56:366–68.
Suggests that the source of Donne's image used in both "The Funerall"
and "The Relique" is the *Speculum Ecclesiae* and/or the *De Principis*

Instruction of Giraldus Cambrensis, in which the author describes the exhumation of the bones of Arthur and reports that tresses of a woman's hair, presumably Guinevere's, were found intertwined about the bones. The Cambrensis manuscripts were in Robert Cotton's library, to which Donne had access. William Camden, Cotton's antiquarian friend, published his *Britannia* in 1586 in which he describes the exhumation (but without reference to the hair and bones). Suggests that Donne read Camden, asked for his source, and was directed to the Cambrensis manuscripts.

▪§ 430. DANIELS, EARL. *The Art of Reading Poetry.* New York: Farrar & Rinehart, Inc. vii, 519 p.

Explication of "A Valediction: forbidding mourning" and "A Valediction: of weeping" (pp. 214–19). Comments on the "bracelet of bright haire" image in "The Relique" and the "subtile wreath of haire" image in "The Funerall" (pp. 225–26). Explication of "Death be not proud" (pp. 275–78).

▪§ 431. DONNE, JOHN. *The Complete Poetry and Selected Prose of John Donne & The Complete Poetry of William Blake*, with an introduction by Robert Silliman Hillyer. Modern Library Giant, G70. New York: Modern Library, lv, 1045 p.

In addition to giving a biographical and critical sketch of Donne and Blake, Hillyer compares and contrasts the two. Links them together because both had a "common desire to escape from the stylistic fatigue of their periods, and to speak out" (p. xviii), and both "exorcise, though in differing terms, the illusions of stupidity, greed, and cynicism from which we have fashioned the realm of our sorrow" (p. lv).

▪§ 432. FRANÇON, MARCEL. "Un Motif de la Poésie Amoureuse au XVIᵉ Siècle." *PMLA*, 56:307–36.

Considers the popular Renaissance theme in love poetry of the desire of the lover to be transformed into something dear and near to the beloved. Traces the tradition of the flea poem from Ronsard to Carew and Cleveland. Discusses Donne's "The Flea" briefly as being outside the main tradition.

▪§ 433. MATHEWS, ERNST G. "John Donne's 'Little Rag.'" *MLN*, 56:607–9.

Finds evidence to show that an allusion to Montemayor in a letter to Sir Robert Ker (*Letters*, 1651, p. 299) is not to Montemayor's *Diana* but more likely to the first four lines of El Comendador Escrivá's "Canción" printed in the *Cancionero generale de Hernando del Castillo*. Montemayor wrote a gloss on the work, and Donne presumed incorrectly that the lines were by Montemayor. See also T. Edward Terrill, *MLN*, 43 (1928):318–19.

434. MATTHIESSEN, F. O. *American Renaissance: Art and Expression in the Age of Emerson and Whitman.* London, Toronto, New York: Oxford University Press. xxiv, 678 p.

Donne is mentioned frequently throughout (pp. 13, 33, 46, 68, 92, 98, 101–6 passim, 113, 114, 117, 128, 129, 131, 168, 246, 247, 248, 395). Discusses Emerson's and Thoreau's critical estimation of Donne and the metaphysical poets and compares and contrasts their own metaphysical strain with that of the seventeenth century (pp. 100–132).

435. MUÑOZ ROJAS, JOSÉ A. "Un Libro Español en la Biblioteca de Donne." *RFE*, 25:108–11.

Comments on what is reputedly the only Spanish book in Donne's library, *Iosephina. Summario de las Excellencias del Glorioso S. Ioseph* (1609) by Geronimo Gracian. Donne refers to the book in No. 18 of the *LXXX Sermons*. Reproduces the title page of Donne's copy in the British Museum which contains his signature and motto. See also R. C. Bald, *N&Q*, 193 (1948):302.

436. NANINCK, JOEP. "Roud Huygens' vertalingen mit het Engels van Donne." *Tijdschrift voor Tool en Lettern*, 29:143–71.

Maintains that Huygens, Donne's Dutch translator, took many liberties with the form of the poems. Through slight alterations and mistranslations he made them seem coarse and bourgeois. Argues that the theory that Huygens was influenced by Donne is unnecessary, since Huygens's poetic style was the same even before he translated Donne. Points out that Donne's obscurity lies in the thoughts themselves while it is Huygens's language that makes his thought obscure. Discusses Vondel's criticism of Donne and states that Vondel's criticism is directed toward the Donne created by Huygens more than against Donne himself.

437. NEWDIGATE, B. H. "Donne's 'Letters to Severall Persons of Honour.'" *N&Q*, 180:441.

Summarizes the conclusions of Roger E. Bennett, *PMLA*, 56:120–40, and suggests that "the haphazard arrangement of the letters, or what appears to be such, and especially the absence of dates from so many of them are not due to the incompetence of the younger Donne, but that they were deliberately contrived to lessen the risk of detection in what must rank henceforth as a notable literary fake."

438. OAKE, ROGER B. "Diderot and Donne's ΒΙΑΘΑΝΑΤΟΣ." *MLN*, 56:114–15.

In the article on suicide in the *Encyclopédie*, there is a review of Donne's tract in which it is suggested that Donne became Dean of St. Paul's after the publication of *Biathanatos*. Questions whether ignorance or intention account for the error, since the facts of Donne's biography were readily available in French at the time.

✑§ 439. POTTER, GEORGE REUBEN. "A Protest Against the Term *Conceit*," in *Renaissance Studies in Honor of Hardin Craig*, ed. Baldwin Maxwell *et al.*, pp. 282–91. Stanford: Stanford University Press. Reprinted in *PQ*, 20 (1941):474–83.

Surveys the changing denotative and connotative meanings of *conceit* and urges that it be discontinued as a critical term. Comments on the confusion of the term as applied to Donne.

✑§ 440. RANSOM, JOHN CROWE. "Eliot and the Metaphysicals." *Accent*, 1:148–56.

Reprinted with slight revision in *The New Criticism* (Norkfolk, Conn.: New Directions, 1941), pp. 175–92.

Attacks Eliot's concept of "unified sensibility" as ineffectively descriptive of what happens in the metaphysical conceit. Uses Donne to illustrate the notion of the metaphysical conceit as a functional metaphor, which "has no explicit tenor or fact-structure but only a 'vehicle' covering it" (p. 154) and which functions as both structure and texture in the poem. Comments in particular on the compass image in "A Valediction: forbidding mourning."

✑§ 441. SIMPSON, EVELYN MARY. "The Text of Donne's 'Divine Poems.'" *E&S* of 1940, Oxford: The Clarendon Press, pp. 88–105.

Discusses the Dobell MS. at Harvard with particular reference to the divine poems. Maintains that the manuscript is very important, because (1) it contains poems not in the 1633 edition that were first published in the less trustworthy edition of 1635; (2) some of the readings of the manuscript are superior to those of the 1635 edition; (3) certain features shared with other manuscripts suggest an earlier draft than that used for the 1633 edition.

✑§ 442. SIMPSON, PERCY. "King James on Donne." *TLS*, 25 October, p. 531.

Reports that in a notebook of the Archdeacon Plume (MS. 30, Folio 17 verso) in the Plume Library at Maldon the following comment is found: "K. James said Dr. Donns uerses were like ye peace of God they passed all understanding." Sometimes this gibe is said to have been made concerning Bacon's *Novum Organum*. Inquires if someone knows of a contemporary authority for fixing the gibe on Bacon rather than on Donne. For a reply by N. E. McClure, see *TLS*, 17 January, p. 31.

✑§ 443. WHITE, WILLIAM. "John Donne Since 1900: A Bibliography of Periodical Articles." *BB*, 17:86–89, 113, 165–71, 192–95.

Published as a pamphlet, Boston: F. W. Faxon Co., Inc., 1942.

More than 500 items (partially annotated listed alphabetically under the headings Periodical Articles, Donne Portraits, Reprints of Donne's Poems, Book Reviews, Brief Publishers' Notices, Addenda.

1942

⋘§ 444. BATTENHOUSE, ROY W. "The Grounds of Religious Toleration in the Thought of John Donne." *Church History*, 11:217–48.

Analysis of Donne's views on religious toleration viewed from four major standpoints: (1) his critical and questioning attitude toward authority; (2) his skepticism regarding metaphysical definitions; (3) his "fundamentalist" reduction of dogma; (4) his "instrumentalist" attitude toward the Church and the sacraments. Lists and comments on Donne's sources and authorities.

⋘§ 445. BENNETT, R. E. "John Donne and the Earl of Essex." *MLQ*, 3:603–4.

Challenges the notion, implied by Walton, that Donne was "merely another of the young men who placed all their hopes in the Earl of Essex" (p. 604). Points out that during the Island Voyage (1597), Donne was not with Essex but was in Lord Thomas Howard's squadron and that Donne chose Henry Percy, Earl of Northumberland, to tell George More of Donne's marriage to More's daughter. Northumberland was by that time opposed to Essex and the faction.

⋘§ 446. BRANDENBURG, ALICE STAYERT. "The Dynamic Image in Metaphysical Poetry." *PMLA*, 57:1039–45.

Discusses metaphysical images in terms of their dynamic quality. The dynamic image, in contrast to the static image, "describes the way in which objects act or interact" (p. 1039). "Donne's interest in the intricate processes of the mind led him to use a mechanical or dynamic type of imagery—an imagery that was original, exact, intellectual, and, on the whole, unemotional. His most remarkable achievement was his success in writing poems that are, in spite of the neutrality of the figures through which he expressed his thought and feelings, full of intense emotion" (p. 1045).

⋘§ 447. BROOKS, CLEANTH. "The Language of Paradox," in *The Language of Poetry*, ed. Allen Tate, pp. 37–61. Princeton: Princeton University Press.

Reprinted with slight alterations in *The Well Wrought Urn: Studies in the Structure of Poetry* (New York, 1947; London, 1949), pp. 3–20.

Argues that "paradox is the language appropriate and inevitable to poetry" (p. 37). Much of the discussion (pp. 46–59) is given over to a close reading of "The Canonization," in which the poem is seen as a parody of Christian sainthood, "but it is an intensely serious parody of a sort that modern man, habituated as he is to an easy yes or no, can hardly understand" (p. 48).

≈§ 448. COOPER, HAROLD. "John Donne and Virginia in 1610." *MLN*, 57:661–63.

In 1610 (N.S.) John Chamberlain in a letter to Dudley Carleton stated that Donne was seeking the office of secretary of Virginia. The author believes that this indicates Donne's "efforts to bolt from a frustrated circumstance" (p. 662). Points out Donne's interest in Virginia in several poems and a sermon. Suggests that "Elegie V: His Picture" may have been written in 1610.

≈§ 449. DUNCAN, EDGAR HILL. "Donne's Alchemical Figures." *ELH*, 9:257–85.

Reprinted in *Discussions of John Donne*, ed. Frank Kermode (Boston: D. C. Heath & Co., 1962), pp. 73–89.

Examines more than twenty figures to show the skill with which Donne adapted certain alchemical concepts to poetic ends and to clarify for modern readers some of the obscurity in those figures that depend on unfamiliar alchemical notions. Especially helpful are comments on Stanza 3 of "The Canonization" and on "A nocturnall upon S. Lucies day."

≈§ 450. HARDY, EVELYN. *Donne: A Spirit in Conflict*. London: Constable & Co. Ltd. xi, 274 p.

Biography of Donne with emphasis on the psychological and environmental tensions that produced in him a spirit of conflict, frustration, and genius. Appendix I (p. 260), a genealogical chart of Donne's maternal ancestors; Appendix II (pp. 261–63), a description of extant portraits and engravings of Donne; Appendix III (pp. 261–65), an analysis of Donne's handwriting; Appendix IV (pp. 266–67), a chronological table of the first publication of his major works.

≈§ 451. HEYWOOD, TERENCE. "Some Notes on English Baroque." *Horizon*, 2:267–70.

Briefly contrasts Crashaw and Donne. Calls Donne "a sort of Barocco–Palladian compromise" (p. 269). Likens Donne's conceits and rhythms in verse and his spiral movement in prose to baroque architecture and painting. Points out that the compass image in "A Valediction: forbidding mourning" can be found in Omar Khayyam.

≈§ 452. LEGOUIS, PIERRE. "Some Lexicological Notes and Queries on Donne's *Satires*." *SN*, 14:184–96.

A special edition of this volume was published as *A Philological Miscellany: Presented to Eilbert Elkwall*, Pt. I. (Uppsala, 1942).

Discusses "words that resisted explanation after the O. E. D. had been anxiously consulted" (p. 184).

❧ 453. McClure, N. E. "King James on Bacon." *TLS*, 17 January, p. 31.

Reply to Percy Simpson, *TLS*, 25 October 1941, p. 531. Suggests that the gibe of King James was directed at Bacon, not Donne. John Chamberlain in a letter addressed to Sir Dudley Carleton (February 3, 1620–21) wrote: "On Saterday the Lord Chauncellor was created Vicount St. Albanes.... The King cannot forbeare sometimes in reading his last booke to say that yt is like the peace of God, that passeth all understanding."

❧ 454. Maycock, Hugh. "John Donne. Dean of St. Paul's." *Cambridge Review*, 63:164–65.

Brief biographical sketch.

❧ 455. Milgate, W. "Donne the Lawyer." *TLS*, 1 August, p. 379.

Notes that Donne was highly regarded as a lawyer and that on June 13, 1628, he, along with several others, was commissioned to examine the proceedings of a Prerogative Court in Canterbury concerning the will of Thomas Payne of Plymouth. Details of the Commission can be found in a Latin document in the State Papers, Coll. Sig. Man. Car. I, Vol. viii, No. 44 (an abstract is included in *Calendar of State Papers, Domestic, Charles I, 1628–29*, ed. J. Bruce, p. 208).

❧ 456. ———. "The Importance of John Donne." *Southerly* (Sydney), 2:33–34.

Abstract of an address given on May 27, 1942, to the English Association (Sydney). Surveys Donne's contribution to literature and criticism in the twentieth century. "He raises so many fundamental questions of form, subject-matter and imagery in poetry, that it becomes a testing ground for critical opinion, revealing in sharp outline the powers and failings of the critic" (p. 34).

❧ 457. Praz, Mario. "John Donne e la poesia del suo tempo," in *Machiavelli in Inghilterra ed Altri Saggi*, pp. 219–37. Roma: Tumminelli.

2d ed., 1943.

An Italian translation of "Donne and the Poetry of His Time," in *A Garland for John Donne 1631–1931*, ed. Theodore Spencer (Cambridge: Harvard University Press, 1931), pp. 51–71.

❧ 458. Richards, I. A. "The Interaction of Words," in *The Language of Poetry*, ed. Allen Tate, pp. 65–87. Princeton: Princeton University Press.

Maintains that one can "understand no word except in and through its interactions with other words" (p. 74). Uses the first twelve lines of *The first Anniversary* and the first stanza of Dryden's *Ode: To the Pious Memory of the accomplished young lady, Mrs. Anne Killigrew* to contrast "two very different types of the interactions of words" (p. 74).

◄§ 459. SIMPSON, EVELYN M. "A Donne Manuscript in St. Paul's Cathedral Library." *PQ*, 21:237–39.

Describes a manuscript volume containing five sermons from the seventeenth century, four of which are Donne's. Inscribed "SERMONS/ MADE BY I. DONNE/ doctor of Deuinty and/ Deane of Pauls/[rule]/ An°: Domini: 1625." Knightly Chetwode is the copyist.

◄§ 460. ———. "Queries from Donne." *N&Q*, 182:64.

Three queries about minor references in *Essayes in Divinity* (1651).

◄§ 461. SMITH, RONALD GREGOR. "Augustine and Donne: A Study in Conversion." *Theology* (London), 45:147–59.

Comparative studies of the religious personalities and conversions of Saint Augustine and Donne. "Towards two human beings similar in character and passions and longing for salvation God inscrutably chose to act in different ways. In consequence, the one has become a gigantic figure in the history of human experience, as well as a person most knowable and real to the readers of his story, while the other has in the eyes of most men dwindled to the proportions of an impressive but rather unsuccessful poet and writer of sermons" (p. 159).

◄§ 462. SOMMERLATTE, KATHERINE. "Churchill and Donne." *The Saturday Review of Literature*, 25 (December 5): p. 27.

Asks if lines 429–31 of *The first Anniversary* are perhaps the source of Winston Churchill's famous phrase "blood, sweat, and tears."

◄§ 463. STEIN, ARNOLD. "Donne and the Couplet." *PMLA*, 57:676–96.

Analyzes Donne's various experimentations with the couplet and suggests that "Like the writers of anti-Ciceronian prose, he is trying to convey the energetic spontaneous flow of ideas in corresponding rhythms and music" (p. 696). A revolt against "easy knowledge" and effeminate fastidiousness.

◄§ 464. TITUS, O. P. "Science and John Donne." *The Scientific Monthly*, 54:176–78.

Outlines Donne's biography and his interest in and confusion about the New Science. Suggests that the modern world, like Donne's world, is "all in peeces" and that perhaps the present age has much to learn from Donne's approach to the problem.

⏵§ 465. Tuve, Rosemond. "Imagery and Logic: Ramus and Metaphysical Poetics." *JHI*, 3:365–400.

Examines Renaissance imagery in the light of rhetorical training, especially Ramist logic. Maintains that much confusion and uncertainty
about the nature and function of Renaissance images result from "an
insufficient understanding of the relation of the origin and function of
images in sixteenth- and seventeenth-century practice to the poetic theory
of their creators" (p. 369). Discusses in detail the images in "A Valediction: of weeping."

1943

⏵§ 466. Allen, Don Cameron. "Dean Donne Sets His Text." *ELH*,
10:208–29.

From a study of all the biblical references in the *LXXX Sermons* of
1640, the author concludes that Donne was not as learned as is sometimes suggested. "When we study Donne's method in a sermon, or in
all the sermons of a definite year, or in all his quotations from a given
book of the Bible, we find that he selects his texts as he pleases, that he
is governed by no particular preferences, and that he does not seem to
make the slightest attempt to secure the best reading" (p. 228). From
Donne's uses of the Hebrew Bible, the author concludes, "There is little
doubt that Donne knew enough Hebrew to find the place in the text of
the Bible and to make reasonable translations. The fact that he seldom
ventured beyond this and that he does not compare his text regularly
indicates that his scholarship was extremely limited" (p. 229). More
revealing perhaps are Donne's uses of the Greek Bible: "His scholarship
is far below that of the average preacher of his age. It is not impossible
that his knowledge of Greek was very limited, for it has been long ob-
served that there is virtually no Greek influence in his secular verse"
(p. 222). Donne uses the Vulgate and the Authorized Version. "The
Authorized Version is, of course, Donne's English Vulgate; in fact, his
ordinary method of citing a text is to give the Latin of the Vulgate followed by the English of the Authorized Version" (p. 226).

⏵§ 467. ———. "John Donne and Pierio Valeriano." *MLN*, 58:610–12.

Cites several passages from the works of Giovanni Pierio Valeriano
di Belluno to suggest that Donne derived some of his more difficult
symbolism from his source. For a reply by Thomas O. Mabbott, see
MLN, 60 (1945):358.

⏵§ 468. ———. "John Donne's Knowledge of Renaissance Medicine."
JEGP, 42:322–42.

Surveys Donne's knowledge of general medical concepts of his age as
well as his particular knowledge of anatomy, physiology, pathology, and

methodus medendi, as these concepts are reflected in his poetry and prose. Maintains that Donne "was more interested in medicine than he was in those problems of cosmology and astronomy about which scholars have been so agitated in their attempts to prove that Donne was well-read in the 'quantum theories' of his day" (p. 322). Reviews Donne's interest in Paracelsus and concludes that "Ninety per cent of Donne's medical allusions belong to traditional medicine and have no paracelsian flavor about them" (p. 326).

◄§ 469. DAVIES, HUGH SYKES. "Donne and the Metaphysicals," in *The Poets and Their Critics: Chaucer to Collins,* pp. 63–89. Pelican Books. Harmondsworth Middlesex: Penguin Books.
Revised ed., 1960.
Collection of critical comments on Donne and the metaphysical poets from Chapman to Eliot.

◄§ 470. DOUGLAS, LORD ALFRED BRUCE. *The Principles of Poetry: An Address Delivered by Lord Alfred Douglas Before the Royal Society of Literature....* London: Richards Press. 25 p.
Attacks primarily two heresies found among many modern poets: (1) the antiformal tendency, and (2) the art for art's sake theory. Calls Donne "an exotic in English verse" (p. 21). States that Donne's reputation has never been very high. "It is only in recent years that it has been enormously and absurdly inflated just because his technique (or lack of it) has so much in common with modern writers" (p. 21). Concludes, "It was not till our own time that anything quite so bad was perpetrated on so large a scale as Donne's work" (p. 22).

◄§ 471. DUNCAN, EDGAR H. "Donne's 'A Valediction: Forbidding Mourning.'" *Expl,* 1:Item 63.
Response to P. K.'s query in the *Expl,* 1:Question 30, whether or not there is a figurative reference to alchemy in Stanzas 4 and 5 of "A Valediction: forbidding mourning." Paraphrases the stanzas and concludes that several alchemical concepts inform the imagery.

◄§ 472. EDITORS. "Donne's Song, 'Go and Catch a Falling Star.'" *Expl,* 1:Item 29.
Comments on Donne's use of magical incantation and the charmed number seven in the poem. Comments on mandrake root.

◄§ 473. GRIERSON, H. J. C. "A Spirit in Conflict." *Spectator,* 170:293.
Corrects a mistake perpetuated by, but not invented by, Evelyn Hardy in *Donne: A Spirit in Conflict* (1942). Concerns a Latin verse letter addressed to a certain Dr. Andrewes. The letter is an apology from the doctor to Donne for his children's having destroyed one of Donne's

books; the doctor sent a manuscript copy of the book in reparation. The old story, beginning with Gosse, is that one of Donne's children destroyed a book belonging to Bishop Andrewes.

◄§ 474. MEMORABILIST. "Some Notes on Donne." N&Q, 184:77, 165–66.

Challenges Milgate's statement in the *Southerly*, 2 (1942):33–34 that "In this century for the first time since his own day, John Donne has emerged as a landmark in our literary development." Cites several nineteenth-century enthusiasts (especially Coleridge). Attempts to show that the capitals, spellings, and commas in Donne's verse are intentional and intelligible and help us understand how Donne would have his poetry read.

◄§ 475. MILES, JOSEPHINE. "Some Major Poetic Words." *University of California Publications in English*, 14:233–39.

Comparisons and generalizations based on lists of the ten words (excluding prepositions, conjunctions, etc.) most frequently used by each of twenty-one poets from Chaucer to Housman (based on concordances existing at the time of the writing). For Donne the list includes *love* (500), *make* (370), *man* (360), *death* (320), *soul* (300), *good* (260), *see* (240), *think* (230), *know* (220), *go* (200).

◄§ 476. SIMPSON, PERCY. "The Rhyming of Stressed and Unstressed Syllables in Elizabethan Verse." MLR, 38:127–29.

Shows that the practice of rhyming stressed and unstressed syllables (for example, tie and bodie) was an acceptable practice among the Elizabethans. Illustrates the point from Donne, Peele, Chapman, and Jonson. Shakespeare and Marlowe avoid the practice.

◄§ 477. TILLYARD, E. M. W. *The Elizabethan World Picture*. London: Chatto & Windus Ltd. vii, 108 p.

Many reprints.

Brief mentions of Donne throughout. Discusses "The Extasie" as an "exercise of self-knowledge and an analysis of man's middle state" (pp. 71–73).

◄§ 478. ———. "A Note on Donne's *Extasie*." RES, 19:67–70.

Sees "The Extasie" as more than a love poem. Maintains that it is centrally concerned with "the basic constitution of man and man's place in the order of creation" (p. 67). "The *Extasie* shows us love as a part of the great human business of living as human being should" (p. 70).

1944

◄§ 479. CAMPBELL, HARRY M. "Donne's 'Hymn to God, My God, in
My Sickness.'" *CE*, 5:192–96.
Reprinted in *Readings for Liberal Education*, Part II: "Introduction
to Literature," eds. Louis G. Locke, William M. Gibson, and George
Arms (Rinehart & Co.: New York, 1948), pp. 500–504.
Close reading of the poem.

◄§ 480. GARDNER, HELEN. "John Donne: A Note on Elegy V, 'His Picture.'" *MLR*, 39:333–37.
Explication of lines 11–20 based on the Pauline antithesis (1 Cor. 3:1–
2) between milk for babes and meat for adults, especially as the passage
was expressed and elaborated upon in contemplative literature. Points out
that Donne frequently uses mystical theology in his love poetry but
rarely so in his religious verses and sermons. Surveys the seventeenth-
century Anglican mistrust of mysticism and private prayer.

◄§ 481. GARROD, H. W. "The Date of Donne's Birth." *TLS*, 30 December, p. 636.
Presents evidence to suggest that Donne was probably born on August
16, 1571. For a reply by W. Milgate, see *N&Q*, 191 (1946):206–8.

◄§ 482. GILPATRICK, NAOMI. "Autobiographies of Grace." *CathW*,
159:52–57.
The *Confessions* of Saint Augustine, Bunyan's *Grace Abounding*, and
Donne's poems are discussed as searches for grace. Very little on Donne.

◄§ 483. MOLONEY, MICHAEL FRANCIS. *John Donne: His Flight from
Mediaevalism.* Illinois Studies in Language and Literature, 29, No.
2–3. Urbana: The University of Illinois Press. 223 p.
Rejects the viewpoint that Donne was completely adherent to either
medieval thought or to the New Science. Places him in the troubled
middle position of being unable totally to abandon medieval concepts
or to accept totally the New Pagan naturalism of the Renaissance. Although Donne toyed with the New Science in his poetry, he in no way
saw it as a challenge to the stability of traditional Christianity. The conflict in his poetry stems from his rejection of the Thomistic belief in the
unification of flesh and spirit, thought and sense, and his unsatisfying
acceptance of Renaissance naturalism, which held that "the sensory
and intellectual are not complementary but antagonistic" (p. 212). This
conflict produced the distinguishing qualities of his poetry, increased intellectualism and a peculiar blend of passion and thought. Comments
on the "artistic aridity of the religious poems" (p. 212) and concludes

that Donne could not have been a mystic in the medieval sense of the word. States that Donne is a link between the Elizabethans and the neo-classicists and, through the neoclassicists, the nineteenth century. The break between intellect and sense, which exists to the present day, is a result of the denial of the medieval synthesis of flesh and spirit, and the reliance on intellect in the poetic creation is a result of dissatisfaction with the New Paganism.

⮑§ 484. ROSENTHAL, M. L., W. C. HUMMEL, AND V. E. LEICHTY. *Effective Reading: Methods and Models*. Boston: Houghton Mifflin Co. viii, 528 p.

Close reading of "Song: Goe, and catche a falling starre" (pp. 406–13). Short comment on "At the round earths imagin'd corners, blow" and a comparison of the two poems.

⮑§ 485. SIMPSON, EVELYN M. "Notes on Donne." *RES*, 20:224–27.

Three separate notes: (1) identifies the "two reverend men" of *Satyre IV* (l. 56) as John Reynolds and Lancelot Andrewes; (2) emends the phrase "ast ego vicissim Cicero" in a letter written by Donne to a friend at the outset of the Island Voyage (see *A Study of the Prose Works of John Donne*, by Simpson, 1924, p. 248) to read "ast ego vicissim risero," a quotation from Horace (*Epode* XV. 24, l. 3); (3) describes a heretofore unidentified manuscript of Donne's poems in the Rawlinson MSS. in the Bodleian.

⮑§ 486. STEIN, ARNOLD. "Donne and the Satiric Spirit." *ELH*, 11:266–82.

In an effort to account for Donne's satiric spirit, the author anatomizes the various forms and possible causes of Donne's melancholy and discusses the relationship between this melancholy and his skepticism.

⮑§ 487. ———. "Donne's Harshness and the Elizabethan Tradition." *SP*, 41:390–409.

"In this essay, based primarily on the *Satires*, we are to study the so-called 'harshness' of Donne; not only the characteristics for which he has been *called* harsh, but the ones by which he himself intended to *be* harsh, and the reasons for this intention" (p. 390). Links Donne's harshness with the same impulse that led anti-Ciceronian prose writers to cultivate a deliberate harshness, in an attempt to counteract effeminate smoothness, soft harmony, and sweetness.

⮑§ 488. ———. "Donne's Prosody." *PMLA*, 59:373–97.

Examines and classifies systematically some of the chief ways in which Donne departs from acceptable Elizabethan metrical practice: by defect of a syllable, by stress–shift, by stress–shift by attraction, and other such devices. Maintains that failure to understand the ways in which stress–shifts function in Donne's poetry makes it impossible to read the lines metrically, and such ignorance accounts in part for the harsh criticism levelled against Donne in the eighteenth and nineteenth centuries and leads modern readers to read the lines as if they were free verse or even prose.

◆§ 489. ———. "Meter and Meaning in Donne's Verse." SR, 52:288–301.

Insists that "people who read Donne as if he were prose miss almost as much of his point and emphasis as those who try to read him as if each line were composed of five model iambs" (p. 298). Shows that Donne's observance of and departures from the iambic pattern create much of the beauty and intellectual strength of his poetry. Catalogues some of Donne's more obvious departures, which Donne employs in order to suggest his exact meaning. Suggests that Donne is less unique in his metrical practice than sometimes thought.

◆§ 490. SVENDSON, KESTER. "Donne's 'A Hymne to God the Father.'" Expl, 2:Item 62.

Reply to a query posed by E. P. S. in Expl, 2 (1943):Question 6. Discusses the text of lines 14–15 of the poem and explicates them. "The spinning of the thread refers, through the metaphor of the three fates, to the drawing of the last breath. Unless the dead have the grace of a proper burial, they wander on the shores of the Styx. Donne will similarly 'perish on the shore' unless he makes a proper end through the grace of the Son of God, who at this moment ('as he shines now') vouchsafes enough grace to Donne for him to achieve genuine penitence and some confidence of a good end. 'And heretofore' is Donne's recognition that he could have acted upon this grace earlier."

◆§ 491. SYPHER, WYLIE. "The Metaphysicals and the Baroque." PR, 11:3–17.

Reprinted in Partisan Reader, eds. William Phillips and Philip Rahv (New York: The Dial Press, 1946), pp. 567–81.

Maintains that our "professed admiration of Donne is in a sense hollow and affected, and our depreciation of Milton wilful. The fact is that Milton is more characteristic of his century than Donne.... If we understand the baroque, it is a questionable tactic to elevate Donne at the expense of Milton" (p. 4). Proceeds to survey baroque "manners" in sculpture, painting, architecture, and principally in poetry. Concludes, "Donne, then, stands in genuine relationship with Milton. Both must be seen against the authentic 'movement' of the seventeenth century. When thus seen, Milton is the greatest of the baroque poets, the most polyphonic" (p. 17).

1945

◆§ 492. ALLEN, DON CAMERON. "Two Annotations on Donne's Verse."
  MLN, 60:54–55.
(1) Explains the phrase "The diamonds of either rock" (l. 6) in "A
Valediction: of my name, in the window" by referring the reader to
Anselmus Boetius de Boot's *Gemmarum et Lapidum Historia* (1609).
(2) Comments on lines 72–73 of *Satyre III*: "though truth and falshood
bee/ Neare twins, yet truth a little elder is." Points out Samuel Butler's
use of the notion later on and suggests Tertullian's "Adversus Praxen"
as the original source of the idea.

◆§ 493. ———. "John Donne's 'Paradise and Calvarie.'" *MLN*,
  60:398–400.
Discusses the commingling of two legends that inform lines 21–22
of "Hymne to God my God, in my sicknesse": (1) the legend that a
tree grew from Adam's dead mouth from which the cross of Christ was
in time made and (2) the legend that Adam's grave was the locus of
the cross.

◆§ 494. BUSH, DOUGLAS. *English Literature in the Earlier Seventeenth
  Century, 1600–1660.* Oxford: The Clarendon Press. vi, 621 p.
  Revised ed., 1962.
General critical and historical survey of the literature of the period
in which Donne is mentioned throughout. Donne's poetry is treated
principally in Chapter IV (pp. 104–69, especially pp. 129–36), and the
prose in Chapter X (especially pp. 302–9). Because of the chronological
limits of the study, the author does not discuss in detail Donne's major
love poems but restricts his attention to *The Progresse of the Soule*, some
of the occasional verses, the two *Anniversaries*, and the divine poems,
which, as he notes, is "an uneven and arbitrary but considerable slice"
(p. 130). Challenges the notion of "unified sensibility" and questions
the critical enthusiasm of those modern critics who have exalted Donne
frequently at the expense of Milton. Bibliography (pp. 524–27).

◆§ 495. CHASE, RICHARD. *Quest for Myth.* Baton Rouge: Louisiana
  State University Press. xi, 150 p.
Discusses poetry as myth and examines briefly Donne's "Epithalamion
made at Lincolnes Inne" (pp. 114–16). Considers Donne's conceits,
particularly the conceit "oft did we grow/ To be two Chaosses" in "A
nocturnall upon S. Lucies day" (ll. 24–25), as "a kind of shorthand
myth" (pp. 121–23).

◆§ 496. DANIELLS, ROY. "Baroque Form in English Literature." *UTQ*, 14:393–408.

Discusses Donne briefly as representative of the baroque form in poetry: "Donne's capacity for operating on a number of planes of thought at once and for moving irregularly from one to the other is masterly, and has obvious analogues in other baroque design" (p. 398).

◆§ 497. GARROD, H. W. "The Latin Poem Addressed by Donne to Dr. Andrews." *RES*, 21:38–42.

Translates and explains the Latin poem "De libro cum mutuaretur." Dates the poem as 1612 and shows that the person addressed is not Lancelot Andrewes. Challenges a number of misconceptions about the poem.

◆§ 498. ———. "Donne and Mrs. Herbert." *RES*, 21:161–73.

Examines the relationship between Donne and Magdalen Herbert. Attempts to date several of the poems that have been usually associated with Mrs. Herbert and questions the evidence of some of those believed by Grierson and others to have been written to her. Also comments on Lord Herbert of Cherbury.

◆§ 499. KNIGHTS, L. C. "On the Social Background of Metaphysical Poetry." *Scrutiny*, 13:37–52.

Reprinted in *Further Explorations* (Stanford: Stanford University Press, 1965), pp. 99–120.

Discusses "only a very few of the ways in which it is possible to work out *from* literature—from Metaphysical poetry—to 'the life of the time' in the early seventeenth century" (p. 39). Maintains that it is "much more likely that the distinctive note of Metaphysical poetry—the implicit recognition of the many-sidedness of man's nature—is in some ways socially supported; that—to borrow some phrases from a suggestive passage in Yeats' criticism—'unity of being' has some relation to a certain 'unity of culture' " (p. 42). Uses Donne's poetry throughout to illustrate the social and cultural milieu of his time.

◆§ 500. MABBOTT, THOMAS O. "John Donne and Valeriano." *MLN*, 60:358.

Challenges Don Cameron Allen's suggestion, *MLN*, 58 (1943):610–12, that Donne used Valeriano as a source for his comments on the symbolic meaning of the coinage of Darius. Concludes, from the viewpoint of a numismatic scholar, that Donne "either had read a more correct numismatic work than Valeriano's, or modified his ideas after personal examination of an ancient Persian coin."

&§ 501. MEMORABILIST. "Sir Richard Baker on John Donne." N&Q, 188:257.

Reprints (with slight variations) R. G. Howarth's objections in *Southerly*, 4 (1944):43, to Evelyn Hardy's *Donne: A Spirit in Conflict* (London: Constable & Co., Ltd., 1942).

&§ 502. MILES, JOSEPHINE. "From *Good* to *Bright*: A Note in Poetic History." *PMLA*, 60:766–74.

Traces the "developing relation of the standard epithets *good* and *bad* to the qualities epithets *bright* and *dark* through the work and the concordance listing of four or five poets on either side of 1740" (p. 866). Donne is discussed as a pre-1740 representative.

&§ 503. POTTER, GEORGE R. "Hitherto Undescribed Manuscript Versions of Three Sermons by Donne." *JEGP*, 44:28–35.

Describes three sermons that appear in a manuscript in the Harvard Library under the number "Nor 4506." The manuscript was formerly owned by P. J. Dobell and is indicated as "Do" in Keynes's bibliography.

&§ 504. PRAZ, MARIO. *La Poesia Metafisica Inglese del Seicento: John Donne*. Roma: Edizione Italiane. 173 p.

In revised form as *John Donne*. Torino: S.A.I.E., 1958. 277 p.

"Il presente corso riprende e rielabora uno studio già da me pubblicato in *Secentismo e marinismo in Inghilterra* (Firenze, Casa Editrice «La Voce», 1925)." Two introductory chapters: "Seguardo Generale al Secentismo Europeo," a general survey of that mode of poetry variously called secentismo, Marinism, Gongorism, euphuism, and metaphysical, and "La Poesia «Metafisica» in Inghilterra," a survey of some of the antecedents of metaphysical poetry in England before Donne. The remainder is a revision of the Donne section of *Secentismo e Marinismo in Inghilterra*, intended primarily for university students.

&§ 505. RAINE, KATHLEEN. "John Donne and the Baroque Doubt." *Horizon*, 11:371–95.

Sees the tension between the unified medieval theological view of man and the world and the fragmented scientific materialism of the seventeenth century as the conflicting polarities that shape the life and poetry of Donne. "The greatness of Baroque art, therefore, may be seen to be not in its destructive elements, but in its attempt to reconcile those kinds of knowledge that at certain times seem impossible to reconcile, except in art" (p. 374). Discusses the conceit as the primary vehicle in baroque poetry for holding together "the tremendous forces of the temporal and the eternal, felt, as they were at that time, to be pulling apart" (p. 375).

◄§ 506. SCOTT, WALTER SIDNEY. *The Fantasticks: Donne, Herbert, Crashaw, Vaughan.* London: John Westhouse. 170 p.

General introduction to the four poets with selections. The introduction to Donne (pp. 10–18) stresses Donne's search for "life-synthesis" or integration in his life and poetry. "Donne experienced, as perhaps few before him, and very few after him, the utter nausea of longing; he knew the pain, physical in its intensity, of desiring most passionately that for which his soul hungered, knowing that this intense need could never be satisfied in this life, and that he was condemned to bear the cross—of all crosses the heaviest—of a desire that must of necessity remain unsatisfied and unfulfilled" (p. 17). Selected verse (pp. 19–53).

◄§ 507. UMBACH, HERBERT H. "The Merit of Metaphysical Style in Donne's Easter Sermons." *ELH*, 12:108–29.

Attempts to show "where Donne is metaphysical as a preacher and that, considered in the context of his times, his sermons have the merit of not being extremely metaphysical for one so gifted in thought and expression" (p. 110). Limits the discussion to eleven Easter sermons and considers them under five headings: (1) a partiality for strange and unexpected figures of rhetoric; (2) an ingenious straining after wit; (3) an attaching of exaggerated importance to particular words and phrases; (4) a parading of authorities and sources with learned paraphrases; (5) an elaboration of outline divisions.

◄§ 508. WIGGINS, ELIZABETH LEWIS. "Logic in the Poetry of John Donne." *SP*, 42:41–60.

Points out some of the "relatively unfamiliar terms and methods of formal logic in some passages [of Donne's verse] which might appear at first glance to be quite free from such connotation" (p. 43). Concludes that Donne "would, no doubt, have reasoned keenly and effectively without the influence of formal logic; with it, he was able to infuse into his poetry a certain element of exquisite subtlety which is the very essence of his 'metaphysical' verse" (p. 60).

◄§ 509. WILSON, F. P. *Elizabethan and Jacobean.* Oxford: The Clarendon Press. vi, 144 p.

Reprinted 1946.

Points out some main differences between Elizabethan and Jacobean literature. Donne is mentioned throughout. Brief comparison of Donne and Andrewes as writers of sermons (pp. 44–45). Comparison of Jonson and Donne as lyric poets (pp. 54–55). Discussion of Donne's break with Elizabethan verse (pp. 54–59). Comparison of Donne and Raleigh (pp. 58–59) and Donne and Herbert (p. 65).

1946

◆§ 510. ANON. "The Bell Tolls." *Scholastic*, 49:19.
Short biographical sketch with many factual errors. Short comments on the poetry. Part of "Meditation XVII" from the *Devotions* is reproduced as verse.

◆§ 511. ALLEN, DON CAMERON. "Donne's Specular Stone." *MLN*, 61:63–64.
Explains the references to the "specular stone" in "The undertaking" (ll. 5–9) and in the fifth letter "To the Countesse of Bedford" (ll. 28–30) by referring to Anselmus Boetius de Boot's *Gemmarum et lapidum historia* (1609).

◆§ 512. ———. "Donne, Butler, and ?" *MLN*, 61:65.
Notes that the anonymous author of *The Surfeit of A. B. C.* (1656) makes a critical comment on Donne's style that resembles closely one made by Butler in his *Note-Books*. Suggests that Butler got his comment from *The Surfeit*. For a reply by Norma E. Bentley, see *MLN*, 61:359–60.

◆§ 513. ———. "Donne Among the Giants." *MLN*, 61:257–60.
Considers Donne's position on the reality of historical giants as reflected in *The first Anniversary* (ll. 135–44). Traces the historical controversy that raged from earliest Christian times. Augustine and subsequent theologians had refuted the notion of the ancients about giants, but certain Renaissance archeological findings challenged their conclusions. Apparently Donne preferred "this tangible evidence to the authority of the learned bishop" (p. 260).

◆§ 514. BENTLEY, NORMA E. "In Defense of Butler." *MLN*, 61:359–60.
Reply to Don Cameron Allen, *MLN*, 61:65. Defends Samuel Butler's comments on Donne by suggesting that they refer to the poetry, not to the poetry and prose, and by showing that Butler's comments are not as negative, perhaps, as Allen suggests.

◆§ 515. DELATTRE, FLORIS. "De la chanson Élizabéthaine au Poème Métaphysique." *ML*, 28:91–96.
Expanded version printed in Floris Delattre and Camille Chemin, *Les Chansons Élizabéthaines* (Paris: Didier, 1948), pp. 219–29.
In contrast to the Elizabethan lyricist, who stressed musicality, generalized emotional experience, and exquisite form, Donne and the metaphysicals are seen as rejecting traditional views of beauty and classical allusion, stressing muscular tone, and revolting against rhythmical regularity in their search for individual psychological reality. Sees a likeness

between the metaphysical poets and the Puritans, both of whom explored individual consciousness and retained music in a privileged position.

◆§ 516. DUNLAP, RHODES. "Donne as Navigator." TLS, 28 December, p. 643.
Comments on lines 59–63 of "A Valediction: of the booke."

◆§ 517. EVERSON, WILLIAM. "Donne's 'The Apparition.'" Expl, 4:Item 56.
Reply to C. William Miller and Dan S. Norton's explication of "The Apparition," Expl, 4:Item 24.

◆§ 518. GARDNER, HELEN L. "Notes on Donne's Verse Letters." MLR, 41:318–21.
Explains three passages from the verse letters: (1) the letter to the Countess of Bedford, which begins "Madame, Reason is our Soules left hand," (2) the fourth stanza of the letter to Lady Bedford, which begins "Madame, You have refin'd mee, and to worthyest things," and (3) the letter to the Countess of Huntingdon, which begins "Madame, Man to Gods image; Eve, to mans was made."

◆§ 519. GILBERT, ALLAN H. "Donne's 'The Apparition.'" Expl, 4:Item 56.
Reply to C. William Miller and Dan S. Norton's explication of "The Apparition," Expl, 4:Item 24. Maintains that the suggestion that syphilis is indicated in the phrase "a cold quicksilver sweat" is an overinterpretation.

◆§ 520. GRIERSON, H. J. C. "John Donne." TLS, 20 July, p. 343.
Responds to John Sparrow's "Donne's 'Anniversaries,'" TLS, 29 June, p. 312.

◆§ 521. JONES, H. W. "John Donne." TLS, 20 July, p. 343.
Brief reply to John Sparrow's "Donne's 'Anniversaries,'" TLS, 29 June, p. 312.

◆§ 522. LEDERER, JOSEF. "John Donne and the Emblematic Practice." RES, 22:182–200.
Discusses the possible influence of the emblem tradition on Donne's imagery. Cautions, "How far some of his images were really drawn from actual emblem books remains, of course, impossible to demonstrate incontrovertibly. But critical shifting of Donne's imagery will show that there are several possibilities of establishing a correspondence with the emblematic practice without unduly stressing direct influences; for the

purpose of the collected evidence is to illustrate Donne's participation in the general style-currents of his age and the effect it had on his creative process" (p. 185). Discusses the compass image in "A Valediction: forbidding mourning" (pp. 196–200). See also Doris C. Powers, *RES*, n.s., 9 (1958):173–75.

◄§ 523. MILCH, WERNER J. "Metaphysical Poetry and the German 'Barocklyrik.' " *Comparative Literature Studies* (Cardiff), 23–24: 16–22.

Suggests areas of comparative studies between individual German "barock" poets and the English metaphysicals as well as between the larger aspects of each movement. Sees the "barock" poets and the metaphysicals as "the last great European attempt to bring about a unified world of thought since the rift between contemplative and the active life, between unquestioned faith and scientific urge had become the central feature of all philosophy" (p. 20). Admits that there was no German counterpart to Donne, but mentions Andreas Gryphius as the most outstanding German "barock" poet. Maintains, "There are four great men determining the trend of thought and letters at the beginning of the century: Jonson and Donne in this country, Opitz and Jacob Boehme in Germany. The equivalent of the 'sacred trend' among Donne's followers appears in German literature as Jacob Boehme's influence upon Baroque-authors" (p. 19).

◄§ 524. MILES, JOSEPHINE. "Major Adjectives in English Poetry from Wyatt to Auden," in *The Vocabulary of Poetry, Three Studies*. University of California Publications in English, 12(1942–46):305–426. Berkeley and Los Angeles: University of California Press.

Composed of two parts and discusses the language of some major poets. I. Introduction: Glass to Pattern (pp. 305–21): various tabulations and discussion of major adjectives used by twenty-five representative poets, including Donne. II. Four Poets of Discourse: Wyatt, Donne, Pope, Wordsworth (pp. 322–59): extended critical discussion of Donne's language based primarily on the preceding data.

◄§ 525. MILGATE, W. "The Date of Donne's Birth." *N&Q*, 191:206–8.

Challenges H. W. Garrod's suggestion, *TLS*, 30 December 1944, p. 636, that Donne was probably born on August 16, 1571. Reviews the evidence and argues for some time from January 22 to February 12, 1572, as most likely.

◄§ 526. ———. "A Note on Donne." *Southerly* (Sydney), 6:120–21.

Corrects two errors in his review of *Donne: A Spirit in Conflict*, Evelyn Hardy, that appeared in *Southerly*, 5 (1944).

◆§ 527. MILLER, C. WILLIAM, AND DAN S. NORTON. "Donne's 'The Apparition.'" *Expl*, 4:Item 24.

Explication of "The Apparition." Points out that the phrase "a cold quicksilver sweat" suggests a common cure for syphilis. For a reply by William Everson, see *Expl*, 4:Item 56, and by Allan H. Gilbert, see *Expl*, 4:Item 56.

◆§ 528. MINTON, ARTHUR. "Donne's 'The Perfume.'" *Expl*, 4:Item 50.

Brief explication of "The Perfume" with special attention to lines 53–70. For a reply by Henry Ten Eyck Perry, see *Expl*, 5:Item 10.

◆§ 529. O'CONNOR, WILLIAM VAN. "Nature and the Anti-Poetic in Modern Poetry." *JAAC*, 5:35–44.

Points out the kinship between modern poets and the metaphysicals, particularly their acceptance of the physical and their cultivation of the antipoetic. Uses Donne as illustration throughout. Parallels Shapiro's "The Fly" and Donne's "The Flea." Concludes, "It seems more than accidental that the 'ugly' should be functional (Shakespeare abounds in illustrations) in the poetry of the two periods, one an age discovering man's relationship with the physical, the other an age striving somewhat desperately to rediscover it" (p. 44).

◆§ 530. PERRY, HENRY TEN EYCK. "Donne's 'The Perfume.'" *Expl*, 5:Item 10.

Brief explication of "The Perfume," in part a reply to Arthur Minton, *Expl*, 4:Item 50.

◆§ 531. SIMPSON, EVELYN M. "The Date of Donne's 'Hymne to God my God, in my Sicknesse.'" *MLR*, 41:9–15.

Reply to John Sparrow, *MLR*, 19(1924):462–66. Challenges Sparrow's dating the poem as the winter of 1623. Basing her argument primarily on evidence found in the poem and secondarily on evidence from the manuscript tradition, the author concludes that the poem was more likely written during Donne's last illness, as Walton suggested in the *Life*.

◆§ 532. SPARROW, JOHN. "A Motto of John Donne." *TLS*, 30 March, p. 151.

Notes that in section 20 of *The Remedy of Prophaneness* (1637), Bishop Hall reports that Donne frequently used the motto "Blessed be God that he is God, divinely like himself" and that he had seen the motto written in Spanish in Donne's hand on several occasions. Confirms Walton's account in the 1658 edition of the *Life* that Donne frequently used the saying as a prayerful ejaculation. Notes that in John Minsheu's *Guide into the Tongues* (1617) Donne's name appears as one of the subscribers.

⊷§ 533. ———. "Donne's 'Anniversaries.' " *TLS*, 29 June, p. 312.

Reproduces and comments on an errata slip (27 corrections) of the *Anniversaries* pasted inside a hitherto unknown 1612 copy of the poems. For replies, see H. J. C. Grierson, *TLS*, 20 July, p. 343 and H. W. Jones, *TLS*, 20 July, p. 343.

⊷§ 534. STAUFFER, DONALD A. *The Nature of Poetry*. New York: W. W. Norton & Co., Inc. 291 p.

Uses Donne to illustrate his conclusions in this generic study of the nature of poetry. See particularly the following: Donne's use of grammatical ellipsis (pp. 73–74) and his use of paradox and intensity (pp. 85–87), the imagery of "Batter my heart" (pp. 135–36) and "At the earths imagin'd corners, blow" (pp. 139–40), the balancing of the concrete and abstract in "The Flea" (pp. 151–53), the tension arising from metrical and rhetorical patterns as illustrated in eight lines from "The Extasie" (pp. 219–21), and a short discussion of the structure of "Lovers infinitenesse" (pp. 240–42).

⊷§ 535. STEIN, ARNOLD. "Donne's Obscurity and the Elizabethan Tradition." *ELH*, 13:98–118.

Studies "the mechanical aspects of Donne's obscurity against the backgrounds of the broad Elizabethan tradition, the special satiric tradition, and some of the literary currents active at the end of the century" (p. 98). Suggests that Donne's cultivated obscurity comes from his desire to stimulate the fit and to discourage the unfit reader, from the Elizabethan understanding of the tradition of obscurity in classical satire, and from the late Elizabethan attitude against popular art.

⊷§ 536. VALLETTE, JACQUES. "Un Précurseur anglais des poètes contemporains." *Le Monde*, 20 June, p. 3.

Brief comment on Donne's relevance to the twentieth century and his relationship to modern poets.

⊷§ 537. WELLEK, RENÉ. "The Concept of Baroque in Literary Scholarship." *JAAC*, 5:77–109.

Surveys the use of the term *baroque* particularly as it is applied to literature. Mentions Donne in several places in connection with baroque sensibility and the history of the term. Bibliography of writings on baroque in literary scholarship (pp. 97–109).

1947

⊷§ 538. ALLEN, DON CAMERON. "Donne's Phoenix." *MLN*, 62:340–42.

Comments on lines 18–22 of "An Epithalamion, Or mariage Song" in which Donne shows his awareness of the controversy that raged over the authenticity of the phoenix and the theological squabble about whether or not the bird, if it existed, was allowed on Noah's Ark. Donne believed it was not on the Ark.

≈§ 539. ATKINS, J. W. H. *English Literary Criticism: The Renascence.* London: Methuen and Co., Ltd. xi, 371 p.

2d ed., 1951; reprinted, 1955.

Comments on Carew's "Elegy upon the death of the Dean of St. Paul's Dr. John Donne" (pp. 298–99) and briefly summarizes Ben Jonson's remarks on Donne (p. 310).

≈§ 540. BOURNE, RAYMUND. "John Donne and the Spiritual Life." *PoetryR*, 38:460–61.

Reply to G. A. Wagner, *PoetryR*, 38:253–58. In contrast to Wagner, who asserts that Donne's principal contribution to literature was his "insight into the mysteries of the spiritual life" (p. 254), the author concludes that "Donne had his own interesting methods of imparting his views on any subject that appealed to him, but that one may look to his poetry as a questionable source of enlightenment in spiritual matters" (p. 461). For a reply by John Nance, see *PoetryR*, 39 (1948):91–92.

≈§ 541. BOYCE, BENJAMIN. *The Theophrastan Character in England to 1642.* Cambridge: Harvard University Press. ix, 324 p.

Brief comments on Donne's character "A Dunce" (pp. 145, 241–42).

≈§ 542. BROOKS, CLEANTH. "The Language of Paradox," in *The Well Wrought Urn: Studies in the Structure of Poetry*, pp. 3–20. New York: Reynal & Hitchcock.

Reprinted (in part) in *John Donne· A Collection of Critical Essays*, ed. Helen Gardner (1962), pp. 100–108.

Reprinted in *Discussions of John Donne*, ed. Frank Kermode (1962), pp. 64–72.

First appeared in *The Language of Paradox*, ed. Allen Tate (1942), pp. 37–61. Slightly revised here.

≈§ 543. DAY-LEWIS, CECIL. *The Colloquial Element in English Poetry.* The Literary and Philosophical Society of Newcastle upon Tyne. 31 p.

Defines the colloquial in English poetry and discusses its value and its application. Praises Donne for shattering conventions and for his combination of directness and dialectic, realism and fancy, deliberate roughness, hesitation, parentheses, and afterthoughts in such a way that a colloquial element is given to passionate argumentation (pp. 12–15).

≈§ 544. FAUSSETT, HUGH I'ANSON. "Donne's *Holy Sonnets*," in *Poets and Pundits: Essays and Addresses*, pp. 130–34. London: Jonathan Cape, Ltd.

Reprint of introduction to a limited edition of *Holy Sonnets* (1938). Places the poems in a biographical framework, suggesting that they reflect the mood and preoccupations of Donne after the death of Anne More in 1617.

✠§ 545. GEGENHEIMER, ALBERT FRANK. "They Might Have Been Americans." *SAQ*, 46:511–23.
Speculates on Donne's career had he been appointed secretary of Virginia in 1610.

✠§ 546. HAYWARD, JOHN. "The Nonesuch Donne." *TLS*, 5 July, p. 377.
Points out that the 1945 edition of *The Complete Poetry and Selected Prose of John Donne* (Nonesuch) contains errors and misprints for which he is not responsible. The text was entirely reset in 1945 without consulting the editor.

✠§ 547. HICKEY, ROBERT L. "Donne and Virginia." *PQ*, 26:181–92.
Traces Donne's interest in Virginia, particularly his association with the Virginia Company and the famous sermon he preached before the Company on November 13, 1622. Argues that the commendatory verse, "To his friende Captaine Iohn Smith, and his Worke," which appears in Smith's *Generall Historie of Virginia* (1624) was written by Donne.

✠§ 548. HOWELL, A. C. "John Donne's Message for the Contemporary Preacher." *Religion in Life*, 16:216–33.
Briefly comments on Donne's life and background, comments on his methods of preaching and the craftsmanship of his sermons, enumerates generally the themes developed in the sermons, and comments on several aspects of his style and eloquence as a preacher in order to show how relevant Donne's sermons are to the contemporary preacher.

✠§ 549. JOHNSON, STANLEY. "John Donne and the Virginia Company." *ELH*, 14:127–38.
Describes Donne's relations with the Virginia Company, comments on the occasion of his famous sermon preached before the Company on November 13, 1622, and points out the relevance of the theme of the sermon at the time of its delivery.

✠§ 550. KEISTER, DON A. "Donne and Herbert of Cherbury: An Exchange of Verses." *MLQ*, 8:430–34.
Gives reasons for believing that Sir Herbert's satirical poem, "The State Progress of Ill," was sent to Donne. Sees a relationship between this poem and Donne's "To Sr Edward Herbert. at Julyers."

❧§ 551. MARTZ, LOUIS L. "John Donne in Meditation: The *Anniversaries.*" *ELH,* 14:247–73.

Reprinted in *Discussions of John Donne,* ed. Frank Kermode (1962), pp. 90–105.

In much revised form, this article appears as part of *The Poetry of Meditation: A Study in English Religious Literature of the Seventeenth Century* (1954), pp. 220–48.

Challenges fragmentary approaches to the *Anniversaries* and shows how "each poem is carefully designed as a whole, and the full meaning of each grows out of a deliberate articulate structure" (p. 248). Sees the design of each poem as a combination of two traditions, the Petrarchan and the tradition of methodical religious meditation. Concludes that the two poems differ greatly in structure, imagery, and value. "The *First Anniversary,* despite its careful structure, is, it must be admitted, successful only in brilliant patches; but I think that it can be shown that the *Second Anniversary,* despite some flaws, is as a whole one of the great religious poems of the seventeenth century" (p. 248).

❧§ 552. MILCH, WERNER. "Deutsche Barocklyrik und 'Metaphysical Poetry.' " *Trivium,* 5:65–73.

Comments on the contemporaneity of metaphysical poets and the German baroque. Compares Donne with Böhme, Opitz, and Gryphius. States that German baroque poetry was without a real leader whereas the English metaphysicals had one in Donne. Discusses the religious, political, and philosophical situation in England and Germany in the seventeenth century.

❧§ 553. MOLONEY, MICHAEL F. "John Donne and the Jesuits." *MLQ,* 8:426–29.

Catalogues Donne's early references to the Jesuits and discusses various political and personal reasons that account for his hostility toward them. Points out that Donne remained sympathetic toward the English recusants during this period.

❧§ 554. NEILL, KERBY. "Donne's 'Aire and Angels.' " *Expl,* 6:Item 8.

Short explication of the poem, particularly the second stanza. Challenges J. B. Leishman's reading in *Metaphysical Poets* (1934), p. 44. Sees a relationship between the theme of "Aire and Angels" and "The Extasie." For a reply by Frank Huntley, see *Expl,* 6 (1948):Item 53.

❧§ 555. ONG, WALTER J. "Wit and Mystery: A Revaluation in Mediaeval Latin Hymnody." *Speculum,* 22:310–41.

Suggests that revaluation of metaphysical wit opens new possibilities for reconsidering long neglected medieval Latin liturgical verses that employ wit. Primarily considers the verse of Adam of Saint Victor and Thomas Aquinas. Briefly shows the similarity of the verbal play of the former and Donne's "A Hymne to God the Father" (p. 315).

✑§ 556. ROBERTS, DONALD RAMSEY. "The Death Wish of John Donne." *PMLA*, 62:958–76.

Suggests that Donne had a death wish, "that it was persistent, even lifelong, and that a full understanding of this wish throws considerable light not only upon Donne's temperament and certain of his actions, but also upon certain aspects of his work and philosophy" (p. 958). Examines *Biathanatos*, *Pseudo-Martyr*, and several of the sermons, as well as a few poems as reflecting Donne's intellectual and emotional preoccupation with death. The author suggests that this preoccupation may have originated with his early encounter with Jesuit fanaticism.

✑§ 557. ROTH, REGINA. "Donne and Sonnets IX and X," in *Gifthorse: A Yearbook of Writing*, pp. 15–18. Columbus: Association of Graduate Students in English, The Ohio State University.

Close reading of "Death be not proud" and "If poysonous mineralls" in which the two sonnets are contrasted primarily in terms of tone.

✑§ 558. SIMPSON, EVELYN M. "Donne's Sermons." *TLS*, 15 March, p. 115.

Announces intention of doing a complete edition of the *XXVI Sermons* in collaboration with G. R. Potter. Discovered at least 46 corrections were made while the original was passing through the press.

✑§ 559. STEPHENS, JAMES. "The 'Prince of Wits': An Appreciation of John Donne." *The Listener*, 37:149–50.

Reprinted in *James, Seumas & Jacques: Unpublished Writings of James Stephens*, ed. Lloyd Frankenburg (New York: The Macmillan Co., 1964), pp. 202–6.

Brief evaluation of Donne as poet with a biographical resumé.

✑§ 560. TUVE, ROSEMOND. *Elizabethan and Metaphysical Imagery: Renaissance Poetic and Twentieth-Century Critics*. Chicago: University of Chicago Press. xiv, 442 p.

Reprinted, Chicago: University of Chicago Press (Phoenix Books), 1961.

Extracts appear in *Discussions of John Donne*, ed. Frank Kermode (1962), pp. 106–17.

Reconsideration of Elizabethan and metaphysical modes of expression in terms of their contemporary habits of thought, principally in terms of Renaissance theories of rhetoric and logic. An inquiry into the nature and function of imagery and a corrective evaluation of twentieth-century critical approaches to Renaissance poetry. Many of the so-called unorthodox and new qualities of Donne's verse are seen as less novel than many contemporary critics suggest and are viewed as part of a large and consistent tradition.

❧ 561. WAGNER, G. A. "John Donne and the Spiritual Life." *PoetryR*, 38:253–58.

Maintains that Donne's principal contribution to literature was his "insight into the mysteries of the spiritual life" (p. 254). Delineates the spiritual values that Donne communicates through his verse, such as his concern for the role of the body, his attitudes toward suffering, his respect and eagerness for change, the value of the inner self, his constant striving for love and unity. Suggests that Donne anticipates many of the contemporary conclusions about these problems. Compares Donne and Baudelaire. For a reply by Raymund Bourne, see *PoetryR*, 38:460–61.

❧ 562. WASSERMAN, EARL R. *Elizabethan Poetry in the Eighteenth Century*. Illinois Studies in Language and Literature, 32, No. 3. Urbana: University of Illinois Press. 291 p.

Discusses Donne's importance in the light of the general renewed interest in Elizabethan poetry during the eighteenth century. Shows that, although Donne was frequently attacked for his rough meter and extravagance, his satirical poetry, as well as his witty lyrics and even his devotional poetry, was widely read, admired, and imitated by other poets.

1948

❧ 563. BALD, R. C. "A Spanish Book of Donne's." *N&Q*, 193:302.

Calls attention to an article by José A. Muñoz Rojas entitled "Un Libro Español en la Biblioteca de Donne" in *RFE*, 25 (1941):108–11.

❧ 564. ———. "William Milbourne, Donne, and Thomas Jackson." *RES*, 24:321–23.

Discusses an unnoticed letter written to John Cosin by William Milbourne that clearly states that the small octavo published under his name in 1638 entitled *Sapientia Clamitans, Wisdome crying out to Sinners to returne from their evill ways: contained in three pious and learned Treatises* was not his own but consisted of two tracts by Thomas Jackson and Donne's *Sermon of Valediction at my going into Germany*. Milbourne apparently admired the three pieces and had them published so that they would be available to a wider audience. He regrets that the title page suggests that he is the author.

᪥§ 565. BETHELL, S. L. "Two Streams from Helicon," in *Essays on Literary Criticism and the English Tradition*, pp. 53–87. London: Dennis Dobson Ltd.

Contrasts two main traditions of English poetry, one represented by Shakespeare and Donne and the other by Spenser, Milton, and Tennyson. Contrasts the language, rhythms, imagery, and subject matter of each tradition. Challenges F. R. Leavis and the *Scrutiny* critics for their assumptions about the superiority of the first group. (First published in the *New English Weekly* during the winter and spring of 1945–1946.)

᪥§ 566. CHRISTENSEN, GLENN J. "Donne's 'The Sunne Rising.' " *Expl*, 7:Item 3.

Reply to Walter Gierasch, *Expl*, 6:Item 47. For a reply by Robert Gale, see *Expl*, 15 (1956):Item 14.

᪥§ 567. DUNLAP, RHODES. "The Date of Donne's 'The Annunciation and Passion.' " *MLN*, 63:258–59.

Dates the poem as 1608, because the only years during Donne's lifetime that Good Friday fell on March 25, which is the Feast of the Annunciation, were 1597 and 1608.

᪥§ 568. FREEMAN, ROSEMARY. *English Emblem Books*. London: Chatto & Windus Ltd. xiv, 256 p.

References to Donne throughout. Short discussion of the source of Donne's compass image in "A Valediction: forbidding mourning" (p. 147).

᪥§ 569. FUSON, BENJAMIN WILLIS. *Browning and His English Predecessors in the Dramatic Monolog*. State University of Iowa Humanistic Studies, ed. Franklin H. Potter, Vol. 8. Iowa City: The State University of Iowa. 96 p.

Although the author excludes most of Donne's dramatic poetry as not fully answering his definition of the dramatic monologue, he suggests that Donne's "real contribution to the genre lay in an unusual fusion of internal drama with psychological subtlety—something rare before Browning" (p. 59).

᪥§ 570. FUSSEL, E. S. "Milton's 'Two-Handed Engine' Yet Once More." *N&Q*, 193:338–39.

Points out a parallel between Milton's controversial image and lines 43–47 of Donne's "To the Countesse of Bedford" ("T'have written then, when you writ, seem'd to mee").

⊷§ 571. GARDNER, HELEN. "John Donne: An Elizabethan Master of
      Contemporary British Poetry." *British Africa Monthly*, 15:31–32.
Brief survey of Donne's life and works. Maintains that "when our age
comes to take its place in the histories of literature he will be recognized
as one of its masters" (p. 31).

⊷§ 572. GIERASCH, WALTER. "Donne's 'The Sunne Rising.' " *Expl*, 6:
      Item 47.
Explicates the poem primarily in terms of the evolution of Donne's
use of the term *unruly*. For a reply by Glenn J. Christensen, see *Expl*,
7:Item 3.

⊷§ 573. GRIERSON, H. J. C. "John Donne and the 'Via Media.' " *MLR*,
      43:305–14.
Reprinted in *Criticism and Creation: Essays and Addresses* (London:
Chatto & Windus Ltd., 1949), pp. 49–66.
Reviews Donne's attitudes and convictions concerning the truth and
reasonableness of the Anglican position. Donne accepted the Church
of England not only as a *via media* between the extremes of Rome and
Geneva but also as a church that stands "midway between the corruption into which the Church of Rome had fallen and the perfect Church
of Christ" (p. 313).

⊷§ 574. HOWARTH, R. G. "John Donne, an Evicted Minister." *N&Q*,
      193:41.
Asks if the John Donne referred to as having been in Bedford Gaol
with Bunyan in M. P. Wilcock's *Bunyan Calling* (1943) is a descendant
of the poet.

⊷§ 575. HUNTLEY, FRANK L. "Donne's 'Aire and Angels.' " *Expl*, 6:Item
      53.
Reply to Kerby Neill, *Expl*, 6 (1947):Item 8. Concentrates on the last
three lines of the poem. Maintains that the central problem of the poem
is not which love is purer, man's or woman's, but rather how to resolve
the disparity between the body and soul.

⊷§ 576. HUSAIN, ITRAT. *The Mystical Element in the Metaphysical
      Poets of the Seventeenth Century*. Edinburgh: Oliver and Boyd.
      351 p.
Contains an introductory chapter on the general characteristics of
mysticism, followed by individual studies of Donne, Herbert, Crashaw,
Henry and Thomas Vaughan, and Traherne. Attempts "to establish the
amount of personal spiritual experience which lies behind the work of
these poets" (Foreword by Evelyn Underhill). Tries "to estimate the
content of the religious thought of these poets in order to determine the

nature and significance of the mystical element in their poetry . . ." (p. 13). Chapter II, "The Skeptical, Scholastic and Mystical Elements in John Donne's Thought" (pp. 37–119), surveys Donne's knowledge of and attitude toward Skepticism and Scholasticism and concludes that Donne "was interested in different schools of philosophy; he knew the sceptical philosophers, like Sextus Empiricus, the Greek philosophers, like Plato and Socrates, and the whole body of scholastic philosophy before and after St. Thomas Aquinas, and his critics like Duns Scotus and Occam—he had read all these philosophers with special reference to his own ever-deepening religious life, but in his later years he took up a position which is essentially that of a mystic" (p. 118). Bibliography.

᪐§ 577. ———. "John Donne's Seals." *N&Q*, 193:567.
Asks if any of the seals of Christ crucified on an anchor which Donne had made and sent to his friends are extant.

᪐§ 578. JOHNSON, STANLEY. "Sir Henry Goodere and Donne's Letters."
MLN, 63:38–43.
Maintains that the letter addressed "To Sr Henry Goodere," which appears in *Letters to Severall Personages* (1651) was probably written by Donne for Goodere to the Earl of Salisbury. Shows that on several occasions Donne was asked by Goodere to compose letters for his use and that occasionally Goodere adapted Donne's letters for his own purposes.

᪐§ 579. MAXWELL, J. C. "A Note on Donne." *N&Q*, 193:4.
Emends the line "They are not so contrary as the North and South Poles; and that they are connatural pieces" in *Letters to Severall Personages* (1651), p. 29, to read "They are not so contrary as the North and South Poles; and yet they are connatural pieces."

᪐§ 580. MILES, JOSEPHINE. *The Primary Language of Poetry in the 1640's*. University of California Publications in English, Vol. 19, No. 1. Berkeley and Los Angeles: University of California Press; London: Cambridge University Press. 160 p.
Incorporated into *The Continuity of Poetic Language: Studies in English Poetry from the 1540's to the 1940's* (Berkeley and Los Angeles: University of California Press; London: Cambridge University Press, 1951).
Distinguishes the major poetic vocabulary of the 1640s from the language that preceded and followed it. A descriptive evaluation of Donne's vocabulary (see especially pp. 70–72) and a discussion of his influence on the vocabulary of his followers.

◄§ 581. NANCE, JOHN. "John Donne and the Spiritual Life." *PoetryR*, 39:91–92.

Reply to Raymund Bourne, *PoetryR*, 38 (1947):460–61, who, in turn, had criticized G. A. Wagner, *PoetryR*, 38 (1947):253–58. Defends what he calls Wagner's "brilliant exposition of John Donne's anticipations of the commonplaces of contemporary metaphysical conclusions" (p. 91).

◄§ 582. NIMS, EDWIN. *The Christ of the Poets.* New York and Nashville: Abingdon-Cokesbury Press. 256 p.

Discusses the various attitudes towards Christ expressed by poets from Spenser to certain modern American Negro poets. Chapter III, "John Donne: Preacher and Poet" (pp. 48–64), summarizes some of the general notions about Donne's life and work held in the 1930s and 1940s. Sees the poetry as autobiographical statement and utilizes it as a commentary on Donne's attitude toward Christ. Sees Christ as the central theme of Donne's religious poems.

◄§ 583. O'CONNOR, WILLIAM VAN. "The Influence of the Metaphysicals on Modern Poetry." *CE*, 9:180–87.

In revised form, this article appears in *Sense and Sensibility in Modern Poetry* (Chicago: University of Chicago Press, 1948), pp. 81–92.

Surveys the importance of Donne and the metaphysicals on certain modern poets, especially Eliot, Stevens, Yeats, Aiken, Edith Sitwell, the Fugitive Poets, Lowell, and Wylie.

◄§ 584. POLICARDI, SILVIO. *John Donne: e la poesia metafisica del XVII secolo in Inghilterra.* Padova: CEDAM. 154 p.

Biographical and personality sketch of Donne. Discusses such themes as the struggle of body and soul in poetry, Donne's fear of and fascination tion with death, and the evolution of his attitudes towards love as seen in the poetry. Points out medieval elements, especially in the *Anniversaries*. Contrasts Donne's love poetry with that of the Elizabethans and finds it more realistic and less classical. Suggests that the development of metaphysical wit was the direct and ultimate result of the exaggerated importance given by the Scholastics to the study of logic and traces the development of this trend through the poetry of the *trovatori* of the Middle Ages, Dante, Petrarch, and Marino.

◄§ 585. RYAN, JOHN K. "The Reputation of St. Thomas Aquinas Among English Protestant Thinkers of the Seventeenth Century." *The New Scholasticism*, 22:1–33, 126–208.

Investigates certain representative English Protestant thinkers of the seventeenth century to determine the reputation of Thomas Aquinas in the period. Surveys Donne's Catholic background and his understanding of and respect for Scholastic thinking in general and Aquinas in particular (pp. 7–22).

◄§ 586. SIMPSON, EVELYN M. "Donne's Spanish Authors." *MLR*, 43: 182–85.

While recognizing that Donne read and knew many Spanish theological and philosophical works written in Latin, the author points out that there is little evidence to show that Spanish literature or the writings of the Spanish mystics exercised much influence on Donne's work.

◄§ 587. URE, PETER. "The 'Deformed Mistress' Theme and the Platonic Convention." *N&Q*, 193:269–70.

Sees the theme of deformed beauty in Donne's "Elegie II: The Anagram," as well as in Cleveland, Corbet, Suckling, Beedome, and Shirley, as a manifestation of the Platonic cult, which insisted on the beauty of the soul over the physical beauty of the mistress.

◄§ 588. WENDELL, JOHN P. "Two Cruxes in the Poetry of Donne." *MLN*, 63:477–81.

Suggests that many difficult passages in Donne's poetry can be clarified by comments found in the sermons. (1) Comments on the specular stone by referring the reader to the *Fifty Sermons* (1649), No. 27, p. 230; and (2) explains the difficult lines 518–20 in *The Progresse of the Soule* by referring to *LXXX Sermons* (1640), No. 17, p. 167.

◄§ 589. WILLIAMS, ARNOLD. *The Common Expositor: An Account of the Commentaries on Genesis 1527–1633.* Chapel Hill: University of North Carolina Press. ix, 297 p.

Studies what Genesis meant to the Renaissance. Donne is mentioned throughout. Notes that "Donne summarized the attitude among Protestants to Catholic commentators as well as anyone else" (p. 33). Indicates how Donne utilized traditional exegesis and how he sometimes departed from the tradition.

1949

◄§ 590. ALLEN, DON CAMERON. *The Legend of Noah: Renaissance Rationalism in Art, Science, and Letters.* Illinois Studies in Language and Literature, 33. Urbana: University of Illinois Press. vii, 221 p.

Studies the relationship between reason and faith in the Renaissance. Discusses briefly Donne's distrust of reason (pp. 30–33, 36), his use of the legend of Noah in "Hymne to God my God, in my sicknesse" (p. 113), and his utilization of the story in *The first Anniversary* (pp. 147–48).

◄§ 591. ————. "John Donne and the Tower of Babel." *MLN*, 64:481–83.

Comments on lines 417–22 of *The second Anniversarie* and on certain lines in the Nativity Sermon of 1624, in which Donne suggests two objections to the notion of the Tower of Babel: (1) that there is not enough material in this world to construct such a tower; (2) that the earth would be too small a foundation for the tower. Outlines contemporary and traditional thinking on the problem.

◄§ 592. BALD, R. C. "Donne's Activities." *TLS*, 13 May, p. 313.

Questions two statements made by Augustus Jessopp in his biography of Donne and repeated by later scholars: (1) that Donne actively assisted Thomas Morton in his controversy with the Catholics during the years 1605–1609, and (2) that Donne was on intimate terms with Sir Francis Bacon between 1606 and 1610.

◄§ 593. ————. "Donne's Travels." *SCN*, 7:1.

Abstract of a paper presented at the MLA Convention of 1948. Suggests that 1591 is a more likely date than 1595 for Donne's early travels. Mentions that Donne went abroad in 1605–1606 as a travelling companion to Sir Walter Shute. Possibly it was on this occasion, rather than in 1591, that Donne visited Spain.

◄§ 594. BEALL, CHANDLER B. "A Quaint Conceit from Guarini to Dryden." *MLN*, 64:461–68.

Discusses the sexual significance of the word *die* in sixteenth- and seventeenth-century poetry. Uses "The Canonization," "The Dampe," and "The Prohibition" as illustrations. Suggests that the success of Guarini's madrigal, sometimes called "Concorso d'occhi amorosi," contributed in making familiar this celebrated euphemism.

◄§ 595. BIRRELL, T. A. "Donne's Letters." *TLS*, 4 November, p. 715.

Reply to I. A. Shapiro, *TLS*, 21 October, p. 681. Only incidentally mentions Donne.

◄§ 596. BOASE, ALAN M. "Poètes Anglais et Français de l'Époque Baroque." *RSH*, 55–56:155–84.

Points out that there is a poetry comparable to English metaphysical poetry in France of the late sixteenth and early seventeenth centuries. Uses Donne as the touchstone of the comparison. Outlines major features of Donne's poetry, stressing in particular the quality of *raisonnment passionné*. Compares Donne to Malherbe, La Ceppède, Drelincourt, Mottin, Théophile, Sponde, and D'Aubigny.

❧§ 597. CLEVELAND, EDWARD D. "Donne's 'The Primrose.'" *Expl*,
    8:Item 4.

Explicates the number crux in the poem, based in part on the total sense of the poem and part on Pythagorean and Christian number philosophies.

❧§ 598. DANBY, JOHN F. "The Poets on Fortune's Hill: Literature and
    Society, 1580–1610." *The Cambridge Journal*, 2:195–211.

In expanded form in *Poets on Fortune's Hill: Studies in Sidney, Shakespeare, Beaumont & Fletcher* (London: Faber and Faber, Ltd., 1952), pp. 21–45.

Evaluates the effects of Elizabethan social stratification and patronage on the poets and poetry of the time. Sees Donne as a gentleman-poet who is essentially a misfit in the world of patronage. "He makes metaphysics out of the poet and patron relation; and a poet-patron relation out of metaphysics" (p. 207).

❧§ 599. EMPSON, WILLIAM. "Donne and the Rhetorical Tradition."
    KR, 11:571–87.

Reprinted in *Elizabethan Poetry: Modern Essays in Criticism*, ed. Paul J. Alpers (New York: Oxford University Press, 1967), pp. 63–77.

Challenges Rosemond Tuve's statements in *Elizabethan and Metaphysical Imagery* (1947) for their overenthusiastic emphasis on the influence of rhetorical training on such poets as Donne. Debates her answer to the question of how far the meanings of words in the poetry of the period are to be narrowed by historical considerations. Argues against the use of the term *catechresis* as proof that Donne "was only applying the rules of rhetoric in a particularly vigorous and stringent manner" (p. 572). Objects to the thesis on the grounds that "it tends to explain things away" (p. 578) and uses as proof the example of Donne's repeated use of the separate planet trope to show that it was not only a standard trope but rather a subtle kind of truth, "something so real that he could brood over it again and again" (p. 578). While Miss Tuve objects to critics who emphasize overtones that lead away from the apparent meaning, Empson sees this suggestive quality in Donne as a mark of his greatness. Objects to her analysis of the differences between Romantic and seventeenth-century poets on the ground that, while not as self-conscious as the Romantics, poets like Donne were expressing their unconscious also and would have been aware of it.

❧§ 600. GARDNER, HELEN. "A Crux in Donne." *TLS*, 10 June, p. 381.

Reply to Leslie Hotson, *TLS*, 16 April, p. 249, and to J. C. Maxwell, *TLS*, 6 May, p. 297. Disagrees with their readings of lines 21–30 of "Farewell to love."

➣§ 601. GROS, LÉON-GABRIEL. "Du raisonnement en Poésie." *Cahiers du Sud*, 293:3–9.

Critical preface to a group of translations into French of several seventeenth-century poems, including "The Flea" and "The Extasie." Evaluates metaphysical poets primarily in terms of Eliot's criticism.

➣§ 602. HAMILTON, G. ROSTREVOR. "The Tell-Tale Article," in *The Tell-Tale Article: A Critical Approach to Modern Poetry*, pp. 3–59. London: William Heinemann, Ltd.

Comments on the effects of the noticeable frequency of the definite article in modern verse. "When in a large sample from Donne—7,000 words from his lyrics, plus 4,000 odd of *The Second Anniversary*—one finds that the over-all percentage is less than 2, there is reason for surprise. I have not come across so abnormally low a figure in any other writer. The contrast between the modern poet's 9 or 10 can be no accident, and is the more remarkable because the modern poet acknowledges Donne as one of his masters" (p. 7). Discusses the effects of Donne's sparing use of the definite article on his poetry (especially pp. 30–34) and contrasts Eliot and Donne (pp. 35f.) to show that Eliot's style is markedly different from Donne's.

➣§ 603. HARRIS, VICTOR. *All Coherence Gone*. Chicago: University of Chicago Press. x, 254 p.

Summarizes sixteenth- and seventeenth-century commentaries on the problem of decay and disorder in the universe, with emphasis on two representative spokesmen in the dispute, Godfrey Goodman and George Hakewill. Suggests that Donne best represents the literal cosmology of corruption, especially in *The first Anniversary*. Donne laments the decay of all the world's beauty, which originated from man's fall. He sees specific signs of decay in the refusal of man to recognize the world's decline and his own doom, but man can be saved if he will realize his weakness and the mutability of the world. Donne finds a resolution of this decay in the distinction between body and soul, between the temporary and the permanent, between a contempt for the world and a contemplation of the glories of the afterlife. Some of Donne's other poems and particularly the sermons emphasize the corruption of all the parts of the universe, though the corruption of man gets special attention. Death is the result of man's sin, but death in this world results in the glories of the next.

➣§ 604. HENDERSON, HANFORD. "Donne's 'The Will.'" *Expl*, 7:Item 57.

Explicates line 15 of "The Will," which is "My mony to a Capuchin." Capuchins, reformed Franciscan friars conspicuous in their zeal for poverty, wore habits that had no pockets.

•❧ 605. Hoноff, Curt. "John Donne." *Hochland*, 41:138–47.

Biographical sketch with some discussion of Donne's intellectual development. Finds similarities between Donne and a number of German poets. Calls attention to the modernity of Donne's verse. Compares Donne's rediscovery by Gosse, Grierson, and Eliot to the rediscovery of Hölderlin in Germany.

•❧ 606. Hotson, Leslie. "A Crux in Donne." *TLS*, 16 April, p. 249.

Explains lines 21–30 of "Farewell to love" by commenting on the obsolete use of the conjunction *because* with the subjunctive. For a reply by J. C. Maxwell, see *TLS*, 6 May, p. 297 and Helen Gardner, *TLS*, 10 June, p. 381.

•❧ 607. Keynes, Geoffrey. "Books from Donne's Library." *TCBS*, 1:64–68.

Lists twenty additional books from Donne's library that were not recorded in the second edition of Keynes's *Bibliography of Dr. John Donne* (1932).

•❧ 608. Matsuura, Kaichi. "A Study of Donne's Imagery." *Studies in English Literature* (Tokyo), 26:125–84.

In revised form this article appears as part of *A Study of the Imagery of John Donne* (Tokyo: Kenkyusha, Ltd., 1953), pp. 1–64.

Discusses Donne's imagery under four headings: (1) The Ptolemaic Universe Imagery, (2) The New Philosophy and the Decay of Man and the World, (3) Man and Angels, (4) The Soul and Body. States that the primary objective is not to consider the style or idiosyncrasies of Donne's style nor the inner qualities of Donne's temperament, such as his tastes and character, but rather to gather up "those images which are drawn from matters belonging to his Scholastic views of the universe and man and his outlook upon the mundane world, and to arrange them in co-ordination to see whether we cannot join these pieces into a whole picture of his conception of the whole world" (p. 126). Argues that many of Donne's images, although frequently employed to express ideas quite irrelevant to the images themselves, are suggestive "of his deeper thoughts and prophetic visions of the world-policy and the destiny of his fatherland" (p. 126).

•❧ 609. Maxwell, J. C. "A Crux in Donne." *TLS*, 6 May, p. 297.

Reply to Leslie Hotson, *TLS*, 16 April, p. 249. Comments on lines 21–30 of "Farewell to love." For a reply by Helen Gardner, see *TLS*, 10 June, p. 381.

•❧ 610. Milgate, W. "Dr. Donne's Art Gallery." *N&Q*, 194:318–19.

Suggests that Donne had some twenty pictures in his possession, at least two by distinguished painters.

✎§ 611. MURRAY, W. A. "Donne and Paracelsus: An Essay in Interpretation." *RES*, 25:115–23.

Discusses various ways that Donne utilizes concepts and words from the alchemical and medical writings of Paracelsus. Detailed examination of "Loves Alchymie" and "A nocturnall upon S. Lucies day."

✎§ 612. PAFFORD, J. H. P. "John Donne's Library." *TLS*, 2 September, p. 569.

Two additional books, bound in one volume, known to have been in Donne's library: (1) Creccelius (Joannes). *Collectiones ex historijs, de origine et fundatione omnium fere monasticorum ordinum in specie,* &c. Francofvrti, 1614, and (2) Pareus (David). *Irenicum: sive, De unione et synodo evangelicorum conciliandu,* &c. Heidelbergac, Francofort, 1614.

✎§ 613. PATTISON, BRUCE. *Music and Poetry of the English Renaissance.* London: Methuen & Co., Ltd. ix, 220 p.

Comments briefly on Donne's having initiated a separation between music and poetry that widened throughout the seventeenth century (pp. 198–200).

✎§ 614. POWELL, A. C. "John Donne's Library." *TLS*, 23 September, p. 617.

Lists four books preserved in the Library of Chichester Cathedral bearing Donne's signature and Italian motto: (1) *De Formica.* Auctore Jeremia Wilde Augustano. Ambergae, 1615. Bound with *De Bonis Ecclesiae, ante legem, sub evangelio* ... per Christophorum Binderum. Tubingac, MDCXV, and *Locmani sapientis Fabulae et selecta quaedam Arabum Adagia.* Leidae, 1615; (2) *Tractatus de rebus ecclesiae non rite alienatis recuperandis* ... Auctore ... Alphonso Villagut. Bononiae, 1606; (3) *Tractatus de Sacrosancta universali Ecclesia* ... Rudolpho Cupers authore. Venetiis, MDLXXXVIII; (4) *Passio Typica* seu Liber unus Typorum veteris Testamenti ... Autore Friderico Balduino ... Wittenbergae, 1619.

✎§ 615. SCOTT, W. S. "John Donne and Bermuda." *Bermuda Historical Quarterly,* 6:77–78.

Suggests that Donne may have had Bermuda in mind when he wrote Stanzas 2 and 3 of "Hymne to God my God, in my sicknesse."

✎§ 616. SHAPIRO, I. A. "The Date of Donne's Poem 'To Mr. George Herbert.'"*N&Q,* 194:473–74.

Dates the Latin and English verses entitled "To Mr George Herbert, with one of my Seal«s» of the Anchor and Christ" as probably composed about January of 1615.

≈§ 617. ———. "Two Donne Poems." *TLS*, 9 April, p. 233.

Objects to Sparrow's dating of *The first Anniversary*, *TLS*, 26 March, p. 208. Maintains that the poem was written "some months" after Elizabeth Drury's death (see line 39) and that *The second Anniversarie, Of the Progresse of the Soule* was written on the occasion of the first anniversary of her death. Objects to the title *Anniversaries* being applied to the two poems.

≈§ 618. ———. "Donne's Letters." *TLS*, 21 October, p. 681.

Asks for assistance in locating the manuscripts of several Donne letters. For a reply by T. A. Birrell, see *TLS*, 4 November, p. 715.

≈§ 619. SIEGEL, PAUL N. "Donne's Paradoxes and Problems." *PQ*, 28: 507–11.

Challenges Evelyn Simpson's too serious evaluation of *Paradoxes and Problemes*. Their essential spirit is one of cynical wit and skeptical irony, not serious philosophical speculation. Describes them as "ostentatious in their parade of immorality. Their purpose was to give the feeling of participation in something delightfully wicked. Towards this end, Donne used ideas in whatever way suited him" (p. 508).

≈§ 620. SPARROW, JOHN. "Two Epitaphs by John Donne." *TLS*, 26 March, p. 208.

Establishes Donne's authorship of two generally unknown Latin epitaphs inscribed on monuments in the parish church of Hawsted in Suffolk, one in honor of Sir Robert Drury and the other in honor of Elizabeth Drury.

≈§ 621. SPITZER, LEO. "Three Poems on Ecstasy," in *A Method of Interpreting Literature*, pp. 1–63. Northampton, Mass.: Smith College.

Reprinted in *Essays on English and American Literature* by Leo Spitzer, ed. Anna Hatcher (Princeton: Princeton University Press, 1962), pp. 139–79.

Defense of *explication du texte* in which the author supports his argument by dealing comparatively with three poems on ecstatic union: Donne's "The Extasie" (pp. 5–21), Saint John of the Cross's "En una noche oscura" (pp. 21–44), and a scene from Wagner's *Tristan und Isolde* (pp. 45–56).

≈§ 622. TATE, ALLEN. "Johnson on the Metaphysicals." *KR*, 11:379–94.

Reprinted in *The Forlorn Demon: Didactic and Critical Essays* (Chicago: Henry Regnery Co., 1953), pp. 112–30.

Reprinted in *Collected Essays* (Denver: Alan Swallow, Publisher, 1959), pp. 488–506.

Reconsideration of Dr. Johnson's views on the metaphysicals. In particular, a contrast in the use of figurative language, with Dr. Johnson and his critical assumptions on one side and the metaphysical poets on the other. Donne is used only to illustrate certain generic comments about the use and function of figurative language.

◄§ 623. THOMSON, PATRICIA. "John Donne and the Countess of Bedford." *MLR*, 44:329–40.
Discusses two major causes for the cooling of the friendship between Donne and the Countess, beginning in 1614: (1) the influence on the Countess of Dr. John Bruges, a Puritan preacher and physician, who became the Countess's spiritual adviser, and (2) the financial difficulties of the Countess during this period.

◄§ 624. WALLERSTEIN, RUTH C. "Rhetoric in the English Renaissance: Two Elegies," in *English Institute Essays* of 1948, ed. D. A. Robertson, Jr., pp. 153–78. New York: Columbia University Press.
Comparative study of Milton's *Lycidas* and Donne's elegy on Prince Henry in the light of seventeenth-century poetic and rhetorical theory. "Donne's is a theological elegy, primarily an immediate expression of thought and feeling, cast secondarily into a dramatic invention, which gives it a simple and passionate vesture, if hardly sensuousness" (p. 171).

◄§ 625. WARD, ELIZABETH. "Holy Sonnet X." *English "A" Analyst*, 12:1–4.
Close reading of "Death be not proud," in which the author shows how the whole poem is built around a central extended conceit, the confutation of Death.

◄§ 626. WINTERS, YVOR. "The Poetry of Gerard Manley Hopkins." *HudR*, 1:455–76; 2:61–93.
Compares Donne's "Thou hast made me," Robert Bridges's *Low Barometer*, and Hopkins's "No worst, there is none."

1950

◄§ 627. ANON. "Poets and Editors." *TLS*, 22 September, p. 597.
Comments on the relationship between the current popularity of certain past writers and the skill of their modern editors. Illustrates the general point by discussing Donne's reputation, in part the result of Grierson's edition and excellent subsequent editions and selections.

◄§ 628. ALLEN, DON CAMERON. "Three Notes on Donne's Poetry with a Side Glance at *Othello*." *MLN*, 65:102–6.
(1) Explains the scientific trope in lines 6–9 of "The triple Foole."
(2) Suggests that lines 89–92 of *Satyre III* rephrase a passage from Lu-

ther's *Von weltlicher Oberkeit*. (3) Examines certain religious, scientific, and alchemical notions about the nature of the fire that shall consume the earth at Doomsday. Comments on lines 13–16 of "A Feaver" in the light of the tradition.

⮑§ 629. ARMS, GEORGE, AND JOSEPH M. KUNTZ. *Poetry Explication: A Checklist of Interpretations since 1925 of British and American Poems Past and Present*. New York: The Swallow Press and William Morrow & Co. 187 p.
Revised ed., by Joseph Kuntz (Denver: The Swallow Press, 1962).
Lists explications for forty-eight of Donne's poems (pp. 56–62).

⮑§ 630. BALL, LEE, JR. "Donne's 'The Computation.' " *Expl*, 8:Item 44.
Discusses the basic unifying conceit of the poem. The twenty-four hours that have passed since the friend's departure are represented by twenty-four hundred years.

⮑§ 631. BUSH, DOUGLAS. "The New Science and the Seventeenth-Century Poets," in *Science and English Poetry: A Historical Sketch, 1590–1950*, pp. 27–50. New York: Oxford University Press, Inc.
Reprinted, Oxford University Paperback, 1967.
Examines Donne's reaction to the new science (pp. 33–37) and concludes that "with all his curiosity and knowledge Donne is no scientific modernist. Like Spenser, he is instinctively attached to the medieval religious conception of a fixed world-order with its interrelated parts, and that great structure seems to be disintegrating" (p. 35). The scientific allusions, images, and language in Donne's poetry come primarily from alchemy, astronomy, astrology, the bestiaries, and emblem books. "In short, much of Donne's 'science' was the kind of thing used by the unlearned Shakespeare and others, it was of course no less legitimate; Donne, like them, was not concerned with the scientific truth of such items, but with their value for the illustration of actual ideas and emotions" (p. 33).

⮑§ 632. DANBY, JOHN F. "Jacobean Absolutists: The Placing of Beaumont and Fletcher." *Cambridge Journal*, 3:515–40.
Reprinted as "Beaumont and Fletcher: Jacobean Absolutists," in *Poets on Fortune's Hill: Studies in Sidney, Shakespeare, Beaumont & Fletcher* (London: Faber and Faber, Ltd., 1952), pp. 152–83; reprinted, Port Washington, N. Y.: Kennikat Press, 1966.
Reprinted as *Elizabethan and Jacobean Poets: Studies in Sidney, Shakespeare, Beaumont & Fletcher* (London: Faber and Faber, Ltd., 1964).
Comparison of the social position and the effects of this positioning

on the work of Donne, Beaumont, and Fletcher (see especially pp. 519–23), in which the author claims that all three were "involved in the same degeneration of a tradition, impelled by similar bread-and-butter needs" (p. 522). All three are said to have occupied, more or less, the same social and literary position. Unlike the tone of independence and stand on truth contained in the *Satyres* and the *Songs and Sonets*, Donne's *Letters to Severall Personages* and *Anniversaries* are characterized by a false fabrication of compliments.

⊷§ 633. FAERBER, HANSRUEDI. *Das Paradoxe in der Dichtung von John Donne.* Zürich: AG. Rüschlikon. 84 p.
Analyzes the uses and function of paradox in Donne's religious and secular poetry. Divided into five major sections: (1) Einleitung (pp. 5–7); (2) Die Religiöse Dichtung (pp. 8–33); (3) Die Liebesdichtung (pp. 34–54); (4) Die «Verse Letters» (pp. 55–64); (5) Die Wesensart des Donn'schen Paradox (pp. 65–74). Three appendices: (1) Paradoxes and Problems (pp. 75–76); (2) Die Häufigfeit der logischen Partikeln (Tabelle) (p. 77); (3) Die geringe Verwendung von Paradoxa in den *Anniversaries* (pp. 78–79). Bibliography (pp. 82–83).

⊷§ 634. CIERASCH, WALTER. "Donne's 'Negative Love.'" *Expl*, 9: Item 13.
Paraphrases the argument of the poem.

⊷§ 635. GLECKNER, ROBERT F., AND GERALD SMITH. "Donne's 'Love's Usury.'" *Expl*, 8:Item 43.
Close reading of the poem, particularly stressing the "wealth of connotation, innuendo, and punning" contained in the poem.

⊷§ 636. HAYDN, HIRAM. *The Counter-Renaissance.* New York: Charles Scribner's Sons. xvii, 705 p.
Extensive survey of the Counter Renaissance in which Donne is mentioned frequently. One section, "The Bell Tolls for Universal Law" (pp. 160–66), contains a discussion of the *Anniversaries*. "Trapped in the transitional period between two confident and optimistic world orders, Donne peculiarly summarizes and symbolizes the dilemma bequeathed by the Counter-Renaissance" (p. 165).

⊷§ 637. KEAST, WILLIAM R. "Johnson's Criticism of the Metaphysical Poets." *ELH*, 17:59–70.
Re-evaluates Johnson's criticism of the metaphysical poets. Points out that Johnson's knowledge of Donne was extensive and covered nearly the whole of the corpus, whereas many modern critics base their judgments on a relatively select few of Donne's poems.

⋙ 638. ———. "Killigrew's Use of Donne in 'The Parson's Wedding.'" *MLR*, 45:512–15.

Demonstrates that Thomas Killigrew in *The Parson's Wedding* appropriated certain lines from Donne's *Songs and Sonets*: "A Lecture upon the Shadow" (ll. 25–26), "Breake of day" (l. 13), and "Loves Alchymie" (ll. 1–5). "The way in which Killigrew introduces the lines he has drawn from Donne clearly implies that he supposed the lines, if not the poems themselves, would be recognized by his audience" (p. 515).

⋙ 639. KEISTER, DON A. "Donne's 'The Will,' 40–41." *Expl*, 8:Item 55.

In part a reply to Thomas O. Mabbott, *Expl*, 8:Item 30. Suggests that the "brazen medals" (l. 40) perhaps refer to commemorative medals that have no real metallic worth and are only valuable because of the associations attached to them. If this association is lost, the medal is worthless. Also suggests that perhaps Donne is referring to "bread tokens," popular in certain German towns, which could be used to purchase bread, unlike the "brazen medals," which buy nothing.

⋙ 640. LEES, F. N. "The Early References to John Donne." *N&Q*, 195:482.

Reply to one item in W. Milgate's "The Early References to John Donne," *N&Q*, 195:291.

⋙ 641. LEISHMAN, J. B. "Was John Donne a Metaphysician?" *The Listener*, 43:747–48.

Argues that, although Donne used the terms and techniques of professional philosophy in his poetry and had an intellectual interest in philosophical questions, he is not necessarily a philosophical poet in the way in which Wordsworth or Rilke, for example, are. "Behind his occasional affectation of the metaphysics, as behind the habitually rigorous argumentation of his poems, there lies, not any central vision or point of view, but some mood of satire or of tenderness, or, to use his own word, some 'concupiscence' of wit" (p. 748).

⋙ 642. LOUTHAN, DONIPHAN. "The *Tome-Tomb* Pun in Renaissance England." *PQ*, 29:375–80.

Points out Donne's use of the "tome-tomb" pun in "The Canonization" (ll. 28–30), "The Autumnall" (l. 45f.), and especially in "A Valediction: of the booke" (ll. 19–27). Indicates how the pun is also utilized in the sermons and in the fourth epistle to the Countess of Bedford ("This twilight of two yeares," ll. 13–15). Concludes, "In Renaissance England a *tome-tomb* pun was abnormal but possible, according to phonological evidence. The relative infrequency of the abnormal pronunciation, as shown by the paucity of rhymes indicating such a pronunciation, should lead us to examine each potential pun of this type with the greatest of care, to determine whether or not its context makes an ambiguity inevitable" (p. 380).

◄§ 643. MABBOTT, THOMAS O. "Donne's 'The Will,' 40–41." *Expl*, 8:Item 30.

Suggests that "brazen medals" refers to Roman coins that were sought by collectors because of their beauty and historical interest but were of no use to the poor man, since he could not spend them. Suggests that Donne was a coin collector. For a reply by Don Keister, see *Expl*, 8:Item 55.

◄§ 644. MAHOOD, M. M. *Poetry and Humanism.* New Haven: Yale University Press. 335 p.

Reprinted, Port Washington, N. Y.: Kennikat Press, 1967.

Donne is mentioned frequently in this study of Christian humanism and the arts; two chapters are specifically devoted to him. In "Donne: The Progress of the Soul" (pp. 87–130), the author traces Donne's spiritual and intellectual development. Donne's poetry and prose reveal his gradual but insistent movement toward theocentric humanism, in which the tensions of his age as reflected in his soul are finally reconciled into an integrated perception and response. In "Donne: The Baroque Preacher" (pp. 131–68), the author discusses the major themes and qualities of the baroque in the plastic arts as well as in literature. Donne's sermons are discussed as reflecting the essential features of the baroque spirit and temperament and also as reflecting the major thematic concerns of the baroque artist.

◄§ 645. MILGATE, W. "The Early References to John Donne." *N&Q*, 195:229–31, 246–47, 290–92, 381–83.

List of references to Donne with comments and notes during and shortly after his lifetime. Suggests that Donne's contemporaries prized his wit and his satirical and rhetorical skills much more than those elements are prized by modern critics. For a reply to one item, see F. N. Lees, *N&Q*, 195:482.

◄§ 646. MOLONEY, MICHAEL F. "Donne's Metrical Practice." *PMLA*, 65:232–39.

Maintains that "the most significant technical features of Donne's verse are the consistent employment of elision and the consistent rejection of a fixed iambic rhythm through the utilization of stress-shift. With regard to the first he was no more revolutionary than Milton, if the greatest critic of Miltonic prosody is correct. With regard to the second, he had ample lyric and dramatic precedent. Indeed, unless Shakespeare and Milton are revolutionary, Donne was of the centre not eccentric" (p. 239). Places Donne in the tradition of Renaissance metrical practice.

•⊰§ 647. NICOLSON, MAJORIE HOPE. *The Breaking of the Circle: Studies in the Effect of the "New Science" upon Seventeenth Century Poetry*. Evanston: Northwestern University Press. xxii, 193 p.
  Revised ed., New York: Columbia University Press, 1960.

Donne is referred to throughout this study of the impact of the New Science on the literary imagination of the seventeenth century. Argues that, with the encroachment of the mechanistic view of the world, the cosmological metaphors (especially the circle), which grew out of an earlier world view, ceased to have the force of actuality and became reduced to mere simile. "The Death of a World" (pp. 65–104) contains a close reading of *The first Anniversary*, which the author calls a threnody, "a dirge upon the decay and death of man, of the world, of the universe" (p. 65). The interpretation of the poem rests primarily upon a complex identification of Elizabeth Drury as Astrea, the Virgin Mary, the idea of Woman, and especially Queen Elizabeth. Maintains that "when Donne uses the more common 'she,' he is speaking of a real person. When he uses the 'double shee,' he is writing in symbolic, universal, and abstract terms about what he called 'The Idea of a Woman' " (p. 71).

•⊰§ 648. OCHOJSKI, PAUL M. "Did John Donne Repent His Apostasy?" *ABR*, 1:535–48.

Reviews Donne's Catholic connections and background. Argues that Donne, "who even after he became an Anglican divine still showed marked sympathy with the persecuted Catholics of England, found no peace in his new-found Church and regretted, if he did not repent, the apostasy" (p. 535). Characterizes Donne's love poetry as "unbridled sensuality preversely [sic] blended with Scholastic terminology" (p. 541).

•⊰§ 649. SHAPIRO, I. A. "The 'Mermaid Club.' " *MLR*, 45:6–17.

Indicates Donne's association with the famous club and disclaims Shakespeare's association with the group.

•⊰§ 650. SPROTT, S. ERNEST. "The Legend of Jack Donne the Libertine." *UTQ*, 19:335–53.

Reviews the reasons for the modern assumption that Donne was a libertine in his youth and concludes that the legend was created mostly by Donne himself by the references to his sins of his youth, which appear in his sermons and letters. The notion is supported by modern critics who read the love poems as if they were autobiographical statements.

Points out that Donne's contemporaries held no such views and that
Donne's protestations of guilt may be seen, for the most part, as an
attempt of the preacher and divine "to impute nothing to another that
he would not confess himself" (p. 343).

⏤§ 651. TURNELL, MARTIN. "John Donne and the Quest for Unity."
    Nineteenth Century and After, 147:262–74.
    Revised version in *Commonweal*, 57 (1952):15–18.
    Shows that Donne's poetry is not a "heap of broken images" but
rather underlying it is a search for that which is permanent and true.
"It is an attempt to recover or to reconstruct a unity which he felt that
the world had once possessed, but lost" (p. 273). The *Songs and Sonets*
are seen as attempts to find the "soul's rest" in sexual love; the *Anniversaries* illustrate the consequences of the lack of unity in the world; and
the religious poems show Donne's continuing search for unity in theology. While the author rejects the modern attempt to parallel the seventeenth century and the modern world, he maintains that "The secret of
Donne's present appeal lies partly in the fact that the problem of the
One and Many, of unity and multiplicity, is a perennial problem which
underlies the specific circumstances of different ages" (p. 274).

⏤§ 652. UNGER, LEONARD. *Donne's Poetry and Modern Criticism*. Chi-
    cago: Henry Regnery Co. xii, 91 p.
    Reprinted in *The Man in the Name: Essays on the Experience of
Poetry* (Minneapolis: The University of Minnesota Press, 1956), pp.
30–104.
    Examines some of "the criticism employing the word [metaphysical]
and some of the literature embraced by it, to make the category tighter
and clearer, or else to discover that it is unfit for categorical pretension—
at least beyond its historical origin" (p. 3). Chapter I, "The Critics:
Modern Definitions of 'Metaphysical,'" reviews the critical comments
of Grierson, Eliot, Williamson, Ransom, Tate, and Brooks on the nature
of metaphysical poetry, particularly on Donne's poetry. Chapter II, "The
Poems: Donne's *Songs and Sonets*," analyzes several of Donne's poems
to determine the validity of the critical assertions of the above critics.
Chapter III, "The Problems: Definitions and Evaluation," presents
broad generalizations based on the preceding analyses and discusses the
complexity of Donne's poetry. Concludes that "there is no basis for
regarding structure *determined by metaphor* as an absolute standard of
evaluation, that Donne's poetry is not generally characterized by such a
structure" (p. 82). "The value of a poem is not, so to speak, already
predicted by the definition of a characteristic style. It is determinable
only in so far as analysis may show a particular poem to have elements
that are valuable according to the interests of a reader" (p. 86). Examines the relationship between reader and the poem.

≈§ 653. WALLERSTEIN, RUTH. *Studies in Seventeenth-Century Poetic.*
    Madison: University of Wisconsin Press. x, 419 p.

In "The Laureate Hearse: The Funeral Elegy and the Seventeenth-Century Aesthetic" (pp. 3–148), the author discusses the development of the funeral elegy from Donne to Dryden and analyzes a number of elegies written on the death of Prince Henry to illustrate how different concepts and assumptions about the nature of poetry and the function of ornament in the century shaped the poets' work and consequently produced quite different kinds of poems. Discusses Donne's "Elegie upon the untimely death of the incomparable Prince Henry" (especially pp. 60–95) to show that the originality of Donne's poem comes not from its theme but rather from "the view from which Donne attacks it, the depth of his interpretation, the mode of expression and completeness with which he developed the techniques of expression . . ." (p. 69). Illustrates how Donne's poem rests upon Saint Augustine's theory of rhetoric.

≈§ 654. WILCOX, JOHN. "Informal Publication of Late Sixteenth-Century Verse Satire." *HLQ*, 13:191–200.

Argues that Donne, like Harington, Davies, Hall, and others, wrote satirical verse to attract the attention and patronage of the court, not because they were reacting to the corruption of the age.

≈§ 655. WILEY, MARGARET L. "John Donne and the Poetry of Scepticism." *Hibbert Journal*, 48:163–72.

Reprinted in *The Subtle Knot: Creative Scepticism in Seventeenth-Century England* (London: George Allen & Unwin Ltd., 1952), pp. 120–36.

Cites numerous examples from Donne's poetry and prose to illustrate his essential skepticism concerning human knowledge and certainty. "Thus the conclusion of Donne, worked out on one of those plateaus on which he so rarely came to rest, was that although man's knowledge cannot equal God's, he knows enough for the conduct of his own life, and in living worthily he approximates as nearly as possible the divine pattern" (p. 172).

1951

≈§ 656. ATKINS, J. W. H. *English Literary Criticism: 17th and 18th Centuries.* London: Methuen & Co., Ltd. xi, 383 p.

Brief discussion of Dryden's criticism of Donne (pp. 138–39) and Johnson's comments on the metaphysical poets (pp. 284–85).

◄§ 657. ATKINSON, A. D. "Donne Quotations in Johnson's Dictionary." N&Q, 196:387–88.
Comments on the 384 quotations ascribed to Donne in Johnson's dictionary. Indicates the distribution of the quotations among Donne's works.

◄§ 658. BACHRACH, A. G. H. "Sir Constantyn Huygens and Ben Jonson." Neophil, 35:120–29.
Brief comments on Donne's acquaintance with Huygens, his Dutch translator.

◄§ 659. BATESON, F. W. "Contributions to a Dictionary of Critical Terms. II. Dissociation of Sensibility." EIC, 1:302–12.
Traces the development of Eliot's notion of "dissociation of sensibility" to the critical writings of Remy de Gourmont, particularly his Problème du Style (1902), which provided Eliot "with a framework to which his own critical ideas and intuitions—even then incomparably profounder and more original than Gourmont's—were able to attach themselves" (p. 308). "What he has done . . . has been to transfer to the nation Gourmont's analysis of the mental processes of the individual. The unified sensibility that Gourmont found in Laforgue, Mr. Eliot finds in the England of the early seventeenth century" (p. 307). Points out certain inconsistencies in Eliot's use of the term "dissociation of sensibility" and traces the evolution of Eliot's thinking. Concludes, "Its use today as a loose, honorific synonym for 'taste' and 'personality' can only be deprecated" (p. 312). For a reply by Eric Thompson, see EIC, 2 (1952):207–13; Bateson replies to Thompson, 2(1952):213–14.

◄§ 660. BETHELL, S. L. The Cultural Revolution of the Seventeenth Century. London: Dennis Dobson, Ltd. 161 p.
Contains two parts: (1) an examination of dissociation of sensibility, specifically as related to theological questions; (2) a study of Vaughan. Donne is mentioned throughout. Discusses Donne's attitude concerning the relation of faith and reason (pp. 23–27), his attitudes toward the New Philosophy, and his uses of metaphysical and analogical thought (pp. 87–94).

◄§ 661. BLACKBURN, WILLIAM. "Lady Magdalen Herbert and Her Son George." SAQ, 50:378–88.
Briefly comments on Donne's relationship with Magdalen Herbert.

◄§ 662. BROOKS, CLEANTH. "Milton and the New Criticism." SR, 59: 1–22.
Points out that, while Milton and Donne each use metaphor differently, they are not as radically opposed as certain critics suggest. Explores

the complexities of some of Milton's metaphors and suggests that Milton is easier to misread than Donne, whose technique forces one to examine his work closely. In Donne, "The metaphysical complexity stands guard over the inner meanings" (p. 21).

⊷§ 663. BROWER, REUBEN ARTHUR. *The Fields of Light: An Experiment in Critical Reading.* New York: Oxford University Press. xii, 218 p.

Reprinted as a Galaxy Book, 1962.

Tries "to demonstrate some methods of reading analysis and to use them in discovering designs of imaginative organization in particular poems, plays, and novels" (p. xi). In discussing tonal patterns, the author compares Donne's "Show me deare Christ" with Hopkins's "Thou art indeed just, Lord, if I contend" (pp. 25–27, 57). In an analysis of sound, the author interprets Donne's "At the round earths imagin'd corners, blow" (pp. 67–70, 76). In an analysis of what the critic calls the "key design" of a poem, he gives a reading of "The Extasie" (pp. 77–83, 91, 92).

⊷§ 664. CRUTTWELL, PATRICK. "Physiology and Psychology in Shakespeare's Age." *JHI*, 12:75–89.

Attempts "to describe some theories of what we should now call physiology and psychology that were current in sixteenth and early seventeenth-century England, to examine their appearances in the imaginative writing of the age, especially Shakespeare's, and to analyze any effects they may have had on such writing" (p. 75). Four examples are drawn from Donne: two from "The Extasie" (ll. 61–62, 7–8) and two from *The second Anniversarie* (ll. 244–46, 254–58).

⊷§ 665. DONNE, JOHN. *The Prayers of John Donne.* Selected and Edited from the Earliest Sources, with an Essay on Donne's Idea of Prayer by Herbert H. Umbach. New York: Bookman Associates. 109 p.

Reprinted, New Haven: College and University Press, 1962.

General introduction (mostly selected passages from Donne's sermons, letters, and poems) to Donne's concept of the nature of prayer and a brief survey of the devotional principles that governed his prayer life (pp. 13–42). Selected prayers (pp. 43–92) divided into five groups: (1) from the *Divine Poems,* (2) from *Essays in Divinity,* (3) from *Devotions upon Emergent Occasions,* (4) from the sermons, and (5) miscellaneous. Notes: textual and explanatory (pp. 93–109).

⊷§ 666. HARDING, D. W. "Coherence of Theme in Donne's Poetry." *KR,* 13:427–44.

Reprinted in expanded version in *Experience into Words: Essays on Poetry* (London: Chatto & Windus Ltd., 1963), pp. 11–30.

Psychoanalytic discussion of Donne's mind as reflected in his work, mainly the poetry. Suggests that Donne continually projects his mind forward to a phase of life yet to come. In his love poetry, Donne is not so much concerned with celebrating sex but rather projects the possibility of extending the duration of the ecstatic moment, motivated by a feeling of fear that the moment will pass without having been fully responded to and savored. Suggests that Donne's ambiguous attitude toward women arises perhaps out of the fact that life seemingly failed to provide him with a satisfactory replacement for the child–mother relationship of affection and sensuous satisfaction. Donne projects his mind toward death in his work in an attempt in some way to convert his fear of it into longing and desire.

◄§ 667. HENN, THOMAS RICE. "The Ballad *The Twa Corbies* and Donne's A *Valediction: forbidding mourning*," in *The Apple and the Spectroscope*, pp. 15–24. London: Methuen & Co., Ltd.
Brief critical reading of "A Valediction: forbidding mourning."

◄§ 668. ING, CATHERINE. *Elizabethan Lyrics: A Study in the Development of English Metres and Their Relation to Poetic Effect*. London: Chatto & Windus Ltd. 252 p.
Part of this essay is reprinted in *Discussions of Poetry: Form and Structure*, ed. Francis Murphy (Boston: D. C. Heath & Co., 1964), pp. 179–200.
Donne is mentioned frequently. Two extended discussions of his verse: (1) a comparison of Wyatt and Donne concerning their concept of the function of the lyric (pp. 18–20); (2) a discussion of Donne's metrical practice (pp. 231–36). States that care for the metrical patterns in Donne's verse frequently helps to clarify and deepen understanding of his meaning.

◄§ 669. JACK, IAN. "Pope and 'The Weighty Bullion of Dr. Donne's Satires.'" *PMLA*, 66:1009–22.
Considers Pope's debt to Donne as a satirist and studies "the scope and nature of the changes which Pope made when he imitated two of Donne's *Satyres*" (p. 1009). Suggests that Pope has more in common with Donne than has been generally thought.

◄§ 670. LEGOUIS, PIERRE. "Le Thème du Rêve Dans le 'Clitandre,' de Pierre Corneille et 'The Dreame,' de Donne." *RHT*, 3:164–66.
Discusses the possible influence of Donne's "The Dreame" on a scene from Corneille's *Clitandre*. See also Pierre Legouis, *RHT*, 4 (1952): 377–78.

᪥ 671. LEISHMAN, J. B. *The Monarch of Wit: An Analytical and Comparative Study of the Poetry of John Donne.* London: Hutchinson University Library. 278 p.

Several editions and reprints.

Pages 9–26 reprinted in *Seventeenth Century English Poetry: Modern Essays in Criticism,* ed. William Keast (New York: Oxford University Press, 1962), pp. 75–91.

Chapter I of the 5th edition (1962) reprinted in *John Donne: A Collection of Critical Essays,* ed. Helen Gardner (Englewood Cliffs, N. J.: Prentice-Hall, Inc., 1962), pp. 109–22.

General comprehensive study of Donne's poetry. Surveys Donne's position in the critical history of seventeenth-century poetry, outlines the main events of his life, discusses the merits of the term *metaphysical* as applied to Donne's verse. Comments on the major categories of the poetry and evaluates various critical opinions of previous scholars and critics. More than a third of the study is devoted to the *Songs and Sonets,* which are divided, primarily on the basis of tone, into seven major categories, ranging from the outrageous, paradoxical, cynical poems to the serious analyses of love. Stresses in particular the dramatic qualities of Donne's poetry.

᪥ 672. LOUTHAN, DONIPHAN. *The Poetry of John Donne: A Study in Explication.* New York: Bookman Associates. 193 p.

Analyzes a number of Donne's poems in order to arrive at an evaluation of Donne's poetry in general. States that "many misconceptions of Donne criticism are due directly to superficial reading of the poems, and importation of patterns which patently do not fit them" (Foreword). Makes generic comments about Donne's uses of language, metaphor, images, etc., but these comments arise from discussions of individual poems. Explicates the following in some detail: "A Valediction: of weeping," "A Valediction: forbidding mourning," "Elegie XVI: On his Mistris," "Elegie XIX: Going to Bed," "Elegie XVIII: Loves Progress," "An Epithalamion, Or mariage Song on the Lady Elizabeth, and Count Palatine being married on St. Valentines day," "The Flea," "The Extasie," *Satyre II,* "Aire and Angels," "The Canonization," "Holy Sonnets XII, XIV, XVII," "A nocturnall upon S. Lucies day," "Twicknam garden," "Farewell to love." In an appendix, entitled "Empson's Idle Tears," the author challenges Empson's comments on "A Valediction: of weeping" which appear in *Seven Types of Ambiguity.* Bibliography.

᪥ 673. MAIN, W. W. "Donne's 'Elegie XIX, Going to Bed.'" *Expl,* 10:Item 14.

Explication of lines 25–26 of the poem: "Licence my roaving hands, and let them go,/ Before, behind, between, above, below." Suggests that the left hand caresses the lady while the right makes the sign of the cross.

◆§ 674. MAXWELL, J. C. "Donne and the 'New Philosophy.'" *DUJ*, n.s., 12:61–64.

Argues that convincing evidence is lacking to prove that the New Philosophy profoundly disturbed Donne. Asserts that Donne utilized the sciences for his own poetic ends; he was less concerned with the sciences per se, more with the poetic truth that could be expressed by using such analogies and novel illustrations.

◆§ 675. MILES, JOSEPHINE. "The Language of the Donne Tradition." *KR*, 13:37–49.

Reprinted in revised form in *Eras and Modes in English Poetry* (Berkeley and Los Angeles: University of California Press, 1957), pp. 20–32.

Argues that to understand the "Donne tradition," one must not only consider style, images, meters, etc. but also the tradition of language. Studies Donne's vocabulary and his choice of words. Compares Donne and Eliot to show that in language Eliot cannot be said to be in the Donne tradition. "Where the Donne tradition uses verbs, Eliot uses nouns and adjectives. Where the Donne tradition uses words of evaluation like *good* and *false*, Eliot uses words of sense like *white* and *dry*. Where the Donne tradition uses strong external controls in line-and-sentence-structure, Eliot uses powerful internal connections. The two characteristics closest to a bond are the characteristics of strong negatives and of colloquial speech; but here too the differences persist: Eliot's negatives are of sense rather than of abstract standard; and his speech is not his own, but quoted; his not the drama, but the observation" (p. 46).

◆§ 676. PRAZ, MARIO. "The Critical Importance of the Revived Interest in Seventeenth-Century Metaphysical Poetry," in *English Studies Today*, ed. C. L. Wrenn and G. Bullough, pp. 158–66. London: Oxford University Press.

Maintains that "the revaluation of Donne has not only resulted in a change of perspective in literary criticism, but has also furthered the reaction against the critical standards and the poetic theory of romanticism: Donne, we may say without fear of exaggeration, has had in the last thirty years a catalytic function" (p. 166). Maintains, "The discovery of the metaphysicals has been more than a literary fashion, has resulted not only in the adoption of certain images, in the cult of certain conceits and imaginative processes: it has rather amounted to the awareness of a similar disposition of spirit, of the same complexity in facing life, of the same ironical reaction" (p. 163).

◆§ 677. SHAPIRO, I. A. "Carew's 'Obsequies to the Lady Anne Hay.'"
    N&Q, 196:7–8.
Discusses the possibility that Donne and Carew knew each other personally through a mutual friend, James Hay, Earl of Carlisle. Concludes
that there is no convincing evidence to prove that Carew and Donne were,
in fact, personally acquainted.

◆§ 678. SIMPSON, EVELYN M. "The Biographical Value of Donne's
    Sermons." RES, n.s., 2:339–57.
Discusses Donne's sermons during the years 1625–1628, a period for
which there is little other biographical material, in order to give some
notion of Donne's spiritual development and mental outlook during this
crucial period of his life. Critical comments on the theme and style of
individual sermons. Concludes that Donne "retained his intellectual
vigour, and also his poetic power of weaving magical word patterns, but
his outlook on life had become that of an old man, with his hopes set on
death and the life beyond the grave" (p. 357).

◆§ 679. SMITH, HAROLD WENDALL. "'The Dissociation of Sensibility.'"
    Scrutiny, 18:175–88.
Re-examination of Eliot's concept in which the causes for the split between thought and feeling is traced to its social and religious roots. Suggests that Eliot, in his evaluation of Donne, canonizes his own poetic
tastes and reflects the tensions of his own sensibility. By the time of
Donne, "The two realms of abstract and sensible had already been divided; it was in the distance which separated them that the 'metaphysician' worked between them, and Eliot's very term 'unification' implies
both elements must have been clearly distinguishable and in need of
being utterly fused into one" (p. 178). Donne's central preoccupation in
his poetry is "the relationship of ideas—a fundamentally abstract interest" (p. 178).

◆§ 680. STEIN, ARNOLD. "Structures of Sound in Donne's Verse." KR,
    13:20–36, 256–78.
Part of the essay is reprinted in slightly expanded form in KR, 18
(1956):439–43.
Maintains that English verse allows and frequently uses an accentual
rhythm, which sometimes counterpoints and sometimes overrides the
iambic syllabic meter. Points out that such rhythms are characteristic of
Donne's particular poetic voice. Suggests that "the sensuous qualities of
sound in Donne's verse are usually rhetorical . . ., to reinforce emphasis
on ideas or on visually perceived images that express a rationally perceiv-
able thing" (p. 22). Discusses four different but related ways sound is
used in Donne's verses: (1) "as almost an abstract vehicle," (2) "as naturalistic imitation," (3) "as a contributing metaphor," and (4) "almost
as a complete metaphor" (p. 22).

⋙ 681. Van Doren, Mark. *Introduction to Poetry.* New York: William Sloane Associates, Inc. xxviii, 568 p.

Reprinted, 1962, 1966.

Close reading of "A Lecture upon the Shadow" (pp. 26–31). For a reply by Peter R. Moody, see *Expl,* 20 (1962):Item 60.

⋙ 682. White, Helen C. "John Donne and the Psychology of Spiritual Effort," in *The Seventeenth Century: Studies in the History of English Thought and Literature from Bacon to Pope,* by Richard Foster Jones and Others Writing in His Honor, pp. 355–68. Stanford: Stanford University Press; London: Oxford University Press.

Sees Donne's interior search for God throughout his life as the main force in his spiritual development and progress. Outlines the complexity of the tensions in Donne's spiritual life. Comments on his continuing spiritual combat against the warring elements in his soul and his search not only for a more perfectly realized knowledge of God but also, more essentially, for a complete spiritual integration with and experience of God. "Donne could and did free himself of various specific forms of lust and pride, but he never lost the sense of the continuing struggle. It is from the inside that he speaks always of the nature and psychology of sin" (p. 362).

⋙ 683. ———. "John Donne in the Twentieth Century." *SCN,* 9:2.

Abstract of a paper given at the MLA Convention of 1950. Brief general statement about the development of the criticism of Donne in the first half of the century.

⋙ 684. Williamson, George. *The Senecan Amble: A Study in Prose Form from Bacon to Collier.* Chicago: University of Chicago Press. 377 p.

Detailed history and critical evaluation of Senecan prose style in the seventeenth century. Considers Donne a Senecan, but there is little extended commentary on his prose style. Brief comparison of Donne and Andrewes (pp. 243–45) in which the author points out that Donne's sermons are more schematic and less pointed than Andrewes's.

1952

⋙ 685. Allen, Don Cameron. "The Double Journey of John Donne," in *A Tribute to George Coffin Taylor,* ed. Arnold Williams, pp. 83–99. Chapel Hill: University of North Carolina Press.

Adduces a number of reasons why Donne abandoned *The Progresse of the Soule* and why it is an artistic failure and why *Of the Progresse of the Soule (The second Anniversarie)* is "one of the great poems of the English language" (p. 93). "Without question the warping of the pre-text of the first poem was governed by the head, and when the heart rebelled, the whole inspiration volatilized and left the poet in that cold state of frustration that poets know so well. The second poem is the child of a passionate *sursum* in which the sensibilities carried the intellectual receptivities with them as companions in art" (p. 99).

◄§ 686. BAKER, HERSCHEL. *The Wars of Truth: Studies in the Decay of Christian Humanism in the Earlier Seventeenth Century.* Cambridge: Harvard University Press. xi, 390 p.

Broad study of the decline of Christian humanism in the earlier seventeenth century. The author states that he is "concerned with the traditional and the emerging concepts of 'truth'—theological, scientific, political, and other—whose collision generated such heat and even light in the age of Milton.... Yet in attempting to seek out the origin of this transformation in the early Renaissance and to sketch the progress through the earlier seventeenth century I have sought to indicate the intellectual and emotional pressures which shaped men's conception of 'truth' and of their capacity to attain it, and to suggest some of the consequences for literature" (p. vii). Places Donne within the intellectual framework of his time. Sees Donne as revealing "a typical seventeenth-century flexibility of mind; and when he is reworking the hallowed formulas of pessimism he stays pretty closely within his ecclesiastical tradition" (p. 59). States that especially in the *Anniversaries* "we find the most notorious Jacobean statement of the old doubts and fears... Donne's threnody is unique in the quality and complexity of its emotion, yet thematically it suggests dozens of Renaissance moralists" (p. 75).

◄§ 687. BALD, R. C. "Donne's Early Verse Letters." *HLQ*, 15:283–89.

Assigns the compact group of thirteen verse letters that appear in *Letters to Severall Personages* to the years 1592–1594, thereby challenging Grierson's dating of them from 1597 to about 1607–1608.

◄§ 688. ———. "Donne's Letters." *TLS*, 24 October, p. 700.

Part of a debate on Donne's "earliest-known prose letter" in the Burley MS. For a complete listing of replies and arguments, see Entry 723.

◄§ 689. ———. "Donne's Letters." *TLS*, 19 December, p. 837.

Part of a debate on Donne's "earliest-known prose letter." For a complete listing of replies and arguments, see Entry 723.

◄§ 690. BARUCH, FRANKLIN R. "Donne and Herbert." *TLS*, 30 May, p. 361.

Points out that Herbert in "The Church Porch" (Stanza 14) appropriates line 30 from Donne's "To Mr Tilman after he had taken orders." For a reply by J. B. Leishman, see *TLS*, 24 October, p. 391.

᳁§ 691. Bateson, F. W. "The Critical Forum: 'Dissociation of Sensibility.'" EIC, 2:213–14.
Reply to Eric Thompson, EIC, 2:207–13, who challenges Bateson's
attack on the notion of "dissociation of sensibility" in EIC, 1 (1951):
302–12. Insists that "however much we dress it up, the Dissociation
of Sensibility cannot be made respectable. It's a lovely mouthful, full of
sound and fury, but unfortunately it doesn't signify anything" (p. 214).

᳁§ 692. Bewley, Marius. "Religious Cynicism in Donne's Poetry."
KR, 14:619–46.
Surveys Donne's religious cynicism by focusing attention in particular
on the two Anniversaries, which are described as "one of the most successfully private jokes ever made, for their point is still generally missed"
(p. 622). Maintains that what the poems are, in effect, "celebrating—
albeit secretly celebrating—is Donne's apostasy from the Roman Catholic Church" (p. 622). Reviews Donne's Catholic connections and
concludes, "One is tempted to say that Donne used much more energy
getting out of the Roman Church than he used getting into the Anglican
one" (p. 646). Suggests that the "Songs and Sonets, in their inculcation
of an outrageous cynicism, in their abuse of religious imagery, in their
distortion of scholastic philosophical concepts, in their cavalier employment of logic, represent many years in Donne's private guerilla war-
fare against the dispositions of faith. The final victory is symbolized
in those two masterpieces of religious cynicism, The First and Second
Anniversaries" (p. 645).

᳁§ 693. Borges, Jorge Luis. "El 'Biathanatos,'" in Otras Inquisiciones
(1937–1952), pp. 107–11. Buenos Aires: Sur.
Trans. into English by Ruth L. C. Simms with an introduction by
James E. Irby in Other Inquisitions 1937–1952 (Austin: University of
Texas Press, 1964).
Suggests that underlying the obvious intention of Biathanatos, which
is to defend suicide, there is a secondary thesis—that Christ, in effect,
committed suicide, that Christ, like Samson, died voluntarily.

᳁§ 694. Bush, Douglas. English Poetry: The Main Currents from
Chaucer to the Present. New York: Oxford University Press. ix,
222 p.
General survey of Donne's poetry (especially see pp. 56–60). Qualified
praise of Donne: "His technique is exciting but, once grasped, is fairly
obvious, and other rewards are not inexhaustible, whereas Spenser continually reveals new depths and overtones" (p. 57).

❧ 695. CAZAMIAN, LOUIS. *The Development of English Humor*. 2
     Parts. Durham: Duke University Press. viii, 421 p.
Studies the development of English humor from the Old English
period to the Renaissance. Discusses Donne's humor primarily in terms
of his use of the conceit (see especially pp. 362–66).

❧ 696. DONNE, JOHN. *The Complete Poetry and Selected Prose of John
     Donne*. Edited with an introduction by Charles M. Coffin. New
     York: Modern Library. xliii, 594 p.
General critical introduction to Donne's twentieth-century reputation, his life, and his poetry and prose (pp. xvii–xxxvi). Note on the
text (pp. xxxvii–xxxix), in which the editor announces that he is essentially reproducing Hayward's Nonesuch text with some rearrange-
ment and with a few additions. Selected bibliography (pp. xl–xliii).
No notes or commentary.

❧ 697. ———. *The Divine Poems*. Edited with introduction and com-
     mentary by Helen Gardner. Oxford: Clarendon Press. xcviii, 147 p.
     Reprinted, 1959.
Pages xxi–xxxvii reprinted with slight alterations in *John Donne: A
Collection of Critical Essays*, ed. Helen Gardner (1962), pp. 123–36.
General introduction to Donne's religious verse, divided into two
parts: (1) a discussion of the general characteristics of the religious
poetry and of the sensibility that informs it (pp. xv–xxxviii); (2) an
extensive discussion of the dating, ordering, and interpretation of the
Holy Sonnets (pp. xxxvii–lv). In the "Textual Introduction" (pp. lvi–
xcvi) the editor gives a full account of the text of the poems in manuscripts and in the first two editions. The text (pp. 1–53) is followed by a
detailed commentary on the poems; particularly noteworthy is the attention given to problems of prosody (pp. 54–113). Seven appendices:
(1) Donne's View on the State of the Soul after Death (pp. 114–17);
(2) Verbal Alterations in the *Divine Poems* in the edition of 1635
(pp. 118–120); (3) The Interpretation of Donne's Sonnet on the Church
(pp. 121–27); (4) Donne and Tilman: their Reluctance to take Holy
Orders (pp. 127–32); (5) The Date of "Hymn to God my God, in my
sickness" (pp. 132–35); (6) "Paradise and Calvarie" (pp. 135–37);
(7) Donne's Latin Poem to Herbert and Herbert's Reply (pp. 138–47).

❧ 698. ———. *Essays in Divinity*. Edited by Evelyn M. Simpson. Ox-
     ford: The Clarendon Press. xxix, 137 p.
Consists of an introduction (pp. ix–xxxvii), in which the *Essayes in
Divinity* are primarily considered for their importance in an understanding of the development of Donne's thought; a bibliographical note
(pp. xxviii–xxix); a note (p. xxx), the text (pp. 1–100); a commentary
on the sources of the *Essayes* (pp. 101–8), and notes (pp. 109–37).

ఆర్‌§ 699. ———. " 'La Corona': Seven Sonnets by John Donne Set for Mixed Chorus a capella by A. Didier Graeffe." SCN, 10, No. 1 (Special supplement).

Thirty-page score of a modern musical setting for the La Corona sequence.

ఆర్‌§ 700. ELDREDGE, FRANCES. "Further Allusions and Debts to John Donne." ELH, 19:214–28.

States that "Insofar as one can judge from what is extant in print, the borrowings by common readers from Donne's phrases and figures are more extensive than from any other non-dramatic poet of the period. By their direct use of phrases and images lingering in their minds, these common readers of the first half of the seventeenth century make more explicit for us the general admiration of Donne's wit with which we are already familiar from research on manuscript copies; and they increase our knowledge of the widespreadness of the influence already traced with considerable thoroughness by examiners of 'the Donne tradition' through his more important imitators. Until the fundamental change in literary taste of the post-Restoration period, Donne was vividly alive not only in particular poet-followers but in the general language of literacy" (p. 228). Supports these conclusions by an extensive survey of many of the contemporary allusions and borrowings from Donne by those not ordinarily associated with the Donne tradition.

ఆర్‌§ 701. FIEDLER, LESLIE. "Archetype and Signature: A Study of the Relationship Between Biography and Poetry." SR, 60:253–73.

Reprinted as "Archetype and Signature: The Relationship of Poet and Poem," in No! in Thunder: Essays on Myth and Literature (Boston: Beacon Press, 1960), pp. 309–28.

Uses two of Donne's poems to illustrate his theory of the relationship between the poet's life and the poem. Shows that lines 5 and 11 of "A Hymne to God the Father" require some biographical information on the reader's part in order to realize the pun. Suggests that a more complex situation exists in line 24 of "Loves Alchymie" ("they'are but Mummy, possest"). Since the dictionary is not conclusive about the usage of the word mummy in Donne's time, the author argues that "we must turn to his life itself, to Donne's actual relations with his mother; and beyond that to the science of such relationships." Concludes that there is a possible Oedipal archetype operative in the line. Perhaps Donne is referring not only to his mother but also to the Catholic Church, his great Mother, "which his actual mother represented not only metaphorically but in her own allegiance and descent."

☙ 702. FRYE, RONALD MUSHAT. "John Donne, Junior, on 'Biathanatos':
    A Presentation Letter." N&Q, 197:495–96.
Reproduces a letter dated July 29, 1649, that discusses *Biathanatos*,
which was written by Donne's son to Sir Constantine Huygens, Donne's
Dutch translator. Found in the Princeton Theological Seminary Library
in a copy of the undated first edition of Donne's treatise.

☙ 703. JACOBSEN, ERIC. "The Fable Is Inverted or Donne's Aesop."
    C&M, 13:1–37.
Traces the verbal and pictorial tradition of the fable of King Log and
King Stork from Aesop to the sixteenth century. Comments on Donne's
use of the fable in lines 1–4 of "The Calme."

☙ 704. JANSON, H. W. *Apes and Ape Lore*. Studies of the Warburg
    Institute, 20, ed. H. Frankfort. London: The Warburg Institute
    University of London. 384 p.
Discusses Stanza XLVI–XLIX of *The Progresse of the Soule* in which
Donne makes use of ape lore (pp. 272–75, 283–85).

☙ 705. LEGOUIS, PIERRE. "L'État présent des controverses sur la poésie
    de Donne." EA, 5:97–106.
Summarizes for the French reader the critical debate on Donne's
poetic reputation, especially the work of J. E. V. Crofts, C. S. Lewis,
Joan Bennett, J. B. Leishman, and Doniphan Louthan.

☙ 706. ———. "Le Thème du Rêve dans 'Le Clitandre,' de Pierre
    Corneille, et 'The Dreame,' de Donne." RHT, 4:377–78.
Suggests that Corneille was a close acquaintance of Constantine
Huygens and possibly through him became acquainted with Donne's
poetry. In the revision of *Clitandre*, made between 1657 and 1660, Corneille inserted the dream passage, which closely resembles Donne's
poem. See also Pierre Legouis, RHT, 3 (1951):164–66.

☙ 707. LEISHMAN, J. B. "Donne and Herbert." TLS, 24 October, p.
    391.
Reply to Franklin R. Baruch, TLS, 30 May, p. 361. Points out that
not only did F. E. Hutchinson in his edition of Herbert note that line
30 of Donne's "To Mr Tilman after he had taken orders" appears in
Stanza 14 of Herbert's "The Church Porch," but also that it appears,
slightly revised, in *The Country Parson* (p. 277, l. 29).

☙ 708. MAZZEO, JOSEPH ANTHONY. "A Critique of Some Modern Theo-
    ries of Metaphysical Poetry." MP, 50:88–96.
Reprinted in *Seventeenth Century English Poetry: Modern Essays
in Criticism*, ed. William R. Keast (New York: Oxford University Press,
Inc., 1962), pp. 63–74.

Reprinted in *Discussions of John Donne*, ed. Frank Kermode (Boston: D. C. Heath & Co., 1962), pp. 118–25.

Reviews several major modern theories about the nature of metaphysical poetry, such as the notion that metaphysical poetry is a decadent and exaggerated use of the Petrarchan and troubadour tradition, is accounted for by the influence of Ramistic logic, is closely allied to the baroque, or is related closely to the emblem tradition. Approaching the problem from the perspective of sixteenth- and seventeenth-century critics, especially Giordano Bruno, Baltasar Gracián, and Emmanuele Tesauro, the author finds all modern theories wanting and at times inconsistent. Argues that "The principle of universal analogy as a poetic, or the poetic of correspondences, offers . . . a theory of metaphysical poetry which is simpler, in great harmony with the evidence, and freer from internal contradictions than the major modern theories that have yet been formulated" (p. 89). Points out that, according to the contemporary critics, "the conceit itself is the expression of a correspondence which actually obtains between objects and that, since the universe is a network of universal correspondences or analogies which unite all the apparently heterogeneous elements of experience, the most heterogeneous metaphors are justifiable. Thus the theorists of the conceit justify the predilection of the 'school of wit' for recondite and apparently strained analogies by maintaining that even the more violent couplings of dissimilars were simply expressions of the underlying unity of all things" (pp. 88–89).

≈§ 709. Novarr, David. "Donne's Letters." *TLS*, 24 October, p. 700.
Part of the long debate on Donne's "earliest-known prose letter." For a complete listing of replies and arguments, see Entry 723.

≈§ 710. Potter, George R. "Donne's Development in Pulpit Oratory as Shown in His Earliest Extant Sermons." *SCN*, 10:13.
Abstract of a paper delivered at the MLA meeting of 1951. Traces Donne's development as a preacher by indicating that his earliest sermons lack many of those positive qualities of style and sensibility that are reflected in his later sermons.

≈§ 711. Raiziss, Sona. *The Metaphysical Passion: Seven Modern American Poets and the Seventeenth-Century Tradition*. Philadelphia: University of Pennsylvania Press. xv, 327 p.
Discusses Donne throughout in this examination of the metaphysical tradition in the work of T. S. Eliot, John Crowe Ransom, Allen Tate, Robert Penn Warren, Hart Crane, Elinor Wylie, and Archibald MacLeish. States that "If, from many of Donne's poems, we remove a seventeenth-century construction here and there or revert an inversion, we discover the experience and language of contemporary writing"

(p. xiii). In Part I (pp. 3–56) the temper of metaphysical poetry is examined, its subject matter, methods, moods, and wit. In Part II (pp. 59–164) the sources of the metaphysical impulse are discussed, those critical tensions and conflicts that are parallel in the seventeenth and twentieth centuries. In Part III (pp. 167–241) the seven poets are examined in the light of the preceding comments.

❧ 712. SHAPIRO, I. A. "The Burley Letters." *TLS*, 12 September, p. 597.
Part of a long debate on Donne's "earliest-known prose letter" in the Burley MS. For a complete listing of replies and arguments, see Entry 723.

❧ 713. ———. "The Burley Letters." *TLS*, 26 September, p. 629.
Part of long debate on Donne's "earliest-known prose letter" in the Burley MS. For a complete listing of replies and arguments, see Entry 723.

❧ 714. ———. "Donne's Birthdate." *N&Q*, 197:310–13.
Presents the extant evidence for Donne's birthdate, particularly a hitherto unnoted clue found on his portrait in the Deanery of St. Paul's. Concludes that "there can be no doubt that Donne was born between 24 January and 19 June, 1572" (p. 312).

❧ 715. SIEGEL, PAUL N. "Donne's Cynical Love Poems and Spenserian Idealism." *SCN*, 10:12.
Abstract of a paper given at the MLA meeting of 1951. Maintains that Donne's love poems are not simply reactions to the idealism of Spenser but are conscious parodies of the kind of humanistic idealism *The Faerie Queene* represents.

❧ 716. SIMON, IRÈNE. "Some Problems of Donne Criticism." *RLV*, 18:317–24, 393–414; 19:14–39, 114–32, 201–2.
Reprinted, *Some Problems of Donne Criticism*, Langues Vivantes, No. 40. (Bruxelles: Marcel Didier, 1952), 76 p.
Studies Donne's poetic diction and its relationship to his attitude toward his subject matter. Challenges certain modern estimates of the poet. States, "We now begin to see that the theory of sensuous vs dissociation of sensibility really tells us more about Eliot than about Donne" (p. 137). Discusses the functional nature of Donne's images and conceits, his experimentation with techniques and syntax in his verse, and the organic structural design of his poems, all of which are considered indicative of his intellectual temperament. The following poems are given extended treatment: "The Crosse" (pp. 407–9), the two *Anniversaries* (pp. 14–30), *La Corona* (pp. 30–39), *Holy Sonnets* (pp. 114–

21), "A Hymne to God the Father" (pp. 127–29), and "Hymne to God my God, in my sicknesse" (pp. 129–31). In a postscript (pp. 201–2), the author summarizes some of the major points in *The Divine Poems*, ed. Helen Gardner (1952) and agrees, except for minor exceptions, with her conclusions.

✑§ 717. SKINNER, M. "John Donne Not in Germany in 1602." *N&Q*, 197:134.

Presents evidence to show that it was not John Donne who was the Queen's emissary in Germany in 1602, as Gosse had suggested, but Sir Daniel Dunne.

✑§ 718. SMITH, HALLETT. *Elizabethan Poetry: A Study in Conventions, Meaning, and Expression*. Cambridge: Harvard University Press. viii, 355 p.

Reprinted, Ann Arbor: University of Michigan Press, 1968 (Ann Arbor Paperbacks).

Discusses Donne's five satires (pp. 223–27). General comment on the nature of Elizabethan satire (pp. 194–256).

✑§ 719. SWINNERTON, FRANK. *The Bookman's London*. Garden City, N. Y.: Doubleday & Co., Inc. ix, 161 p.

Brief biographical sketch of Donne and Jonson, with some comparisons and contrasts (pp. 16–20). Jonson "was moralist and extrovert, as Donne was casuist, sensualist, and metaphysician" (p. 20).

✑§ 720. THOMPSON, ERIC. "The Critical Forum: 'Dissociation of Sensibility.'" *EIC*, 2:207–13.

Challenges F. W. Bateson, *EIC*, 1 (1951):302–12. Suggests that Eliot's study of F. H. Bradley is central in understanding his concept of "dissociation of sensibility." For a reply by Bateson, see *EIC*, 2:213–14.

✑§ 721. THOMSON, PATRICIA. "The Literature of Patronage, 1580–1630." *EIC*, 2:267–84.

Surveys the effects of patronage on English literature from 1580–1630. Contrasts Donne and Daniel (pp. 280–84). Argues that "the desire to please brought out the worst in Donne. In his Anniversaries and his verse letters there intrudes a note of falsity and strain which results from it: the subtlety put to false use, an irritating cleverness, an inhibiting self-consciousness" (pp. 280–81). For a reply by J. W. Saunders, see *EIC*, 3 (1953):109–14.

❧§ 722. TURNELL, MARTIN. "Donne's Quest for Unity." *Commonweal*, 57:15–18.

Revised and shortened version of his earlier article by the same title in *Nineteenth Century and After*, 147 (1950):262–74.

❧§ 723. WHITLOCK, BAIRD W. "Donne's 'First Letter.'" *TLS*, 22 August, p. 556.

Argues that Donne's "earliest-known prose letter" (see Simpson, *Study of the Prose Works of John Donne*, pp. 303–4) taken from the Burley MS. is falsely attributed to Donne. Sets up a long debate in the *TLS*; see the following: I. A. Shapiro, *TLS*, 12 September, p. 597; Baird W. Whitlock, *TLS*, 19 September, p. 613; I. A. Shapiro, *TLS*, 26 September, p. 629; Baird W. Whitlock, *TLS*, 3 October, p. 645; R. C. Bald, *TLS*, 24 October, p. 700; David Novarr, *TLS*, 24 October, p. 700; Baird W. Whitlock, *TLS*, 14 November, p. 743; R. C. Bald, *TLS*, 19 December, p. 837.

❧§ 724. ———. "The Burley Letters." *TLS*, 19 September, p. 613.

Part of a long debate on Donne's "earliest-known prose letter" in the Burley MS. For a complete listing of replies and arguments, see Entry 723.

❧§ 725. ———. "Donne's Letters." *TLS*, 3 October, p. 645.

Part of a long debate on Donne's "earliest-known prose letter" in the Burley MS. For a complete listing of replies and arguments, see Entry 723.

❧§ 726. ———. "Donne's Letters." *TLS*, 14 November, p. 743.

Part of a long debate on Donne's "earliest-known prose letter" in the Burley MS. For a complete listing of replies and arguments, see Entry 723.

1953

❧§ 727. ANON. "The Preacher of Paradox." *TLS*, 28 August, p. 548.

In part a review of the first volume of *The Sermons of John Donne*, eds. George R. Potter and Evelyn M. Simpson, but more than three-fourths of the essay is concerned with the religious sensibility of sermons. Attempts to show that, although the poems are more greatly valued by modern readers, "nothing is really missing from the sermons."

❧§ 728. ALLEN, D. C. "A Note on Donne's 'Elegy VIII.'" *MLN*, 68:238–39.

In the elegy Donne refers to the siege of Sancerra in 1573 (ll. 9–12). Reproduces a passage from Jean DeLery's *Histoire Memorable de la Ville de Sancerre* (1574) to illustrate the desperation of the occasion that Donne refers to.

◄§ 729. BALD, R. C., ED. *An Humble Supplication to Her Maiestie* by Robert Southwell. Cambridge: Cambridge University Press. xxii, 80 p.

Suggests in Appendix III, "Donne and Southwell" (pp. 70–80) that certain references in the third chapter of the *Pseudo-Martyr* possibly refer to Southwell's *An Humble Supplication*. Detailed account of Donne's relationship with the Jesuits before he chose to declare himself an Anglican. States that Donne "is almost certain to have known Southwell" (p. 78).

◄§ 730. BETHELL, S. L. "Gracián, Tesauro, and the Nature of Metaphysical Wit." *Northern Miscellany of Literary Criticism*, 1:19–40.

Reprinted in *Discussions of John Donne*, ed. Frank Kermode (Boston: D. C. Heath & Co., 1962), pp. 136–49.

While agreeing basically with Rosemond Tuve's fundamental position in *Elizabethan and Metaphysical Imagery* (1947), the author attempts "to supplement and somewhat rectify her account of metaphysical poetry by means similar to her own, that is by going to contemporary theorists" (p. 20). Since early seventeenth-century England produced almost no theorists on the nature of wit, the author gives an account of metaphysical wit and the nature of the conceit based primarily on a reading of Baltasar Gracián's *Agudeza y Arte de Ingenio* (1642) and Emanuele Tesauro's *Il Cannocchiale Aristotelico* (1654). "Gracián and Tesauro are engaged with the general nature and specific modes of the conceit rather than with the wider functions of literary criticism, so what they have to say applies almost as much to English as to Spanish or Italian poetry. There is, of course, no suggestion that they are 'sources' of anything or 'influences' on anybody. But, coming as they do after Europe had been soaked for a half a century in metaphysical wit, we might expect them to articulate the methods by which poets and other writers had been perhaps only half-consciously working" (p. 22). After outlining the major tenets of the two theorists, the author, by way of illustration, comments on the nature of wit in Donne's compass image in "A Valediction: forbidding mourning," lines 19–21 of "The good-morrow," lines 27–29 of "The Sunne Rising," and gives a rather extensive treatment of wit in "The Flea."

◄§ 731. BORGERHOFF, E. B. O. " 'Mannerism' and 'Baroque': A Simple Plea." *CL*, 5:323–31.

Argues that in spite of the controversial nature of the terms *baroque* and *Mannerism* both have a literary usefulness. Mentions Donne as a mannerist poet.

♨ 732. Brown, Nancy P. "A Note on the Imagery of Donne's 'Loves Growth.'" *MLR*, 48:324–27.

Comments on the use of recent astronomical observations in Stanza 2 of "Loves growth" and suggests that the poem was possibly composed some time after the publication of Galileo's letter by Kepler in 1611.

♨ 733. Collins, Carvel. "Donne's 'The Canonization.'" *Expl*, 12: Item 3.

Comments on the structure of the poem, "The poem divides powerfully into two halves which are mirror images of each other in their outlines though they are the exact reverse of each other in the thought and feeling which fill those outlines."

♨ 734. Davenport, A. "Notes on 'King Lear.'" *N&Q*, 198:20–22.

Points out that Edgar's speech: "A servingman, proud in heart and mind" (III, iv, ll. 87–101) may have been suggested by Donne's elegy "The Perfume" (ll. 12–60).

♨ 735. Donne, John. *The Sermons of John Donne*. Edited, with Introductions and Critical Apparatus, by George R. Potter and Evelyn M. Simpson. Berkeley and Los Angeles: University of California Press; London: Cambridge University Press, 1953–62. 10 vols.

Each volume of this edition has been entered as a separate item in the bibliography. Volume I (1953), II (1955), III (1957), IV (1959), V (1959), VI (1953), VII (1954), VIII (1956), IX (1958), X (1962).

♨ 736. ———. *The Sermons of John Donne*. Edited, with Introductions and Critical Apparatus, by George R. Potter and Evelyn M. Simpson. Vol. I. Berkeley and Los Angeles: University of California Press; London: Cambridge University Press. xiv, 354 p. 10 vols.

Pages 83–84 and 88–103 are reprinted in *John Donne: A Collection of Critical Essays*, ed. Helen Gardner (1962), pp. 137–51.

Preface (pp. v–ix); Table of Contents (pp. xi–xii); List of Illustrations (p. xiii); A List of Abbreviations Used in Introductions and Critical Apparatus (p. xiv); General Introductions: I. On the Bibliography of the Sermons (pp. 1–32), II. On the Manuscripts (pp. 33–45), III. On the Text (pp. 46–82), IV. The Literary Value of Donne's Sermons (pp. 83–103); Explanatory Notes to Text and Critical Apparatus (pp. 104–6); Abbreviations and Variant Forms Used for Scriptural References in Margins of Text (pp. 107–8); Introduction to the Sermons in Volume I (pp. 109–147); The Sermons (pp. 149–318); Notes to the Sermons in Volume I (pp. 319–44); Index to the Introductions (pp. 345–54). Nine sermons preached from April 30, 1615, to April 19, 1618.

⊸§ 737. ⸻. *The Sermons of John Donne*. Edited, with Introductions and Critical Apparatus, by Evelyn M. Simpson and George R. Potter. Vol. VI. Berkeley and Los Angeles: University of California Press; London: Cambridge University Press. vi, 374 p. 10 vols.

Table of Contents (pp. v–vi); List of Illustrations (p. viii); Introduction (pp. 1–36); The Sermons (pp. 37–364); Textual Notes to the Sermons in Volume VI (pp. 365–74). Eighteen sermons preached from May 1623 to January 1626.

⊸§ 738. DUNCAN, JOSEPH E. "The Intellectual Kinship of John Donne and Robert Browning." *SP*, 50:81–100.

In revised form appears as Chapter III of *The Revival of Metaphysical Poetry* (Minneapolis: University of Minnesota Press, 1959), pp. 50–68.

Surveys the important similarities and differences in the philosophical ideas and aesthetic theories of Donne and Browning. Points out that "Although in a few cases Browning apparently borrowed directly from Donne, he more frequently received from the earlier poet broad suggestions for his poetic structures, techniques, and imagery. Browning probably was in some measure influenced by Donne in his development of the dramatic monologue, in his experimentation with conversational metrics and idiom, and in his use of metaphysical logic, conceits, and wit" (p. 100). Browning manifested his admiration for Donne in his letters as well as in his poetry. Concludes that Browning's style "resembles Donne's more closely than that of any of his other predecessors" (p. 100).

⊸§ 739. ⸻. "The Revival of Metaphysical Poetry, 1872–1912." *PMLA*, 68:658–71.

Reprinted in *Discussions of John Donne*, ed. Frank Kermode (Boston: D. C. Heath & Co., 1962), pp. 126–35.

In revised form appears as Chapter IV of *The Revival of Metaphysical Poetry* (Minneapolis: University of Minnesota Press, 1959), pp. 113–29.

Traces the development of Donne's reputation from 1872 (Grosart's edition) to 1912 (Grierson's edition) to show that "Grierson's edition and the reviews that acclaimed it marked the end of the first stage of the metaphysical revival" (p. 658). Points out that Grierson's edition "was no doubt in part the cause of the enthusiasm about Donne that reached a scholarly climax in 1931 with the observance of the tercentenary of the poet's death. It was also the result of the increased interest in Donne's poetry and personality that began during the later decades of the nineteenth century. Similarly, Eliot's essays were not so much a new note as a sensitive formulation of ideas that had become familiar by 1912" (p. 658). Discusses in particular the late nineteenth-century fascination with Donne the man and surveys the background of Eliot's criticism.

⋖§ 740. EMSLIE, McD[ONALD]. "A Donne Setting." N&Q, 198:495.

Reports an anonymous musical setting of the first stanza of "Sweetest love, I do not goe" and inquires if anyone has discovered other seventeenth-century musical settings of Donne's verse not already generally known.

⋖§ 741. FISCH, HAROLD. "Alchemy and English Literature." PLPLS, 7: 123–36.

Discusses the importance of alchemical thinking on imaginative literature, especially during the seventeenth century, and its importance in challenging Aristotelian thinking. Comments briefly on Donne's use, both serious and satirical, of alchemical images (pp. 129–30).

⋖§ 742. GARDNER, HELEN. "Donne's 'Divine Poems.'" TLS, 30 January, p. 73.

Reply to a review of The Divine Poems (1952), that appeared in TLS, 9 January, p. 23. Defends the choice of retaining "thy little booke" in line 8 of the sixth of the La Corona sonnets and of retaining "dearth" in line 6 of "Holy Sonnet IV: At the round earths imagin'd corners, blow." (According to Grierson's numbering, this poem is "Holy Sonnet VII.")

⋖§ 743. ———. "None Other Name: John Donne on the Unity of the Church." Sobernost, 3:7–12.

Comments on Donne's attitude toward Christian unity: "Donne writes and speaks as a member of a Church which, unlike the Roman and Genevan Churches, did not hold a theory of the Church which 'unchurched' other Churches. . . . [Nevertheless, the] disunion of Christendom is plainly a cause of grief to him, and he writes on the topic more often, with more fervour and with more eloquence than do his contemporaries" (p. 9). Short biographical sketch.

⋖§ 744. HERMAN, GEORGE. "Donne's Holy Sonnets, XIV." Expl, 12: Item 18.

In part a rejection of J. C. Levenson's interpretation of the first quatrain of "Batter my heart," Expl, 11:Item 31. Sees an extended trinitarian metaphor throughout the poem—"though I cannot say that I fully realize it." Comments on various possible puns and extended verbal play in the poem. For a reply by J. C. Levenson, see Expl, 12 (1954):Item 36 and by George Knox, see Expl, 15 (1956):Item 2.

⋖§ 745. HUSAIN, ITRAT. "Donne's 'Pseudo-Martyr.'" TLS, 12 June, p. 381.

Announces that he is preparing a definitive edition of the Pseudo-Martyr and would like information concerning the copy of the treatise Donne gave to King James on January 24, 1610.

👉§ 746. HYNES, SAM L. "A Note on Donne and Aquinas." *MLR*, 48: 179–81.

Discusses the role that the aesthetics of Aquinas play in the structure of *The first Anniversary*.

👉§ 747. JOHNSON, S. F. "Donne's Satires, I." *Expl*, 11:Item 53.

In part a reply to Stanley Sultan's inquiry in *Expl*, 11:Question 6. Calls *Satyre I* a "modernized version of the traditional debate of body and soul." Sees the protagonist as sober John Donne and the antagonist as wild Jack. "The basic contrast is between naked virtue and naked lust, between soul and body."

👉§ 748. LEVENSON, J. C. "*Holy Sonnets, XIV.*" *Expl*, 11:Item 31.

Explicates the first quatrain of "Batter my heart" and maintains that the various metaphors "coherently suggest a single situation: God is a tinker, Donne a pewter vessel in the hand of God the artisan." For a reply by George Herman, see *Expl*, 12:Item 18. Levenson answers Herman in *Expl*, 12 (1954):Item 36. See also George Knox, *Expl*, 15 (1956):Item 2.

👉§ 749. LORA, JOSÉ GARCÍA. "Un Aspecto de John Donne: Su Originalidad." *Insula*, 86 (Supplemento):3–4.

States that the originality of Donne results from the fusion and assimilation of various impressions that come from a multiplicity of sources, the ability of his consciousness to fuse disparate parts of his knowledge and sensibility into one unified response. Thereby Donne expresses the total value that the total sum of these factors holds for him. While breaking all the conventions, Donne brings together the world of science and the world of letters. In advance of his time, Donne achieves a kind of symbiosis.

👉§ 750. LOWE, ROBERT LIDDELL. "Browning and Donne." *N&Q*, 198: 491–92.

Points out Browning's admiration and knowledge of Donne and states that Stanzas 5 and 6 of "Childe Roland to the Dark Tower Came" were possibly suggested by the opening stanza of "A Valediction: forbidding mourning."

👉§ 751. MALLOCH, A. E. "The Unified Sensibility and Metaphysical Poetry." *CE*, 15:95–101.

Attempts to limit more precisely the terms *unified sensibility* and *metaphysical poetry* and to indicate the relationship between the two. "The relation of the unified sensibility to metaphysical poetry is the relation of poetic process to poetic technique. Certain techniques can validly be said to distinguish Donne, Herbert, Crashaw, and Marvell as a school (and there are significant differences within that school). The unification or dissociation of sensibility, on the other hand, is a judgment on a poet's mode of creation, whatever the nature of his techniques" (pp. 100–101).

◄§ 752. MATSUURA, KAICHI. *A Study of Donne's Imagery: A Revelation of His Outlook on the World and His Vision of a Universal Christian Monarchy.* Tokyo: Kenkyusha Ltd. xiii, 157 p.

Studies the imagery in both the poetry and prose, especially the sermons, and attempts to depict Donne's vision and outlook on man and his universe. Donne is said to be "not merely a poet and preacher, but also a kind of Hebraic prophet who did something towards the making of the destiny of the modern 'chosen people' to play the most important part in the vital task of our century to regenerate and reorganize the world" (p. 157). Attempts "to gather those images which are drawn from matters belonging to his Scholastic views of the universe and man and his outlook upon the mundane world, and to arrange them in coordination to see whether we cannot join these pieces into a whole picture of his conception of the whole world" (p. vi). Ten chapters: (1) The Ptolemaic Universe Imagery, (2) The New Philosophy and the Decay of Man and the World, (3) Man and Angels, (4) The Soul and Body, (5) Love, Friendship, and Universal Brotherhood, (6) Nature and Law, (7) Donne's Conception of Monarchy as the Ideal Form of Human Society, (8) Rhetorical Parallelism Between Israel and England, (9) Donne's Vision of an Imperialistic Mission for England Manifested in His Rhetorical Conceits, (10) John Donne and the Modern World-Policy of the Anglo-Saxon Nations.

◄§ 753. MILGATE, W. "References to John Donne." *N&Q*, 198:421–24.

Adds early references to Donne to his earlier listing in *N&Q*, 195 (1950):229–31, 246–47, 290–92, 381–83. "The references to Donne, however laudatory, offer depressing evidence of the lack of serious and discriminating discussion of what to us seem to be his essential qualities as a poet, or even of his poems in the light of what in contemporary aesthetic might have been considered important" (p. 424). Corrects several misprints in his earlier article. See also D. J. Drinkwater, *N&Q*, 199 (1954):514–15.

◄§ 754. MORAN, BERNA. "Some Notes on Donne's Attitude to the Problem of Body and Soul." *Ingiliz Filolojisi Dergisi*, 3:69–76.

Reviews Donne's changing attitudes toward the relationship of the body and the soul. Concludes that "from the metaphysical point of view the relation of body and soul is natural, but after the Original Sin it has become, mortally unnatural—hence the body's corrupting influence. The body was considered by Donne, in his middle years, also as a means of inheriting Original Sin, but later he dismissed this view and cleared the body of such responsibility. In his sermons both the body and soul are equally innocent and equally responsible in this respect" (p. 76).

⥲§ 755. MORRIS, DAVID. *The Poetry of Gerard Manley Hopkins and T. S. Eliot in the Light of the Donne Tradition: A Comparative Study.* Schweizer Anglistische Arbeiten, 33 Band. Bern: Francke. 144 p.

Analyzes the debt of modern poetry to Donne—particularly the poetry of Hopkins and Eliot, who are discussed in the light of the Donne tradition. The basic elements of the tradition discussed are intellectual complexity, "passionate thinking"—the fusion of thought and feeling, wit, the conceit, and the analytical method. Stresses in particular how Eliot and Hopkins are like Donne in certain technical matters.

⥲§ 756. MOURGUES, ODETTE DE. *Metaphysical Baroque & Précieux Poetry.* Oxford: The Clarendon Press. vii, 184 p.

Compares those French poets whom the author considers *metaphysical*—a term she distinguishes from *baroque* and *précieux*—and certain late sixteenth- and seventeenth-century English poets, in particular Donne. Suggests that "there exists in French poetry, not a metaphysical school, but a metaphysical 'line' beginning as early as 1544 with Scève's *Délie*, dodging the Pléiade, running in an underground way through scientific poetry, coming to the surface again at the end of the sixteenth century and giving its last scattered manifestations in some minor poets of the mid-seventeenth century" (p. 10).

⥲§ 757. POTTER, GEORGE R. "Problems in the Editing of Donne's Sermons," in *Editing Donne and Pope* by George R. Potter and John Butt, pp. 1–10. Los Angeles: William Andrews Clark Memorial Library.

States basic views on the nature of textual criticism. Outlines some of the major problems that Evelyn Simpson and he encountered in their editing of Donne's sermons and gives the rationale behind many of the final decisions and solutions to a number of those problems.

⥲§ 758. ROSS, MALCOLM M. "A Note on the Metaphysicals." *HudR,* 6:106–33.

Discusses the decline of Christian poetic sensibility in the seventeenth century. Argues that this change can best be seen in "those Christian symbols which at one and the same time are rooted in dogma and which convey—or seek to convey—the immediate sense of existence" (p. 107). Comments on the breakdown of the Christian symbol from analogy to mere metaphor as a result of the reform of Christian dogma. In Donne, "true analogy and mere metaphor co-exist in an uneasy, although fruitful, state of tension" (p. 112).

✒§ 759. SAUNDERS, J. W. "Donne and Daniel." *EIC*, 3:109–14.
    In part a reply to Patricia Thomson, *EIC*, 2 (1952):267–84, in which the author challenges the linking of Donne and Daniel together as professional writers. "Donne ... is fundamentally the courtly amateur, fighting for self-realization, while Daniel is always the professional, secure in a backwater of patronage. To talk of the 'frustrations and anxieties' caused by Donne's unhappiness as a 'public' poet is either to confine the point to a few transitional poems that don't matter, or to fall into a contradiction of terms" (p. 114).

✒§ 760. SPARROW, JOHN. "More Donne." *TLS*, 13 March, p. 169.
    Two brief notes: (1) suggests that a Platin folio of 1599, *Annales Magistratuum et Provinciarum SPQR*, compiled by Stephanus Vivandus Pighius Campensis, bearing the bookplate of the Bridgewater Library, was probably owned by Donne; (2) comments on the Latin inscription that appears under the engraving of Donne in his shroud on the frontispiece of *Deaths Duell*.

✒§ 761. SULTAN, STANLEY. "Donne's *Satires*, I." *Expl*, 11:Question 6.
    Asks if there is some allegorical or symbolic meaning at the center of the poem. For a reply by S. F. Johnson, see *Expl*, 11:Item 53.

✒§ 762. TATE, ALLEN. "The Point of Dying: Donne's 'Virtuous Men.'" *SR*, 61:76–81.
    Reprinted in *The Forlorn Demon* (Chicago: Henry Regnery Co., 1953), pp. 171–76.
    Reprinted in *Collected Essays* (Denver: Alan Swallow Publisher, 1959), pp. 547–52.
    Detailed analysis of the first two stanzas of "A Valediction: forbidding mourning."

✒§ 763. WHITLOCK, BAIRD W. "'Cabal' in Donne's Sermons." *N&Q*, 198:153.
    Suggests that Donne coined a new meaning for the familiar word *cabal* in his sermon "On Trinity Sunday," No. 41 of the *LXXX Sermons* (p. 411) which should be recorded as a first in the *OED*.

✒§ 764. WRIGHT, HERBERT G. "Some Sixteenth and Sevententh Century Writers on the Plague." *Essays and Studies*, n.s., 6:41–55.
    Briefly discusses Donne's experience of and reaction to the plague of 1625 (p. 47).

1954

ఆక్ర్ 765. ADAMS, ROBERT MARTIN. "Donne and Eliot: Metaphysicals."
KR, 16:278–91.

Reprinted in revised form as "Metaphysical Poets: Ancient and Modern," in *Strains of Discord* (Ithaca: Cornell University Press, 1958), pp. 105–20.

Compares Donne and Eliot as metaphysical poets. "A good deal has been made of Mr. Eliot's phrase 'dissociation of sensibility' as describing an element which unites the two metaphysical ages, though precisely on what terms has never been made too clear. Eliot seems to have meant at different times that Donne did *not* suffer from dissociation of sensibility and was therefore a model for our times, or that he *did* and was therefore akin to them. The confusion is significant, not merely careless; the rather complex fact seems to be that Donne did suffer from 'dissociation of sensibility,' exploited the fact energetically, and felt rather strongly that he shouldn't—being in all respects like Eliot" (p. 280). Both poets are said to manipulate dramatic contexts, and Eliot's use of Frazer, Weston, and others is compared to Donne's use of religion and the New Science. Concludes that "a basic psychological element in the metaphysical style of Eliot, as of Donne, seems to be the assertion of temperament over logical or conventional categories; and this assertion cannot help involving a poet in self-dramatization" (p. 289).

ఆక్ర్ 766. ALLEN, D. C. "Donne's 'The Will.'" MLN, 69:559–60.

Suggests that there is a possible analogue to "The Will" in *Grunnii Corococtae porcelli testamentum*, published by Soncinus in 1505 and reprinted in 1520 and 1522. This treatise was inserted by Alexander Brassicanus in his *Proverbiorum symmicta* in 1529 and was frequently reissued thereafter.

ఆక్ర్ 767. BENNETT, J. A. W. "A Note on Donne's *Crosse*." RES, n.s., 5:168–69.

Gives various sources for Donne's conceits in lines 17–24 of "The Crosse." Concludes that "all of the likenesses that Donne here assembles were noticed and collected by early Christian writers" (p. 169). Suggests that perhaps Donne derived his collection from Lipsius's *De Cruce* (I, ix).

ఆక్ర్ 768. BRYAN, R. A. "A Sidelight on Donne's 17C Literary Reputation." SCN, Summer:21.

Abstract of a talk given at SAMLA in 1953. Based upon an examination of commonplace books in the Folger's Halliwell Collection, the author points out that apparently Donne's elegies, followed by the shorter love lyrics, were most popular during the seventeenth century.

Suggests that this in part explains the decline of Donne's reputation as a serious poet during the century. For a reply by R. G. Howarth, see *N&Q*, n.s., 5 (1958):43.

◆§ 769. ———. "A Sidelight on Donne's Seventeenth-Century Literary Reputation." *SAB*, 19:11.

Another abstract of a talk given at SAMLA in 1953. See Bryan, *SCN*, Summer:21.

◆§ 770. BUTOR, MICHEL. "Sur 'Le Progrès de l'Âme' de John Donne." *Cahiers du Sud*, 38:276–83.

Explication of *The Progresse of the Soule*. Concludes that Donne is being sarcastic about Christianity in general. Relates the poem to Donne's life.

◆§ 771. COFFIN, CHARLES M. "Donne's Divinity." *KR*, 16:292–98.

In part a review of Vols. I and VI of *The Sermons of John Donne*, eds. George R. Potter and Evelyn M. Simpson (1953). Essay develops into an independent study of Donne as preacher. Maintains that Donne did not need to develop technically as a preacher after his ordination; he learned what to preach, not how. In particular, he learned to preach more emphatically on God's immanence than on His transcendence.

◆§ 772. CRUTTWELL, PATRICK. *The Shakespearean Moment and Its Place in the Poetry of the 17th Century*. London: Chatto & Windus Ltd. 262 p.

Argues that at the end of the sixteenth century Donne and Shakespeare were both participating with the same qualities in the richest moment in English poetry. "The mature Shakespearean or metaphysical style— which, it must be repeated, is the same style used for different purposes and in different *milieux*—emerged in the last years of the sixteenth century and remained the most fruitful style for the first few decades of the next." Discusses some of the common qualities of both poets: both are dramatic, both recognized the complex, both juxtaposed clashing elements. The new style is characterized by the abandonment of poetic diction, by a greater concentration of meaning, by fewer words, by complex syntax and rhythm, by a sense of humor and irony, by Donne's total rejection of classical mythology. Discusses the *Anniversaries* and Shakespeare's last plays as bridges between the human and divine, the body and the soul. The common quality is their inclusiveness—their ability to "concentrate on to a single point a wide range of different orders of experience" (p. 105). Discusses the conditions of life that allowed for the building of bridges between all subjects and things and elaborates on what caused the end of the metaphysical style—Puritanism, the Commonwealth Interregnum, the resultant differences in thinking about the human condition.

◄§ 773. DONNE, JOHN. *The Sermons of John Donne.* Edited, with Introductions and Critical Apparatus, by Evelyn M. Simpson and George R. Potter. Vol. VII. Berkeley and Los Angeles: University of California Press; London: Cambridge University Press. vi, 463 p. 10 vols.

Table of Contents (pp. v–vi); List of Illustrations (p. vii); Introduction (pp. 1–48); The Sermons (pp. 49–451); Textual Notes to the Sermons in Volume VII (pp. 453–63). Eighteen sermons preached between 29 January 1625/26 and Whitsunday, 1627. "In this volume and in Volume VIII we find Donne at the summit of his power as a preacher" (p. 1).

◄§ 774. DRINKWATER, D. J. "More References to John Donne." *N&Q*, 199:514–15.

Adds several more references to Donne to W. Milgate's list in *N&Q*, 195 (1950):229–31, 246–47, 290–92, 381–83 and in *N&Q*, 198 (1953): 421–24. Agrees with Milgate that Donne's influence "is more far-reaching than profound, the trend being to bizarre conceit in many who lacked the intellect and creative ability to render this poetry" (p. 515).

◄§ 775. EVANS, B. IFOR. *Literature and Science.* London: George Allen and Unwin Ltd. 114 p.

Discusses Donne's "creative scepticism" (pp. 19–20). Donne is said to be "the first outstanding creative writer to be disturbed by the new learning in science and astronomy" (p. 19).

◄§ 776. GRANSDEN, K. W. *John Donne.* Men and Books Series. London: Longmans, Green and Co., Ltd. viii, 197 p.

General introductory study of the life and work of Donne for the general reader. Announces that this study is not a reassessment of Donne but rather is intended to serve as a "companion" for the general reader. Divided into five major parts: (1) the life (pp. 1–48); (2) the metaphysical school (pp. 49–53); (3) the secular poems (pp. 55–124); (4) the divine poems (pp. 125–47); and (5) the prose works (pp. 149–91). Selected bibliography.

◄§ 777. HUNT, CLAY. *Donne's Poetry: Essays in Literary Analysis.* New Haven: Yale University Press; London: Geoffrey Cumberlege, Oxford University Press. xiii, 256 p.

Proposes "to take a few poems and scrutinize them in detail, and then proceed from these particularities to some general conclusions and speculations about Donne's work and about Donne himself" (p. vii). Close readings of the following poems (pp. 1–118): "The Indifferent," "Elegie XIX," "Love's Alchymie," "The Blossome," "The good-morrow," "The Canonization," and "Hymne to God my God, in my sicknesse." Numerous other poems are mentioned briefly. In "Some Conclusions" (pp. 118–201), the author evaluates Donne's artistry and sensibility, outlines the major qualities of his verse, and challenges several current critical notions about the nature of Donne's genius. Concludes that "Certainly a solid reason behind the fad of Donne's poetry in our time is that his work dramatizes, with exciting vividness and conclusive particularity, the truth that not only love and matter but also abstract thought and art—in fact, to summarize what, for all practical philosophic purposes, this series adds up to, that we ourselves—are much odder than we thought" (p. 201). Notes (pp. 205–53). Index: Works by Donne Discussed (pp. 255–56).

⋙ 778. KERMODE, FRANK. "Donne Allusions in Howell's Familiar Letters." N&Q, 199:337.

Notes two possible allusions to Donne in James Howell's *Epistolae Ho-Elianae*, one from "Goodfriday, 1613. Riding Westward" and one from "The Canonization."

⋙ 779. KEYNES, GEOFFREY. "John Donne's Sermons." TLS, 28 May, p. 351.

Describes a manuscript acquired at a sale of the remaining portion of the Bridgewater Library (Sotheby's, March 19, 1951) in which, scattered among miscellaneous items, are eight of Donne's sermons. See also Keynes *Bibliography of Donne* (3d ed.), pp. 25–26.

⋙ 780. KUHLMANN, HELENE. "John Donne, Betrachtungen über Elend und Grösse der Menschen." NS, n.s., 3:452–58.

Quotes frequently from the *Devotions* to show how they can help us with modern problems. Donne is said to view all people as on constant move, through misery, on the way to God. Donne's thoughts are not so much philosophical speculations as they are reflections of a simple soul that loves God.

⋙ 781. LEVENSON, J. C. "Donne's 'Holy Sonnets,' XIV." Expl, 12:Item 36.

In part a reply to George Herman, *Expl*, 12 (1953):Item 18, who attacked Levenson's earlier explication of "Batter my heart" in *Expl*, 11 (1953):Item 31. Reconsiders several of his earlier statements. See also George Knox, *Expl*, 15(1956):Item 2.

⋙ 782. LEWIS, C. S. *English Literature in the Sixteenth Century Excluding Drama*. The Oxford History of English Literature, eds. F. P. Wilson and Bonamy Dobrée, III. Oxford: The Clarendon Press. vi, 696 p.

Donne is discussed in several places. Short discussion of Donne's *Satyres* (pp. 469–70) in which Donne and Lodge are contrasted and

Donne and Hall are compared as formal satirists. Describes the satires as being shaggy, unmetrical in versification, disgusting in diction, obscure in thought, and generally tedious. Donne's early poetry is discussed under three categories (pp. 546–51): (1) the Ovidian pieces; (2) those poems which "though not all satiric, all use the violently contorted metre which one kind of Elizabethan satirist favoured" (p. 547); (3) the lyrics. Contrasts Donne and Shakespeare in both versification and temper and concludes that the essential feature of Donne's poetry is *Sprechgesang*: "a speaking tone against a background of imagined metrical pattern" (p. 550). Bibliographical note (pp. 639–40).

◄§ 783. McCANN, ELEANOR M. "Donne and St. Teresa on the Ecstasy." *HLQ*, 17:125–32.

Attributes no direct debt of Donne to Saint Teresa but points out the many similarities between "The Extasie" and the middle portions of Teresa's *Vida*. Concludes, "Although far apart in history, politics, and religion, Donne and Teresa have left records of their ecstatic experience which illuminates not only the life of love but each other as well" (p. 132).

◄§ 784. MARTZ, LOUIS L. *The Poetry of Meditation: A Study in English Religious Literature of the Seventeenth Century*. Yale Studies in English, 125. New Haven: Yale University Press; London: Oxford University Press. xiv, 375 p.
Revised ed., 1962.
Pages 135–44 are reprinted in *The Modern Critical Spectrum*, eds. Gerald Jay Goldberg and Nancy Marmer Goldberg (1962), pp. 244–50.
Pages 211–48 (with revisions from the 2d ed.) are reprinted in *Seventeenth Century English Poetry: Modern Essays in Criticism*, ed. William Keast (1962), pp. 141–17
Pages 220–23 and 228–48 are reprinted in *John Donne: A Collection of Critical Essays*, ed. Helen Gardner (1962), pp. 152–70.
The aim of this study is "to modify the view of literary history which sees a 'Donne tradition' in English religious poetry. It suggests instead a 'meditative tradition' which found its first notable example not in Donne but in Robert Southwell" (p. 3). Sees Donne's originality, "not as a meteoric burst, but part of a normal, central tendency of religious life in his time" (p. 2). Suggests that the metaphysical poets, though widely different, are "drawn together by resemblances that result, basically, from the common practice of certain methods of religious meditation" (p. 2). Donne is mentioned throughout, but in particular the following may be noted: a discussion of the structural relationship between the *Holy Sonnets* and Ignatian meditation (pp. 43–56); a discussion of *La Corona* poems in the light of contemporary meditative practices (pp. 107–12); comments on Donne's meditations on death (pp.

137–44); discussion of the relationship between Donne and Herbert (pp. 143–49, 261–69) and between Donne and Sidney (pp. 266–69). Chapter 6, "John Donne in Meditation: the *Anniversaries*" (pp. 211–48) is a revised version of an article that appeared in *ELH*, 14 (1947): 247–73. Appendix 2 (pp. 353–56) is entitled "The Dating and Significance of Donne's *Anniversaries*."

785. POTTER, GEORGE REUBEN. "John Donne: Poet to Priest," in *Five Gayley Lectures 1947–1954*, eds. L. B. Bennion and G. R. Potter, pp. 105–26. Berkeley and Los Angeles: University of California Press; London: Cambridge University Press.

Discusses Donne's development as a preacher, how in time the truths of religion that he held intellectually became part of his deepest convictions and sensibility. Traces briefly Donne's growing sense and adaptation of his religious sensibilities to the needs and circumstances of the various audiences to which he preached. "Donne did not achieve this balance of tactfulness with sincerity, of adaptability with artistic integrity, merely by learning the tricks of the trade, by perfecting a technique; although he of course did that too. But his main effort involved a study of himself and a study of people whom he was addressing" (p. 112). Concludes with a study of Donne's prose style, how as preacher he "retrained himself—as an artist" (p. 119).

786. ROPE, H. E. G. "The Real John Donne." *Irish Monthly* (Dublin), 183:229–34.

Argues that Donne was a formal apostate and heretic. "It is theologically impossible for an instructed Catholic to lose the Faith inculpably, and without a mortal sin against Faith." Maintains that "it is utterly beside the mark to speak of the 'holiness' of Donne, who persisted in apostasy" (p. 230).

787. SAWIN, LEWIS. "The Earliest Use of 'Autumnal.'" *MLN*, 69: 558–59.

Points out that the earliest recorded use of the word *autumnal*, meaning past the prime of life, given in the *OED* is 1656 in a work entitled "A Discourse of auxiliary Beauty." Cites Donne's use of the word in "The Autumnall" (title and l. 2) and Jonson's use of it in *Epicoene* as certainly antedating 1656.

788. SHARP, ROBERT L. "Donne's 'Good-Morrow' and Cordiform Maps." *MLN*, 69:493–95.

Comments on the imagery of lines 12–18 of the poem. Donne is saying "that each heart [of the two lovers] is a hemisphere: the two hearts together make one world" (p. 495). Points out that existing cordiform maps depict such hearts, "each a hemisphere and both together forming one world" (p. 495).

◄§ 789. STEVENSON, DAVID L. "Among His Private Friends, John Donne?" SCN, 12:7.
Abstract of a paper given at the MLA meeting of 1953. Points out three hitherto unnoticed borrowings from Shakespeare: (1) Metempsychosis, Stanza 5 (Shakespeare's Sonnet 129, ll. 1–2); (2) "Lovers infinitenesse" (Romeo and Juliet, II, ii, ll. 126–35); and (3) "Death be not proud" (King John, IV, xv, l. 87). "In each instance of borrowing, Donne creates a wholly self-contained passage, existing in its own right. Yet in each case he enriches both his own work and that of Shakespeare by a variety of competitive intellectualism."

◄§ 790. UMBACH, HERBERT H. "When a Poet Prays." Cresset, 17:15–23.
Discusses the literary significance of Donne's prayers, surveys Donne's own comments on the nature of prayer, and examines several representative prayers.

◄§ 791. WALLERSTEIN, RUTH. "Sir John Beaumont's 'Crowne of Thornes,' A Report." JEGP, 53:410–34.
Brief comparison of Beaumont and Donne (pp. 432–34). Points out that both "share a large area of culture, of intimate habit of thought and imagination than Spenser and Beaumont" (p. 432).

◄§ 792. WARNKE, FRANK J. "Two Previously Unnoted MSS. of Poems by Lord Herbert of Cherbury." N&Q, 199:141–42.
Discusses the authorship of "Inconstancy" and dismisses Donne as the likely author.

◄§ 793. WARREN, AUSTIN. "The Very Reverend Dr. Donne." KR, 16:268–77.
Suggests that Donne was neither a rake nor a saint. Presents Donne as a "Reformed Christian," who "had passed from Rome through scepticism to a Christianity partly pragmatic, partly personal—which is Anglican negatively or politically rather than positively" (p. 270). Discusses Donne as a student of the Bible and comments on the literary merits of his sermons. "Donne was not an original or systematic theologian; but he was a great preacher: I venture to think a greater preacher than poet, able to express in that medium, and in that middle period of his life, a range and depth which the poems rarely reach" (p. 276).

◈§ 794. WHITLOCK, BAIRD W. "The Dean and the Yeoman." N&Q, 199:374–75.

Records an incident, found in the *Repetory Book* of the Court of Alderman in the London Records Office dated 12 March 1629/30, of Donne's having a yeoman arrested for refusing to kneel during divine services. Mentions Donne's apparent conviction that kneeling during prayer is necessary for salvation (*LXXX Sermons*, pp. 72–73).

◈§ 795. ———. "John Syminges, A Poet's Step-Father." N&Q, 199: 421–24, 465–67.

Biographical account of Donne's first stepfather. Makes minor corrections in N&Q, 200 (1955):132–33.

◈§ 796. WILEY, MARGARET. "The Poetry of Donne: Its Interest and Influence Today." *Essays and Studies*, n.s., 7:78–104.

Comments on "some of the main points of likeness between the earlier poets—particularly Donne—and their present-day descendants" (p. 80). Maintains that the kinship between the seventeenth and the twentieth centuries "penetrates far deeper than that relatively superficial kind: rooted as it is in broadly similar social conditions, which, in the literature of both ages, evoked certain responses that correspond strikingly in spirit and technique" (pp. 79–80). Compares Donne to Eliot, Yeats, and Dylan Thomas.

1955

◈§ 797. BLUNDEN, EDMUND. "Some Seventeenth-Century Latin Poems by English Writers." *UTQ*, 25:10–22.

Translation of Donne's Latin poem to Dr. Andrews, "De libro cum mutuaretur &c." with a brief comment.

◈§ 798. BUSH, DOUGLAS. "Seventeenth-Century Poets and the Twentieth Century." *Annual Bulletin of the Modern Humanities Research Association*, No. 27:16–28.

Traces the fortunes of the Donne revival from the nineteenth through the twentieth century and gives reasons why Donne and the other metaphysical poets achieved such extraordinary attention from both scholars and practicing poets, especially during the 1920s and 1930s, and why there is somewhat of a decline in interest since that period, especially among practicing poets. Considers the effects of the metaphysical revival on the fate of Milton in the twentieth century and concludes that "Milton, far from having been dislodged from his throne, appears to sit more securely than ever on a throne that has partly new and even more solid foundations. Amateur criticism restored Donne and banished Milton, scholarly criticism kept Donne and restored Milton" (pp. 26–27).

✒§ 799. COLERIDGE, SAMUEL TAYLOR. *Coleridge on the Seventeenth Century.* Edited by Roberta Florence Brinkley with an introductory essay by Louis I. Bredvold. Durham, N. C.: Duke University Press. xxxviii, 704 p.

Collection of Coleridge's comments on the seventeenth century arranged under seven headings: (1) the seventeenth century in general, (2) the philosophers, (3) the divines, (4) science, (5) literary prose, (6) poetry, and (7) the drama. Donne is mentioned throughout. Note in particular Coleridge's comments on Donne's sermons (pp. 163–205), the letters (pp. 428–31), and the poetry (pp. 519–30).

✒§ 800. DAVENPORT, A. "An Early Reference to John Donne." *N&Q,* 200:12.

Suggests three references to Donne's *Satyre IV* in William Fennor's *The Counter's Commonwealth.*

✒§ 801. DONNE, JOHN. *The Sermons of John Donne.* Edited, with Introductions and Critical Apparatus, by George R. Potter and Evelyn M. Simpson. Vol. II. Berkeley and Los Angeles: University of California Press; London: Cambridge University Press. x, 466 p. 10 vols.

Preface to Volume II (pp. v–vi); George R. Potter, 1895–1954 (p. vii); Table of Contents (pp. ix–x); List of Illustrations (p. xi); Introduction (pp. 1–46); The Sermons (pp. 47–363); Appendix A: The Ellesmere Manuscript and Its Significance Relative to the Sermons (pp. 365–71); Appendix B: Earlier Text of Sermon No. 11 (pp. 373–90); Textual Notes to the Sermons of Volume II (pp. 391–462); Corrigenda and Addenda for Volume I (pp. 463–66). Eighteen sermons preached at Lincoln's Inn and Whitehall.

✒§ 802. ELMEN, PAUL. "John Donne's Dark Lantern." *PBSA,* 49:181–86.

Argues that it is more likely that Donne wrote "darke lanterne" rather than "glasse lanterne" in line 26 of "The Litanie."

✒§ 803. EMSLIE, MACDONALD. "Barclay Squire and Grierson's Donne." *N&Q,* 200:12–13.

Points out several errors in Squire's musical transcriptions contained in Grierson's *The Poems of John Donne* (1912).

✒§ 804. ESCH, ARNO. *Englische Religiöse Lyrik des 17. Jahrhunderts: Studien zu Donne, Herbert, Crashaw, Vaughan.* Tübingen: Max Niemeyer. xi, 225 p.

Studies the problems of religious poetry of the period by analyzing and comparing the works of individual poets. Chapter II deals specifically with Donne's poetry. Maintains that the religious poetry cannot be understood without a knowledge of the love poetry. Points out likenesses and differences. Comments on the fact that in the religious poetry Donne uses several different forms: the sonnet, the verse epistle in heroic couplets, and the litany. Compares the *La Corona* sonnets with the *Holy Sonnets* and finds distinct differences. Analyzes the verse epistles and the litany forms and concludes that for his religious poetry Donne could not use the experimental verse forms found in the *Songs and Sonets* because the content of the poems demanded traditional forms.

◄§ 805. Evans, Maurice. "Donne and the Elizabethans," in *English Poetry in the Sixteenth Century*, pp. 161–75. London: Hutchinson's University Library.

Challenges the notion that Donne was "the great iconoclast who, single-handed, overthrew the tyranny of Petrarch and replaced the outworn conventions of Elizabethan poetry by a new strain of realism" (p. 161). Relates Donne to the main stream of Elizabethan poetry and defines what is original in his verse. States that "Donne's greatest achievement was to develop the dramatic impulse in non-dramatic poetry" (p. 168).

◄§ 806. Francis, W. Nelson. "Donne's 'Goodfriday 1613. Riding Westward.' " *Expl*, 13:Item 21.

Paraphrase of the poem. Concludes, "The notably powerful aspect of the poem derives from the way in which an apparently trivial and meaningless circumstance—riding westward on Good Friday—is heightened, first by cosmological imagery, then by layer upon layer of symbolic meaning."

◄§ 807. Grenander, M. E. "Donne's 'Holy Sonnets,' XII." *Expl*, 13: Item 42.

Comments on the paradoxes in "Holy Sonnet XII: Why are wee by all creatures waited on?" The crowning paradox is that "all things except man, even God, are 'creatures' in that they are all subservient to man. But in another sense all things, except the Creator, including man, are 'Creatures' in that they are all creations of God."

◄§ 808. Groom, Bernard. "The Spenserian Tradition and Its Rivals up to 1660," in *The Diction of Poetry from Spenser to Bridges*, pp. 48–73. Toronto: University of Toronto Press; London: Geoffrey Cumberlege, Oxford University Press.

Studies the diction of English poetry from Spenser to Bridges and describes Donne as an anomaly. "On the historical aspects of Donne's diction two points are clear. One is the general truth of the statement made by Grierson and Smith that 'Donne's avoidance of words felt at once to be "poetic" is almost without parallel in English poets'; the other is the attraction which his 'strong lines' and 'masculine expression' exercise at certain times—though not always" (p. 64). Insists that a close examination of Donne's diction "shows his position to be similar to that of Robert Browning: that is, he read widely in other men's poetry, reproducing various words and phrases—including 'poetic' ones —but giving to what he borrowed the impress of his own character" (p. 65). Suggests that the "novelty of Donne's diction lies largely in its grammar; he uses words according to the logic of his meaning, not for metaphor" (p. 65).

❧ 809. MALLOCH, A. E. "Donne's *Pseudo-Martyr* and *Catalogus Librorum Aulicorum.*" *MLN*, 70:174–75.
Argues that if Items 2 and 5 of the *Catalogus* are read, as he suggests certain passages of the *Pseudo-Martyr* should be read, not as statements of bitter anti-Protestantism but as indications of Donne's "willingness to recognize the imperfections of that cause which has his allegiance," then Mrs. Simpson's dating of the *Catalogus* as 1604 or 1605 is historically convincing and decisive.

❧ 810. NOVAK, MAX. "An Unrecorded Reference in a Poem by Donne." *N&Q*, 200:471–72.
Points out a possible reference to Campion's *Lorde's Mask* in "An Epithalamion, Or mariage Song on the Lady Elizabeth, and Count Palatine."

❧ 811. SAWIN, LEWIS. "Donne's 'The Canonization,' 7." *Expl*, 13:Item 31.
Comments on line 7 of the poem: "Or the Kings reall, or his stamped face." Points out that *reall* is a Spanish coin, frequently bearing the king's image. "The line has two meanings: 'the king's actual face and his face on a coin,' and 'the king's royal coin, his stamped face'."

❧ 812. SLEIGHT, RICHARD. "John Donne: 'A Nocturnall Upon S. Lucies Day, Being the Shortest Day,' " in *Interpretations: Essays on Twelve English Poems*, ed. John Wain, pp. 31–58. London: Routledge and Kegan Paul, Ltd.
Reprinted, 1962.
Close reading of the poem. Sees it primarily as a movement from despair to acceptance of death. Discusses the style of the poem to illustrate how Donne's roughness reinforces the statement of the poem.

✑§ 813. SPARROW, JOHN. "Donne's Books in the Middle Temple." *TLS*, 29 July, p. 436; 5 August, p. 451.

Describes and classifies seventy-eight books from Donne's library recently discovered in the Library of the Middle Temple, presumably bought *en bloc* soon after Donne's death.

✑§ 814. SYPHER, WYLIE. *Four Stages of Renaissance Style: Transformations in Art and Literature 1400–1700.* Anchor A44. Garden City, N.Y.: Doubleday & Co., Inc. 312 p.

Studies the development of Renaissance style from 1400 to 1700, showing relationships between literature and the fine arts. Donne and other metaphysical poets are discussed as examples of the mannerist style. In art history, Mannerism "represents a 'formal dissolution of a style'—the style of renaissance art founded upon the concepts of proportion and harmony and unity" (p. 102). In literature, this style exemplifies Eliot's notion of "dissociation of sensibility" and Grierson's idea that Donne "and the truly 'metaphysical' poets of the seventeenth century are 'more aware of disintegration than of comprehensive harmony'" (p. 103). Discusses, among others, the following traits that make Donne a Mannerist: tortured thoughts, extraordinary ambiguities, unexpected points of view, perverse and equivocal images and metaphors, an intellectual manner, dramatic self-awareness, and a subjective view of reality.

✑§ 815. WARNKE, FRANK J. "Marino and the English Metaphysicals." *SRen*, 2:160–75.

Points out that "any sequential reading of Donne and Marino reveals differences in techniques and visions which are as striking as the similarities, and in some ways more striking" (p. 160). Their various uses of the paradox epitomize the differences between the two. Marino's paradoxes are usually ornamental, verbal, incidental; Donne's are integral. Maintains that Marino's style "differs from that of the school of Donne in its sensuous diction, in its diffuse imagery, in its tangential structure, and in its tendency toward exclamation rather than argumentation" (p. 169). Also, Marino's poetry differs from that of the metaphysicals "in its use of mythological reference and pastoral machinery, in its auditory smoothness, in its sensuous imagery, and in its diffuse metaphorical patterns. It differs further in its continued use of the characteristic Renaissance forms of epic, sonnet, and madrigal" (p. 174). The true English equivalents of Marino are Giles and Phineas Fletcher.

✑§ 816. WATSON, GEORGE. "Hobbes and the Metaphysical Conceit." *JHI*, 16:558–62.

Argues that the metaphysical conceit was killed by a change in critical theory and illustrates this change by referring to the critical writings of Hobbes. In time, the conceit was dismissed as mere sound. For a reply by T. M. Gang, see *JHI*, 17 (1956):418–21.

⋙ 817. WHITLOCK, BAIRD W. "Ye Curioust Schooler in Cristendom." *RES*, n.s., 6:365–71.

Presents the text of a letter written in 1625 by Edward Alleyn to his father-in-law, John Donne. Considers what evidence it affords of Donne's character in his later years and particularly his attitude toward his son-in-law. "Its importance lies in its being the only known letter to Donne which paints a completely dark picture of him" (p. 365). For two corrections in the transcription, see *RES*, n.s., 8 (1957):420–21.

⋙ 818. ———. "Donne at St. Dunstan's." *TLS*, 16 September, p. 548; 23 September, p. 564.

Study of references to Donne found in the *Churchwardens' Account* and the *Vestry Minutes* of St. Dunstan's in the London Guildhall Library. "They show the close relationship between St. Dunstan's and Donne's other parish in Sevenoaks; they show children being sent to Virginia, another of Donne's interests; they show the business relationships of friends of Donne like Sir Julius Caesar, Sir Robert Rich, and Izaak Walton with the parish; and they show the interests of the church in giving help to needy sailors of all countries and to unmarried mothers and orphans" (p. 564).

⋙ 819. ———. "John Syminges." *N&Q*, 200:132–33.

Minor corrections of the author's biographical sketch of Donne's stepfather in *N&Q*, 199 (1954):421–24, 465–67.

⋙ 820. ———. "The Orphanage Accounts of John Donne, Iron-monger." *The Guildhall Miscellany*, 4:22–29.

Description of the proceedings recorded in the Orphans Accounts of the City of London concerning Donne's legacy. "Such an account, however, although revealing little of Donne's life, serves to round out our knowledge of social forces at work in his life, and for that reason is worthwhile" (p. 22).

1956

⋙ 821. ANON. "Donne's Poetry." *TLS*, 27 April, p. 253.

Reply to Joan Grundy, *TLS*, 27 April, p. 253. Part of a debate on Donne's relation to poetic tradition. For a complete listing of replies, see Entry 822.

◦§ 822. ANON. "Poetic Tradition in Donne." *TLS*, 16 March, p. 164.

Essentially a review of *Donne's Poetry: Essays in Literary Analysis*, Clay Hunt (1954). Challenges certain comments Hunt makes on Donne's relation to the poetic tradition. Several replies: Joan Grundy, *TLS*, 27 April, p. 253, and a reply by the reviewer, *TLS*, 27 April, p. 253. In his review, the author states that Donne "must have felt that the death of his wife was a judgment on him for leaving the Roman Church" and that he had "no great enthusiasm for Elizabeth." These comments elicited replies from Helen Gardner and J. B. Leishman, *TLS*, 11 May, p. 283; a reply from the reviewer, *TLS*, 11 May, p. 283; a reply to the reviewer by Helen Gardner, *TLS*, 25 May, p. 320 and by Evelyn M. Simpson, *TLS*, 25 May, p. 320.

◦§ 823. ANON. "Poetic Tradition in Donne." *TLS*, 11 May, p. 283.

Reply to Helen Gardner and J. B. Leishman, *TLS*, 11 May, p. 283, who challenge the reviewer's comments that Donne "must have felt that the death of his wife was a judgment on him for leaving the Roman Church" and that Donne had "no great enthusiasm for Elizabeth." For a complete listing of replies, see Entry 822.

◦§ 824. ALLEN, D. C. "Donne's Compass Figure." *MLN*, 71:256–57.

Suggests that Donne may have borrowed his compass image in "A Valediction: forbidding mourning" from the *Rime* of Guarini. Points out analogues in Jean Edouard du Monin's *Le Phoenix* (Paris, 1585) and in Père Mersenne's *Quaestiones in Genesim* (Paris, 1623).

◦§ 825. CHATMAN, SEYMOUR. "Mr. Stein on Donne." *KR*, 18:443–51.

Reply to Arnold Stein, *KR*, 18:439–43. Challenges Stein's interpretation of "Elegie X: The Dreame."

◦§ 826. COBB, LUCILLE S. "Donne's 'Satyre II,' 71–72." *Expl*, 14:Item 40.

Suggests a solution to the crux in lines 71–72 of *Satyre II*. The word *asses* is a Norman French legal term meaning "acquiescence" and the word *wedges* means "ingot." Thus the lines can be paraphrased to read: "Like the ingot in its mold, the dishonest lawyer must shape his words to fit the pattern required by the court; and in so doing 'hee' is enduring a forced acquiescence, like that endured by the ingot. For him, the forcing agent is the 'barre'; for the ingot, it is a 'block'." For a reply by Vernon Hall, Jr., see *Expl*, 15 (1957):Item 24 and by Thomas O. Mabbott, see *Expl*, 16 (1957):Item 19.

◦§ 827. ———. "Donne's 'Satyre II,' 49–57." *Expl*, 15:Item 8.

Explicates lines 49–57 of *Satyre II* by commenting on the legal significance of the terminology in the passage, particularly the specific meaning of the phrase "continuall claimes."

⊷§ 828. COLIE, ROSALIE L. "Huygens Hath Donne," in *Some Thankful-nesse to Constantine: A Study of English Influence upon the Early Works of Constantijn Huygens*, pp. 52–71. The Hague: Martinus Nijhoff.

Discusses Huygens's translation of nineteen of Donne's poems into Dutch (1630–1633). In addition to being an admirer of Donne as a poet, Huygens also was enthusiastic about him as a preacher.

⊷§ 829. COX, R. G. "A Survey of Literature from Donne to Marvell," in *From Donne to Marvell*, ed. Boris Ford, pp. 43–85. The Pelican Guide to English Literature, 3. Baltimore: Penguin Books, Inc.

Reprinted several times.

Reprinted with revisions, 1960, 1962.

Very general survey of the poetry and prose from Donne to Marvell in which Donne is viewed both as a continuation of the past and as one of the principal progenitors of the new fashions in poetry. Those elements usually associated with his verse, such as dramatic realism, fusion of passionate feeling with logical argumentation, wit, the use of the conceit, colloquial vigor, surprising imagery and diction, concentration, etc., are all briefly commented on. Without ascribing to the notion of "schools," the author contrasts Donne and Jonson as the two most formative influences on seventeenth-century poetry. Donne's poetry is used as a touchstone in describing the devotional lyrics of Herbert, Crashaw, Vaughan, and lesser poets; comments on Donne's influence on the Cavaliers and on his relationship to Marvell. Very brief discussion of the prose.

⊷§ 830. ———. "The Poems of John Donne," in *From Donne to Marvell*, ed. Boris Ford, pp. 98–115. The Pelican Guide to English Literature, 3. Baltimore: Penguin Books, Inc.

General summary of some of the basic characteristics of Donne's poetry: realistic expressiveness, intensity and concentration, metrical experimentation, variations in tone, characteristic imagery drawn not only from the familiar but also from medieval theology and contemporary science, surprise, wit, uses of the conceit, the blend of passion and thought, etc. Considers Donne's poems under three major categories, each corresponding roughly with various periods of Donne's life: (1) the love poetry, (2) the occasional pieces, verse letters, and miscellaneous poems, and (3) the religious verse.

⊷§ 831. CROSS, K. GUSTAV. " 'Balm' in Donne and Shakespeare: Ironic Intention in *The Extasie*." *MLN*, 71:480–82.

Suggests that Donne's use of *balm* in line 6 of "The Extasie" may be derived from Shakespeare's metaphorical use of the term as *sweat* in *Venus and Adonis* (1. 27) and that the seventeenth-century reader would have recognized not only the erotic but also ironic elements in the line. Challenges Grierson and others who have perhaps taken the poem too seriously.

⮐§ 832. DENONAIN, JEAN-JACQUES. *Thèmes et formes de la poésie "métaphysique": Étude d'un aspect de la littérature anglaise au dix-septième siècle.* Publications de la Faculté des Lettres d'Alger, 18. Paris: Presses Universitaires de France. 548 p.

Attempts to define as precisely as possible the nature of metaphysical poetry. Donne is used throughout as a touchstone. After an introduction (pp. 5–18) in which the author states his purpose and challenges several of the better known definitions, the book divides into five major parts: (1) a tentative definition of metaphysical poetry (pp. 21–95); (2) an analysis of major themes in metaphysical poetry (pp. 99–326); (3) a discussion of the psychological processes by which the themes of the poetry are developed and expanded (pp. 329–64); (4) a study of poetic forms utilized by the metaphysical poets (pp. 367–449); (5) a conclusion in which the author seeks to discern the unifying characteristics of metaphysical poetry (pp. 453–80). Four sections of the book deal specifically with Donne: (1) the love poetry of Donne (pp. 103–45); (2) the religious inspiration in Donne's poetry (pp. 146–59); (3) Donne's uses of image, metaphor, and conceit (pp. 383–88); (4) Donne's poetic technique (pp. 410–25). Among the several appendices, some deal specifically with Donne: (1) a chronological listing of Donne's life and works (pp. 483–84); (2) an analysis of "The Primrose" (pp. 490–500); (3) an analytical table of Donne's use of accents in a selected number of poems (p. 501); (4) an analytical table of the prosodic structure of Donne's poetry (pp. 502–4); (5) a comparative table of kinds of strophes used by the metaphysical poets (p. 515). Bibliography.

⮐§ 833. DONNE, JOHN. *The Sermons of John Donne.* Edited, with Introductions and Critical Apparatus, by Evelyn M. Simpson and George R. Potter. Vol. VIII. Berkeley and Los Angeles: University of California Press; London: Cambridge University Press. vi, 396 p. 10 vols.

Table of Contents (pp. v–vi); List of Illustrations (p. vii); Introduction (pp. 1–34); The Sermons (pp. 35–372); Textual Notes to the Sermons in Volume VIII (pp. 373–89); Appendix: Sermon No. 5 and the Commentaries of Pererius and Cornelius à Lapide (pp. 391–96). Sixteen sermons preached between Trinity Sunday, 1627, and Easter, 1629.

⮐§ 834. ———. *The Songs and Sonets of John Donne.* An *Editio minor* with Introduction and Explanatory Notes by Theodore Redpath. London: Methuen & Co., Ltd. li, 156 p.

Reprinted with minor corrections, 1959, 1964, 1967.

Introduction (pp. xv–li) divided into several separate sections: (1) The status of the 'Songs and Sonets' in English poetry; (2) The place of the 'Songs and Sonets' within Donne's work; (3) Groupings within the 'Songs and Sonets'; (4) The 'Songs and Sonets' and the tradition of the English love lyric; and (5) Notes on the text and canon. The text (pp. 1–137) is modernized and the punctuation is modified. Explanatory notes for each poem are printed on the pages facing the text. Four appendices: (1) Would Donne's revised text necessarily be the authentic text? (p. 138); (2) "Specular Stone" ("The Undertaking" l. 6) (pp. 139–40); (3) "Aire and Angels" (ll. 24, 26–28) (pp. 140–44); (4) "Farewell to Love" (ll. 23–30) (pp. 145–49). Selected bibliography.

835. FORD, BORIS, ED. *From Donne to Marvell.* The Pelican Guide to English Literature, 3. Baltimore: Penguin Books, Inc. 277 p.
Reprinted with revisions, 1960, 1962, 1963, 1965.
Donne is mentioned throughout this collection of essays on seventeenth-century topics. Essays in which he is principally treated have been entered as separate items in the bibliography. Selective bibliography of Donne and Donne criticism (pp. 257–58).

836. GALE, ROBERT L. "Donne's 'The Sunne Rising,' 27–30." *Expl,* 15:Item 14.
An addition to Glenn J. Christensen's note in *Expl,* 7 (1948):Item 3. Paraphrases lines 27–30 of the poem to read: "You, sun, being old, want to be at ease; you may, if you only realize that you may, warm the world by warming us." Cites other poems to support his reading.

837. GANG, T. M. "Hobbes and the Metaphysical Conceit—A Reply." *JHI,* 17:418–21.
In part a reply to George Watson, *JHI,* 16 (1955):558–62. Challenges Watson's interpretation of Hobbes's critical writings. Second part of essay is devoted to a discussion of the metaphysical conceit. Comments on the compass image in "A Valediction: forbidding mourning." "What makes this conceit characteristically 'metaphysical' is not the wildness of the comparison, but the fact that the comparison is between a concrete thing and an abstraction, and that the double meanings are produced by taking the concrete part of the comparison 'seriously,' that is, writing literally about the vehicle of the metaphor" (p. 421). Comments briefly on "A Feaver."

838. GARDNER, HELEN. "The Historical Sense," in *The Limits of Criticism: Reflections on the Interpretation of Poetry and Scripture,* pp. 40–63. London: Oxford University Press.
Comments on Donne's insistence on the primary importance of understanding the literal sense of Scripture, by which Donne also includes

the figurative, metaphorical, and parabolic levels of meaning but de-emphasizes the spiritual or mystical level of interpretation. Suggests that how Donne handles "passages of Scripture has some bearing on our reading of Donne's poetry" (p. 51). States that in modern critical evaluations of the poetry, "We are avoiding its true seriousness and finding seriousness in its levity, if we concentrate upon the imagination's power to perceive analogies and neglect its primary power to apprehend and express what touches the mind and heart. Where this is lacking metaphysical poetry is tedious trifling, or, to use the language of its own age, the mere 'itch of wit' " (pp. 51–52).

≈§ 839. ———. "Donne and the Church." *TLS*, 25 May, p. 320.
Reply to the anonymous reviewer, *TLS*, 11 May, p. 283, who had claimed that Donne "must have felt that the death of his wife was a judgment on him for leaving the Roman Church." For a complete listing of replies, see Entry 822.

≈§ 840. ———, AND J. B. LEISHMAN. "Poetic Tradition in Donne."
    TLS, 11 May, p. 283.
Reply to an anonymous reviewer, *TLS*, 16 March, p. 164, who stated that Donne "must have felt that the death of his wife was a judgment on him for leaving the Roman Church" and that Donne had "no great enthusiasm for Elizabeth." For a complete listing of replies, see Entry 822.

≈§ 841. GOLDBERG, M. A. "Donne's 'A Lecture Upon the Shadow.' "
    Expl, 14:Item 50.
Maintains that if the central image and idea "are examined against the background of Paracelsus and the neo-Platonists, a tradition in which Donne was immersed, then the conceit becomes wholly consistent, a complexity of meaning becomes pervasive, and much of the relationship between secular and divine in the poet becomes clarified." Argues that the speaker "is urging a unity of body and mind to achieve the *spiritus* attainable only after a true *coniunctio*." For a reply by John D. Russell, see *Expl*, 17 (1958):Item 9 and by Nat Henry, see *Expl*, 20 (1962):Item 60.

≈§ 842. GRUNDY, JOAN. "Donne's Poetry." *TLS*, 27 April, p. 253.
Part of a debate on Donne's relation to poetic tradition. For a complete listing of replies, see Entry 822.

≈§ 843. HERMAN, GEORGE. "Donne's 'Goodfriday, 1613. Riding Westward.' " *Expl*, 14:Item 60.
Divides the poem into three parts, lines 1–10, 11–32, 33–42, and suggests that this division "might well suggest that, triptych-like, the two

shorter passages hinge upon the central one, and perhaps further that some condition in the first passage is affected by events in the middle section so as to produce the situation found in the third." Concludes, "The movement is spatial rather than temporal; the poet's task is that of establishing the proper perspective between himself and his Redeemer. This is accomplished by presenting physically similar but emotionally contrasting views of the poet, as if appearing on opposite sides of the central panel of a triptych." Comments briefly on lines 19–20, 21, and 27.

◄§ 844. HICKEY, ROBERT L. "Donne's Art of Preaching." *TSL*, 1:65–74.
Examines several of Donne's comments on preaching in order to reconstruct his theory about the art. Calls Donne a "confirmed Augustinian, both in theology and rhetoric" (p. 65), who "believed that the best style for the sermon is the temperate and ornamental style, the 'moderate' style described by Cicero in the *Orator* and discussed by St. Augustine in *De Doctrina Christiana*, IV, 21, 25 as the style used by the teachers of the church, especially Ambrose and Cyprian" (p. 67). Suggests that if one collected all of Donne's comments on rhetoric and the art of preaching they would offer "a fairly comprehensive handbook of logic and rhetoric comparable to *De Doctrina Christiana*" (p. 74).

◄§ 845. HINDLE, C. J. "A Poem by Donne." *TLS*, 8 June, p. 345.
Reply to James E. Walsh, *TLS*, 6 April, p. 207. Walsh points out that parts of "Goe, and catche a falling starre" were printed in an anonymous work entitled *A Helpe to Memory and Discovrse* (London, 1630) in a special section at the end with a separate title page reading "Table-talk, as Mysicke to a Banqvet of Wine." Hindle points out that "Table-talk" was first published separately in 1621, though no copy of the book can now be found. Suggests that possibly Donne's poem was published nine or ten years earlier than Walsh suggests.

◄§ 846. KNOX, GEORGE. "Donne's 'Holy Sonnets,' XIV." *Expl*, 15:Item 2.
In part a reply to J. C. Levenson, *Expl*, 11 (1953):Item 31 and George Herman, *Expl*, 12 (1953):Item 18. Maintains that the trinitarian reference in line 1 determines the structure of the whole poem.

◄§ 847. KORNINGER, SIEGFRIED. *Die Naturaufassung in der Englischen Dichtung des 17. Jahrhunderts*. Weiner Beiträge zur Englischen Philologie, 64. Wein-Stuttgart: Wilhelm Braumüller. 260 p.
Investigates changing attitudes toward nature in the seventeenth century. Points out that up to the beginning of the period the Ptolemaic attitude prevailed, but in the course of the century there was a turnabout and the Copernican attitude was accepted. By using poetry as

his source material, the author studies two groups of questions: (1) How does man face his environment, what does he understand of it, and how does he depict it? (2) To what extent is his attitude toward nature expressed in his poetic works, and what inspirations and artistic impulses does the poetry derive from the investigation of nature? Donne uses concepts from both the Old and New Philosophies, which indicates that he did not take sides in the dispute. Even the famous lines from *The first Anniversary*, which seem to express his despair over the new discoveries, must be understood in their context and should not be overinterpreted. Finds in Donne's poetry an interest in nature and natural phenomena, which he shared with most of his contemporaries.

᪣ 848. Krieger, Murray. *The New Apologists for Poetry*. Minneapolis: University of Minnesota Press. xiv, 225 p.

Offers an analysis of "The Canonization" (pp. 12–18, 25, 26) by way of illustrating some of the central concepts of his study. Finds the meaning of the poem to reside in the "complex of internal relations" (p. 18). The poem shows the reader "some interrelationships among the problems of love, of religion, and of the worldly life in the many views it has simultaneously brought before him. If it gives him no single answer, it shows him why no single answer will do. For the poem is argument only as it is perverted and even parodied argument; and, as argument, it is convincing, and seriously convincing, only as it is nonsensical" (p. 18).

᪣ 849. Malloch, A. E. "The Techniques and Function of the Renaissance Paradox." *SP*, 53:191–203.

Critical discussion of the Renaissance paradox that draws heavily on Donne. Shows that the primary function of the paradox is not to deceive but "by a show of deceit to force the reader to uncover the truth" (p. 192). Emphasizes the dramatic nature of the paradox and discusses the relation of paradox and the Scholastic *quaestio disputata*.

᪣ 850. Maud, Ralph. "Donne's *First Anniversary*." *Boston University Studies in English*, 2:218–25.

In part a rejoinder to Louis Martz in *The Poetry of Meditation* (New Haven: Yale University Press, 1954), pp. 221–35. Sees an integral relationship between the meditations and the eulogies. Suggests that the impact of Elizabeth Drury in the poem comes from the implication that the world is presently corrupt in its purest part. There are two levels of intensity of meditation: first, meditation on the pervasiveness of original sin; second, comment on the shattered hope of seeing perfection even in that which is the nearest to perfect—Elizabeth. The meditations deal with the first level; the eulogies comment on the second.

⊷§ 851. MILLER, HENRY KNIGHT. "The Paradoxical Encomium with
   Special Reference to Its Vogue in England, 1600–1800." MP,
   53:145–78.
Defines the paradoxical encomium as "a species of rhetorical jest or display piece which involves the praise of unworthy, unexpected, or trifling
objects" (p. 145) and traces the history of the genre from the earliest
periods of Greek rhetoric with special attention to the flourishing of it
in England from 1600–1800. Cites Donne's "Paradox I" and "Paradox
III" as belonging to the tradition.

⊷§ 852. NOVARR, DAVID. "Donne's 'Epithalamion Made at Lincoln's
   Inn': Context and Date." RES, n.s., 7:250–63.
Contrasts the crude and scoffing elements in the poem with Donne's
other epithalamia and accounts for the difference by suggesting that the
poem is a satiric entertainment, written to celebrate a mock wedding
held as part of the revels at Lincoln's Inn. Tentatively proposes that
Donne wrote the poem for a performance at the Midsummer revels in
1595.

⊷§ 853. ORNSTEIN, ROBERT. "Donne, Montaigne, and Natural Law."
   JEGP, 55:213–29.
Argues that Donne and Montaigne were independent of each other
and of the libertine tradition when they criticized the concept of Natural
Law. Maintains that "Like Renaissance Libertines, they denied that
nature established immutable and categorical imperatives. But unlike
the Libertines, they affirmed in unmistakable terms, the rule of reason
in human life" (p. 214).

⊷§ 854. PETER, JOHN. Complaint and Satire in Early English Literature.
   Oxford: The Clarendon Press. 323 p.
References throughout to the Satyres. Compares and contrasts Donne
with Marston, Gilpin, Lodge, and other of the Renaissance formal
satirists. Stresses Donne's originality in his experimentations with the
genre. "Donne is much more than a product of his general situation:
rather he is a seminal agent, an individual and distinguished mind whose
satires, circulating in manuscript, did much to accelerate the sophistication of this sort of poetry" (p. 133). Donne is interested in presenting
his own moods rather than in merely documenting abuses.

⊷§ 855. PHELPS, GILBERT. "The Prose of Donne and Browne," in From
   Donne to Marvell, ed. Boris Ford, pp. 116–30. The Pelican Guide
   to English Literature, 3. Baltimore: Penguin Books, Inc.
Reprinted with revisions, 1960, 1962, 1963, 1965.
Compares the prose of Donne and Browne and asserts that Donne "is
more immediately engaged with his material—that even in his flippancy

he is the more serious writer" (p. 117). Donne is said to express the "passionate re-creation of an experience" (p. 120) in his prose, while Browne is said to create by means of "a deliberate, architectonic effect" a kind of "distancing of emotion" (p. 120).

◄§ 856. ROONEY, WILLIAM J. " 'The Canonization'—The Language of Paradox Reconsidered." *ELH*, 23:36–47.

Challenges Cleanth Brooks's dictum in *The Well Wrought Urn* (New York, 1947), p. 3, that "there is a sense in which paradox is the language appropriate and inevitable to poetry." Disagrees with Brooks's reading of "The Canonization" and presents his own reading. Maintains that Brooks misinterprets both the tone and structure of the poem. Concludes his argument by saying, "It is one thing to say that a poem is *made of paradoxical meanings* and quite another thing to conclude that the poem *functions to convey* a paradox, serious or otherwise" (p. 46).

◄§ 857. SIMPSON, EVELYN M. "Donne and the Church." *TLS*, 25 May, p. 320.

Reply to the anonymous reviewer, *TLS*, 16 March, p. 164, who claimed that Donne "must have felt that the death of his wife was a judgment on him for leaving the Roman Church." For a complete listing of replies, see Entry 822.

◄§ 858. SMITH, A. J. "Two Notes on Donne." *MLR*, 51:405–7.

(1) An explanation of the crucial analogy "thy love may be my loves spheare" in lines 23–27 of "Aire and Angels." (2) Note on the punctuation of line 10 in "Since she whom I lov'd," in which Helen Gardner's emendation is challenged. For a reply by Helen Gardner, see *MLR*, 52 (1957):564–65.

◄§ 859. STEIN, ARNOLD. "Donne's Prosody." *KR*, 18:439–43.

Reprinted in a slightly expanded form from "Structures of Sound in Donne's Verse," *KR*, 13 (1951):20–36, 256–78. Interpretation of the meter of "Elegie X: The Dreame." For a reply by Seymour Chatman, see *KR*, 18:443–51.

◄§ 860. TILLYARD, E. M. W. *The Metaphysicals and Milton.* London: Chatto & Windus Ltd. vii, 87 p.

Maintains that Milton was "a great figure looking back to the Middle Ages and forward to the spirit and achievements of eighteenth-century puritanism. But his larger surprises and ironies are in harmony with the requirements of his age and of course are largely inspired by them. He was very much of a person, yet he did not thrust his personality overmuch into his poetry and he chose to inhabit the general centre rather than to construct a private bower, or perform dazzling acrobatics, near the circumference. He is more like Jonson and Marvell than he is like Donne and Crashaw. Donne, on the other hand, was a great innovator but with a narrower, more personal talent. He made people heed him, he stirred them up, he contributed to the age's vitality. But he remains the exception, and his admirers will do him no good in the long run if they pretend he was anything else" (p. 74). In Appendix A (pp. 77–78) the author interprets lines 2 and 9 of "Since she whom I lov'd," and in Appendix B (pp. 79–84) comments on "The Extasie," noting that Donne's real interest in the poem is "in the basic constitution of man and man's place in the order of creation" (p. 79). Comments on Donne throughout.

◄§ 861. UNGER, LEONARD. *The Name in the Name: Essays on the Experience of Poetry*. Minneapolis: University of Minnesota Press. x, 242 p.

Two essays in this collection challenge certain modern critical assumptions about the nature of metaphysical poetry, especially Donne's poetry. Chapter III, "Donne's Poetry and Modern Criticism" (pp. 30–104), is a reprint of the book by the same title (1950). Chapter IV, "Fusion and Experience" (pp. 105–40), continues the argument of the earlier essay and deals primarily with the concept of "unified sensibility," a notion the author considers invalid as used by modern criticism. Discusses the criticism of Williamson, Eliot, Ransom, Brooks, and Tate.

◄§ 862. WALSH, JAMES E. "A Poem by Donne." *TLS*, 6 April, p. 207.

Points out that parts of "Goe, and catche a falling starre" were printed in an anonymous work entitled *A Helpe to Memory and Discovrse* (London, 1630) in a special section at the end with a separate title page reading "Table-Talke, as Mysicke to a Banqvet of Wine." For a reply by C. J. Hindle, see *TLS*, 8 June, p. 345.

◄§ 863. WELLEK, RENÉ. "The Criticism of T. S. Eliot." *SR*, 64:398–443.

Reviews Eliot's basic comments on Donne and metaphysical poetry (pp. 437–40). Points out that, although Eliot's criticism proved to be an important impetus to the so-called Donne revival, his ideas are, for the most part, neither original nor consistent. Eliot was the first critic to link the metaphysicals so definitely with the French symbolists. Critics fail to note that many of Eliot's comments on Donne are guarded and frequently not laudatory: "Eliot's sympathy for Donne is thus far from perfect" (p. 438).

1957

◄§ 864. ALVAREZ, A. "John Donne and his Circle." *Listener,* 57:827–28.
Considers the relationship between Donne's poetry and its audience.
Points out that Donne was not, like Spenser, a professional writer but
was a wit and a member of a "young, literary, middle-class intellectual
élite" who were not interested in being instructed in philosophy. Thus,
Donne did not articulate a particular aesthetic theory nor concern himself with the literary world as such, and, with few exceptions, he did not
appear in the anthologies of the period. Unlike Spenser, who was concerned with perfecting his art in an effort to reach as many people as
possible and to be as pleasing as possible in order to convey the great
moral truths of the philosophers, Donne was "interested in poetic form
inasmuch as it could be bullied into giving direct and natural expression
to what he had to say for himself; and in that the philosophers were
merely accessories to his wit" (p. 828).

◄§ 865. BRADBROOK, F. W. "John Donne and Ben Jonson." *N&Q,* n.s.,
    4:146–47.
Points out several parallels between Donne's poetry and Jonson's
Volpone, particularly how both poets employ images of coining and
wealth to express emotion.

◄§ 866. COANDA, RICHARD. "Hopkins and Donne: 'Mystic' and Meta-
    physical." *Renascence,* 9:180–87.
Examines some of the chief resemblances between Donne and Hopkins and concludes, "Their best religious verse is most similar: Donne
prefigures Hopkins, and Hopkins writes like a nineteenth-century
Donne" (p. 187).

◄§ 867. CUNNINGHAM, J. S. "At John Donne's Death Bed." *DUJ,* 18:28.
Original poem on Donne's death.

◄§ 868. DONNE, JOHN. *The Sermons of John Donne.* Edited, with In-
    troductions and Critical Apparatus, by George R. Potter and
    Evelyn M. Simpson. Vol. III. Berkeley and Los Angeles: Uni-
    versity of California Press; London: Cambridge University Press.
    ix, 434 p. 10 vols.
Table of Contents (pp. v–vi); List of Illustrations (p. vii); Prefatory
Note (p. ix); Introduction (pp. 1–43); The Sermons (pp. 45–387);
Textual Notes to the Sermons in Volume III (pp. 389–434). Eighteen
sermons preached from April, 1620, to the middle of February 1621/22.

✍§ 869. EMERSON, KATHERINE T. "Two Problems in Donne's 'Farewell to Love.'" *MLN*, 72:93–95.
Comments on two difficult passages in "Farewell to love," lines 28–30 and lines 39–40.

✍§ 870. EMPSON, WILLIAM. "Donne the Space Man." *KR*, 19:337–99.
Asserts that Donne believed in the plurality of worlds. Suggests that, as an Anglican preacher, Donne was in a good position, both in conscience and in knowledge, to be concerned with what was considered by some to be a heretical idea because it seemed to question the uniqueness of Christ. Refutes numerous contentions of other critics who fail to recognize this belief in Donne and attempts to explicate the idea of separate planets in such poems as "The good-morrow," "The Extasie," and "Aire and Angels." For a reply by Toshihiko Kawasaki, see *Studies in English Literature* (Tokyo), 36 (1960):229–50.

✍§ 871. GARDNER, HELEN LOUISE, ED. *The Metaphysical Poets*. Penguin Poets, D38. Harmondsworth, Eng.: Penguin Books.
Reprinted, 1959, 1961, 1963, 1964.
Revised ed., 1966.
2d ed., 1967.
Important general introduction to the main characteristics of metaphysical poetry. Anthology.

✍§ 872. ———. "Another Note on Donne. 'Since she whome I lov'd.'" *MLR*, 52:564–65.
Reply to A. J. Smith, *MLR*, 51 (1956):405–7, and to a review of *The Poetry of John Donne: A Study in Explication*, Doniphan Louthan (1951), by Joan Bennett, *MP*, 50 (1952–53):278. Maintains that "The contrast on which the sonnet is built is that between the highest human love we know on earth and the love of God which is the soul's reward in Heaven" (p. 564).

✍§ 873. HAGSPIAN [HAGOPIAN], JOHN V. "Some Cruxes in Donne's Poetry." *N&Q*, n.s., 4:500–502.
Three comments on Grierson's text: (1) in the "Epithalamion made at Lincolnes Inne," the author retains *will* in line 47 and rejects Grierson's emendation of *nill*; (2) in the verse letter "To Sr Henry Wotton. Sir, more then kisses" the author rejects the parentheses inserted by Grierson in line 26; (3) in "Holy Sonnet XI: Spit in my face you Jewes," he supports Grierson's reading of *you* in line 1 and rejects Helen Gardner's emendation of *yee*.

ᏝᏚ 874. HALL, VERNON, JR., "Donne's 'Satyre II,' 71–72." *Expl*, 15:Item 24.

In part a reply to Lucille S. Cobb's reading of lines 71–72 of *Satyre II*, *Expl*, 14 (1956):Item 40. Reads *asses* as the plural of *as*, a Roman coin. "Thus Donne is saying that the lawyer endures the shaping of his conscience to the case as the asses bear the weight of the hammer which gives them their imprint." Comments on several other minor points in the poem. See also Thomas O. Mabbott, *Expl*, 16:Item 19.

ᏝᏚ 875. HILBERRY, CONRAD. "The First Stanza of Donne's Hymne to God my God, in my sicknesse.'" *N&Q*, n.s., 4:336–37.

Relates the image of the tuning of an instrument in the first stanza with the traditional symbol of Christ crucified as a harp or lute. Seen in this light, the first stanza "is transformed from a picture of a pleasant exercise in anticipation, to a quiet statement of the agony, excruciating as Christ's, which must be endured on the way to redemption" (p. 337). The first stanza introduces the Resurrection-out-of-agony motif and is consistent with the rest of the poem.

ᏝᏚ 876. KERMODE, FRANK. *John Donne*. Writers and Their Works, No. 86. London: Longmans, Green and Co., Ltd. 48 p.

Reprinted, 1961, 1964.

General critical introduction of Donne's life and works. Rejects the notion of "dissociation of sensibility" and finds in Donne's wit the most significant feature of his art, agreeing with Praz that Donne appeals to the reader "whom the *rhythm of thought* itself attracts by virtue of its own peculiar convolutions" (p. 9). Singles out "A nocturnall upon S. Lucies day" as Donne's finest poem. Maintains that Donne drew heavily on the Middle Ages and the Church Fathers and regarded modern science more or less as an illustration of the fallibility of all human knowledge. Nearly half the study is devoted to Donne's religious career and development. "Donne's acceptance of the established Church is the most important single event of his life, because it involved all the powers of his mind and personality" (p. 27). Selected bibliography.

ᏝᏚ 877. ⸻. "'Dissociation of Sensibility': Modern Symbolist Readings of Literary History," in *Romantic Image*, pp. 138–61. London: Routledge and Kegan Paul, Ltd.

The relevant parts of this chapter that deal with Donne and the seventeenth century are explored in a much expanded form in *KR*, 19:169–94.

ᏝᏚ 878. ⸻. "Dissociation of Sensibility." *KR*, 19:169–94.

Attacks the theory of "dissociation of sensibility." Points out that the tension between reason and theological truth was not confined to nor begun in seventeenth-century England. As far as poetry is concerned, especially metaphysical poetry, the theory is an "attempt on the part of Symbolists to find an historical justification for their poetics" (p. 194). Discusses how the term and concept are closely bound up with the Donne revival. In a much revised form, the same ground is covered in " 'Dissociation of Sensibility': Modern Symbolist Readings of Literary History," in *Romantic Image* (London: Routledge and Kegan Paul, Ltd., 1957), pp. 138–61.

⏴⑧ 879. LEGOUIS, PIERRE. "Donne, l'amour et les critiques." *EA*, 10:115–22.

Review of three items: Clay Hunt's *Donne's Poetry: Essays in Literary Analysis* (1954), David Novarr's "Donne's 'Epithalamion Made at Lincoln's Inn': Context and Date," *RES*, n.s., 7 (1956):250–63, and Theodore Redpath's *The Songs and Sonets of John Donne* (1956). Accuses the three of anachronistic moral preoccupations, abuse of autobiographical interpretation, and an overly zealous tendency to find erotic wordplay in the poems.

⏴⑧ 880. MABBOTT, THOMAS O. "Donne's 'Satyre II," 71–72." *Expl*, 16: Item 19.

In part a reply to Lucille S. Cobb, *Expl*, 14 (1956):Item 40, and Vernon Hall, Jr., *Expl*, 15:Item 24. Comments on the possible numismatic pun in lines 71–72 of the poem.

⏴⑧ 881 MADISON, ARTHUR L. "Explication of John Donne's 'The Flea.' " *N&Q*, n.s., 4:60–61.

Paraphrases the argument of the poem and points out, in particular, the dramatic and humorous elements in it. Sees the poem not as an impassioned plea but rather as "a little intellectual game indulged in by the two lovers, both of them knowing what the outcome will be, but enjoying the game for its own sake" (p. 61).

⏴⑧ 882. MAIN, C. F. "New Texts of John Donne." *SB*, 9:225–33.

Describes the texts of certain Donne poems in the Harvard MS. Eng. 686, an early commonplace book compiled some time between 1623 and 1635. Especially important are the variant readings of "Elegie XIX: Going to Bed."

⏴⑧ 883. MALLOCH, A. E. "The Definition of Sin in Donne's *Biathanatos*." *MLN*, 72:332–35.

Points out that Donne contradicts Saint Augustine's definition of sin by quoting from two others, seemingly from Saint Thomas, but in fact from the *Tabula Aurea* (1473) of Peter of Bergamo, a fifteenth-century Dominican whose work serves as headings for an index of Saint Thomas's work. Reference to Saint Thomas does not support the particular twist

Donne gives these definitions. Suggests that this illustrates the spirit of Donne's approach in *Biathanatos*, which is primarily a piece of paradoxical argumentation.

◄§ 884. MAZZEO, JOSEPH A. "Notes on John Donne's Alchemical Imagery." *Isis*, 48:103–23.

Reprinted in *Renaissance and Seventeenth-Century Studies* (New York: Columbia University Press; London: Routledge and Kegan Paul, Ltd., 1964), pp. 60–89.

Examines the extensive use of alchemical imagery in Donne's poetry and, to a lesser degree, in his prose. Points out that such a survey "reveals the extraordinary skill and precision with which he adapted these figures to the use of his art, and his work demonstrates an exact knowledge of all the ideas involved" (p. 121). Analogy was so basic to the intellectual temper of Donne's age that it is wrong to see such figures as purely rhetorical adjuncts to style. It is possible that much of Donne's knowledge of alchemy was unconscious, simply a part of his intellectual heritage. However, it seems clear that he knew Paracelsian theory thoroughly, at times disagreeing with it. In Donne's work there is no concrete statement on his opinion of alchemy, but the internal evidence shows that he had a great interest in it and a firm understanding of its principles. At times he satirized the charlatanry in contemporary practice. Special attention is given to "A nocturnall upon S. Lucies day."

◄§ 885. MILES, JOSEPHINE. *Eras & Modes in English Poetry*. Berkeley and Los Angeles: University of California Press. xi, 233 p.

Questions the theory of dividing English poetry arbitrarily into historical periods and defines three recurrent modes in poetry based upon the various kinds of sentence structure and word usage favored by English poets: the clausal or predicative, the phrasal or sublime, and the balanced, or classical. Considers the clausal or active predicative mode as the most English and traces it to Chaucer. It is in this mode that such a variety of poets as Skelton, Wyatt, Donne, Cowley, Wordsworth and Coleridge in the *Lyrical Ballads*, Byron, Browning, and even such moderns as Frost and Auden belong. The clausal mode lends itself to passionate argumentation, natural discourse in verse, abrupt movement, clausal connective, and a preponderance of verbs over adjectives. Chapter II, "The Language of the Donne Tradition" (pp. 20–32) is a revision of an article by the same title in *KR*, 13 (1951):37–49. In Appendix A (pp. 215–30) the author shows, by means of a statistical table, that Donne belongs to the clausal mode. In Appendix B (pp. 231–33) she lists the fifty-two words most frequently used by Donne.

✒§ 886. NATHANSON, LEONARD. "The Context of Dryden's Criticism of Donne's and Cowley's Love Poetry." N&Q, n.s., 4:56–59.

Maintains that Dryden and William Walsh, as well as certain other minor neoclassical critics, were disapproving of the love poetry of Donne and Cowley as well as of the poetry of Petrarch and others, because to them the concepts of nature and decorum were violated by literary adornment and intellectual elaboration in this kind of verse. The neoclassical critics insisted that the function of love poetry was to win the lady, not to achieve literary fame and advancement. See also Nathanson's follow-up note in N&Q, n.s., 4:197–98.

✒§ 887. ———. "Dryden, Donne, and Cowley." N&Q, n.s., 4:197–98.

Footnote to the author's earlier essay in N&Q, n.s., 4:56–59. Points out that Rène Rapin in his *Reflexions sur la Poëtique* (1674) criticized Ronsard in much the same terms that Dryden and Walsh censured Donne and Cowley for troubling the mind of the fair sex with learning in their amorous verse.

✒§ 888. NOSEK, JIŘÍ. "Studies in Post-Shakespearian English: Prose Style." *Philologica* (Prague), 3, No. 2:101–44.

Detailed linguistic analysis of some of the basic elements of seventeenth-century prose style, including examples drawn from Donne.

✒§ 889. NOVARR, DAVID. "The Dating of Donne's *La Corona*." PQ, 36:259–65.

Reviews the evidence for the dating of the *La Corona* poems and concludes that "they were written shortly before the *Holy Sonnets*, that is, late in 1608 or early in 1609" (p. 265).

✒§ 890. PARISH, JOHN E. "Donne as a Petrarchan." N&Q, n.s., 4:377–78.

Challenges Theodore Redpath in *The Songs and Sonets of John Donne* (1956), who places "Loves Deitie" and "Twicknam garden" among those poems in which Donne expresses his hostility toward women. Suggests that Donne uses conventional Petrarchan attitudes in both poems.

✒§ 891. SMITH, A. J. "Donne in His Time: A Reading of 'The Extasie.'" *Rivista di Letterature Moderne e Comparate* (Firenze), 10:260–75.

Close reading of "The Extasie" in which the author argues that the modern reader can be easily misled unless he makes an effort to read the poem as it would have been understood in Donne's time. Explicates many of the difficult passages in the light of seventeenth-century thinking and concludes that basically the poem is "a witty love poem in the accepted convention of witty love poems. It works towards two salient positions, both of which are perfectly stock in the verse-conventions of the period, but which are normally treated as irreconcilable, and indeed mutually exclusive. It is built upon a well-known fictional situation. It employs throughout accepted figures and traditional devices of wit, such as the fusion of identities, and the religio amoris, both to make its points and as the points made. Its methods are the popular ones, ingenious play of figure, argument by conceit, and straightforward, if hypersubtle, pleading in a brief" (p. 272).

◄§ 892. ———. "Sources of Difficulty and of Value in the Poetry of John Donne." *Letterature Moderne*, 7:182–90.
Challenges the contemporary theorizers on Donne who, following the lead of Dr. Johnson, have failed to recognize that Donne's style is "nothing more occult, or less remote, than the sixteenth century tradition of wit" (p. 183). Claims that "What was new about Donne's poetry—and it is new only in a limited sense—was that the poet found his mode of witty presentation in a thorough-going application of argumentative techniques" (p. 184). Analyzes the rhetorical wit of "Aire and Angels."

◄§ 893. STAMM, RUDOLF. *Englische Literatur.* Wissenshaftliche Forshungsberichte Geisteswissenshaftliche Reihe Herausgegeben von Professor Dr. Kal Hönn, Band 2. Bern: A. Francke. 422 p.
Brief bibliographical essay on scholarship and criticism concerning Donne from 1935 to 1955 (pp. 160–66).

◄§ 894. WARNKE, FRANK J. "Donne's 'The Anniversarie.'" *Expl*, 16: Item 12.
Suggests that the figurative development and the metrical movement of the poem militate against the seemingly serenely affirmative statement of the poem. "The poem is not simply a passionate lyric outcry. Rather, it *is* such an outcry but manages simultaneously to be a powerful dramatic expression of the tension prevailing between the lover's desperate desire for permanence and his unwilling knowledge that such permanence can never be."

◄§ 895. WHITLOCK, BAIRD W. [Correction of transcript of Edward Alleyn's letter to Donne]. *RES*, n.s., 8:420–21.
Corrections and alternate readings suggested by R. C. Bald of the author's transcription of Edward Alleyn's letter to Donne, which was published in *RES*, n.s., 6 (1955):365–71.

1958

◄§ 896. ADAMS, ROBERT M. *Strains of Discord: Studies in Literary Openness.* Ithaca, N.Y.: Cornell University Press. xi, 220 p.
In this study of *open form*, which the author defines as "literary form (a structure of meanings, intents, and emphases, i.e. verbal gestures)

which includes a major unresolved conflict with the intent of displaying its unresolvedness" (p. 13), Donne is mentioned in several places. In Chapter IV, "Metaphysical Poets, Ancient and Modern," the first section of this tripartite essay subtitled "Donne and Eliot" (pp. 105–20), is a much revised version of an article that first appeared in *KR*, 16 (1954):278–91. Maintains that the most distinguishing feature of metaphysical poetry is wit, a "wit based upon a difficult metaphor, intellectual or abstract in its nexus, rather than naturalistic, involving more often an esoteric analogy than a superficial, single-level physical resemblance, and giving always the sense of a difficulty overcome" (p. 107). Emphasizes the dramatic elements in the poetry of Donne and Eliot, who are used as key representatives in a comparison of what the author calls "ancient and modern" metaphysical poetry. Comments on *Satyre III* (pp. 9–13).

⋙ 897. BOTTRALL, MARGARET. *Every Man a Phoenix: Studies in Seventeenth-Century Autobiography.* London: John Murray (Publishers), Ltd. v, 174 p.

References to Donne throughout this study of the emergence of autobiography as a literary genre. Comments on the *Devotions upon Emergent Occasions* (pp. 23–25), which is called "primarily a book of penitential self-revelation" (p. 23).

⋙ 898. BROOKE-ROSE, CHRISTINE. *A Grammar of Metaphor.* London: Seeker & Warburg. xl, 343 p.

Shows that metaphor is more than simply a mental process through which one thing is called another. Since the metaphor is expressed in words and "a metaphoric word reacts on other words to which it is syntactically and grammatically related" (p. 1), the author analyzes this complex relationship as used by different major poets from Chaucer to Eliot. Donne is mentioned frequently. Includes a summary of the author's analyses of Donne's use of metaphor (pp. 296–300).

⋙ 899. BUSH, DOUGLAS. "Tradition and Experience," in *Literature and Belief*, ed. M. H. Abrams, pp. 31–52. English Institute Essays, 1957. New York: Columbia University Press.

Reprinted in *Engaged and Disengaged* (Cambridge: Harvard University Press, 1966), pp. 143–63.

Concerned with the non-Christian's response to and experience of poetry that is rooted in Christian belief. Makes several references to Donne. Suggests that "the great poetry of religious meditation, the poetry that really comes home to modern readers who do not share the beliefs it embodies, is that which extends beyond the particular creed and personality of its author, which grows out of and embraces general human experience" (pp. 40–41). States that Donne's religious poems do not do this, "They have their technical and aesthetic interest, which is considerable but not inexhaustible; yet, with a few exceptions, I do not think that, after the first impact, they wear very well" (p. 39).

⊷§ 900. Cross, Gustav. "Another Donne Allusion." N&Q, n.s., 5:532–33.
Points out an allusion to the first line of "Twicknam garden" in George Etherege's first play, *The Comical Revenge; or, Love in a Tub* (IV, v, l. 41). Etherege's adaptation helps explain the meaning of "surrounded with teares" since he writes "drown'd in tears."

⊷§ 901. Donne, John. *The Sermons of John Donne*. Edited, with Introductions and Critical Apparatus, by Evelyn M. Simpson and George R. Potter. Vol. IX. Berkeley and Los Angeles: University of California Press; London: Cambridge University Press. vi, 444 p. 10 vols.
Table of Contents (pp. v–vi); List of Illustrations (p. vii); Introduction (pp. 1–44); The Sermons (pp. 45–411); Textual Notes to the Sermons in Volume IX (pp. 413–444). "This volume falls into two parts. The first contains the series of dated sermons up to the point at which the beginning of Donne's fatal illness forced him to stop preaching and retire into the country; the second contains a number of undated sermons, some of which may go back to 1624 or 1625" (p. 1).

⊷§ 902. Falk, Ruth E. "Donne's 'Resurrection, imperfect.'" *Expl*, 17: Item 24.
Paraphrases the poem and concludes that the primary meaning is contained in the tag phrase, *Desunt caetera*, which can be translated either as "the rest is lacking" or "the rest are missing," and the word *imperfect* in the title.

⊷§ 903. Hagopian, John V. "A Difficult Crux in Donne's *Satyre II*." *MLN*, 73:255–57.
Challenges Grierson's emendation and reading of lines 71–73 of the satire. If *like* is read as an adverb meaning *as* or as an adjective meaning *similar*, then the lines make sense as they stand in the 1633 edition.

⊷§ 904. ———. "Donne's 'Love's Diet,' 20–24." *Expl*, 17:Item 5.
Challenges Grierson's paraphrase of line 21 of "Loves diet" and suggests an interpretation, which, the author claims, is consistent with Donne's typically scornful and bravado attitude toward the vanity of women.

◄§ 905. HICKEY, ROBERT L. "Donne's Art of Memory." *TSL*, 3:29–36.
Maintains that the range, variety, and quality of the imagery in Donne's sermons can best be accounted for by understanding Donne's belief that "the ends of persuasive discourse, i.e. *docendum, movendum, delectandum*, are achieved by evoking the faculty of memory instead of, or in addition to, appealing to the understanding or attempting to influence the will" (p. 29). Shows that Donne, accepting for the most part the Renaissance theories about the soul and the operations of the mind, came to recognize that memory was the unique faculty of the soul in the listener through which persuasion could be most effectively achieved. "The remarkable range of Donne's imagery in his sermons, his references and allusions drawn from virtually all possible fields of knowledge, his examples, illustrations and analogies, his piling of metaphor upon metaphor, even the redundancy and superfluity of his tropes and figures, are the result of his efforts to evoke the memory of each of his listeners" (p. 33).

◄§ 906. HOWARTH, R. G. "References to John Donne." *N&Q*, n.s., 5:43.
Challenges the scholarly procedure and conclusions of those who fail to examine manuscript and printed sources to verify their critical opinions. Suggests that his own collection of mentions of and allusions to Donne, to appear in the revised edition of Keynes's bibliography, agrees basically with the conclusions of R. A. Bryan, *SCN*, (Summer 1954):21, who pointed out that "Donne's most popular poems were his elegies. His love lyrics were second in popularity; but the shorter, simpler lyrics were preferred to those like *The Extasie* now highly regarded."

◄§ 907. HUGHES, MERRITT Y. "The Seventeenth Century," in *Contemporary Literary Scholarship: A Critical Review*, ed. Lewis Leary, pp. 67–82. New York: Appleton-Century-Crofts, Inc.
General review of some of the more significant critical estimates of Donne and Milton. Comments on variously changing attitudes toward Donne's use of science and the New Philosophy.

◄§ 908. JOSEPH, BROTHER, FSC. "Donne's 'A Valediction: forbidding mourning,' 1–8." *Expl*, 16:Item 43.
Comments on the word *melt* (l. 5) and shows how it functions as part of the images of silence, which predominate in the first three stanzas of the poem. Sees a parallel between Donne's use of the word and Banquo's comment in *Macbeth* (I, iii, l. 81).

◄§ 909. KEYNES, GEOFFREY. *A Bibliography of Dr. John Donne, Dean of Saint Paul's*. 3d ed. rev. Cambridge: Cambridge University Press. xviii, 285 p.
Only one new entry among the early editions of Donne's work, a

hitherto unrecorded variant of the *Three Sermons*. Includes five new works containing previously unrecorded pieces by Donne. A number of additions to two of the appendices: (1) the number of books known to have survived from Donne's library is increased from 61 to 197, and (2) over 40 double-column pages contain important references to and criticism of Donne from 1597 to 1957. Contains 13 more illustrations, lists reviews for the first time, and contains a new section entitled "Selected Poems." Identifies entries for the first time by *STC* and *Wing* numbers.

⌁§ 910. ———. "Dr. Donne and Scaliger." *TLS*, 21 February, pp. 93, 108.

Describes a recently discovered book from Donne's library, *Opus Novum de emendatione temporum in octo libros tributum* by Joseph Scaliger (Paris, 1583). Opposite the title page on the flyleaf is a heretofore unknown four-line epigram by Donne, "the longest verse writing in Donne's own hand that is so far known" (p. 108). Gives John Sparrow's translation from Latin to English. Facsimile reproduction of the epigram (p. 93). See also John Sparrow, *TLS*, 28 February, p. 115.

⌁§ 911. LEGOUIS, PIERRE. "John Donne and William Cowper: A Note on *The Task*, III, 712–24." *Anglia*, 76:536–38.

Points out possible echoes of Donne's "Confined Love" and "Holy Sonnet XVIII: Show me deare Christ" in Cowper's poem. "An unconscious echo is the utmost we might conjecture" (p. 538). Cowper states in a letter of July 31, 1790, that he had read Donne's work many years before. He also indicates in several places that Donne is an ancestor of his mother.

⌁§ 912. MACKLEM, MICHAEL. *The Anatomy of the World: Relations Between Natural and Moral Law from Donne to Pope*. Minneapolis: The University of Minnesota Press. viii, 139 p.

Studies the development of the relationship between natural and moral law in the period between Donne and Pope. "Both Donne and Pope were working within established schemes of belief. The prevailing assumptions within each were controlled by a theory of law and of the relationship between law and the natural and moral agent. For Donne this relationship is productive of disorder in both man and the world; for Pope it is productive of order. The difference is not simply that between affirmative and negative answers to the question of the existence of evil. It is rather that between a conception of evil as sin or the consequences of sin and a conception of evil as a condition of existence" (p. 4). Starting with the concept of disorder, as evidenced in *The first Anniversary* (ll. 201–14), the author shows how a very different view had established itself by 1670, when Burnet published *Sacred Theory of the*

Earth and was subsequently attacked by a number of his contemporaries who not only denied Burnet's point that mountains and seas were signs of corruption resulting from the Fall but who insisted that these phenomena represented God's power and wisdom. Gives an account of the development of thought and sensibility that culminated in Pope's *Essay on Man* (Epistle I, ll. 171–72). Two appendices: (1) a checklist of short titles of the Burnet Controversy (pp. 97–99), and (2) "Moral Gravitation: a Metaphor of Moral Order" (pp. 100–102).

≈§ 913. MACLURE, MILLAR. *The Paul's Cross Sermons 1534–1642.* Toronto: University of Toronto Press; London: Oxford University Press. vii, 261 p.

Traces the history of the outdoor sermon during and after the English Reformation and the changes it underwent as a result of political and theological conflict. Mention is made of Donne throughout concerning those sermons given at Paul's Cross.

≈§ 914. MARSHALL, WILLIAM H. "Elizabeth Drury and the Heathens." *N&Q,* n.s., 5:533–34.

Suggests that Donne in the *Anniversaries* portrays Elizabeth Drury as representing not only redeemed man but also unfallen man. Elizabeth, unlike the rest of mankind, knows God intuitively and possesses "essential joy." Heathens in their worship of various idols succeed only in acquiring an imperfect fragmentary vision of the one transcendent God; their joys are "accidentall joyes."

≈§ 915. ———. "A Possible Interpretation of Donne's 'The Second Anniversary' (Lines 33–36)." *N&Q,* n.s., 5:540–41.

Suggests that lines 33–36, in which Donne envisions his commemorative verses in honor of Elizabeth Drury as repopulating the wasteland created by her death, Donne portrays the girl as a father (she will never be a mother) who plays the male role to the necessarily feminine muse. Seen in this light, the poems are "legitimate" and properly bear her name. Suggests that perhaps Donne is responding to the unfavorable criticism that had been levelled against *The first Anniversary.*

≈§ 916. MASOOD-UL-HASAN. *Donne's Imagery.* Aligarh: Muslim University. 95 p.

Proposes "to study the images subject-wise rather than through an analysis of a few individual poems. As such, it is not only a study of the sources of imagery but, also, an attempt at the appraisal of the fascinating interaction of images which is the very breath of Donne's poetry." Catalogues and discusses images, metaphors, and conceits from the areas of sex, religion, law, philosophy, geography, chemistry, astronomy, coins, voyages, law, politics, foods and banquets, architecture and horticulture, music, war, death, popular beliefs, superstitions, magic and witchcraft, and the senses. Maintains that these images "are not mere rhetorical devices employed to make the verses more effective and ornate, but they are integral with his thinking and constitute the very texture of his thought" (p. 1). Selective bibliography (pp. 89–91).

⋙ 917. MURRAY, W. A. "Donne's Gold-Leaf and his Compasses."
    MLN, 73:329–30.
Points out that there is a transitional association between the image of gold leaf and the compass image that follows in "A Valediction: forbidding mourning" (ll. 21–36). The chemical symbol for gold, found in Paracelsian medical and alchemical texts, was a point surrounded by a circle. Notes that in one such tract, entitled *Paragranum*, the main features of Donne's complex image are suggested.

⋙ 918. NOVARR, DAVID. *The Making of Walton's Lives*. Cornell Studdies in English, eds. M. H. Abrams, Francis E. Mineka, and William M. Sale, Jr., 41. Ithaca, N.Y.: Cornell University Press. xvi, 527 p.
Discusses Walton's biographical methodology and intention and also makes important comments on the subjects of the *Lives*. Although Donne is mentioned throughout, Part I, "The Earliest Life and Its Revisions" (pp. 19–126), is devoted to a study of *The Life and Death of Dr Donne* (1640) and its subsequent revisions, as well as to an examination of Walton's relationship with Donne. Says that "The revisions of the Life of Donne are a cumulative monument to Walton's veneration for Donne" (p. 125). Appendix B: "Walton and the Poems about Donne's Seal" (pp. 503–6).

⋙ 919. POWERS, DORIS C. "Donne's Compass." *RES*, n.s., 9:173–75.
Suggests that, although Donne may have derived his compass image in "A Valediction: forbidding mourning" from Guarini's "Riposte dell' Amante" (Venice, 1598) as Josef Lederer suggests in *RES*, 22 (1946): 198f., it is also possible that Donne, like Guarini, was influenced by the device of a compass inscribing a circle on a tablet used by Christophe Plantin, the sixteenth-century Belgian printer. Donne had at least two volumes with the Plantin device in his library. An image in "Loves Progress" (ll. 79–80), an early poem, indicates the possibility that Donne was acquainted with the device and recognized its poetic possibilities.

⋙ 920. PRAZ, MARIO. *The Flaming Heart: Essays on Crashaw, Machiavelli, and Other Studies in the Relations between Italian and English Literature from Chaucer to T. S. Eliot*. Anchor Books A132. Garden City, N.Y.: Doubleday & Co., Inc. 390 p.
In "The Politic Brain: Machiavelli and the Elizabethans" (pp. 90–

145), the author discusses *Ignatius his Conclave* (pp. 134f.). "Donne's Relation to the Poetry of His Time" (pp. 186–203), which originally appeared in *A Garland for John Donne 1631–1931*, ed. Theodore Spencer (Cambridge: Harvard University Press; London: Oxford University Press, 1931), appears in a much revised form, pp. 53–72.

☙ 921. ———. *John Donne*. Torino: S.A.I.E. 277 p.
Revision of *La Poesia Metafisica Inglese del Seicento: John Donne* (Roma, 1945).

☙ 922. Press, John. *The Chequer'd Shade: Reflections on Obscurity in Poetry*. New York: Oxford University Press. 229 p.
Reprinted as an Oxford Paperback, 1963.
Points out that obscurity in Donne's poetry frequently arises from the poet's complex patterns of thought. "A great deal of Donne's obscurity springs from his complete fidelity to the intricate nature of his chosen themes, his determination that the most delicate nuances of every subtle concept shall be revealed in all their bewildering variety" (pp. 25–26). Suggests that modern ignorance of the philosophical notions that inform the poems rather than intrinsic difficulty of the lines has increased the problem. Several comments on the relationship of Donne's obscurity to that of Eliot and Yeats.

☙ 923. Richmond, H. M. "Donne and Ronsard." *N&Q*, n.s., 5:534–36.
Points out three parallels between Donne and Ronsard: (1) "Holy Sonnet XIV: Batter my heart" and *Amours* (ii. l. 9); (2) "Negative love" and Ronsard's madrigal beginning "L'homme est bien sot"; (3) "The Canonization" and "Elegie à Marie." Concludes, "In style, theme, and allusion, Ronsard leads the way for Donne in the three examples which I have given" (p. 536).

☙ 924. Russell, John D. "Donne's 'A Lecture Upon the Shadow.'" *Expl*, 17:Item 9.
In part a reply to M. A. Goldberg, *Expl*, 14 (1956):Item 50. Argues against the reading of the poem against a background of Paracelsian and Neoplatonic thinking. Donne deliberately makes the imagery of the poem inconsistent in order to point out that there is really no affinity between love (man-controlled) and the diurnal cycle. For a reply by Nat Henry, see *Expl*, 20 (1962):Item 60.

☙ 925. Seng, Peter J. "Donne's Compass Image." *N&Q*, n.s., 5:214–15.
Quotes from an anonymous poem found in a commonplace book in the Folger Library manuscript collection (452.5, fols. 25^v–26), transcribed some time between 1620 and 1630, to demonstrate that the com-

parison of lovers to compasses in the seventeenth century was not as unusual as Dr. Johnson perhaps thought.

⋙ 926. SHAPIRO, I. A. "Walton and the Occasion of Donne's *Devotions*." *RES*, n.s., 9:18–22.

Discusses Donne's illness of 1623, the occasion of his writing the *Devotions*, and identifies the specific illness as relapsing fever, which Donne himself alludes to when he concludes his meditations by having his physicians warn of "the fearful danger of relapsing." Discounts Gosse's theory that the illness resulted from a chill after the Law Sergeant's Feast of October 1623; likewise discredits Walton's account, in which Walton confuses a later illness of 1625 with the one of 1623 and therefore assigns the *Devotions* erroneously to this later date.

⋙ 927. SMITH, A. J. "The Metaphysic of Love." *RES*, n.s., 9:362–75.

Reprinted in *Discussions of John Donne*, ed. Frank Kermode (Boston: D. C. Heath & Co., 1962), pp. 150–60.

After summarizing the works of several major love philosophers who were popular in Renaissance Italy and well known in England by the seventeenth century, the author shows that, contrary to claims made by modern critics, "The Extasie," for all its witty brilliance, is not a seduction poem, nor a statement of an individual metaphysic of love, nor basically an introspective piece, nor an expression of personal passion. Maintains that "Beyond doubt, it is the work of a strongly original and variously gifted personality, with a fine dramatic sense and feeling for language. But these gifts appear to be exercised in that dressing-up, representing of received positions, which Italian critics of the Renaissance regarded as the essentials of poetic process. Only, Donne's chief vivifying resource is what his age called 'wit' " (p. 375).

⋙ 928. SOENS, A. L. "Casaubon and Donne." *TLS*, 2 May, p. 241.

Calls attention to a Latin letter dated February 17 written by John Harington and sent to Isaac Casaubon, then in Paris, along with a copy of Donne's *Pseudo-Martyr*. Points out that "Since Donne's *Pseudo-Martyr* was not entered in the Stationers' Register until December, 1609, and Casaubon left Paris for England in October, 1610, the letter was undoubtedly written in 1610, and the *Pseudo-Martyr* must therefore have been published earlier than February 17 in that year." Points out also that Donne refers twice to Casaubon's still unpublished *De libertate ecclesiastica* (1612) in *Pseudo-Martyr*. Donne apparently had access to one of several copies still in sheets.

⋙ 929. SPARROW, JOHN. "Dr. Donne and Scaliger." *TLS*, 28 February, p. 115.

Adds two more recently discovered items to the list of books from Donne's library: (1) *Compendio dell'Arte Essorcistica* by Girolamo

Menghi (Venice, 1601), and (2) the second part of the same work, *Parte Seconda Dell 'Arte Essorcistica* (Venice, 1601). Reproduces part of a letter by H. W. Garrod, who corrects Sparrow's translation of a four-line Latin epigram discovered by Keynes in Donne's copy of Scaliger's *Opus Novum de emendatione temporum in octo libros tributum*. See also Geoffrey Keynes, *TLS*, 21 February, p. 108.

✺§ 930. STAPLETON, LAURENCE. "The Theme of Virtue in Donne's Verse Epistles." *SP*, 55:187–200.

Examines Donne's use of the word *virtue* in the *Letters to Severall Personages*, which, the author claims, "represent a preparation for the more ambitious as well as more profound *Anniversaries*—and provide a sequel to them as well" (p. 187). At first Donne seems to use the word to mean little more than a renunciation of the corruption of the world of affairs. Later on, however, he "derived some special connotation of the term *virtus* from Paracelsus, and, in a striking manner, combined it with Plato's conception of virtue as indivisible. From the conjunction of these two notions, he originated an almost symbolic term that gives a common focus to his later verse epistles and eventually results in the more animated structure of the Anniversaries" (p. 189).

✺§ 931. WARNKE, FRANK J. "Jan Luykens: A Dutch Metaphysical Poet." *CL*, 10:45–54.

Maintains that, although there are affinities between the poetry of Donne and Luykens, the latter's poetry resembles more closely the work of the later metaphysical poets, like Vaughan.

✺§ 932. WARREN, AUSTIN. "Donne's 'Extasie.' " *SP*, 55:472–80.

Interprets the poem as a meditative one that is neither completely Platonic nor completely anti-Platonic but rather an attempt to find a third position "which is neither Christian and sacramental marriage nor yet the socially and spiritually defiant naturalism he had expressed in poems like 'Communitie' " (p. 474). Argues that the poem reflects Donne's own inner tensions about love philosophies. Calls the hypothetical listener in the poem "the analysing—evaluating lover whose consciousness is the unifying medium of the poem" (p. 480).

✺§ 933. WILSON, EDWARD M. "Spanish and English Religious Poetry of the Seventeenth Century." *Journal of Ecclesiastical History*, 9:38–53.

Comments briefly on the influence of the Ignatian method of meditation on the *Anniversaries* and *Holy Sonnets*. Maintains that there is nothing in Spanish religious poetry of the time that is quite like Donne.

1959

∽§ 934. ALLEN, D. C. "Donne on the Mandrake." *MLN*, 74:393–97.

Comments on various scriptural and classical connotations and explanations of the mandrake. Points out that the plant was thought to increase fertility and act as an aphrodisiac and soporific. Suggests that what Donne is saying in "Goe, and catche a falling starre" is "get with child the thing that gets with child." Compares this reading with Donne's comments on the mandrake in *The Progresse of the Soule*, that the fruit of the plant inflames desire but that the leaves kill the power to conceive.

∽§ 935. ———. "Love in a Grave." *MLN*, 74:485–86.

Points out that Donne's placing of a pair of lovers to bed in a grave ("The Anniversarie," "The Relique") is not as baroque or morbid as certain modern commentators suggest. The idea of the joint burial of heroes and, by extension, lovers, is a notion found in several sources from antiquity, particularly in Ovid.

∽§ 936. ATTAL, JEAN-PIERRE. "Qu'est-ce que la poésie 'métaphysique'?" *Critique* (Paris), 15:682–707.

Review of six critical studies: (1) Denonain's *Thèmes et Formes de la Poésie «Métaphysique»* (1956); (2) Odette de Mourgues's *Metaphysical Baroque and Précieux Poetry* (1953); (3) Alan Boase's *Sponde* (1949); (4) "Poètes Anglais et Poètes Français de l'Epoque baroque," *RHS*, (1949):155–84; (5) Joan Bennett's *Four Metaphysical Poets* (1957); (6) T. S. Eliot's "The Metaphysical Poets" in *Selected Essays* (1953). Argues that metaphysical poetry is indeed metaphysical in that it deals with first principles and first causes, that it is above all concerned with truth rather than beauty, and that it scorns the heritage of the classics and traditional poetic phraseology: "Ils se sont tournés vers quotidien et le familier pour atteindre le«réel»" (p. 706). Compares Donne to Marino and discusses his Platonism. Maintains that Donne's treatment of love is basically mythical.

∽§ 937. BALD, R. C. *Donne & the Drurys*. Cambridge: Cambridge University Press. x, 175 p.

Traces in detail Donne's relationship with Sir Robert Drury and his family. Comments extensively on Donne's continental journey with the Drurys in 1611–1612 and on Drury's long-time patronage. Considers Donne "only in so far as he was in touch with the Drurys; no attempt has been made to tell the full story of his life even during the years of his friendship with them" (p. ix).

⊷§ 938. BOLLIER, E. P. "T. S. Eliot and John Donne: A Problem in Criticism." *TSE*, 9:103–18.

Re-examines Eliot's criticism of Donne and the metaphysicals in the light of the rest of his criticism during the 1920s and 1930s. Discusses *The Sacred Wood* "to establish clearly what Eliot's critical theories and program were and what part Donne played in them" (p. 105). Considers *Homage to John Dryden* Eliot's "best known study of metaphysical poetry and from the point of view of his critical program, his most important" (p. 105). Surveys Eliot's critical statements on Donne written between 1925 and 1929, most of which are unpublished, in which Eliot concluded that the metaphysical poets were less important for his own critical purposes than he had originally thought. And lastly, examines Eliot's definitive estimate of Donne, "definitive, at least, in the sense that he has never modified it since making it in 1931" (p. 105). Concludes that Eliot's "early criticism was not disinterested: it was intended to establish a new hierarchy of English poets in order to create a climate of opinion favorable to new poetry, if only to his own. Later, at the end of the decade, when Eliot's general views had more or less prevailed, he abandoned Donne, after dissociating his own views from the fashionable ones and correcting the impression that he was an unqualified admirer of Donne" (pp. 104–5).

⊷§ 939. BRANTS, J. "John Donne, Dichter en Deken." *Kroniek van Kunst en Kultuur*, 19 (No. 6):68–76.

General introduction for Dutch readers. Comments on recent Dutch translations. Surveys briefly the love poetry, sacred verse, and sermons. Compares Donne to the Dutch poet Jacob Cats.

⊷§ 940. C., S. "Donne's 'The Legacie.'" *Expl*, 18:Question 1.

Inquires about the meaning of line 18 of "The Legacie," in which the speaker of the poem tells of his mistress's heart as having "corners" and "colours." "I take 'colours' to mean that she was wearing the favors of other men, but all I can see in 'corners' is the suggestion that her heart is sharp and cruel instead of curved and gentle." For a reply by S. A. Cowan, see *Expl*, 19 (1961):Item 58.

⊷§ 941. CAREY, J. "Clement Paman." *TLS*, 27 March, p. 177.

Questions Keynes's dating of an early reference to Donne by Paman in *A Bibliography of Donne*, 3d ed. (1958), p. 126. Comments on Paman, an early imitator of Donne. Reproduces Paman's *The Taverne*, an imitation of *Satyre IV* (not cited by Keynes); and points out Donnian echoes in Paman's *The Diamond* and *The departure. To Stella*.

◄§ 942. COLIE, ROSALIE L. "Constantijn Huygens and the Metaphysical
    Mode." GR, 34:59–73.
Examines the religious poetry of Huygens, Donne's Dutch translator,
to determine the extent of Huygens's claim of being a metaphysical poet.
Points out many parallels between the two poets and concludes that
Huygens's "religious poetic, his mode of metaphoric usage, his choice
of matter, all show the poet's persuasive belief in God's original wit and
in his own lesser wit, set to sing his praises of God's creativity, working
simultaneously in the physical and spiritual worlds of which metaphysical
poetry is made" (p. 73).

◄§ 943. DONNE, JOHN. *The Sermons of John Donne*. Edited, with In-
    troductions and Critical Apparatus, by George R. Potter and
    Evelyn M. Simpson. Vol. IV. Berkeley and Los Angeles: Uni-
    versity of California Press; London: Cambridge University Press.
    viii, 419 p. 10 vols.
Prefatory Note (pp. v–vi); Table of Contents (pp. vii–viii); List of
Illustrations (p. ix); Introduction (pp. 1–41); The Sermons (pp. 43–
379); Textual Notes to the Sermons in Volume IV (pp. 381–419).
Fifteen sermons preached from the beginning of 1622 to the middle of
1623, Donne's first year and a half as Dean of St. Paul's.

◄§ 944. ——. *The Sermons of John Donne*. Edited, with Introduc-
    tions and Critical Apparatus, by George R. Potter and Evelyn M.
    Simpson. Vol. V. Berkeley and Los Angeles: University of Cali-
    fornia Press; London: Cambridge University Press. vi, 430 p. 10 vols.
Table of Contents (pp. v–vi); List of Illustrations (p. vii); Introduction (pp. 1–31); The Sermons (pp. 33–389); Textual Notes to the Sermons in V (pp. 391–421). Appendix: Donne's Tenure of the Rectory
of Blunham (pp. 423–30). Nineteen undated sermons that the editors
suggest were preached before the middle of 1623.

◄§ 945. DORSTEN, J. A. VAN. "Huygens en de Engelese 'Metaphysical
    Poets.'" TNTL, 76:111–25.
Reviews scholarly opinion about Donne's influence on Huygens.
Argues that a comparison of translations with the originals cannot prove
anything about the influence or lack of it. There are similarities in the
poetry of Huygens and Donne, especially in its obscurity, but metaphysical poets other than Donne exhibit this feature. Analyzes the metaphysical aspects of two poems by Huygens.

◄§ 946. DUNCAN, JOSEPH E. *The Revival of Metaphysical Poetry: the
    History of a Style, 1800 to the Present*. Minneapolis: University
    of Minnesota Press. 227 p.
Reviews in a broad sense the critical reputation of Donne and the

metaphysical poets in their own time and in subsequent centuries. Emphasizes "the line of successive interpretations, rather than individual evaluations, and treats poetic style as a vital force guiding creative efforts in a later period" (p. 5). Attempts "to show in what ways the metaphysical style, as it was interpreted and varied through successive periods, was both like and unlike the metaphysical style of the seventeenth century." Divided into ten chapters: (1) The Early Conceptions of Metaphysical Poetry (pp. 6–28); (2) Seeds of Revival (pp. 29–49); (3) John Donne and Robert Browning (pp. 50–68); (4) The Beginnings of the Revival in America (pp. 69–88); (5) The Catholic Revival and the Metaphysicals (pp. 89–112); (6) The Metaphysical Revival: 1872–1912 (pp. 113–29); (7) Yeats, Donne and the Metaphysicals (pp. 130–42); (8) Eliot and the Twentieth-Century Revival (pp. 143–64); (9) Metaphysicals and Critics since 1912 (pp. 165–81); and (10) The Metaphysical Florescence (pp. 182–202). Chapter 3 first appeared as "The Intellectual Kinship of John Donne and Robert Browning," SP, 50 (1953):81–100, here slightly revised; Chapter 6 first appeared as "The Revival of Metaphysical Poetry, 1872–1912," PMLA, 68 (1953):658–71, here slightly revised.

᪲§ 947. GAMBERINI, SPARTACO. *Poeti Metafisici e Cavalieri in Inghilterra*. Biblioteca dell «Archivum Romanicum»: Serie I: Storia-Letteratura-Paleografia, Vol. 60. Firenze: Leo S. Olschki. 269 p.

Attempts to discriminate between such critical terms as *wit, conceit, metaphysical poetry, euphuism, baroque,* and *mannerism.* Compares and contrasts Chapman, Donne, and Jonson as leaders of different poetical schools. General survey of Donne's verse for an Italian audience (pp. 39–64). While recognizing that in many ways Donne remained an Elizabethan poet, the author points out that the logical, argumentative quality of Donne's verse has no parallel among his contemporaries. Suggests that, although Donne adapts his verse to various occasions and needs, it has a consistent and constant quality to it. Claims that wit is frequently a cover-up for inner tensions and deep anguish. Gives the poetry a somewhat autobiographical reading.

᪲§ 948. GARDNER, HELEN. "The Argument about 'The Ecstasy,'" in *Elizabethan and Jacobean Studies*, pp. 279–306. Oxford: The Clarendon Press.

Reprinted, 1967.

Outlines the controversy over "The Extasie." "There is no short poem of comparable merit over which such completely divergent views have been expressed, and no lover of Donne's poetry can be happy to leave the question in its present state of deadlock" (p. 279). Maintains that the poem is about ecstasy, not primarily about the rival claims of physical and spiritual love. Suggests that Leone Ebreo's *Dialoghi d'Amore* is a likely source for the poem as well as for "The Dreame." Detailed analysis of the poem to show that the primary subject that Donne explores is the happiness of equal and perfect union between two lovers.

➤§ 949. ———. "Interpretation," in *The Business of Criticism*, pp. 52–75. Oxford: The Clarendon Press.

Comments on "Aire and Angels" by explaining certain intellectual traditions that inform the poem and by discussing several of Donne's other poems, especially "Negative love" and "Farewell to love," which give the critic certain insights into both the statement and the tone of "Aire and Angels." Disagrees in particular with those who regard the last lines of the poem as inconsistent with the rest of it.

➤§ 950. KORNBLUTH, ALICE FOX. "Another Chaucer Pun." *N&Q*, n.s., 6:243.

Suggests that the pun in line 312 of Chaucer's *Troilus*, in which the eyes represent zeros or naught, anticipates Donne's use of similar wordplay in "A Valediction: of weeping."

➤§ 951. MANLEY, FRANCIS. "Chaucer's Rosary and Donne's Bracelet: Ambiguous Coral." *MLN*, 74:385–88.

Discusses several contradictory opinions held concerning the supernatural power of coral. Sometimes it was regarded as a protection against the devil and evil; at other times, it was considered a love charm. In "Sonnet. The Token" Donne rejects the coral bracelet offered by his mistress since he apparently fears that it might protect him against the very thing that he seeks.

➤§ 952. MARTZ, LOUIS L. "Donne and the Meditative Tradition." *Thought*, 34:269–78.

Reprinted as "John Donne: A Valediction," in *The Poem of the Mind* (New York: Oxford University Press, 1966), pp. 21–32.

Argues that the central organizing principle of Donne's poems, which gives them "their distinctive structure, direction, and inclusiveness" (p. 276), is the meditative tradition. "The term 'meditation' . . . does not serve to replace the term 'metaphysical'; it rather intersects the term 'metaphysical,' and serves a different purpose by associating Donne with a particular tradition in European culture. Reading Donne in the context of European meditative literature may help us to see more clearly the nature of his greatness, and to grasp his firm centrality in the life of his age and our own. It may even help to preserve Donne's poetry against the encroaching shadows of myths and archetypes" (p. 277).

➤§ 953. MORAN, BERNA. "Donne's Poem 'The Dream.'" *Litera*, 6:31–33.

Discusses the logical construction of the poem and its unity. Shows how the poem is informed by the Aristotelian–Thomistic system.

◄§ 954. MURRAY, W. A. "What Was the Soul of the Apple?" RES, n.s., 10:141–55.

Interprets The Metempsychosis (The Progresse of the Soule) as an "embryo Fall-poem, different in style and method from later developments of a similar theme in the Anniversaries. It is Donne on the subject of Paradise Lost, characteristically finding his symbols in the attempt of Philo Judaeus to allegorize the story of Genesis" (p. 141). Finds that the essential theme of the poem is moral choice and argues that it shows that moral choice is vitiated by the nature of a fallen world. Sees the poem as a reflection of Donne's mind and mood in 1601. Finds the references to Elizabeth to be complimentary, neither bitter nor antagonistic. The imagery is basically iconographic and is reminiscent of Bosch.

◄§ 955. NEWTON, WILLOUGHBY. "A Study of John Donne's Sonnet XIV." Anglican Theological Review, 41:10–12.

A reading of the sonnet in the light of certain suggestions made by Paul Tillich in Love, Power and Justice (1954).

◄§ 956. PAFFORD, J. H. P. "Donne: An Early Nineteenth-Century Estimate." N&Q, n.s., 6:131–32.

Reprints a poem from Pieces of Ancient Poetry, from unpublished manuscripts and scarce books (1814), which the editor, John Fry, calls "the germ of a small poem by Dr. Donne." Fry assumed that either the poem was a rough first version of "Goe, and catche a falling starre" or perhaps an anonymous source used by Donne. Fry's hostile comments on Donne reflect an assessment of Donne in 1814: "Donne never can be admired, nor ever obtain a second perusal from any mind imbued with the slightest particle of taste, or fancy, or feeling" (p. 132).

◄§ 957. PETERSON, DOUGLAS L. "John Donne's Holy Sonnets and the Anglican Doctrine of Contrition." SP, 56:504–18.

Sees the first sixteen Holy Sonnets (as ordered by Helen Gardner in The Divine Poems) as a unified sequence and suggests that the governing principle of all nineteen of the sonnets is the Anglican doctrine of contrition. The sonnets move from an expression of fear of the Lord to one of love, resulting in genuine contrition for sin as opposed to mere attrition. "To show that the Holy Sonnets have a unity of purpose and theme is not to argue that their value as poetry is thereby enhanced, but, ultimately, responsible criticism will have to take into account the ramifications in individual poems of the theological doctrine which informs the sonnets as a group. For one thing, the meaning of individual sonnets is qualified by their relationships with other sonnets in the group. For another, the terminology of individual sonnets is given finer definition by their theological context than is otherwise possible. Finally, we are brought closer to understanding the sonnets on Donne's terms.

Such a reading ought, at least, to lead to certain revisions of contemporary commonplaces about Donne's neurotic and melancholic faith" (p. 518).

⋙ 958. Praz, Mario. "Donne and Dickens." TLS, 20 February, p. 97.
Points out a parallel between one of Donne's sermons in which he discusses the dust in a church as the remains of dead persons and Dickens's comic treatment of the same subject in *The Uncommercial Traveller*.

⋙ 959. Richmond, H. M. "The Intangible Mistress." *MP*, 56:217–23.
Discusses various treatments of the theme of the unknown or unknowable mistress, a stock theme in Renaissance poetry, as a way of distinguishing what is genuinely metaphysical in metaphysical poetry. Donne, like Ronsard, focuses his attention not only on the lady or her physical charms but on the state of the lover's mind. Donne analyzes an attitude in his poetry instead of creating situations, and he naturally turns to reason and logic to assist him in such analyses. Using "Negative love" as his primary Donnian example, the author shows that the crucial interest in the poem is not in feeling but in thinking. Concludes, "The really interesting point is, however, that the processes which Donne invokes are 'metaphysical' in the strictest sense. For the Renaissance lover no less than for the theologian of the time, the pursuit and definition of the ideal, whether sacred or profane, could proceed only by means of the sole systematic resources available—the intellectual processes of the medieval scholastic thinkers" (p. 219).

⋙ 960. Scott, Robert Ian. "Donne and Kepler." *N&Q*, n.s., 6:208–9.
Explains the involved astronomical metaphor with which Donne begins the "Elegie upon the untimely death of the incomparable Prince Henry" in terms of Kepler's first law of planetary motion. Donne uses the metaphor to illustrate the central importance of reason always coinciding with faith.

⋙ 961. Stephenson, A. A. "G. M. Hopkins and John Donne." *DownR*,
77:300–320.
Compares the devotional poetry of Hopkins and Donne. Discusses Donne's possible influence on Hopkins. Argues that Hopkins's religious poetry is more satisfying than Donne's because his Christian vision was more profound and more inclusive.

⋙ 962. Tillotson, Kathleen. "Donne's Poetry in the Nineteenth Century (1800–1872)," in *Elizabethan and Jacobean Studies*, pp. 307–26. Oxford: The Clarendon Press.
Presents a detailed account of the interest in Donne and his poetry during the nineteenth century, thereby adding more evidence to the

already generally accepted notion that the modern revival of Donne did not suddenly begin in 1912 (Grierson) nor in 1921 (Eliot). To his nineteenth-century reading audience, Donne was an intriguing curiosity and widely appreciated but was considered too risqué for the polite anthologies of the period.

❧ 963. UNTERMEYER, LOUIS. "The Metaphysical Man: John Donne," in *Lives of the Poets: The Story of One Thousand Years of English and American Poetry*, pp. 122–36. New York: Simon & Shuster, Inc.
General introduction to Donne's reputation. Contains a biographical sketch and comments on some of the more salient characteristics of the poetry.

❧ 964. WHITE, WILLIAM. "Sir Geoffrey Keynes's Bibliography of John Donne: A Review with Addenda." *BB*, 22:186–89.
Reviews Keynes's third edition of *A Bibliography of Dr. John Donne* (1958) and adds more than 200 items, mostly critical studies.

❧ 965. WHITLOCK, BAIRD W. "The Heredity and Childhood of John Donne." *N&Q*, n.s., 6:257–62; 348–53.
Gives information on Donne's family background and on the circum-stances of his childhood. Points out that Donne's mother's family con-sisted of lawyers, physicians, dramatists, civil servants, and experienced travellers—all of whom must have had some influence on the young Donne either directly or indirectly through family consciousness. Little is known about Donne's father, and what is known is not particularly flattering. Donne's stepfather, an eminent physician, whose profession constantly brought him in contact with death, may have been influential in shaping the sensibilities of the young Donne. There is more to Donne's background and influences on him than simply the Catholic tradition, which at times has been considered almost as if it were the only factor shaping his personality.

1960

❧ 966. ALLEN, D. C. "The Genesis of Donne's Dreams." *MLN*, 75: 293–95.
In "The Dreame" in the *Songs and Sonets*, as well as in "Elegie X: The Dreame," Donne speculates on the erotic dream of love. States that "Both of these poems are sophisticated variations on a not unusual literary topic, and it might be interesting to know something about their ancestors in order to measure the means by which Donne converted them into baroque renderings" (p. 293). Traces this genesis through several medieval romances and in several Renaissance poets, specifically Sannazzaro, Magny, Baif, Ronsard, and Muret.

↜§ 967. BAUERLE, R. F. "John Donne Redone and Undone." N&Q, n.s., 7:386.

Points out a plagiarized and revised version of "Song: Goe, and catche a falling starre" published anonymously in the London Magazine (June 1741), p. 301. The revision not only reflects the taste of the plagiarist but also indicates that Donne was little known at the time and therefore the plagiarism was not detected.

↜§ 968. CANDELARIA, FREDERICK H. "Ovid and the Indifferent Lovers." RN, 13:294–97.

Demonstrates how Ovid's Amores (II, iv) brings together four poets not usually associated with each other—Marlowe, Donne, Suckling, and Herrick—all of whom either directly or indirectly used Ovid as "a model for a pose that became commonplace in Renaissance poetry, the stance of the indifferent lover" (p. 294). Discusses "The Indifferent" and "Elegie XVII: «Variety»." Concludes that both poems use Ovidian materials for their own purposes and that both end in a manner unlike Ovid's elegy.

↜§ 969. CHAMBERS, A. B. "The Meaning of 'Temple' in Donne's 'La Corona.'" JEGP, 59:212–17.

Considers the significance of the fourth sonnet in the La Corona sequence, "Temple." By referring to a number of glosses on the meaning of Jesus's teaching of the doctors in the Temple, the author argues that "the subject matter of the fourth sonnet looks back to the human frailty of the birth of Jesus, signifies the first manifestation of his divinity, marks his entrance into the ministry, and forecasts the end for which he came" (p. 217). The sonnet "appears in a poem of prayer and praise upon the life of Christ not as an extraneous element but as a thematic part which is in effect a précis of the whole" (p. 217).

↜§ 970. COMBECHER, HANS. "John Donne's 'Annunciation': Eine Interpretation." NS, n.s., 9:488–92.

Detailed analysis of the poem with an attempt at the end to place it in the intellectual context of the age.

↜§ 971. CROSSETT, JOHN. "Bacon and Donne." N&Q, n.s., 7:386–87.

Points out that the famous line from the Devotions, "No man is an Iland" was apparently borrowed by Bacon in his revision of the essay "Of Goodnesse and Goodnesse of Nature" (1625). Also suggests that the mention of Saint Paul at the end of the added passage may be an oblique reference to the Dean of St. Paul's.

◄§ 972. ———. "Did Johnson Mean 'Paraphysical'?" *Boston University Studies in English*, 4:121–24.

Suggests that by studying Johnson's dictionary as well as his general critical vocabulary, a vocabulary taken basically from Longinus, it is possible to trace not only the origin but also the precise meaning of the term *metaphysical* as used by Johnson in *The Lives of the Poets*. Concludes that Johnson merely "substituted 'metaphysical' for the non-existent 'paraphysical,' willingly or otherwise accepting the confusion in the exact meanings of *meta* and *para*; and that he wished 'metaphysical' to express the notion of deviating from nature by being excessive and contrary to nature" (p. 124).

◄§ 973. DUNCAN-JONES, E. E. "The Barren Plane-Tree in Donne's "The Autumnall.'" *N&Q*, n.s., 7:53.

Suggests that the second book of Virgil's *Georgics* (ll. 69–70) may be one likely source of the plane-tree allusion. Apparently the concept was widespread, as indicated by Evelyn's *Sylva* (1664), and therefore there is little reason to assume that Donne borrowed the idea from a passage in William Browne's *Britannia's Pastorals*, Book II, Song IV (1616), as suggested by Jack Lindsay, *TLS*, 19 March 1931, p. 234. On the basis of the allusion Lindsay incorrectly dates the poem as having been written after 1616.

◄§ 974. DURR, R. A. "Donne's 'The Primrose.'" *JEGP*, 59:218–22.

Close reading of the poem in which the author suggests that the poem delineates "in ordered sequence, a fundamental action of the *Songs and Sonets* as a whole. This is the action that originates in the desire to find a true—a fixed and perfect—love and security and rest inherent in it, that in its passage through Donne's astute and honest intellect, tutored by corrosive experience, passes into a cynical disintegration of the hope of realizing that ideal, and concludes in 'gay' abandonment to the sensual flux of casual delights" (p. 218). Maintains that the poem "once recognized as microcosmic of this pattern, may thus afford a point of reference for the reading of Donne's secular verse" (p. 218).

◄§ 975. ELLRODT, ROBERT. *L'Inspiration personnelle et l'esprit du temps chez les poètes métaphysique anglais*. Paris: Jose Corti. 2 vols. in 3.

Part 1 of Volume I is entitled "John Donne et les poètes de la tradition chrétienne" (pp. 80–264). Nine chapters devoted specifically to Donne: (1) Présence, (2) Esprit métaphysique et présence au monde, (3) De l'attention de soi, (4) Conscience de soi, (5) La conscience de soi et les modes de la sensibilité, (6) De la sincérité a l'humour, (7) De l'ambiguité, (8) Le paradox et la pensée chrétienne, (9) La pensée logique et l'abstraction. The author describes these chapters as an "analyse patiente des textes s'est effacée de faire apparaître les modes de conscience, les «formes» de pensée, d'imagination et de sensibilité qui ont determiné dans la poésie de Donne le choix et le traitement des thèmes, et se sont réfletées fidèlement dans les «formes» d'expression littéraire" (p. 257). The purpose of the method is to arrive at the essential traits of Donne's literary personality, what the author calls Donne's "personnalité formelle." A central theme of these chapters is Donne's preoccupation with the consciousness of self and how this is related to his uses of paradox, ambiguity, irony, and dissonance. In the second section of Volume I, entitled "Les poètes de la tradition chrétienne" (pp. 265–452), the author discusses Herbert and Crashaw, both of whom are compared to and contrasted with Donne. Appendix entitled "Le sense de «Anniversaries» de Donne" (pp. 453–54). Part 2 Volume I is divided into two sections: (1) "Poètes de transition" (pp. 9–170)—a study of Lord Herbert of Cherbury, Cowley, and Marvell, and (2) "Poètes mystiques" (pp. 171–399)—a study of Vaughan and Traherne. A conclusion (pp. 400–436) relates the various metaphysical poets to each other. Bibliography (pp. 439–72). In Volume II the author discusses the social, psychological, and literary origins of metaphysical poetry at the turn of the century. An appendix, "Donne et le neoplatonisme de la Renaissance" (pp. 401–10), shows that Donne's poetry reflects the interaction of his own individual mode of consciousness with the intellectual, social, and political milieu of his time.

§ 976. ———. "Chronologie des poèmes de Donne." *EA*, 13:452–63.
Summarizes the position of contemporary criticism concerning the dating of Donne's religious poems, satires, epigrams, epistles, and epithalamia, and undertakes to give his own opinion on the dating of the *Elegies* and the *Songs and Sonets*. Suggests that there is no evidence to support the notion that the cynical and libertine poems were written before Donne's marriage.

§ 977. ESCH, ARNO. " 'Paradise and Calvary': Zu Donnes *Hymne to God, my God, in my sicknesse*, V. 21–22." *Anglia*, 78:74–77.
Discusses lines 21–22 of the poem. Points out that Donne might very well have been familiar with the old Christian belief that paradise and calvary were in the same spot. Cites writers as early as the second century who entertained this belief. The legend of Adam's birth and burial on Golgotha was widely known and part of late Judaism. In *The Progresse of the Soule* there is further mention of this belief.

§ 978. FOX, ROBERT C. "Donne in the British West Indies." *History of Ideas News Letter*, 5:77–80.
Reproduces and comments briefly on a poem about Donne "composed by a young lady," which first appeared in the July 18, 1733, issue of *The Barbados Gazette*.

🔊 979. GARDNER, HELEN. "Donne MSS. for the Bodleian." *TLS*, 11 March, p. 168.

Describes three manuscripts acquired by the Bodleian from the library of Wilfred Merton: the Dowden MS. of the poems, the Dowden MS. of the sermons, and the Wilfred Merton MS. of the sermons. Notes that "Apart from the splendid collection in the possession of Sir Geoffrey Keynes, these were the most important Donne manuscripts still in private hands." States that it is likely that the Dowden MS. of the poems represents Donne's own selection of his works made in 1614.

🔊 980. GRENANDER, M. E. "Holy Sonnets VIII and XVII: John Donne." *Boston University Studies in English*, 4:95–105.

Detailed analysis of "Holy Sonnet VIII: If faithfull soules be alike glorifi'd" and "Holy Sonnet XVII: Since she whom I lov'd hath payd her last debt" as "contrasting examples of two instances of Donne's 'wit' pointed out by Louis I. Bredvold: 'a plain and straightforward reasoning about his subject,' and symbolism, the 'most characteristic form' in which Donne's poetic genius expressed itself" (p. 96).

🔊 981. HENINGER, S. K., JR. *A Handbook of Renaissance Meteorology, with Particular Reference to Elizabethan and Jacobean Literature.* Durham: Duke University Press. xii, 269 p.

Reference work in which meteorological information is gathered together from the natural philosophy of Aristotle, Scripture, classical mythology, and the interrelated tenets of magic, astrology, and folklore. Part I describes the scientific background. Part II stresses that, although Elizabethan and Jacobean poetry and prose are dotted with references to meteorological phenomena, they find their most significant form as metaphor. Part III examines the meteorological imagery in selected creative writers, including Donne (pp. 200–203). Discusses "A Feaver" in detail to illustrate his generalizations and refers to *Satyre I*, "The Storme," "A Valediction: forbidding mourning," "Elegie XVI," and several of the divine poems. A list of passages from Donne that contain meteorological references (pp. 256–57).

🔊 982. HOLLOWAY, JOHN. "Patmore, Donne, and the 'Wit of Love,' " in *The Chartered Mirror: Literary and Critical Essays*, pp. 53–62. London: Routledge and Kegan Paul, Ltd.

American ed., New York: Horizon Press, 1962.

Compares Donne and Patmore. Suggests that Donne's poetry "is almost always creating in his reader's mind a profound impression that behind it there is a rich and wide and sensitive contact with reality.... In Patmore, that is only present from time to time; and too often, the opposite is there: too often, the verse seems to *congeal* between the reader and the realities, and obscures those realities from him" (p. 59).

983. HUGHES, MERRITT Y. "Some of Donne's 'Ecstasies.'" *PMLA*, 75:509–18.

Centering his attention on "The Extasie," the author surveys not only the various critical opinions about the seriousness of Donne's central figure in that poem but also Donne's use if the notion of *ekstasis* in several of his other works, both poetry and prose. Argues, "The only escape from the dilemma of treating Donne as a crude sensualist or as a materialistic philosopher less at home in his own century than in ours is to look at him in his own intellectual tradition." Examines that tradition and concludes that "however solemn a revelation of the nature of their love Donne's lovers may have had in 'The Extasie,' he could not have regarded it as something literally equivalent to the final mystical experience of Plotinus" (p. 515).

984. ISER, WOLFGANG. "Manieristische Metaphorik in der englischen Dichtung." *GRM*, n.s., 10:266–87.

Discusses "Hymne to God my God, in my sicknesse" to contrast Donne with the Elizabethans and to establish the principles by which Donne worked. At the center of Donne's poetry is the meditating ego, the bond that connects various metaphors. Donne's goal is self-analysis. Each stanza of the "Hymne" has as its subject self in relation to the different aspects of learning. The interaction of self and these impersonal aspects creates meaning. Wit makes the *coincidentia oppositorum* of the metaphors possible. Using examples from Yeats and Eliot, the author compares the poetry of the seventeenth and twentieth centuries.

985. KAWASAKI, TOSHIHIKO. "John Donne's Microcosm: Some Queries to Professor Empson." *Studies in English Literature* (Tokyo), 36:229–50.

Reply to Empson's "Donne the Space Man," *KR*, 19 (1957):337–99. Discusses Donne's use of the Scholastic and Hermetic philosophy of microcosm.

986. KUHNRE, W. WILLIAM. "The Exposition of Sin in the Sermons of John Donne." *Lutheran Quarterly*, 12:217–34.

Discusses views on sin that Donne maintains in the sermons. In particular, examines Donne's "biblical and catholic point of view that sin is man's proud attempt to contradict God and, by so doing, man's ultimate contradiction of himself" (p. 218). Considers the forms of sin according to Donne and shows "how closely Donne seems to follow the classic Reformation insight into the sin which lingers in the life of the redeemed, the teaching *simul iustus et peccator*, over which no merit other than Christ's can gain victory" (p. 218).

◄§ 987. LERNER, LAURENCE. "The Truest Poetry is the Most Feigning,"
    in *The Truest Poetry; An Essay on the Question: What is Litera-*
    ture?, pp. 204–18. London: Hamish Hamilton.

Discusses Donne and Auden as poets who successfully arrive at truth
by feigning. Suggests that Donne's reputation waned for two and a half
centuries after his death because "readers were not prepared to be
tolerant about what a poem's true subject was" (p. 206). Insists that
Donne's poems "are about anything except what they profess to be
about: philosophy, medicine, physics, topical references—all things under the sun save love" (p. 208). Considers the *Anniversaries* as perhaps
Donne's most "ingenious fibs" and comments on the quality of feigning
in "Song: Goe, and catche a falling starre," "The good-morrow," "The
Sunne Rising," "The Extasie," and "The Anniversarie."

◄§ 988. MARTZ, LOUIS L. "John Donne: the Meditative Voice." MR,
    1:326–42.

Reprinted in *The Poetry of the Mind* (New York: Oxford University
Press, Inc., 1966), pp. 3–20.

While recognizing to some extent the validity of calling much of
Donne's poetry *metaphysical*, the author suggests that an alternative
term, *meditative*, is also particularly descriptive of certain qualities in
Donne's verse. Finds the best definition of that quality, as it appears
in Donne's verse and in other poems, in two pieces by Wallace Stevens,
"Man and Bottle" and "Of Modern Poetry." Such poetry "destroys the
old romantic tenements, and in their place constructs a stage on which
an insatiable actor presents to the mind the action of an inward search"
(p. 327). Illustrates his concept by commenting on selected poems from
the *Holy Sonnets*, the *Elegies*, the *Satyres* (especially *Satyre* III), "Twicknam garden," and "A nocturnall upon S. Lucies day."

◄§ 989. MILES, JOSEPHINE. *Renaissance, Eighteenth-Century, and Mod-*
    ern Language in English Poetry: A Tabular View. Berkeley and
    Los Angeles: University of California Press; London: Cambridge
    University Press. iii, 73 p.

Presents information gathered from two hundred poets, from Chaucer
to the present, "in such a way as to suggest the basic patterns of relation
between poet and poet in the use of language, and at the same time to
provide the most straightforward chronological arrangement of materials
for those who may have other questions to ask, about single poets, single
eras, single types, or single terms" (p. 1). Tabulates Donne's use of
language.

◄§ 990. ORAS, ANTS. "Shakespeare, Ben Jonson, and Donne," in *Pause*
    Patterns in Elizabethan and Jacobean Drama: An Experiment in
    Prosody, pp. 13–19. University of Florida Monographs, Humanities,
    No. 3. Gainesville: University of Florida Press.

Proposes "to examine verse as such, for its own sake, as one of the principal elements contributing to the total impact of Renaissance drama and determining the special nature of the impression that drama creates" (p. 1). Studies "the incidence of internal pauses in each of the nine possible positions within an iambic pentameter line in relation to the totals of such pauses, regardless of the amounts represented by such totals" (p. 2). Briefly notes that Donne, like Jonson, in the *Satyres, Elegies,* and *Letters to Severall Personages* "in his metrical procedures does the opposite of nearly everything characteristic of the dominant Spenserian school.... [Donne's pauses] occur abundantly all over the line, pauses in the last third of the line become exceptionally frequent, and a far more than Spenserian predilection is shown for the uneven pauses" (p. 18). Later Donne reverts—particularly in his *Holy Sonnets*—"to a type of firm design, with iambic peaks, in some instances reminiscent of Spenser," whereas Jonson continues what the author calls "his rather flat-roofed pattern" (p. 19).

౨§ 991. PERELLA, NICHOLAS. "Armarilli's Dilemma: The *Pastor Fido* and Some English Authors." *CL*, 12:348–59.

Points out that the reference to "nature, injur'd by late law" (l. 30) in "The Relique" probably comes from Guarini's *Pastor Fido* (1590).

౨§ 992. POYNTER, F. N. L. "John Donne and William Harvey." *Journal of the History of Medicine and Allied Sciences*, 15:233–46.

Shows that Donne was interested in medicine throughout his life; therefore the imagery Donne borrowed from medicine was more than merely an attempt to exhibit his learning. Points out a number of possible connections between Donne and Harvey. Suggests that Donne may have attended some of Harvey's lectures and that Harvey apparently borrowed imagery from the *Devotions* to illustrate his theory of the primacy of the heart. Apparently Donne had no knowledge of Harvey's theory of the circulation of the blood.

౨§ 993. QUINN, DENNIS. "Donne and 'Tyr.'" *MLN*, 75:643–44.

In a sermon preached at Lincoln's Inn (*The Sermons of John Donne*, eds. Evelyn M. Simpson and George R. Potter, Vol. II, p. 131), Donne refers to a person named "Tyr," a reference that has puzzled scholars. Suggests that "Tyr" is Lucretius Tiraboscus and that the work referred to is his *Rationes textus hebraei et editionis vulgatae* (Venice, 1572). In another sermon (*Sermons*, Vol. III, p. 315) Donne again makes references that suggest his firsthand knowledge of Tiraboscus's work.

౨§ 994. ———. "Donne's Christian Eloquence." *ELH*, 27:276–97.

Maintains that Donne's method of preaching was not as idiosyncratic as moderns believe nor founded upon the more contemporary Renaissance styles of preaching but that it basically is derived from the traditional Augustinian notion of Christian eloquence and its connection with Scripture. Saint Augustine's theory, found chiefly in Book IV of *De Doctrina Christiana*, maintains that the true aim of the Christian preacher is to win souls by "expressing the truth as it is embodied in the Scriptures" (p. 276). Augustine, like Donne, maintained that the preacher should utilize all devices at his command, rhetorical and otherwise, in interpreting the Bible, but "it is the truth that saves souls, not human argument or devices of language" (p. 277). Unlike much Reformation preaching, which centered on theological doctrines and dogmas, the emphasis of the Augustinian sermon is on love and moral vision. The sermon, therefore, is quite distinct from the lecture. Maintains that in his sermons Donne attempts to re-create the truth of Scripture in the way in which the Bible presents this truth, that he speaks to the soul directly rather than simply to the intellect. Concludes that Donne's "use of Biblical metaphors as the imagery of his sermons derives from the conviction that Scriptural rather than human eloquence saves souls; indeed Donne's own style varies to some extent according to the style of his text. This accords with the traditional effort to imitate Scriptural eloquence. In their very structure, the sermons re-enact the truth which Donne sees in the texts, with the result that the sermons are actions imitative of or analogous to the Biblical action. Finally, the sermons are aimed primarily at the soul through memory rather than through rational intellect; in this they follow the Augustinian conception of memory as a great spiritual faculty" (pp. 296–97).

⤙ 995. SKELTON, ROBIN. "The Poetry of John Donne," in *Elizabethan Poetry*, eds. John Russell Brown and Bernard Harris, pp. 203–20. Stratford-Upon-Avon Studies, 2. New York: St. Martin's Press, Inc.

Critical evaluation of the main characteristics of Donne's poetry. Points out how Donne expanded upon and challenged the poetic conventions of his time in such a way as to produce a new kind of poetry. Although Donne has had considerable influence on the poets who have followed him, few in his own time fully understood the complexity of his verse. "It is, in fact (and perhaps rather oddly), only when we reach Browning that we see any attempt to create a 'Construction of Involvement' of Donnian complexity, and we have to look at the poetry of the twentieth century before we can discover any real development of Donne's methods" (p. 220).

⤙ 996. SMITH, A. J. "New Bearings in Donne: *Aire and Angels*." *English*, 13:49–53.

Reprinted in *John Donne: A Collection of Critical Essays*, ed. Helen Gardner (Englewood Cliffs, N.J.: Prentice-Hall, Inc., 1962), pp. 171–79.

Challenges the validity of such modern critical assumptions as "radical image, baroque tension and doubt, unified sensibility, emotional ap-

prehension of thought, and the like" (p. 49) and states that the foundation of metaphysical poetry "is nothing more occult, or less remote, than
the sixteenth-century tradition of wit" (p. 49). Contends that Donne
"simply brought into poetry for quite orthodox ends the manner of a
game with which every frequenter of the Inns of Court would have been
intimately familiar" (p. 50). By using "Aire and Angels" as an example,
the author shows that, although Donne brilliantly handles Renaissance
commonplaces and thereby produces an excellent poem, the poem essentially makes no significantly new contribution to the philosophy of
love. The question explored and answered in the poem had been treated
at least fifty years earlier by Sperone Speroni in his "Dialogo di Amore."

≈§ 997. SOWTON, IAN. "Religious Opinion in the Prose Letters of John
    Donne." *Canadian Journal of Theology*, 6:179–90.
    Tries "to fill in, from the letters, what we already know of Donne's
opinions on a variety of religious matters" (p. 180).

≈§ 998. STEIN, ARNOLD. "Donne and the 1920's: A Problem in Histor-
    ical Consciousness." *ELH*, 27:16–29.
    Suggests that the poets of the 1920s who championed Donne, led in
part by the critical dicta of Eliot, were perhaps from our historical perspective in error in their historical judgments and in their consequent
enthusiasm, but that we should recognize that real problems confronted
the consciousness of these poets and that Donne, along with the theory
of unified sensibility, partially answered a need.

≈§ 999. WHITLOCK, BAIRD W. "The Family of John Donne, 1588–1591."
    N&Q, n.s., 7:380–86.
    Pieces together the scraps of information available in public records
to trace the misfortunes of the Donne family during the critical years
1588 to 1591. Donne's mother, because of her recusancy, fared rather
poorly, and "none of the family knew how to make a good economic
match" (p. 384). Suggests that, although Donne's Catholic sympathies
may have been weakening during this period, his formal break with the
old faith was still several years in the future. Donne's anxiety about his
family and about the recusants in general is reflected in later letters and
in *Satyre II* (ll. 5–10).

≈§ 1000. WILLIAMSON, GEORGE. *Seventeenth Century Contexts*. Lon-
    don: Faber and Faber, Ltd.; Chicago: University of Chicago Press.
    291 p.
    Contains five essays on Donne. Four were published previously and are
reprinted in this volume: "Mutability, Decay, and Jacobean Melancholy," *ELH*, 2 (1935):121–50; "The Libertine Donne," *PQ*, 13 (1934):
276–91; "Textual Difficulties in Donne's Poetry," *MP*, 38 (1940):37–

42; and "Strong Lines," *ES*, 18 (1936):152–59. "The Convention of *The Extasie*" appears for the first time in this collection. Each item has been entered separately in this bibliography.

◄§ 1001. ———. "The Convention of *The Extasie*," in *Seventeenth Century Contexts*, pp. 63–77. London: Faber and Faber, Ltd.; Chicago: University of Chicago Press.

Reprinted in *Seventeenth Century English Poetry: Modern Essays in Criticism*, ed. William Keast (New York: Oxford University Press, 1962), pp. 132–43.

Comparative study of the uses of the convention of the casuistic dialogue on love found in certain poems of Sidney, Greville, Wither, Lord Herbert of Cherbury, and Donne. Points out that Donne is "interested less in the moral casuistry of love than in the philosophical question provoked by it" (p. 72). Suggests that the debate in "The Extasie" may involve the body and soul rather than the souls of two lovers. Explicates some of the crucial lines of the poem and suggests that Bembo's discussion of love in *The Courtier* is the best introduction to Donne's treatment of love.

◄§ 1002. ZIMMERMAN, DONALD E. *The Nature of Man: John Donne's Songs and Holy Sonnets*. The Emporia State Research Studies, v. 8, no. 3. Emporia: Kansas State Teachers College. 33 p.

Divided into four parts: (1) "The Nature and Devices of Donne's Metaphysics" (pp. 5–10) catalogues the basic characteristics of Donne's style, placing particular emphasis on his use of the "telescoped" image, the dynamic image, and paradox; (2) "Love in the Secular Poems" (pp. 10–17) outlines four major themes developed in Donne's love poetry: sensual love, spiritual love, integrated love, and Petrarchan love; (3) "The Extasie: An Explication" (pp. 17–25) discusses the poem as "primarily a study of the paradox of man" and as "analysis of love" in which Donne reconciles the opposites of body and spirit "in such a way as to leave the basic unity of man intact, or to establish such a unity, without sacrificing one opposite to the other" (p. 17); (4) "The Poet in Prayer" (pp. 25–30) shows that Donne achieved his most mature statement about the nature of man in his religious verse, accepting man as "a mixture of sense and spirit, of various levels of being" (p. 30).

1961

◄§ 1003. ALLEN, D. C. "Donne and the Ship Metaphor." *MLN*, 76:308–12.

Traces the use of the ship of salvation and the ship of love metaphors from their classical origins through Saint Augustine to the Renaissance and discusses Donne's use of them in his poetry and prose, especially in

The Progresse of the Soule (ll. 51–60), "A Hymne to Christ" (ll. 1–4), "Aire and Angels" (ll. 15–18), and in certain of the sermons.

৺§ 1004. ———. "Milton and the Love of Angels." *MLN*, 76:489–90.

Supports Marilla's position in *MLN*, 68 (1953):485–86, that Raphael in *Paradise Lost* (VIII, ll. 620–29) is speaking in terms of ideal lovers, as exemplified by Donne in "The Extasie." Finds support for the argument in Alessandro Piccolomini's *Della Institution Morale* (1542), which maintains that bodies alone and souls in bodies cannot unite but that, like the angels, only those souls freed from the imprisonment of the body can unite to become one.

৺§ 1005. ALVAREZ, A. *The School of Donne.* London: Chatto and Windus Ltd. 202 p.

Proposes "to show how Donne affected the language and form of poetry in a way that is still peculiarly meaningful to us, and is rapidly becoming yet more meaningful.... [The study is] an attempt to define a kind of intelligence which, though it was first expressed at the end of the sixteenth century, is still vital and urgent. For Donne was not only the most supremely intelligent poet in the language, he was also the first Englishman to write verses in a way that reflected the whole complex activity of intelligence" (p. 12). Suggests that an inordinate amount of attention has been given to the imagery and conceits of Donne and his followers and tries "to replace the stress on the element of realism in Donne, the skill by which he created a poetic language in which technique was at the service of a fullness of intelligence" (p. 14). Views the "School of Donne," therefore, as united not so much by various poetical methods and techniques but fundamentally by the intellectual attitude and tone that formed it—the desire to portray dramatically in poetry the complexities of thought and emotion. Discusses in Chapter I those elements in Donne that separate him from the Elizabethan tradition, and in the following chapters discusses the followers of Donne in terms of these distinctions. Appendix I, "Donne's Circle" (pp. 187–95), briefly discusses those friends and acquaintances who surrounded Donne at Oxford and later at Lincoln's Inn. Appendix II, "Attacks on Donne" (p. 196), mentions several contemporary attacks on Donne's poetry. In Appendix III, "Donne and the Miscellanies" (pp. 197–98), the author mentions several of the miscellanies to which Donne contributed.

৺§ 1006. ARCHER, STANLEY. "Meditation and the Structure of Donne's 'Holy Sonnets.'" *ELH*, 28:137–47.

Challenges the position of both Louis Martz (*The Poetry of Meditation*) and Helen Gardner (*The Divine Poems*) that the dramatic openings and the tripartite structure of the *Holy Sonnets* are necessarily the result of the influence of the formal meditation as evidenced in *The*

Spiritual Exercises of Saint Ignatius. Argues that the qualities of the "meditative influence" are found also in Donne's secular poetry and concludes it was unlikely that Donne was influenced by meditative literature in these early, profane poems. Points out that it is unlikely that Donne was introduced to the complexities of formal meditation as a child. Exactly where he found the notion of the tripartite structure is a question that deserves further exploration. Shows that the dramatic openings of the *Satyres* are not unlike those of Persius, and notes that tripartite structure, as evidenced in the Greek chorus, is nearly as old as poetry.

◄§ 1007. CHAMBERS, A. B. "Goodfriday, 1613. Riding Westward: The Poem and the Tradition." *ELH*, 28:31–53.
Traces the tradition of spherical analogy. Like the circles of the fixed stars and of the planets in Plato's view of the macrocosm, passion and reason in man move in opposite directions. That which travels in a westward direction is natural and right, thus reflecting God's will; anything that moves eastward is contrary and wrong. However, the analogy is complicated by Christian symbolism in which the East is the better direction since the risen Christ, the sun–son, is connected with the East. Donne is moving westward, yet his devotion moves him eastward. Through a detailed reading of the poem, the author shows how Donne wittily plays upon the inherent paradox.

◄§ 1008. CLEMENTS, ARTHUR L. "Donne's Holy Sonnet XIV." *MLN*, 76:484–89.
Challenges the notion that "Batter my heart" rigidly divides into three distinct quatrains, each of which reflects the specific action of One Person of the Trinity. Maintains that "each of the other Persons is 'involved' in the activity of any one; in other words, the paradox of three-in-one is truly and profoundly a paradox and is operative as such in the poem" (pp. 484–85). Suggests that the organizing principle is "the paradox of death and rebirth, the central paradox of Christianity" (p. 487).

◄§ 1009. COLLMER, ROBERT G. "The Background of Donne's Reception in Holland." *MissQ*, 14:51–57.
Discusses the cultural and literary background of the "Muiderkring" to whom Huygens presented his translations of Donne. Shows why Donne's poems were favorably received by this illustrious circle of Dutch men of letters.

◄§ 1010. ———. "The Meditation on Death and Its Appearance in Metaphysical Poetry." *Neophil*, 45:323–33.
Examines the *meditatio mortis* and notes some of its appearances and reflections in the poetry of Donne, Herbert, Vaughan, and Crashaw.

Points out a number of ways in which Donne's attitude toward death is reflected in his poetry. For example, Donne's poems on death, informed as they are by wit, tend to lack a suggestion of mystical ecstasy sometimes produced by considering the subject. Also Donne infrequently refers to meditation on his own death, a practice highly recommended to reduce one's attraction to sin, but he does contemplate the grave and speaks of "envisioning the situation of death" (p. 330).

᠍᠍ᦗ 1011. COWAN, S. A. "Donne's 'The Legacie.'" *Expl*, 19:Item 58.
Reply to an inquiry by S. C., *Expl*, 18 (1959):Question 1. Suggests a reading of lines 18 and 19 of "The Legacie," in which the speaker of the poem says that his mistress's heart has both "corners" and "colours." "Because the circle, like God, has neither beginning nor end this geometric form symbolized perfection to correspondence-conscious Renaissance man. Conversely, any object with corners must fall short of perfection. The significance of 'colours' is the plural form, suggesting parti- or vari-colored with the implication of fickleness: a chameleon expediently alters shades; a traitor changes his colors."

᠍᠍ᦗ 1012. CRUM, MARGARET. "Notes on the Physical Characteristics of some Manuscripts of the Poems of Donne and Henry King." *Library*, 16:121–23.
Suggests that "the practice of King and his copyists, which are up to a point easy to trace, may be interesting in relation to the best Donne manuscripts, and that Donne's habits may be partly reflected in King's" (p. 121).

᠍᠍ᦗ 1013. DUNCAN-JONES, E. E. "Donne's Praise of Autumnal Beauty: Greek Sources." *MLR*, 56:213–15.
Suggests that one likely source for "The Autumnall" is an anecdote that was borrowed from Plutarch, which appears in Aelian's *Variae Historiae*, a work Donne knew. Points out that the theme of autumnal beauty is developed in Letter 51 of Philostratus and can also be found in a number of epigrams in *The Greek Anthology*. Many of the epigrams would have been available to Donne in Latin, Italian, and French translations.

᠍᠍ᦗ 1014. ELLRODT, ROBERT. "La vogue de l'image scientifique dans la poésie anglaise du dix-septième siècle." *EA*, 14:346–47.
Briefly discusses the use of scientific imagery before and after Donne. Points out that Donne is not unique in this regard: "L'image scientifique est apparue avant Donne en poésie lyrique et n'est pas essentielle à l'expresion de son génie" (p. 346).

◄§ 1015. FLEISSNER, ROBERT F. "Donne and Dante: The Compass Figure Reinterpreted." *MLN*, 76:315–20.

Argues that the compass figure in "A Valediction: forbidding mourning" is "comparable to and possibly influenced directly" by Dante. Points out that Donne was quite familiar with Dante's works and that he owned a copy of the *Il Convito*. Stresses that both poets emphasize the circle, not the instrument. Maintains, "The object of the speaker's love thus occupies the very center of the circle in the same manner as the figure of Love does for Dante" (p. 317). Suggests several other parallels in the poem that are strikingly similar to Dante.

◄§ 1016. GÉRARD, ALBERT. "Mannerism and the Scholastic Structure of Donne's 'Extasie.'" *Pubs. de l'Univ. de l'État à Elisabethville*, 1:27–37.

Close reading of the poem in which the author shows that Donne adopted the formal structure of scholastic logic. "Its structure is built on a pattern that might be simplified as follows: *videtur quod* love rooted in the body and we behave as though we were bodies; *sed contra*, love incites our souls to act on their own and to reveal themselves as the true essence of our selfhood; *respondeo dicendum* that given the conditions of human nature, the body is necessary to the soul, although it is inferior to it" (pp. 34 35). Relates the poem to sixteenth-century Mannerism.

◄§ 1017. HOLLANDER, JOHN. *The Untuning of the Sky: Ideas of Music in English Poetry 1500–1700*. Princeton: Princeton University Press. xii, 467 p.

Discusses certain beliefs about music in the Renaissance and how English poetry of the sixteenth and seventeenth centuries expressed and employed them. Describes "the successive stages in the de-mythologizing of poetry's view of music" (p. 19). Maintains, "From the canonical Mediaeval Christian view that all human music bears a definite relation to the eternal, abstract (and inaudible) 'music' of universal order, to the completely de-Christianized, use of such notions in late seventeenth-century poetry as decorative metaphor and mere turns of wit, a gradual process of disconnection between abstract musical mythology and concrete practical considerations of actual vocal and instrumental music occurs" (p. 19). Discusses briefly Donne's use of musical conceits (pp. 264–65, 281–83, 301).

◄§ 1018. JONES, EVAN. "Verse, Prose and Pope: A Form of Sensibility." *Melbourne Critical Review*, 4:30–40.

Comparative study of Donne's *Satyre IV* and Pope's version of the work.

❧ 1019. KERMODE, FRANK. "Interesting but Tough." *Spectator*, 206: 298–99.

Review of *The School of Donne*, A. Alvarez, and *The Metaphysical Poets*, Helen Gardner.

❧ 1020. LEISHMAN, J. B. *Themes and Variations in Shakespeare's Sonnets*. London: Hutchinson & Co. (Publishers) Ltd. 254 p.

Discusses the differences between Donne and Shakespeare in their use of Platonism and hyperbole and comments on their motives for writing (pp. 171–77). In particular, see "The 'religiousness' of Shakespeare's Love. Shakespeare and Donne" (pp. 214–31). Sees likenesses between Shakespeare's religious sonnets and some of Donne's serious *Songs and Sonets* in the idea that the poet and his beloved are a whole world in themselves and in the idea of "compensation." Points out that Donne's inspiration was literary (Ovid) and Shakespeare's was real conviction. Donne's poems are theatrical; Shakespeare's, passionate. Donne was assured of the love of his beloved while Shakespeare was not, which creates greater intensity.

❧ 1021. LEVINE, JAY ARNOLD. " 'The Dissolution': Donne's Twofold Elegy." *ELH*, 28:301–15.

Influenced by Ovid's *Amores* (iii, l. 7), three of Donne's English contemporaries, Marlowe, Nashe, and Campion, and one Frenchman, Mathurin Regnier, commented on sexual impotence in their verse in a circumspect way. Proposes "to demonstrate how that Donne disguised the theme so intricately—perhaps as much from expediency as artistic design—that only after the most careful reading can 'The Dissolution' be added to this index of forbidden poems" (p. 303). Through the use of analogues and glosses, drawn especially from the *Hermetica* and other cabalistic writings, the author suggests that "through the catalytic action of alchemical symbolism, the broader patterns of occult doctrine have an important bearing upon 'The Dissolution' " (p. 305). Detailed analysis of the poem. Concludes that the poem is "a two-fold elegy, which wittily fuses the two modes of classical elegiac verse, both the funereal and the erotic" (p. 315).

❧ 1022. LOWE, IRVING. "John Donne: The Middle Way. The Reason-Faith Equation in Donne's Sermons." *JHI*, 22:389–97.

Suggests that Donne has been misunderstood by those who regard him as either a skeptic or fideist of sorts. Points out that in the sermons Donne adheres to the Catholic position that through natural reason man can know God. Reason may on occasion seem subservient to faith in Donne's sermons, but this is true only because reason must always assent to faith. Donne occasionally attacks reason, but he does so only to make his audience value faith more dearly. The sermons are "a veritable defense of reason" (p. 396), but the type of reason Donne defends is not the kind the New Philosophy calls into doubt.

✒§ 1023. McCann, Eleanor. "Oxymora in Spanish Mystics and English Metaphysical Writers." CL, 13:16–25.

Points out that the oxymoron "was the most natural way of expressing a core idea of Spanish mysticism: that the great unifying force of God's love blots out apparent contrarieties in the mind of the truly devout" (p. 16). Notes that in his sermons, in particular, Donne freely uses oxymora, that he refers to Saint Teresa's close associates, and that he owned a copy of *Josefina* by Jerónimo Gracián, the saint's apologist and annotator. Maintains that certain of the traditional oxymora "were transplanted, others hybridized after arriving by ingenious methods of seed dispersal into the English soul-garden" (p. 25).

✒§ 1024. Manley, Frank. "Walton's Angler and Donne: A Probable Allusion." MLN, 76:13–15.

Suggests that a passage in one of Donne's sermons preached December 14, 1617, at Denmark House is the source of Walton's allusion in *The Compleat Angler* (1st ed., p. 29) to the notion that after Solomon was converted, he turned his naturally amorous disposition to the service of God in his writing of the "Song of Songs." Although the sermon was not published until 1661, the author thinks it possible that Walton had heard the sermon, perhaps had seen a copy of the manuscript of it when Donne was preparing his preface for the *Fifty Sermons* of 1649, or in some other way had become familiar with it.

✒§ 1025. Morris, Harry. "In Articulo Mortis." TSE, 11:21–37.

Compares three deathbed poems written within a forty-year period by three different poets, which "capture the emotions of mortality *in extremis*" (p. 21): Southwell's "I Die Alive," Raleigh's "The passionate mans Pilgrimage," and Donne's "Hymne to God my God, in my sicknesse." Shows how Donne appropriates the tradition for his own ends. States that Donne's poem "exhibits as much composure in the face of death as any poem in the language" (p. 33).

✒§ 1026. Mueller, William R. "Donne's Adulterous Female Town." MLN, 76:312–14.

Reads "Batter my heart" in the light of its Old Testament background. Points out that traditionally the prophets denounced the infidelity of communities rather than of individual persons and that frequently Israel's failure to live up to its covenant with God was described in terms of an adulterous relationship between the Israelites and the pagan or false gods. States that Donne's "comparison of himself with an adulterous female town is a part of his Biblical heritage. He, like Israel, had broken the covenant and betrayed God's love. His sonnet pleads for a renewal of the saving covenant through which, paradoxically, man's freedom lies in his bondage to God, his chastity in his ravishment by God" (p. 314).

◄§ 1027. NELSON, LOWRY J. "Poems of Donne," in *Baroque Lyric Poetry*, pp. 121–37. New Haven and London: Yale University Press.

Reprinted, 1963.

Shows Donne's skill in using rhetorical structures and suggests "a way in which his achievement may be brought into a general scheme of European Baroque style in poetry" (p. 121). Discusses in some detail "Loves growth," "The Sunne Rising," "Elegie XII: His parting from her," and "Twicknam garden." States that Donne is "one of the first to make use of a rhetorical situation in the lyric in such a way as to present a complex change, an evolution, in the speaker's attitude" (p. 136).

◄§ 1028. PRAZ, MARIO. "Literary Resurrections." *ES*, 42:357–62.

Discusses the increased interest of the time in such poets as Carew and Vaughan and comments on several attacks on Donne's reputation. States that "Far from 'possessing a mechanism which could devour any kind of experience,' as T. S. Eliot would have it, Donne's sensibility was then extremely limited, and the fact that its limitations are in large measure those of the modern intellectual world, accounts for Donne in our time" (p. 362). Relies heavily on Clay Hunt's *Donne's Poetry* (1954) and agrees with many of its conclusions.

◄§ 1029. SCHWARTZ, ELIAS. "Donne's 'Elegie X (The Dreame).'" *Expl*, 19:Item 67.

In part a reply to Fredson Bowers, *MLN*, 54 (1939):280–82. Rejects Platonic interpretations of the lady's image: "The impressing of the lady's image on the heart of the speaker . . . can only be understood as the imposition of Aristotelian form on matter. The 'Image,' then, is merely the mental picture of the lady in the speaker's mind (St. Thomas' 'phantasm'). It is the mental picture present to the lover during his waking life, which, as long as his love is unattainable, causes him pain." Gives a brief reading of the poem in the light of these suggestions.

◄§ 1030. SOURIS, ANDRÉ, COMP. AND ARR. *Poèmes de Donne, Herbert et Crashaw mis en musique par leur contemporains G. Coperario, A. Ferrabosco, J. Wilson, W. Corkine, J. Hilton.* Transcriptions et réalisation par André Souris après des recherches effectuées sur les sources par John Cutts. Introduction par Jean Jacquot. Paris: Editions du Centre National de la Recherche Scientifique. xix, 26 p.

Discusses the poems of Donne that were put to music by his contemporaries. Music for "Song: Dearest [sic] love, I do not goe," "Song:
Goe, and catche a falling starre," "The Message," "The Expiration"
(2 versions), "Breake of day," and "A Hymne to God the Father."

1031. SPROTT, S. E. *The English Debate on Suicide from Donne to
     Hume*. La Salle, Illinois: Open Court Publishing Co. viii, 168 p.
Comments on the position of *Biathanatos* in the history of the debate
on suicide from 1600 to 1800. Stresses the idea that the treatise was a
relativistic defense of suicide and was a book of its time that commented
seriously on an emerging public issue.

1032. TURNELL, MARTIN. "The Changing Pattern: Contrasts in Mod-
     ern and Medieval Poetry," in *Modern Literature and Christian
     Faith*, pp. 1–21. London: Darton, Longman & Todd.
Discusses the relation between literature and religious belief in six
poets from Chaucer to Eliot. Sees Donne as "at once the last scholastic
and the first modern" (p. 9). Donne's poetry reflects "a change from
the state of spiritual unity to the dualism of the contemporary world"
(p. 9).

1033. ULREY, PAMELA. "The 'One' in Donne's Poetry." *RenP* of
     1958–1960, 76–83.
Discusses how the quest for unity is reflected in both the secular and
religious poems of Donne. Discusses several of the secular poems to
show that "the completeness sought or attained through earthly love
includes, indeed demands, physical union; that union through love, for
lovers, makes love their world of actuality, as opposed to the outside
world which becomes appearance, fantasy, unreality; that this world of
love and completeness transcends the world of appearance with its time
and space limitations; that the principle of unity in love lifts it from
a profane to a religious experience" (p. 78).

1034. WARNKE, FRANK J. *European Metaphysical Poetry*. The Eliza-
     beth Club Series, 2. New Haven and London: Yale University
     Press. xi, 317 p.
In the introduction (pp. 1–86) to this anthology of French, German,
Dutch, Spanish, and Italian metaphysical poetry, the author distinguishes
between baroque and metaphysical style. The latter is seen as one of
the several related styles within the generic category. Discusses Donne's
major characteristics, such as the uses of the functional metaphor, the
intellectual conceit, paradox, irony, uses of rhetoric, psychological pro-
fundity, and complexity. States, "Metaphysical poetry is associated in
the minds of its readers with the work of one man, John Donne. Yet,
since every poet has his individual voice as well as his adherence to a
collective style, one cannot simply make a touchstone of Donne's style

in determining what poetry is Metaphysical; certain of his crucial themes, techniques, and emphases will occur in all Metaphysical poetry but others will not. Metaphysical poetry has, when tried on the ear, a 'metaphysical' sound; that is to say, it sounds significantly like the poetry of John Donne. But each metaphysical poem has also the unique sound of the individual poet" (p. 5). Donne is compared to a number of English and continental poets, such as Huygens, Scève, Jean de Sponde, Bertaut, Durand, Saint-Amant, Théophile, Opitz, Fleming, Schirmer, Campenella, Vondel, Quevedo, Lope de Vega, Chassignet, Gryphius, Dullaert, and Luyken.

✍§ 1035. WEBBER, JOAN. "The Prose Style of John Donne's *Devotions upon Emergent Occasions*." *Anglia*, 79:138–52.

Appears in expanded form in *Contrary Music: The Prose Style of John Donne* (Madison: University of Wisconsin Press, 1963), pp. 183–201.

Comments on three elements of Donne's mature prose style that remain, for the most part, constant: the relatively loose sentence, the use of vivid metaphors and homely analogies, and an associative organization that centers about single words "which, whether metaphorical or not, tend to become symbolic" (p. 138). Points out that Donne's style varies in the three sections of each of the *Devotions* in order "to express different philosophical, ethical and emotional viewpoints" (p. 140). States, "Each unit progresses from negation in the meditations through questioning in the expostulations to affirmation in the prayers" (p. 141). Thus, they represent "a picture of Donne's mind, of three opposing, yet deeply felt conditions: despair, rebellious love, and calm submission. The pattern also has some connection with meditational organization, although it is bolder and more daring than the ordinary spiritual exercise, more expostulatory than the meditational elements in Donne's sermons. Finally, its subject matter is an exploration of the possibilities of knowledge inherent in the three traditional instruments of revelation: the Book of Creatures, the Scriptures, and the Church" (p. 141). Maintains that the *Devotions* "show very clearly that for him self-knowledge involved a recognition of inner tensions and disharmonies. The recognition enabled him to justify and contain these conflicts within a personality—or a style—which is undisputably Donne's. The conflicts themselves, however, are here described in three separate rhetorical modes which reveal for us the separate themes of what he called the 'contrary music' of his sermons" (p. 138).

✍§ 1036. WEIMANN, KARL-HEINZ. "Paracelsus in der Weltliteratur." *GRM*, n.s., 11:241–74.

Points out that Donne and Jonson introduced Paracelsian thought into England at about the same time and probably influenced one another. Donne knew the conceptual world of Paracelsus; however, when he brings it into his poetry, it is not, as in the case of Jonson, to decorate his plot, but to gain new symbols to express his lyrical moods. In Paracelsian thought Jonson looked for new content; Donne looked for new forms for existing content. Comments on the many poems in the *Songs and Sonets*, which derive their mood from the concepts and images of Paracelsian chemistry and medicine, such as "A nocturnall upon S. Lucies day" and "Loves Alchymie."

❧ 1037. WILLIAMSON, GEORGE. *The Proper Wit of Poetry.* Chicago: University of Chicago Press; London: Faber and Faber, Ltd.; Toronto: University of Toronto Press. 136 p.

Traces the changing concept of wit from the Jacobean era through the Caroline and Interregnum periods to the Augustan Age and attempts to indicate what particular fashions prevailed, how each generation understood the nature and function of wit in a slightly different way, and finally how there was a gradual separation of the facetious and the serious, of nature and fancy. Donne is mentioned throughout, but his own wit is treated most fully in Chapter Two, "Jacobean Wit" (pp. 22–42). Claims that for Donne wit was "a way of resolving tensions as well as paradoxes, and included the argumentative element in his poetry" (p. 32). Singles out "The Relique" as representative of the epitome of Donne's wit, although a number of other poems are cited and commented upon.

❧ 1038. WOOLLAM, DAVID H. M. "Donne, Disease and Doctors: Medical Allusions in the Works of the Seventeenth-Century Poet and Divine." *Medical History,* 5:144–53.

Discusses Donne's melancholic disposition and comments on his attitudes toward suffering, disease, death, and doctors. Discusses briefly his knowledge of and use of anatomy and physiology.

1962

❧ 1039. BRYAN, ROBERT A. "John Donne's Poems in Seventeenth-Century Commonplace Books." *ES,* 43:170–74.

Examines the appearance of Donne's poems in 19 seventeenth-century poetical commonplace books discovered in private libraries in the United States. Of the 180 poems by Donne, 93 were love lyrics. The most popular lyric was "Breake of day." On the other hand, "The Extasie" appears only once, and "A nocturnall upon S. Lucies day," "The Blossome," "The Primrose," "The Relique," "The Dissolution," "A Jeat Ring sent," "Negative love," "Farewell to love," and "«Selfe Love»" do not appear at all. Donne's elegies appear 54 times, and 17 of the 20 ascribed to him are found. The two most popular of all of Donne's poems seem to have been "Elegie II: The Anagram" and "Elegie XIX: Going to Bed." Concludes, "The keepers of the commonplace books were most interested in Donne's wit; his ability to be amusing, his ability to shock rather than to instruct the intellect, was more appreciated than his power to excite moral and religious feelings" (p. 172). In all, 80 per cent of the poems are love lyrics or elegies.

⋙ 1040. ———. "John Donne's Use of the Anathema." *JEGP*, 41: 305–12.

Points out that Donne employs in a witty way the language and form of the Roman Catholic rite of excommunication in "The Curse," "The Bracelet," and "The Expostulation." In these poems Donne not only attempts to show the essential holiness of his love and its tokens by parodying religious language but also less obviously satirizes the Catholic rite.

⋙ 1041. BULLOUGH, GEOFFREY. "The Poetry of the Soul's Instrument During the Renaissance," in *Mirror of Minds: Changing Psychological Beliefs in English Poetry*, pp. 1–47. Toronto: University of Toronto Press; London: The Athlone Press.

Discusses briefly Donne's attitude toward the body–mind relationship. States that "Too much has been made of the 'fusion' of thought and feeling in Donne. His work depends rather on an interplay, conflict, and tension between them arising from his sense of the postlapsarian dissonance in man's body and mind" (p. 41). Concludes that Donne's poetry "is based in the paradox of human existence, the 'wearisome condition of humanity,' the limitations of the soul's instruments, and the dramatic quality of his work springs from the effort to resolve dissonance into harmony" (p. 41).

⋙ 1042. DONNE, JOHN. *Poèmes de John Donne*. Traduit de l'anglais par Jean Fuzier et Yves Denis. Introduction de J. R. Poisson. Édition bilingue. Paris: Gallimard. 254 p.

General introduction to Donne for the French reader (pp. 7–22). Biographical information and a brief summary of the intellectual history of the period. Sees similarity between Donne and Sponde, La Ceppède, Scève, and Saint-Amant. Selection of Donne's poetry with French translations (pp. 23–251).

⋙ 1043. ———. *The Sermons of John Donne*. Edited, with Introductions and Critical Apparatus, by Evelyn M. Simpson and George R. Potter. Vol. X. Berkeley and Los Angeles: University of California Press; London: Cambridge University Press. xvii, 479 p. 10 vols.

Foreword by William Farnham (pp. vii–ix); Preface by Evelyn Simp-

son (pp. xi–xiii); Table of Contents (pp. xv–xvii); List of Illustrations
(p. xviii). Part I. Introduction (pp. 3–38); The Sermons (pp. 39–248);
Appendix: The Unidentified Sermon on Psalms 24.7 in the Lothian MS
(First Section) (pp. 249–53); Textual Notes to the Sermons in Volume
X (pp. 255–92). Part II. Chapter I: Donne's Sources (pp. 295–328);
Appendix: List of Hebrew Words on Which Donne Comments in the
Sermons (pp. 329–44); Chapter II: Donne's Sources (continued) (pp.
345–75); Appendix A: List of Identified Passages from St. Augustine's
Works Quoted or Referred to by Donne in the Sermons (pp. 376–86);
Appendix B: List of Medieval and Renaissance Commentators and
Controversialists Quoted by Donne in the Sermons and Other Main
Prose Works (pp. 387–401); Chapter III: The Folios, Composition
and Arrangement (pp. 402–9); Appendix A: List of Variants in Copies
of *XXVI Sermons* (pp. 410–13); Appendix B: List of Sermons in the
Folios, the Present Edition, and Alford's Edition (pp. 414–17); Appendix C: Index of Scriptural Texts of the Sermons (pp. 418–21); Addenda and Corrigenda for Volumes I–IX (pp. 423–46); General Index
to All the Volumes of the Present Edition (pp. 447–79). The first ten
sermons in this volume are undated; the last is dated February, 1631.

≈§ 1044. EVANS, G. BLAKEMORE. "Two Notes on Donne: 'The under-
    taking'; 'A Valediction: of my name, in the window.'" *MLR*,
    57:60–62.
    (1) Explains the ironic use of the "Worthies" in lines 1–4 of "The
undertaking" in light of the tradition of the "boasting Worthies." (2)
Explains lines 5–6 of "A Valediction: of my name, in the window."
Donne may have borrowed from Van Linschoten the idea that there
were two sources for the best of oriental diamonds. Suggests two possible
interpretations for the phrase "diamonds of either rock": "In the first,
Donne says that his mistress's eyes will set at naught (or, perhaps,
simulate) the best oriental diamonds (that is, the diamonds of the two
('either') rocks known as 'old rocks'). In the second, Donne says that
his mistress's eyes will set at naught oriental diamonds of both qualities
(that is, diamonds of both the 'old' and 'new' rocks)" (p. 62). Prefers
the first interpretation but does not rule out the second.

≈§ 1045. GARDNER, HELEN, ED. *John Donne: A Collection of Critical
    Essays.* A Spectrum Book: Twentieth Century Views, S–TC–19.
    Englewood Cliffs, N.J.: Prentice-Hall, Inc.
    Reprinted, 1963.
    Collection of previously published essays from 1896 to 1960. (1) Helen
Gardner, "Introduction." (2) George Saintsbury, "John Donne." Preface to *The Poems of John Donne*, ed. E. K. Chambers, 2 vols. (London,
1896). Reprinted in G. Saintsbury, *Prefaces and Essays* (London, 1933).
A summary of Donne's life is omitted between the first and second para-

graphs. (3) Herbert J. C. Grierson, "Donne's Love-Poetry." From an introductory essay on "The Poetry of Donne," in *The Poems of John Donne*, ed. Herbert J. C. Grierson, 2 vols. (London, 1912), Vol. II, pp. xxxiv–xlix. (4) Pierre Legouis, "The Dramatic Element in Donne's Poetry." From *Donne the Craftsman* (Paris, 1928; London, 1928), pp. 47–61, 71–79. (5) William Empson, "A Valediction: of Weeping." From *Seven Types of Ambiguity*, 3d ed. (London, 1953; reprinted, 1956), pp. 139–48. Original copyright 1930, by Chatto & Windus Ltd. (6) Mario Praz, "Donne's Relation to the Poetry of His Time." First contributed to *A Garland for John Donne*, ed. Theodore Spencer (Cambridge, Mass., 1931; London, 1931), pp. 51–72. Revised and enlarged for inclusion in *The Flaming Heart* (New York, 1958). (7) J. E. V. Crofts, "John Donne: A Reconsideration." First contributed to *E&S* of 1936, 22 (Oxford, 1937), pp. 128–43. (8) C. S. Lewis, "Donne and Love Poetry in the Seventeenth Century." Latter part of an essay contributed to *Seventeenth-Century Studies Presented to Sir Herbert Grierson* (Oxford, 1938), pp. 73–84. (9) Cleanth Brooks, "The Language of Paradox: 'The Canonization.'" From the first chapter of *The Well Wrought Urn* (New York, 1947; London, 1949). (10) J. B. Leishman, "Donne and Seventeenth Century Poetry." Chapter I of *The Monarch of Wit*, 5th ed., rev. (London, 1962). First copyright 1951, by Hutchinson University Library. (11) Helen Gardner, "The Religious Poetry of John Donne." From Part I of the General Introduction to *The Divine Poems*, ed. Helen Gardner (Oxford, 1952), pp. xxi–xxxvii. (Some footnotes are omitted.) (12) Evelyn M. Simpson, "The Literary Value of Donne's Sermons." First contributed as Section IV of the General Introduction to *The Sermons of John Donne*, eds. George R. Potter and Evelyn M. Simpson, 10 vols. (Berkeley, 1953–1962), Vol. I (1953), pp. 83–84, 88–103. (13) Louis L. Martz, "John Donne in Meditation." Slightly altered part of Chapter 6 of *The Poetry of Meditation* (New Haven, 1954), pp. 220–23, 228–48. (14) A. J. Smith, "New Bearings in Donne: 'Air and Angels.'" First contributed to *English*, 13 (1960):49–53, published for the English Association by The Oxford University Press. Chronology of Donne's dates, notes on the editors and authors, and a selected bibliography.

&5 1046. HARDISON, O. B. "The Idea of Elizabeth Drury," in *The Enduring Monument: A Study of the Idea of Praise in Renaissance Literary Theory and Practice*, pp. 162–86. Chapel Hill: The University of North Carolina Press.

Examines the *Anniversaries* as formal epideictic poems. Presents evidence to support the idea that the poems were not considered failures by most of Donne's contemporaries nor by Donne but were regarded as successful poems of praise. Discusses the structure and rhetorical conventions of each poem. Concludes, "Epideictic theory offers a perspective within which the *Anniversaries* can be read without distortion.

They are not lyric responses to a contemporary crisis. They are not Donne's equivalent to the religious devotion. Elizabeth Drury is neither Queen Elizabeth nor a surrogate for the Blessed Virgin, Christ, or the divine *logos*. She is a virtuous young woman concerning whom Donne had received 'good report' and whom he undertook to celebrate in two elegies based on traditional topics and images. If the tradition of praise illuminates the poems, the poems are a convincing demonstration of the richness and vitality of the tradition" (p. 186).

◄§ 1047. HARRIS, VICTOR. "John Donne and the Theatre." *PQ*, 41:257–69.

Challenges the notion that Donne was greatly influenced by the theatre of his time (See Patrick Crutwell, *The Shakespearean Moment and Its Place in the Poetry of the 17th Century*, 1954). Points out that Donne "does show some inclination toward dramatic idiom, some personal ties with people of the theatre, and some indulgence toward show and spectacle. But there is surprisingly little evidence, whether early or late, of any serious taste for the theatre, much less any commitment to it" (p. 261). There are few references to plays and dramatists in his work, and when he does use the theatre, it is usually employed as a symbol for folly, idleness, shame, and degradation. When he refers to actors, Donne usually considers them "dull comedians and motley humourists who inhabit the world of foppery and who like courtiers are to be judged only by their costumes" (p. 263). Donne's hostility is most evident in the sermons.

◄§ 1048. HENRY, NAT. "Donne's 'A Lecture upon the Shadow.'" *Expl*, 20:Item 60.

In part a reply to M. A. Goldberg, *Expl*, 14 (1956):Item 50, and J. D. Russell, *Expl*, 17 (1958):Item 9. Argues that "the speaker is not lecturing a mere mistress but more likely a loved one of many year's association, perhaps a middle-aged wife, but certainly not a new, or young, one." Sees the poem as primarily "a comparison between the youthful and the mature love states (secular, yet with the sexual minimized, if not entirely neglected here) with the purpose of revealing the key to marital content in the latter years of the affiliation." Donne is saying that "love must either grow, or, having reached its highest level, stay there; any diminution from its peak ('first minute, after noon') will bring on its destruction ('night')." For a reply by Laurence Perrine, see *Expl*, 21 (1963):Item 40.

◄§ 1049. JORDAN, JOHN. "The Early Verse-Letters of John Donne." *URev*, 2:3–24.

General critical estimate of the early verse-epistles written between 1592 and 1597, including thirteen verse-letters addressed to friends who are designated only by their initials plus "The Storme" and "The Calme."

❧ 1050. KEAST, WILLIAM, ED. *Seventeenth Century English Poetry: Modern Essays in Criticism.* A Galaxy Book, 89. New York: Oxford University Press. 434 p.
Collection of previously published items. (1) H. J. C. Grierson, "Metaphysical Poetry." From *Metaphysical Lyrics & Poems of the Seventeenth Century* (Oxford, 1921), pp. xiii–xxxviii. (2) T. S. Eliot, "The Metaphysical Poets." From *Selected Essays 1917–1932* by T. S. Eliot, copyright 1932, by Harcourt Brace & World, Inc.; copyright, 1960, by T. S. Eliot. (3) F. R. Leavis, "The Line of Wit." From *Revaluation: Tradition & Development in English Poetry* (London, 1936, 1949; New York, 1947), pp. 10–36. (4) Helen Gardner, "The Metaphysical Poets." From *The Metaphysical Poets* (Oxford, 1961), pp. xix–xxxiv. (5) Joseph Anthony Mazzeo, "A Critique of Some Modern Theories of Metaphysical Poetry." From *MP*, 50 (1952):88–96. (6) J. B. Leishman, "Donne and Seventeenth-Century Poetry." From *The Monarch of Wit* (London, 1951; 3d ed., 1957), pp. 9–26. (7) C. S. Lewis, "Donne and Love Poetry in the Seventeenth Century." From *Seventeenth Century Studies Presented to Sir Herbert Grierson* (Oxford, 1938), pp. 64–84. (8) Joan Bennett, "The Love Poetry of John Donne: A Reply to Mr. C. S. Lewis." From *Seventeenth Century Studies Presented to Sir Herbert Grierson* (Oxford, 1938), pp. 85–104. (9) George Williamson, "The Convention of *The Extasie.*" From *Seventeenth Century Contexts* (London, 1960; Chicago, 1960, 1961), pp. 63–77. (10) Louis L. Martz, "John Donne in Meditation: the *Anniversaries.*" From *The Poetry of Meditation* (New Haven, 1954; London, 1954), pp. 211–48 (with emendations from the 2d ed., paperback, 1962).

❧ 1051. KERMODE, FRANK, ED. *Discussions of John Donne.* Discussions of Literature. Boston: D. C. Heath & Co. ix, 160 p.
Collection of previously published items with an introduction by Frank Kermode. (1) Ben Jonson from *Conversations with William Drummond of Hawthornden.* From *Ben Jonson,* ed. Herford and Simpson (Oxford, 1925), Vol. I, pp. 133, 135f., 138. (2) Thomas Carew, "An Elegie upon the Death of the Deane of Pauls, Dr. John Donne." From Carew's *Poems,* ed. Rhodes Dunlap (Oxford, 1949), pp. 71–74. (3) John Dryden from *An Essay of Dramatic Poesy.* From *Essays of John Dryden,* ed. W. P. Ker (Oxford, 1900), Vol. I, p. 52; Vol. II, pp. 19, 102. (4) Lewis Theobald from "Shakespeare." From *Eighteenth Century Essays on Shakespeare,* ed. D. Nichol Smith (Glasgow, 1903), p. 85. (5) Samuel Johnson, "Metaphysical Wit." From "The Life of Cowley" in *Lives of the English Poets* (1779–1781). (6) Samuel Taylor Coleridge, "Notes on the Poems of Donne." From Roberta F. Brinkley's *Coleridge on the*

Seventeenth Century (Durham, N.C., 1955), pp. 521, 526f, 529f. (7) Anonymous, "Donne's Poems." From the Retrospective Review, 8 (1823):31–55. (8) Thomas DeQuincey, "Donne as Rhetorician." From Works (Edinburgh, 1862), Vol. X, pp. 39–40; reprinted from Rhetoric (1828). (9) Anonymous, "The Poetry of Donne." From Lowe's Edinburgh Magazine, 1 (1846):228–36. (10) John Alfred Langford, "An Evening with Donne." From The Working Man's Friend (1851). (11) George Saintsbury, "An Introduction." From the introduction to the Muses' Library edition of Donne's Poems, ed. E. K. Chambers (1896), pp. xi–xxxiii. (12) Francis Thompson, "Notes on Donne." From Literary Criticism by Francis Thompson, ed. T. L. Connolly (New York, 1948), pp. 68f., 149, 251. (13) Arthur Symons, "John Donne." From Fortnightly Review, n.s., 66 (1899):734–45. (14) W. J. Courthope, "The School of Metaphysical Wit: John Donne." From A History of English Poetry (London, 1903), Vol. III, 147ff. (15) Sir Herbert Grierson, "Donne's Love Poetry." From Donne's Poetical Works, ed. H. J. C. Grierson (Oxford University Press, 1912), Vol. II, xlv–xlvii. (16) William Butler Yeats, "Donne's Sensuality." From The Letters of W. B. Yeats, ed. Allan Wade (1954), p. 570 and from Autobiographies (1955), p. 326. (17) T. S. Eliot, "The Metaphysical Poets." From Selected Essays 1917–1932 by T. S. Eliot, copyright 1932, by Harcourt Brace & World, Inc.; copyright 1960, by T. S. Eliot. (18) Louis I. Bredvold, "The Naturalism of Donne." Abridged from "The Naturalism of Donne in Relation to Some Renaissance Traditions," JEGP, 22 (1923):471–502. (19) F. O. Matthiessen, "Donne and T. S. Eliot." From The Achievement of T. S. Eliot, 3d ed. (Oxford University Press, 1958). (20) George Williamson, "Strong Lines." From Seventeenth Century Contexts (London, 1960; Chicago, 1961). (21) Cleanth Brooks, "The Language of Paradox." From The Well Wrought Urn (New York, 1947; London, 1949). (22) Edgar H. Duncan, "Donne's Alchemical Figures." From ELH, 9 (1942):257–85. (23) Louis L. Martz, "John Donne in Meditation: The Anniversaries." From ELH, 14 (1947):247–73. (24) Rosemond Tuve, "Imagery, Metaphysical and Modern." Extracted from Elizabethan and Metaphysical Imagery (Chicago, 1947). (25) Joseph A. Mazzeo, "Modern Theories of Metaphysical Poetry." From MP, 50 (1952):88–96. (26) Joseph E. Duncan, "The Revival of Metaphysical Poetry, 1872–1912." From PMLA, 68 (1953):658–71. (27) S. L. Bethell, "The Nature of Metaphysical Wit." From Northern Miscellany of Literary Criticism, 1 (1953):19–40. (28) A. J. Smith, "The Metaphysic of Love." From RES, n.s., 9 (1958):362–75.

◄§ 1052. KUNTZ, JOSEPH M. Poetry Explication: A Checklist of Interpretations since 1925 of British and American Poems Past and Present. Revised edition. Denver: Alan Swallow Publisher. 331 p. First ed., 1950. Lists explications for seventy-four of Donne's poems.

~§ 1053. LINNEMAN, SISTER M. ROSE ANN. "Donne as Catalyst in the Poetry of Elinor Wylie, Wallace Stevens, Herbert Read, and William Empson." *XUS*, 1:264–72.

Discusses the direct and indirect influence of Donne on Wylie, Stevens, Read, and Empson. States, "Along with Donne, these poets seek for a cosmological and psychological integration. Their quest for fusion lends function and meaning to the correspondences, conceits, ambiguities, and 'felt-thought' that help to express it" (p. 264).

~§ 1054. MAHONEY, JOHN L. "Donne and Greville: Two Christian Attitudes Toward the Renaissance Idea of Mutability and Decay." *CLAJ*, 5:203–12.

By comparing *The second Anniversarie* and Fulke Greville's *Treatie of Humane Learning*, the author shows that, although both poets were aware of the corruption of man and the universe, each responded to the problem of mutability in different ways. States, "Donne could only lift his eyes from the scene of mutability to envision the constancy of heaven. Greville . . . attempted to reconcile the mutable and the immutable, and, in his own way, effected such a reconciliation by establishing all human knowledge on the only enduring foundation, the word of God" (p. 212).

~§ 1055. MALLOCH, A. E. "John Donne and the Casuists." *SEL*, 2:57–76.

Although fascinated by casuistry, Donne appears to have had serious doubts about the methods employed. Points out, "For if he disagreed with their methods, he also appears to have shared with them many of the habits of thought which produced those methods. Donne is as much a man of contradictions in his attitude toward the casuists as elsewhere. He insists that moral action must proceed from an assent of the self and yet he toys constantly with a literature of casuistry which sets moral action within a legal arena and allows little room for the self" (p. 75).

~§ 1056. MARILLA, E. L. "Some Vagaries in Modern Literary Criticism: Some Instances Touching the Renaissance," in *Studies in English Renaissance Literature*, ed. Waldo F. McNeir, pp. 168–80. Louisiana State University Studies. Humanities Series, No. 12. Baton Rouge: Louisiana State University Press.

Comments on Donne's modern reputation. Points out that the rediscovery of Donne in the nineteenth century was made by men who were willing to overlook his eccentric poetic method for the spiritual fortification, which the poems offered to a religiously frustrated age. His reputation in the twentieth century has been, in large part, the result of the endorsement that his poetry received from the New Critics. States that "it is clear that the virtues of Donne's poetry have been more or less arbitrarily extolled and that his present eminence therefore rests upon precarious ground" (p. 173).

◄§ 1057. MARSH, T. N. "Elizabethan Wit in Metaphor and Conceit: Sidney, Shakespeare, Donne." *EM*, 13:25–29.
Brief comparative study of how Sidney, Shakespeare, and Donne use several common images.

◄§ 1058. MOLELLA, LYNNE. "Donne's 'A Lecture upon the Shadow.'" *Thoth*, 3:69–77.
Close reading of the poem. Sees it as "essentially an impassioned warning rather than simply a measured explanation of the philosophy of love" (p. 70) and as an examination of the power of perfect love. Suggests that Donne fails to resolve the ambivalence of his attitude. Calls the poem "a complex and not entirely successful attempt to reconcile the earthly and the ideal, the dark side of man which is capable of treason and that side of him which yearns for the purity of the noon light. Donne's major fault in this poem is that he is too aware of the equal claims of the opponents, and his hesitancy to award the victory to one of them alone is a mark of his fidelity to the truth of the human predicament" (p. 77).

◄§ 1059. MOODY, PETER R. "Donne's 'A Lecture upon the Shadow.'" *Expl*, 20:Item 60.
In part a reply to Mark Van Doren in *Introduction to Poetry* (1951), pp. 26–31. Argues that the lovers are not walking west to east, as Van Doren suggests, but rather are walking east to west. Therefore, the word *behind* (l. 17) should be seen as referring not to location, but to time. Donne's conclusion is that "growing love rids itself of false pretensions just as shadows dwindle in the morning sun until the perfect point of noon is reached. Afterwards, if love decay, the lovers themselves act falsely to each other as shadows lengthen before them and the light declines. The sun is the power of love which causes shadows to dwindle as love grows in the morning; but the sun is also the same source of light which, in the afternoon, causes shadows to lengthen as love's false disguises increase and love moves toward darkness."

◄§ 1060. MUELLER, WILLIAM R. *John Donne: Preacher*. Princeton: Princeton University Press; London: Oxford University Press. vii, 264 p.
Detailed study of the preacher and the sermons. In Chapter I the author presents a biographical sketch of Donne. In Chapter II he discusses Donne's attitudes on the nature and function of his vocation to the Anglican priesthood and examines some of his fundamental convictions

about the Church and the role of Scripture. Chapter III is a discussion
of Donne's ideas about the nature and function of preaching. Points out
that Donne disapproved of the extemporaneous sermon; his practice was
to prepare each sermon carefully and then, after he had preached it, to
write it down in an extended form for circulation and publication. Discusses the structure, rhetoric, imagery, and tone of the sermons. Chapter
IV consists of comments on the character of Donne's theology and his
awareness of his responsibility as a spokesman for the *via media*. Points
out that for the most part Donne's theological views were formed by
the time he entered the ministry; therefore, little change or development
can be perceived throughout the sermons. Discusses Donne's views on
sin and redemption, grace and free will, death and resurrection. Chapter
V is a general evaluation of Donne's achievement as a preacher and
comments on his reputation both in the seventeenth century and in the
twentieth. Contrasts Donne and Lancelot Andrewes.

൴ 1061. Muñoz Rojas, José A. "Encuentro con Donne." *PSA*, 27:23–
    48.
Appreciative essay on the life and works of Donne intended as an introduction for Spanish-speaking readers. Biographical interpretation of
the poetry. Discusses briefly Donne's knowledge of Spanish authors and
the general influence of Spanish on Donne's works and sensibility.

൴ 1062. Praz, Mario. "Il Barocco in Inghilterra," in *Mannerismo,
    Barocco, Rococo: Concetti e Termini*, pp. 129–46. Problemi At-
    tuali di Scienza e di Cultura, No. 52. Roma: Accademia Nazionale
    dei Lincei.
Trans. into English in *MP*, 61 (1964):169–79.
Maintains that the baroque is essentially alien to English sensibility
and taste. Suggests that Milton, Crashaw, and Dryden were influenced
by baroque models. States that Donne can best be understood as a
mannerist poet. His chief characteristic is neither the use of wit nor the
conceit but the dialectic of an impassioned mind.

൴ 1063. Quinn, Dennis B. "John Donne's Principles of Biblical
    Exegesis." *JEGP*, 41:313–29.
Examines both Donne's statements on biblical exegesis and his general practice in order to define his principles of interpreting Scripture.
Donne reflects the Anglican position of keeping a balance between reason
and faith. Donne maintains that the valid interpretation of the Bible
must rest on faith, as Saint Augustine states, and not exclusively on
reason or scholarship. States that Donne "tried to avoid the errors which
vitiate the interpretations of his day—their tendentiousness, unimagina-
tive literalism, speculative fantasy—as well as the errors of past exegesis—
its allegorical ingenuity, historical and linguistic ignorance, and slavish

devotion to tradition. He espouses the rule of faith as well as the rules of good scholarship" (p. 317). Concludes, "It will not do to see Donne's exegesis as either medieval or 'allegorical' or as modern and 'literal.' He found it possible in both theory and practice to deny neither the letter nor spirit—just as he denied neither reason nor faith, body nor soul, man nor God. The sermons demonstrate once more Donne's astonishing power to unite perennially wedded yet warring forces at the very time when they seemed about to undergo permanent alienation" (p. 329).

ϡ§ 1064. ROONEY, WILLIAM J. J. "John Donne's 'Second Prebend Sermon'—A Stylistic Analysis." *TSLL*, 4:24–34.
Discusses the structure and style of the sermon in order to show that the "resulting design, which extends into every facet of the sermon—even into grammatical arrangement within sentences—is not only an interesting phenomenon in itself, but seems to be, in part at least, a key to much of what Donne does most effectively, not only in his prose, but in his poetry as well" (p. 24). Suggests that there is a counterpoint effect created by the lack of correlation between the rational structure and the emotional meaning.

ϡ§ 1065. SCHOECK, R. J. "The Libraries of Common Lawyers in Renaissance England: Some Notes and a Provisional List." *Manuscripta*, 6:155–67.
Proposes to "gather together some notes on the books and libraries of common lawyers in England down to about 1650 to support the claim that not only were the lawyers learned but that they possessed libraries of significance" (p. 156). Brief statement on Donne's library (p. 164). Notes that Donne's copy of Sir Thomas More's English Works of 1557 is now in the Library of the Catholic University of America.

ϡ§ 1066. SHARP, ROBERT L. "Donne's 'Autumnall' and the Barren Plane Tree." *N&Q*, n.s., 9:210–12.
Traces the origin of the notion of the barrenness of the plane-tree back as far as the pseudo-Aristotelian *De Mundo*, in which the tree is discussed as bearing no edible fruit. The notion of barrenness, once established, is interpreted in various ways by those who follow. Concludes, "Just how Donne would have defined the barrenness of the plane it seems to me there is no way of telling" (p. 212).

ϡ§ 1067. SILHOL, ROBERT. "Réflexions sur les sources et la structure de A *Litanie* de John Donne." *EA*, 15:329–46.
Suggests that Donne's guide in writing "The Litanie" was the litany written in 1544 by Archbishop Cranmer. Seeks to establish in what measure Donne followed the liturgical model. Maintains that the poem is not essentially a sacred poem and should not be considered as a prayer:

"Il nous faut tenir A *Litanie* pour un poème lyrique—profane, presque, a bien des égards—où le poète tente désespérément de se donner confiance, s'addressant en définitive beaucoup plus à lui-même qu'à son créateur. C'est comme expression personnelle, enfin, du conflit entre les appétits de Donne et la morale religieuse, entre sa raison et les dogmes, que le poème prend tout son intérêt" (pp. 345-46).

◄§ 1068. SLOAN, THOMAS O. "A Rhetorical Analysis of John Donne's 'The Prohibition.'" *QJS*, 48:38-45.
Detailed rhetorical analysis of the poem in which the author shows the influence of the Ramist system of logic and rhetoric.

◄§ 1069. STEIN, ARNOLD. *John Donne's Lyrics: The Eloquence of Action*. Minneapolis: University of Minnesota Press. viii, 244 p.
Introduction discusses interest in Donne historically, particularly after World War I, and how his poetry should be read and the metaphysical conceit accepted. "The highest purpose of this book is to gain some insight into the integrity of Donne's poetic mind, and this purpose requires taking seriously two propositions: that Donne is a poetic logician endowed with a talent and love for the unity of imaginative form; and that Donne's poetry, though it is not simple, nevertheless deeply and persistently engages important problems which concern 'simplicity'" (pp. 17-18). Chapter I, "The Questions of Style," examines Donne as "a conscious master of harshness" (p. 24) and proclaims that his verse is both rhetorical and simplistic. Supports this premise with examples of the interrelationship of meter and meaning in Donne's verse. Sees Donne's imagery as visual. Discusses elements of sound, sense, and feeling. Applies his thesis to a detailed analysis of "The good-morrow." Chapter II, "The Forms of Wit," discusses wit generally, then divides Donne's wit into four classes with explanations and examples of each: epigrammatic reversal, inversions, binary forms, and ternary forms. Chapter III, "Burden of Consciousness," discusses the drive to infuse a work with the private and personal aspects of the poet. Considers "negative theology and the mythic" in the light of this sense of consciousness. In "Postscript on Donne's Modern Career," the author accounts for Donne's popularity today. Two appendices deal with an interpretation of a stanza of "Lovers infinitenesse" and with Donne's religious thought, relating the secular poems to the religious ones.

◄§ 1070. WHITLOCK, BAIRD W. "Donne's University Years." *ES*, 43:1-20.
Discusses the influential circle of friends that surrounded Donne as a student at Oxford. Points out that at Oxford Donne read not only classical authors but also was introduced to Spanish literature. Insists, in fact, that "the main contribution of Oxford to Donne seems to have

been his knowledge of and interest in Spanish" (p. 4). Argues that it is highly improbable that Donne ever attended Cambridge. Presents evidence to support the idea that Donne fought in the Low Countries. Maintains that the epigrams are important to an understanding of Donne's later poetry.

❧ 1071. YOUNGREN, WILLIAM. "Generality in Augustan Satire," in *In Defense of Reading: A Reader's Approach to Literary Criticism*, pp. 206–34. New York: E. P. Dutton & Co.
Detailed comparison of *Satyre IV* and Pope's imitation.

1963

❧ 1072. ADAMS, HAZARD. "Metaphysical Poetry: Argument into Drama," in *The Context of Poetry*, pp. 75–99. Boston: Little, Brown & Co.
Outlines the general characteristics of metaphysical poetry, using Donne as an illustration. Short explication of "Twicknam garden." Stresses the dramatic elements in the poetry.

❧ 1073. ANDREASEN, N. J. C. "Theme and Structure in Donne's *Satyres*." SEL, 3:59–75.
Shows how all five of the *Satyres* are interrelated and, taken as a whole, form a sequence. Suggests that they are "built upon a single thematic principle of organization; they are all concerned with presenting an idealistic defense of spiritual values against the creeping encroachment of sixteenth-century materialism" (p. 59). Continuity is achieved in part by the presence of a consistent speaker who is an idealist combatting the materialism of the age and challenging various profane antagonists. Unity is also achieved by the use of a system of interlocking imagery within the individual satires and between satires, and by dramatic tone and techniques. Analyzes the five satires to illustrate their unity.

❧ 1074. BUXTON, JOHN. "The Donne Fashion," in *Elizabethan Taste*, pp. 317–38. London: Macmillan and Co., Ltd.
Discusses Donne as a private poet in contrast to such public poets as Drayton, Daniel, Spenser, and Shakespeare. Maintains that Donne was not "deriding the good taste of the time as old-fashioned; he was exploiting it for the sake of wit, and of a recondite wit that was likely to be enjoyed most by a circle of like-minded friends" (p. 327). Comments on Donne's friends and acquaintances.

❧ 1075. CAREY, JOHN. "John Donne." *Time & Tide*, 44:24, 36.
Brief critical introduction to Donne's life and work.

ᴥᣔ 1076. Chitanand, T. P. "Donne's *The Progresse of the Soule.*" Indian Jour. Eng. Studies, 4:48–68.

Reviews previous criticism and concludes by explicating the poem
as "nothing more more than a satire on the Queen" (p. 66) for her persecution of Donne's kinsmen, the Catholics.

ᴥᣔ 1077. Davis, Kay. "Unpublished Coleridge Marginalia in a Volume
of John Donne's Poetry." N&Q, n.s., 10:187–89.

Notes by Coleridge in Charles Lamb's copy of the 1669 edition of
Donne's poems.

ᴥᣔ 1078. Donne, John. *John Donne: The Anniversaries.* Edited with
introduction and commentary by Frank Manley. Baltimore: Johns
Hopkins Press. viii, 209 p.

Traces the critical history of the *Anniversaries.* Challenges much previous criticism and suggests that the poems can best be understood by
examining them in the light of the tradition of wisdom in the Renaissance. Extensive discussion of Greek, Hebraic, and Christian concepts
of wisdom. Text based on the first editions of 1611 and 1612. Extensive
commentary.

ᴥᣔ 1079. ———. *John Donne's Sermons on the Psalms and Gospels;
With a Selection of Prayers and Meditations.* Edited, with an introduction, by Evelyn M. Simpson. Berkeley: University of California Press; London: Cambridge University Press. 244 p.

The introduction to ten representative sermons gives a brief biographical sketch, stresses that the power of the sermons is a result of Donne's
poetic background and his own intense religious experience. Notes two
great themes of the sermons—the thought of death and the thought of
love—and discusses Donne's affection for the Psalms and the Gospels of
Matthew and John. Explains the method of composition of the sermons and discusses the occasion and artistry of each of the sermons included.

ᴥᣔ 1080. Finkelpearl, P. J. "Donne and Everard Gilpin: Additions,
Corrections, and Conjectures." RES, n.s., 14:164–67.

In part a reply to R. E. Bennett, RES, 15 (1939):66–72. Questions
the allusions to Donne that Bennett proposes occur in Gilpin's work but
suggests a possible reference to Donne in *Skialetheia* in which Gilpin
writes: "folles doe sit/ More honored then the *Prester John* of wit."

ᴥᣔ 1081. Freccero, John. "Donne's 'Valediction: Forbidding Mourning.'" ELH, 30:335–76.

Detailed analysis of the poem "in order to examine its multileveled
coherence" (p. 353). Argues that Donne attempts "rescuing human love

from both the angelic mysticism and the erotic formalism of the Italian tradition and restoring it to its proper domain: humanity" (p. 336). Extensive discussion of the compass image, which is seen as a protest against both neo-Petrarchan and Neoplatonic dehumanizations of love. Suggests that the ultimate source for the compass image is probably Chalcidius' commentary on the *Timaeus*. Sees the compass executing two motions: (1) a circular movement around the circumference of the circle, and (2) a linear movement along the radius of the circle. Thus the movement is spiral. Points out that the spiral is a conventional Platonic symbol for humanity and that the planets were thought to move in a spiral.

§ 1082. Gohn, Ernest S. "Dating Donne and Scholarly Sentimentality." *PMASAL*, 48:609–19.

Maintains that the available external and internal evidence, the usual order of the poems in the earlier editions, and the factual biographical data are all inconclusive, for the most part, in establishing exact dates for individual poems in the *Songs and Sonets*. Challenges scholars who attempt to read the poems as autobiographical.

§ 1083. Guss, Donald L. "Donne and the Greek Anthology." *N&Q*, n.s., 10:57–58.

Points out several parallels between Donne's poems and *The Greek Anthology*, specifically in "The Dampe," "Elegie XIV," "The Flea," and "Elegie IX." Suggests that perhaps the Greek epigram was an influence on Donne's rejection of certain conventional Petrarchan attitudes but concludes that the relation of Donne's work to the Greek epigram is not clear. Recognizes that many of the themes of *The Greek Anthology* were available to Donne in the work of Renaissance poets. Thus the author concludes, "The parallels . . . may serve to reinforce and define the growing critical consciousness that Donne is, after all, a Renaissance poet" (p. 58).

§ 1084. ———. "Donne's Conceits and Petrarchan Wit." *PMLA*, 78:308–14.

Relates Donne's lyrics to the *pre-secentisti* (chiefly Serafino, Tasso, and Guarini). Shows that Donne's poems belong to the unclassical tradition of witty Petrarchism, which "accounts for their sophisticated levity and their dramatic truth, both their epigrammatic neatness and their symbolic import" (p. 308). Both Petrarchist and anti-Petrarchist at the same time, Donne comes "at the end of three centuries of progressive secularization of the *dolce stil novo*" (p. 314).

✍§ 1085. HÖLTGEN, KARL JOSEF. "Eine Emblemfolge in Donne's *Holy Sonnet XIV.*" *Archiv*, 200:347–52.

Certain images in the poem remind one of emblems in contemporary emblem books. Does not attempt to prove that individual works were sources for Donne. The motifs of the emblematic and its methods were so popular that one can simply presuppose the emblematic composition and interpretation principle for the poet and his readers, especially with regard to certain conceits. One of the emblems in the poem is traced in the emblem books.

✍§ 1086. KAWASAKI, TOSHIHIKO. "From Southwell to Donne." *Studies in English Literature* (Tokyo), 39:11–31.

Traces the development of devotional poetry from Southwell through Henry Constable and William Alabaster to Donne. Compares the four poets. Considers the first three as forerunners of metaphysical poetry.

✍§ 1087. KUNA, F. M. "T. S. Eliot's Dissociation of Sensibility and the Critics of Metaphysical Poetry." *EIC*, 13:241–52.

Argues that dissociation of sensibility is "a poetic theory, and nothing more, which cannot be applied to any poetry written before the eighteenth century without distorting all historical truth, and which must not be separated from its original context" (p. 243). Maintains that Eliot's concept can be applied only to modern poetry and that it is primarily the result of Eliot's theorizing about the nature of his own poetry.

✍§ 1088. MISRAHI, VICTOR. "John Donne «en perspective»." *Revue de l'Université de Bruxelles*, 15:297–306.

General introduction to the poetry, with a biographical sketch. Brief summary of the history of criticism of Donne.

✍§ 1089. MOORE, ARTHUR K. "Donne's 'Loves Deitie' and *De Planctu Naturae.*" *PQ*, 42:102–5.

Shows that Donne's philosophy of love in the poem is substantially the same as that of Alain de Lille (Alanus de Insulis) in *Liber de planctu Naturae*.

✍§ 1090. MORILLO, MARVIN. "Donne's 'Farewell to Love': The Force of Shutting Up." *TSE*, 13:33–40.

Close analysis of the poem. Shows that the last sentence is an ironic reversal. Donne presents the tension between the demands of reason and sexual desire. The arguments grow increasingly philosophical until, in Stanza 4, he chooses abstinence. Finding the resolution unsatisfactory, he accepts love in the last line as therapeutic.

◄§ 1091. MORRIS, WILLIAM E. "Donne's Early Use of the Word 'Concoction.'" *N&Q*, n.s., 10:414–15.

Points out that the earliest references to *concoction* in Donne's works
appear in "The Extasie" (l. 27) and *The first Anniversary* (l. 456).
Maintains that the first definite date that can be assigned to Donne's
use of the term is April 30, 1615, for it appears in his earliest surviving
sermon.

◄§ 1092. PAFFARD, M. K. "Donne's 'The Extasie,' 57–60, 68." *Expl*,
22:Item 13.

Suggests that lines 57–60 of the poem contain direct references to
the Incarnation. Paraphrases the line to read: "God's influence cannot
work on man without taking the form of a physical body," or "God cannot perfectly express his love for man without first taking a bodily form
in Christ." Suggests that line 68, "Else a great Prince in prison lies,"
refers also to the idea of the Incarnation.

◄§ 1093. PARISH, JOHN E. "Donne's *Holy Sonnets*, XIII." *Expl*, 22:Item
19.

Suggests that in the poem Donne deliberately offers "an example of
a meditation inadequately devout." Maintains that the argument of the
sonnet is purposely fallacious. The speaker proposes that Christ will be
forgiving and merciful to the sinner because Christ's face is beautiful.

◄§ 1094. ———. "No. 14 of Donne's *Holy Sonnets*." *CE*, 24:299–302.

Reviews and evaluates recent criticism of the poem. Stresses the unity
of the sonnet, in which the full force of the Trinity is implored. Two
traditional metaphors inform the sonnet: (1) the body as a beseiged town,
and (2) storming the lady's heart by force. In the first quatrain the King
(God) seeks admission to the captured city. In the second quatrain the
reader views the lamentable state of the city through the eyes of the
populace. In the sestet the captive Princess (either the soul or reason)
asks for release from her unholy union with the Usurper (Satan).

◄§ 1095. PERRINE, LAURENCE. "Donne's 'A Lecture upon the Shadow.'"
Expl, 21:Item 40.

Reply to Nat Henry, *Expl*, 20 (1962):Item 60. Explication of lines
16–18: "Donne's poem pivots on a sharply defined contrast between
the deliberate deceptions practised by young lovers to conceal their as-
yet-publicly-undeclared love from other people and the deceptions and
disguises which older lovers practise on each other if their loves do not
'at noone stay.'"

✦§ 1096. Ringler, Richard N. "Two Sources for Dryden's *The Indian Emperour*." *PQ*, 42:423–29.

Suggests that one source for Dryden's play is Donne's *The first Anniversary*.

✦§ 1097. Rudd, Nial. "Donne and Horace." *TLS*, 22 March, p. 208.

Points out several of Donne's borrowings from Horace, Juvenal, and Cicero in *Satyre IV*.

✦§ 1098. Samson, Patricia. "Words for Music." *SoR*, 1:46–52.

Notes that unlike Thomas Campion's verse and unlike much Elizabethan verse, metaphysical poetry is generally unsuited for music. Compares Benjamin Britten's settings of the *Holy Sonnets*, which "make Donne's already complex poetry almost impossible to follow, so that the songs are less satisfying in performance than the poems alone are" (p. 46) and Dorian LeGallienne's settings of the same poems, in which the music "is less intrinsically valuable than Britten's, perhaps, but it is closer to the poems, so that although the poems do not gain much, their loss is slighter than in Britten's settings" (pp. 46–47).

✦§ 1099. Sloan, Thomas O. "The Rhetoric in the Poetry of John Donne." *SEL*, 3:31–44.

Discusses the value of analyzing Donne's poetry in the light of specific Renaissance rhetorical theory and practice. Does not claim that Donne is a Ramist but maintains that "Ramism in both its innovative and its traditional features is unquestionably representative of Donne's milieu, and it is therefore serviceable for the analytical operations involved in studying the *rhetorical* foundations of Donne's poetry" (p. 44). Close rhetorical analysis of "The undertaking."

✦§ 1100. Sparrow, John. "Hymns and Poetry." *TLS*, 11 January, p. 32.

Points out that a number of poems by Donne, Herbert, Crashaw, and other religious poets of the period are contained in the *Collection of Hymns* (London, 1754) edited by John Gambold for the "Brethren's Church" of the Moravians. Notes that "Wilt Thou forgive that sin?" is printed, with musical setting, by Pelham Humfrey, in Book I of Playford's *Harmonia Sacra* (1688). For a reply by F. W. Sternfeld, see *TLS*, 1 February, p. 77.

✦§ 1101. Sternfeld, F. W. "Hymns and Poetry." *TLS*, 1 February, p. 77.

Reply to John Sparrow, *TLS*, 11 January, p. 32. Points out that Humfrey's musical setting of "Wilt Thou forgive that sin?" is recorded in an article by Vincent Duckles, "The Lyrics of John Donne as set by his Contemporaries," Seventh International Musicological Congress: Cologne, *Bericht*, Kassel and London, 1959, pp. 91–93.

❧ 1102. Van Laan, Thomas F. "John Donne's *Devotions* and the Jesuit Spiritual Exercises." *SP*, 60:191–202.

Points out parallels between the individual sections of the *Devotions* (title, meditation, expostulation, prayer) and the method of discursive meditation recommended by Saint Ignatius in *The Spiritual Exercises*.

❧ 1103. Webber, Joan. *Contrary Music: The Prose Style of John Donne*. Madison: University of Wisconsin Press. ix, 227 p.

Proposes "to read Donne's prose in the light of the traditions he knew, and to show how and why he made of them what he did" (pp. vii–viii). Chapter I is an analysis in general terms of Donne's prose style in the *Juvenalia, Biathanatos, Essayes in Divinity, Sermons,* and *Devotions* to show how Donne's style changes "to keep pace with his ideas" (p. 13). Chapters II–VI deal exclusively with different aspects of style in the sermons; Chapter II, with sentence structure; Chapter III, with the use of occasional images and metaphors; Chapter IV, with tone of voice; Chapter V, with symbolism and attitude toward language; Chapter VI, with the organization and structure of the sermons. Chapter VII is an expanded version of "The Prose Style of John Donne's *Devotions Upon Emergent Occasions*," *Anglia*, 79 (1961):138–52.

❧ 1104. Williamson, George. "The Design of Donne's *Anniversaries*." *MP*, 60:183–91.

Reprinted in *Milton & Others* (Chicago: University of Chicago Press; London: Faber and Faber, Ltd., 1965), pp. 150–64.

Trans. into Italian by Rosanna Zelocchi in *Convivium*, n.s., 31 (1963): 436–47.

Disagrees with Martz's position that the *Anniversaries* are influenced by *The Spiritual Exercises* of Saint Ignatius. Comments on Dryden's critical evaluation of the poems. Relates the poems to Donne's *Metempsychosis*: "In the *Metempsychosis* he took a satirical view of original sin; in the *First Anniversary* he explored seriously the consequences of original sin in the world he knew; in the *Second Anniversary* he pondered the Christian answer to these consequences and completed the journey of the soul from creation to its potential destiny" (p. 191). Sees Elizabeth Drury as only the occasion for the more serious theme of the poems.

1964

❧ 1105. Allen, D. C. "Donne's 'Sapho to Philaenis.'" *ELN*, 1:188–91.

Points out that the heroine and the mode of Donne's poem were borrowed from Ovid's "Sappho Phaoni." Donne also imitates verses from Sappho's poetry. Philaenis was probably suggested by Calderinus' commentary on Martial.

1106. BALD, R. C. "Historical Doubts Respecting Walton's *Life of Donne*," in *Essays in English Literature from the Renaissance to the Victorian Age*, ed. Millar MacLure and F. W. Watt, pp. 69–84. Toronto: University of Toronto Press.

A "systematic attempt to estimate the degrees of falsification, intentional or unintentional, in what Walton tells us about Donne" (p. 69). Shows that, although Walton's biography remains a charming and sincere portrait of Donne, a number of points are not historically accurate. In a sense the biography is propaganda in that "it seeks to inculcate the religious virtues of penitence and piety" (p. 69).

1107. ———. "A Latin Version of Donne's Problems." MP, 61: 198–203.

Describes a book of problems and paradoxes published in Latin in 1616 by Ludovicus Rouzaeus, which contains translations of thirteen of Donne's problems. Rouzaeus acknowledges the borrowings.

1108. BERRY, LLOYD E. A *Bibliography of Studies in Metaphysical Poetry 1939–1960*. Madison: University of Wisconsin Press. xi, 99 p.

A continuation of Spencer and Van Doren's *Studies in Metaphysical Poetry: Two Essays and a Bibliography* (New York: Columbia University Press, 1939). Lists 1,147 critical studies on the metaphysical poets from 1939 to 1960. "Entries were compiled after a search of more than 1,000 journals, about 480 of which are not listed in the *PMLA* bibliography" (jacket). 522 items specifically on Donne.

1109. BLANCHARD, MARGARET M. "The Leap into Darkness: Donne, Herbert, and God." *Renascence*, 17:38–50.

Contrasts the religious sensibility of Herbert and Donne as it is reflected in their verse. By studying the tone and the visual and auditory imagery in the poems of each, the author concludes that Herbert's relationship to God tends to be personal whereas Donne's tends to be objective. In Herbert's poetry God speaks and is more directly addressed than in Donne's poetry, which "reflects most often a dialectic within himself rather than a dialogue with Divinity—not necessarily because he does not believe that his God can speak to him, but because he does not trust that he is close enough to hear" (p. 39).

1110. BRILLI, ATTILIO. "Gli Amores ovidiani e la poesia di J. Donne." *SUSFL*, 38:100–139.

Studies Donne's erotic love poetry in the light of the Ovidian tradition. Discusses Donne's familiarity with Ovid and comments on Donne's specific uses of the *Amores*.

⋙§ 1111. BROADBENT, J. B. *Poetic Love*. London: Chatto & Windus Ltd. vii, 310 p.

History of love poetry from the twelfth century to the Enlightenment in terms of the problem of duality of the body and soul. Corrects the view on Donne's "unified sensibility": Donne desired it but did not accomplish it. Discusses Donne's religious poetry—its tensions, its mode of argument, its use of human love as image of divine, its presentation of dramatic conflict (pp. 94–111). Compares Donne to Spenser and Sidney (pp. 215–44). States that Donne's poetry includes both Ovidian and Platonic elements, but his best poems go beyond his models to express a spiritual love between human beings that transcends body and soul. Discusses "The good-morrow" and states that Donne was the first to treat love as the nexus between two persons. Calls "The Extasie" the supreme "we" poem in English. Ends with assessment of Donne's imitators.

⋙§ 1112. COLIE, R. L. "The Rhetoric of Transcendence." *PQ*, 43:145–70.

Shows how the "epistemological paradox" became one of the important poetic themes of the late Renaissance and how poetry enriched the paradox by an appropriate rhetoric. Traces the source of all paradox in Western Tradition to Plato. Compares Stoicism and Skepticism and their joining with Christianity in a search for both man's knowing and how he knows. Discusses Donne's *Anniversaries* as Christian poems in the Stoic tradition, which build on paradoxes about difficulties of understanding one's self, the world, and God. Concludes that Donne sees poetry as an instrument of paradox that becomes an instrument of transcendent meaning. Donne's use of solecisms to point to paradoxes is a rhetorical mode of expressing supernal unity. "These poems do not try to set things straight, to make contradictions orderly; they accept contradiction and paradox as the basis of human existence and of human understanding, and simply build upon that acceptance" (p. 170).

⋙§ 1113. COLLMER, ROBERT G. "John Donne, la llave de la poesía inglesa moderna." *Humanitas* (Nuevo León, Mexico), 5:297–307.

Contends that one way of understanding a great deal of modern English and American poetry is to examine Donne's poetry. Points out Donne's place in the development of English poetry, discusses his life and certain historical information, and comments on his essential poetic techniques.

⋙§ 1114. ELLRODT, ROBERT. "Scientific Curiosity and Metaphysical Poetry in the Seventeenth Century." *MP*, 61:180–97.

Attempts to account for scientific curiosity in metaphysical poetry and for differences in the use of science among the various poets. Maintains that Donne did not approach science in the Baconian spirit of utilitarianism nor was his scientific curiosity that of a dilettante. His broad interests reflect Renaissance humanism, resulting in the use of a disparate variety of images. Scientific facts are used as stepping stones toward speculation and apprehension of universal truth, not simply as ornamentation. Donne's approach to science "suggests a constant coexistence of curiosity and weariness . . . paralleled by the coexistence of a rational and critical faculty with a growing tendency to rely on faith" (p. 190). Donne believed in ultimate unity of natural and divine truth, while recognizing that such truth was beyond the grasp of human intelligence.

⊷§ 1115. GERALDINE, SISTER M. "Erasmus and the Tradition of Paradox." *SP*, 61:41–63.
Discusses the *Paradoxes and Problemes* as "the first group of paradoxes written by a major writer in England after Erasmus wrote the Praise in More's home" (p. 60). Compares the use of paradox in the work of Erasmus and Donne.

⊷§ 1116. GROS, LÉON–GABRIEL. *John Donne*. Paris: Éditions Pierre Seghers. 214 p.
Synoptic table of Donne's life, major contemporary events, and major contemporary works in English and European literature. Iconographical documentation. Critical study divided into three chapters: (1) a biographical sketch, (2) a critical estimation of metaphysical poetry with special consideration of Donne's views on love in his poetry, and (3) a brief review of some of the major criticism of Donne, especially the work of Eliot, Leishman, Ellrodt, and Legouis. Text: selections from the love poetry translated into French. Brief extracts from several critics. Selected bibliography.

⊷§ 1117. GUSS, DONALD L. "Donne's 'The Anagram': Sources and Analogues." *HLQ*, 28:79–82.
Argues that Donne's poem is not simply a rhetorical game in the manner of Tasso and the Marinisti but that in some ways it is closer to Gascoigne's "In prayse of a gentlewoman who though she were not very fayre, yet was she as harde favored as might be." Also points out those elements in Donne's description of the lady that resembled Francesco Berni's "Chiome d'argento fine, irte e attorte." Shows that "where Berni and Tasso use epideictic techniques . . . Donne uses demonstrative arguments; where they misapply the high style, Donne demonstrates the paradox that ugliness is beauty" (p. 82).

⋐§ 1118. HALIO, JAY L. "*Perfection* and Elizabethan Ideas of Conception." *ELN*, 1:179–82.

Comments on the Elizabethan proverb, "women receive perfection by men." Derived from Aristotle's theory of conception and generation, the saying suggests that in conception woman contributes the material cause and man contributes the form and efficient cause. Thus the male contributes the sensitive soul, without which the embryo remains imperfect. Helps to explain the use of "perfection" in the "Epithalamion made at Lincolnes Inne."

⋐§ 1119. HAZO, SAMUEL. "Donne's Divine Letter," in *Essays and Studies in Language and Literature*, ed. Herbert H. Petit, pp. 38–43. Duquesne Studies, Philological Series, 5. Pittsburgh: Duquesne University Press.

Points out that in form and technique "The Crosse" resembles the verse letters and that in subject matter and spirit it is in the tradition of the divine poems; hence, the author calls it "a divine letter." Suggests that the poem should be read as a "verse letter on a serious or 'divine' subject rather than a divine poem which occasionally borrows from verse letter conventions" (p. 43). Analyzes the poem. Shows that the whole piece can be seen as "an expanded conceit to the extent that cruciform imagery and symbolism in both the material and spiritual senses are consistently developed and expanded to the final couplet" (p. 43).

⋐§ 1120. HICKEY, RORERT L. "Donne's Delivery." *TSL*, 19:39–47.

Discusses how Donne prepared and presented his sermons and how he used voice and gesture for persuasion. Points out that Donne spoke from carefully prepared notes committed to memory. Later he wrote them out and expanded them to almost double the original length. Discusses the organization of the sermons and comments on what Donne's contemporaries had to say about his delivery.

⋐§ 1121. HOLLAND, NORMAN N. "Clinical, Yes. Healthy, No." *L&P*, 14:121–25.

Reply to Robert Rogers, *L&P*, 14:116–21. Attempts to clarify his use of psychoanalytic study as a means of predicting the appeal of a poem. Discusses "The Relique" and "The Indifferent" and finds that Donne uses sexual and religious love to reduce aggression. Maintains that "The Relique" both "defends against and satisfies the aggressive drives in love by fragmenting the relationship, replacing bodily union with an intellectual and spiritual distancing" (pp. 123–24).

৵§ 1122. HOWARTH, R. G. "Donne Vindicated" in *A Pot of Gillyflowers: Studies and Notes*, pp. 100–101. Cape Town, S. Africa.

Comments briefly on R. C. Bald's findings in *Donne and the Drurys* (1959) about Donne's relationship to Sir Robert and his reasons for writing the *Anniversaries*. Points out that the poems were not written simply to flatter a patron.

৵§ 1123. JACOBSEN, ERIC. "Donne's Elegy VII." *ES*, 45:Supp., 190–96.

Shows that line 22 of the poem, "Inlaid thee, neither to be seene, nor see," is related to the agricultural imagery that precedes and follows it. Disagrees with Grierson's gloss on the line and shows that earlier editors, especially Grosart, were more nearly correct.

৵§ 1124. KRUEGER, ROBERT. "The Publication of John Donne's Sermons." *RES*, 15:151–60.

Using two heretofore unpublished documents to support his conclusions, the author shows that the *LXXX Sermons* of 1640 and the *Fifty Sermons* of 1649 derive from different manuscript collections. Apparently John Donne the younger offered Francis Bowman, an Oxford publisher, fifty of his father's sermons, which he claimed represented all of the extant sermons. Soon afterwards he came upon eighty more that he probably received from Walton through Donne's executor, Henry King. The latter sermons, perhaps prepared for publication by Donne himself, are much more carefully presented and edited.

৵§ 1125. MONTGOMERY, ROBERT L. "Donne's 'Ecstasy,' Philosophy and the Renaissance Lyric." *Kerygma und Dogma*, 4:3–14.

Discusses "The Extasie" in terms of "the evolution of the Renaissance lyric from its early expressiveness to a complex and complicated intellectualization" (p. 4). Focuses on "the methods by which the lyric was intellectualized" rather than on the concepts that inform it. Sees the poem as fusing doctrine and experience in such a way that each element proves the other.

৵§ 1126. NELLIST, B. F. "Donne's 'Storm' and 'Calm' and the Descriptive Tradition." *MLR*, 59:511–15.

Places these two verse letters in the tradition of poems using sea imagery to suggest the place of fortune in men's lives. Like Lucan, but unlike Ovid, Donne presents a dramatic experience rather than a particular event which is described in such a way as to arrive at a moral. Instead of the traditional moral of contempt of the world, he accepts frustration and despair as part of man's humanity.

≈§ 1127. NOVARR, DAVID. "The Two Hands of John Donne."*MP*, 62: 142–54.

Review of five studies on Donne: (1) Arnold Stein, *John Donne's Lyrics: The Eloquence of Action* (1962), (2) *John Donne: The Anniversaries*, ed. Frank Manley (1963), (3) *The Sermons of John Donne*, eds. Evelyn Simpson and George R. Potter, Vol. X (1962), (4) Joan Webber, *Contrary Music: The Prose Style of John Donne* (1963), (5) William R. Mueller, *John Donne: Preacher* (1962).

≈§ 1128. PRAZ, MARIO. "Baroque in England." *MP*, 61:169–79.

Comments on Donne as a Mannerist. Traces briefly the modern interest in Donne and the critical confusion about Donne's relationship to the baroque.

≈§ 1129. RICHMOND, H. M. *The School of Love: The Evolution of the Stuart Love Lyric*. Princeton: Princeton University Press. 337 p.

Points out how "The Flea" differs in mood and attitude from other admonitory poems (pp. 16–17). Discusses "Aire and Angels" and "Negative love" as poems that illustrate the mind of a man consciously seeking a significant relationship with a woman (pp. 32–37). Discusses the influence of Sappho in "The Extasie." Basic theme is the breaking out of the initial trance of love in order to articulate fully the lovers' relationship (pp. 47–49). Comments on "The Dreame" as conforming to dream poems nominally, but on a different mental plane. While the poem evokes a fascination of dreams for the lover, it defines and revokes their dangers to his mental stability and to truth (pp. 53–55). Considers "The Apparition " a poem that makes ridiculous the tradition of cursing an unfaithful mistress by conscious exaggeration and burlesque (pp. 86–87). Compares "The Message" to Carew's "Ask me no more" in terms of syntax (pp. 114–15). Discusses "A Valediction: forbidding mourning" in contrast to Surrey's handling of the theme (p. 150) and comments on "Twicknam garden" as a variation of the classical Polyphemus—Galatea tradition and as a development from Ronsard.

≈§ 1130. RICKEY, MARY ELLEN. "Donne's 'The Relique' 27–28." *Expl*, 22:Item 58.

Shows that kisses of the two lovers in the poem are compared with the *agape* of the early Christian community. By means of the imagery throughout the poem, Donne "designates the two lovers as early saints, living in the time of miracles, showing forth their love through a type of the holy *agape*, and other lovers, by implication, as decadent products of a post-apostolic age, corporeal and appetitive."

◄§ 1131. ROGERS, ROBERT. "Literary Value and the Clinical Fallacy." *L&P*, 14:116–21.

Answers an article by Norman N. Holland, *L&P*, 14:43–55. Discusses "The Relique" to illustrate that aesthetic values must be independent of clinical values. For a reply by Norman N. Holland, see *L&P*, 14:121–25.

◄§ 1132. ROWE, FREDERICK A. *I Launch at Paradise: A Consideration of John Donne, Poet and Preacher*. London: Epworth Press. xiii, 253 p.

Appreciative study of Donne's poems and sermons in a context of his life that is written for both the ordained and lay preaching ministry. Selected bibliography.

◄§ 1133. ROWLAND, DANIEL B. *Mannerism—Style and Mood: An Anatomy of Four Works in Three Art Forms*. New Haven and London: Yale University Press. xii, 136 p.

In an attempt to distinguish Mannerism from Renaissance and baroque modes of expression, the author discusses the style and mood of *The first Anniversary* (pp. 51–82). Compares Donne's style to those of Spenser and Crashaw. Donne creates an unresolved tension in the poem with roughness; use of abstract, conceptual, and functional metaphors; and use of complex structure. In manneristic art, "tension is created not to be resolved but to remain" (p. 77), which may explain in part why critics have disagreed on the success of the poem.

◄§ 1134. SHAWCROSS, JOHN T. "Donne's 'A Lecture upon the Shadow.'" *ELN*, 1:187–88.

Suggests a possible biographical reading of the poem in which Donne reminds his wife in 1601 that love that is concealed is imperfect. "Donne lectures that love must be kept in full and constant light, without even the slightest falsity or disguise between the lovers, or it has expired" (p. 188).

◄§ 1135. SINHA, V. N. "John Donne and the Romantic Theory of Imagination." *Criticism and Research* (Banaras Hindu University), 34–45.

Unable to locate this item.

◄§ 1136. SMITH, A. J. "Theory and Practice in Renaissance Poetry: Two Kinds of Imitation." *BJRL*, 47:212–43.

Historical analysis of the theory of imitation and the degree and manner of its use in the Renaissance. Specifically discusses Donne's place in this history and comments on "The Extasie," "Aire and Angels," and *The first Anniversary*.

⊷§ 1137. Sparrow, John. "George Herbert and John Donne among the Moravians." *BNYPL*, 68:625–53.

Reprinted in *Hymns Unbidden: Donne, Herbert, Blake, Emily Dickinson and the Hymnographers*, Martha Winburn England and John Sparrow (New York: New York Public Library, 1966), pp. 1–28.

Adaptations of Donne's poems that appear in Part I of the Moravian *A Collection of Hymns* (1754). Number 383 in the collection consists of lines from four of Donne's *Holy Sonnets*, and Number 384 comprises the first three stanzas of "The Litanie" with some alterations.

⊷§ 1138. Stephens, James. "John Donne," in *James, Seumas & Jacques: Unpublished Writings of James Stephens*, pp. 202–6. Chosen and Edited with an Introduction by Lloyd Frankenberg. New York: The Macmillan Co.

Written in 1946, this article suggests that Donne lacked a certain simplicity necessary for great poetry. Donne's emphasis on wit is opposed to great poetry. Calls Donne's poetry "the most 'remarkable' collection of poetic material in the English language" (p. 206).

⊷§ 1139. Strong, Roy. "The Elizabethan Malady: Melancholy in Elizabethan and Jacobean Portraiture." *Apollo*, 79:264–69.

Discusses the Lothian portrait of Donne and calls it "the most famous of all melancholy love-portraits" (p. 268).

⊷§ 1140. Sullens, Zay Rusk. "Neologisms in Donne's English Poems." *AION-SG*, 7:175–271.

Word by word check of Donne's English poems against the *OED*. Table I: Words which Donne uses earlier than the earliest *OED* date; Table II: Words for which the *OED* cites Donne as the earliest source; Table III: Word combinations in Donne which the *OED* does not record; Table IV: Meanings which Donne uses earlier than their earliest *OED* date; Table V: Meanings for which the *OED* cites Donne as the earliest source; Table VI: Meanings in Donne which the *OED* does not record.

⊷§ 1141. Vining, Elizabeth Gray. *Take Heed of Loving Me*. Philadelphia and New York: J. B. Lippincott Co. 352 p.

Fictionalized biography of Donne.

⊷§ 1142. Warnke, Frank J. "Sacred Play: Baroque Poetic Style." *JAAC*, 22:455–64.

Discusses how intellectual play, dramatic projection, and mythic embodiment coexist in the work of the baroque poets, including Donne.

◄§ 1143. YOKLAVICH, JOHN. "Donne and the Countess of Huntingdon."
  PQ, 43:283–88.

Traces Donne's acquaintance with the Countess. Points out that as a child she lived in Sir Thomas Egerton's household. Uses this knowledge to refute that Donne's verse letter to her that begins "That unripe side of earth" was written in 1597. The Countess was only a child at that time, and the tone of the piece does not seem appropriate if it were addressed to a child.

1965

◄§ 1144. ANDREASEN, N. J. C. "Donne's *Devotions* and the Psychology of Assent." *MP*, 62:207–16.

Points out that all devotional literature has as its aim the full assent of the meditator, not just his intellectual assent but a full response from the mind, will, and affections. Shows how the *Devotions* achieve this end and are a blend of two devotional genres, the meditational guide book and the spiritual autobiography. Demonstrates how each of the twenty-three individual devotions is a microcosmic pattern of assent and how each corresponds to the pattern of the Ignatian meditation. On the "plot" level, the *Devotions* describe the illness and recovery of one man (Donne); on an allegorical level, they describe the progress of the soul (of Everyman) from sin to regeneration through charity. Shows how the *Devotions* are not egocentric but theocentric.

◄§ 1145. BALD, R. C. "Dr. Donne and the Booksellers." *SB*, 18:69–80.

Discusses briefly Donne's dealings with his publishers and the booksellers. Comments on the speed of publication in the early seventeenth century. Discusses the printing of several of Donne's works; in particular, suggests that the *Devotions* were written in a few weeks, while Donne was convalescing.

◄§ 1146. BENDER, TODD K. "The Platan Tree in Donne, Horace, and Theocritus." *TLS*, 12 August, p. 704.

Suggests that when Donne wrote of the plane-tree in "Elegie IX: The Autumnall," he had in mind Theocritus' *The Epithalamy of Helen*, in which Theocritus describes a cult of Helen of Sparta. For a reply by Helen Gardner, see *TLS*, 26 August, p. 740.

◄§ 1147. BRONZWAER, W. J. M. "Correspondence." *REL*, 6, No. 2:102.

Reply to Hugh Sykes Davies, *REL*, 6, No. 1:93–107, and to Helen Gardner, *REL*, 6, No. 1:108–10. Comments on the use of the pronoun *it* in line 24 of "Aire and Angels" and suggests that the last three lines of the poem contain a chiasmus. See also David W. Lindsay, *REL*, 6, No. 3:106.

৺§ 1148. BRYAN, ROBERT A. "*Translatio* Concepts in Donne's *The Progress of the Soul*," in ... *All These to Teach: Essays in Honor of C. A. Robertson*, eds. Robert A. Bryan, Alton C. Morris, A. A. Murphree, and Aubrey L. Williams, pp. 120–29. Gainesville: University of Florida Press.

Discusses the concepts of the *translatio emperii* and *translatio studii* as related to *The Progresse of the Soule*—the idea of "human history as a westward movement of empire and civilization or humane learning from one epoch and country to another epoch and country, a movement normally originating in the East and moving westward across the globe of Europe" (p. 123). Shows how Donne, like Raleigh before him, inverts honorific associations of the concepts with the intention of satirizing the English court.

৺§ 1149. BUCKLEY, VINCENT. "John Donne's Passion." *CR*, 8:19–31.
Discusses the quality of "poetic passion" in Donne's poetry.

৺§ 1150. CALLARD, J. "Donne's Books." *TLS*, 23 December, p. 1204.
Records the discovery of a book from Donne's library, found at the Chapter Library at Windsor Castle: Conrad Schleussburg's *Haereticorum Catalogus* (1599).

৺§ 1151. CAREY, JOHN. "Notes on Two of Donne's *Songs and Sonets*." *RES*, n.s., 16:50–53.
(1) Comments on "O more then Moone," line 19 of "A Valediction: of weeping." Points out that Elizabeth was frequently called the moon, Cynthia, Diana, etc. by Renaissance poets. Perhaps disgusted with such hyperbole, Donne is saying, in a "deliberate gesture of insubordination" (p. 51), that his lady is more than merely a sovereign. On the basis of this evidence, the author suggests that the poem was probably written before 1603 and not long after 1595. (2) Challenges the notion that "The Extasie" is a seduction piece or a wooing poem. Points out that the poem is in the past tense and that the person addressed is not the lady but a hypothetical listener.

৺§ 1152. CHARI, V. K. "The Dramatic in Donne." *Indian Journal of English Studies* (Calcutta), 6:19–32.
Contends that Donne's poems are dramatic in only a rudimentary way. The style is sometimes dramatic, but the mode is argumentative. Compares Donne to Browning to illustrate the point.

৺§ 1153. CLAIR, JOHN A. "Donne's 'The Canonization.'" *PMLA*, 80: 300–302.
Maintains that the poem has more unity than has been usually recognized and that the central metaphor of canonization is carried out in all

five of the stanzas. Shows how the poem follows closely the *processus* of canonization in the Roman Catholic Church of Donne's time. Moves from proof of personal sanctity, to proof of heroic virtue, to proof of miracles, to the examination of the burial place and the writings of the saint, and at last to the full declaration of sainthood and the veneration of the saint. Sees a parallel between the role of the antagonist in the poem and the function of the devil's advocate in the *processus*.

≈§ 1154. COLLMER, ROBERT G. "Donne and Charron."*ES*, 46:482–88.
Points to close parallels between *Biathanatos* and Pierre Charron's *De la Sagesse* (1601). Although Donne does not indicate his indebtedness nor does he quote from Charron's book, it is possible that he knew the study. All that can be said with certainty is that Charron clearly anticipates several of Donne's arguments in *Biathanatos*.

≈§ 1155. ———. "Donne's Poetry in Dutch Letters." *CLS*, 2:25–39.
Discusses the possible influence of Donne on a group of Dutch poets of the seventeenth century called the *Muiderkring*, which consisted of such men as P. C. Hooft, Constantijn Huygens, Jacob Cats, Joost van den Vondel. Concludes that, although the poets of this group were generally enthusiastic about Donne's poetry, there was no great following of him among the Dutch. Summarizes diverse scholarly opinion on the influence of Donne on Huygens.

≈§ 1156. ———. "The Function of Death in Certain Metaphysical Poems." *McNR*, 16:25–32.
Reprinted in *Brno Studies in English* (Brünn), 6 (1966):147–56.
Discusses the handling of death in the poetry of Donne, Herbert, Crashaw, and Vaughan. Although Donne presents more variations on the theme than do the others, he fails to offer a completely coherent, well-developed view on the subject. Death for Donne was primarily a force of division, not one of union or gain. Donne plays with the concept of death in poetry, using it, as he used geography or medicine, for poetic and dramatic effects.

≈§ 1157. CORNELIUS, DAVID K. "Donne's 'Holy Sonnet XIV.' " *Expl*, 24:Item 25.
Argues that the poem can be seen as "a development in three images corresponding respectively to Father, Son, and Holy Ghost, and reflecting successively the attributes Donne associated with the Persons—power, wisdom, and love." Supports this view by referring to the sermons.

≈§ 1158. DANIELS, EDGAR F., AND WANDA J. DEAN. "Donne's 'Elegy VII,' 22." *Expl*, 24:Item 34.
Discusses the word *inlaid* (l. 22). Challenges Grierson's comments and suggests that *inlaid* is perhaps a past participle of *lay in*, which is de-

fined in the *OED* as "to enclose or reserve (a meadow) for hay." Such a reading is more clearly related to the images of land, which both precede and follow the word, than Grierson's interpretation.

◆§ 1159. DAVIES, HUGH SYKES. "Text or Context?" *REL*, 6, No. 1: 93–107.

Defense of close reading. Challenges Helen Gardner in *The Business of Criticism* (1959) and shows how their separate critical approaches account for wide differences in the interpretation of "Aire and Angels." Disputes with Miss Gardner mostly on the basis of syntax, the use of the pronoun *it* (l. 23), the use of the word *spheare* (l. 24), and the distinction between two kinds of purity as that of thin air and thickened air. Interprets the conclusion of the poem as being consistent with the tone and attitude conveyed in the beginning, not a reversal in attitude toward women. For a reply by Helen Gardner, see *REL*, 6, No. 1:108–10. See also W. J. M. Bronzwaer, *REL*, 6, No. 2:102, and David W. Lindsay, *REL*, 6, No. 3:106.

◆§ 1160. DEMARAY, JOHN G. "Donne's Three Steps to Death." *Person*, 46:366–81.

Discusses the development of Donne's skepticism and divides it into three stages: (1) From 1601 to 1611, Donne believed in a rationally ordered universe, the laws of which could best be learned by studying Scripture; (2) in 1611, Donne recognized that the order of nature was threatened with destruction, yet he still sought for meaning in this world; (3) by 1612, Donne had reached the final stage of his skepticism and rejected reason and embraced faith, asserting that divine order can be found only in heaven.

◆§ 1161. DOBB, CLIFFORD. "Donne's Books." *TLS*, 30 December, p. 1213.

Records the discovery of a book from Donne's library: Giovanni Francesco Bordoni's *De rebus praeclare gestis a Sixto V. Pon. Max.* . . . *Carminum liber primus* (1588). For a reply by John Sparrow, see *TLS*, 6 January 1966, p. 9.

◆§ 1162. DONNE, JOHN. *John Donne: The Elegies and The Songs and Sonnets.* Edited with introduction and commentary by Helen Gardner. Oxford: Clarendon Press. xcix, 272 p.

General critical introduction to Donne's love poetry (pp. xvii–xxx); discussion of the canon and the dating of the *Elegies* (pp. xxxi–lxii); detailed discussion of the manuscripts and early editions (pp. lxiii–xcv). The poems (pp. 1–108). Commentary on individual poems (pp. 109–230). Appendix A: Verbal Alterations in the *Elegies* and *Songs and Sonets* in the edition of 1635 (pp. 231–37); Appendix B: Musical Settings of

Donne's Poems (pp. 238–47); Appendix C: Lady Bedford and Mrs. Herbert (pp. 248–58); Appendix D: "The Ecstasy" (pp. 259–65); Appendix E: The Marshall Engraving and the Lothian Portrait (pp. 266–70).

◄§ 1163. FORSTER, LEONARD. "Donne's Books." TLS, 9 December, p. 1159.

Points out that there are at least two known books in Donne's library that are in German and suggests that Donne probably knew the language. For a reply by John Sparrow, see TLS, 6 January 1966, p. 9, and by I. A. Shapiro, see TLS, 20 January 1966, p. 48.

◄§ 1164. GARDNER, HELEN. "Correspondence." REL, 6, No. 1:108–10.

Reply to Hugh Sykes Davies, REL, 6, No. 1:93–107. Maintains that "Aire and Angels" deals with man's love finding a fit embodiment in woman's love, not with a comparison of the purity of men's and women's love. See also David W. Lindsay, REL, 6, No. 3:106, and W. J. M. Bronzwaer, REL, 6, No. 2:102.

◄§ 1165. ———. "Donne's Platan Tree." TLS, 26 August, p. 740.

In part, a reply to Todd K. Bender, TLS, 12 August, p. 704. Maintains that references to Xerxes and the plane-tree are so common in the literature of the Renaissance that no specific source for Donne's reference is necessary.

◄§ 1166. GERALDINE, SISTER M. "John Donne and the Mindes Indeavours." SEL, 5:115–31.

Attempts to catalogue Donne's statements and assumptions about the relation of the intellect to virtue by a discussion of Satyre III, portions of Machiavelli's trial in Ignatius his Conclave, and references in the sermons. Both Satyre III and Ignatius his Conclave present a scale of ungodliness in terms of knowledge and ignorance. Donne's bête noir is the use and misuse of reason to destroy the consciences of others. Discusses the term light and its implications for Donne. Distinguishes three kinds of knowledge: (1) useless or misdirected knowledge; (2) humane learning; and (3) knowledge of Scripture and the things of God. To Donne the last type is essential to Christian living; salvation depends on the Word. Uses sermons to illustrate that only by the Word can man come to faith, but to Donne the Word is the mediation between God and man. Concludes that the language of satire, in contrast to the inspired words of the sermon, appeals only to the intellect; but if it is used to correct devious thinking, it too is one kind of word analogous to the Word.

◄§ 1167. GORLIER, CLAUDIO. "Il poeta e la nuova alchimia." *Paragone*, 16:clxxxii, 55–78; clxxxiv, 43–80.

Discusses Donne in contrast to the Elizabethan poets, particularly Shakespeare. Detailed comparison of "Lovers infinitenesse" to Shakespeare's "Sonnet 40." Shows that Donne always goes beyond his *point de départ* in sensual reality or individual experience to a universal or metaphysical resolution. In Part 2, compares Donne and the Elizabethans in regard to metrics and music. Finds more use of enjambment in Donne, a cadence nearer that of prose, a style that is freer in structure and better adapted to the development of an argument, a certain directness and economy in syntax, and a freedom in lexical innovation peculiar to baroque poetry. Extended analysis of "A nocturnall upon S. Lucies day." Comments on the twentieth-century revival of interest in Donne.

◄§ 1168. GUSS, DONALD L. "Donne's Petrarchism." *JEGP*, 64:17–28.

Shows how Donne belongs to the Petrarchan tradition. Points out a number of analogues between Donne's poems and those of Petrarch and his followers, especially the Italians. Suggests that what is original in Donne is his dramatic imagination and illustrates how both "The Apparition" and Stanza 3 of "The Canonization" are dramatic realizations of commonplace Petrarchan conceits.

◄§ 1169. HERBOLD, ANTHONY. " 'Seeking Secrets or Poëtiquencsse': Donne's Dialectics in the Divine Poems." *MSpr*, 59.2//–94.

Discusses the divine poems as dialectical. Donne searches for "an equilibrium between balanced polarities" (p. 280). Shows how the tension, the dramatic quality, the imagery and conceits, the rhetoric and diction reflect the dialectical flux of alternatives and contraries.

◄§ 1170. HUGHES, RICHARD E. "John Donne's 'Nocturnall Upon S. Lucies Day': A Suggested Resolution." *Cithara*, 4:60–68.

Contends that the poem is not a lament for the Countess of Bedford's death "but for her renunciation of Donne's friendship; and that the poem represents an attempt on Donne's part to convince Lucy of his own conversion which he has undergone through her example" (p. 62).

◄§ 1171. HUNTER, JIM. *The Metaphysical Poets*. Literature in Perspective. London: Evans Brothers Limited. 160 p.

Introductory study of metaphysical poetry intended for the "ordinary man who reads for pleasure" (p. 5). Uses Donne as a touchstone for discussions of the times, the characteristics of metaphysical poetry, verse forms, diction, imagery, and critical estimate through the years. Chapter 6 (pp. 90–107) is solely concerned with Donne: short biographical sketch, description of the poetry and prose, comments on his earnestness, and defense of his good taste and "roughness." Selected bibliography.

◆§ 1172. KLINE, GEORGE L. " 'Elegy for John Donne' by Joseph Brod-
sky." *RusR*, 24:341–53.
Introduction and complete translation from the Russian of an original
modern poem on Donne.

◆§ 1173. LeCOMTE, EDWARD. *Grace to a Witty Sinner: A Life of Donne*.
New York: Walker & Co. 307 p.
Biographical study. Last chapter reviews the Donne revival in the
twentieth century. Appendix contains twenty-three letters by Donne. Selected bibliography.

◆§ 1174. LINDSAY, DAVID W. "Correspondence." *REL*, 6, No. 3:106.
Reply to Hugh Sykes Davies, *REL*, 6, No. 1:93–107, and to Helen
Gardner, *REL*, 6, No. 1:108–10. Argues that "Aire and Angels" must be
interpreted as a whole in order to make sense of the conclusion. Lines
23–28 show that the extravagant compliments paid the lady in lines 1–22
were paid only to her physical beauty, a "cryptic insult." See also W. J. M.
Bronzwaer, *REL*, 6, No. 2:102.

◆§ 1175. LOW, DONALD A. "An Eighteenth-Century Imitation of
Donne's First Satire." *RES*, n.s., 16:291–98.
Discusses and reproduces an imitation of Donne's *Satyre I* found in a
commonplace book in York Minister Library belonging to William
Mason, Thomas Gray's biographer.

◆§ 1176. MELLER, HORST S. "The Phoenix and the Well-Wrought Urn."
TLS, 22 April, p. 320.
Suggests that a woodcut and sonnet frequently found in the Giolitine
editions of *Il Petrarcha* (1544–1560) may have supplied Donne with the
initial inspiration as well as several details for "The Canonization." *Il
Petrarcha* contains an emblematic design of an urn surmounted by a
phoenix and celebrates the immortality of the love of Petrarch and Laura.
The sonnet mentions Laura as a saint and invites lovers to prostrate
themselves in adoration. See also A. J. Smith, *TLS*, 13 May, p. 376.

◆§ 1177. MENASCÉ, ESTHER. "John Donne: Ultimo poeta del Medioevo,"
in *Studi di letteratura, storia e filosofia in onore di Bruno Revel*, pp.
393–414. Biblioteca dell' «Archivum Romanicum», Series 1: Storia,
letteratura, paleografia, v. 74. Firenze: L. S. Olschki.
Maintains that since the rediscovery of Donne by Eliot and other
critics in this century, attention has always been directed toward the
showing of the modernity of Donne. Sees a predominance of medieval
aspects in his works and finds them particularly evident in the *Anniversaries*. Sets out to reverse the judgment of Jonson and many later critics
concerning the lack of worth of these poems and discusses the theory of

Marjorie Nicolson in *The Breaking of the Circle* that the poems are a veiled tribute to Elizabeth I. Suggests that the theme of *The first Anniversary* is the fragility of the world and that the theme of *The second Anniversarie* is the glory of eternal life. Discusses evidences of Donne's medieval outlook.

৺§ 1178. MORRIS, WILLIAM E. "Donne's 'The Sunne Rising,' 30." *Expl*, 23:Item 45.

Challenges Redpath's reading of line 30 of the poem. Shows how Donne wittily transforms the sun into a cube. Since the lovers' bed is its center, the walls of the room are its circumference. "As the lovers have made the 'square' of the bed into the globe of the world, the speaker at last attempts to force the sphere of the sun into the cube of the room, and thus to make the room of their loving an everywhere, with the sun warmly boxed in."

৺§ 1179. PARISH, JOHN E. "The Parley in 'The Extasie.'" *XUS*, 4:188–92.

Discusses military imagery in the poem. Suggests that "two equal Armies" (l. 13) refers to the bodies of the lovers, which lie like "sepulchrall statues" (l. 18) while their souls negotiate. The speakers in the parley are the king–general and the queen–general of the two armies who decide to join forces. The "great Prince in prison" (l. 68) is the child desired by the lovers.

৺§ 1180. PIRIE, ROBERT S. "Donne's Books." *TLS*, 23 December, p. 1204.

Records the discovery of a book from Donne's library: Richard Mountagn's *A Gagg for The New Gospel, No: A New Gagg For An Old Goose* (1624).

৺§ 1181. RALEIGH, KAREN M. "The Extasie." *Lit*, No. 6:44–49.

Very general and brief comments on the style of Donne's love lyrics, followed by a short explication (mostly paraphrase) of the essential statement of "The Extasie."

৺§ 1182. RASPA, ANTHONY. "Theology and Poetry in Donne's *Conclave*." *ELH*, 32:478–89.

Studies *Ignatius his Conclave* in the light of several of Donne's other works of the same period in order to show that "he held a fundamentalist view of the created universe and history" (p. 489). Suggests that Donne cast his attack on innovators in the form of a mock vision of hell in order to satirize the fictionalized mental picture required of exercitants of *The Spiritual Exercises* of Ignatius.

◄§ 1183. Ringler, Richard N. "Donne's Specular Stone." MLR, 60: 333–39.

Shows that Donne's knowledge of the specular stone was derived from Guido Pancirollus who, in his Rerum memorabilium iam olim deperditarum (1599), confused specular stone and phengites. Shows that Donne was generally familiar with the work of Pancirollus. Helps explain the references to specular stone in several of Donne's works, particularly Stanza 2 of "The undertaking," which the author maintains could not have been written before 1599.

◄§ 1184. Sen, Sunil Kanti. Metaphysical Tradition and T. S. Eliot. Calcutta: Firma K. L. Mukhopadhyay. viii, 126 p.

Proposes "(1) to examine the nature of metaphysical poetry and its roots in the general sensibility of the age, (2) to analyse the neo-classical shift of taste and the romantic practices which are directly responsible for the rejection of the metaphysical tradition and (3) to investigate the nature and extent of Eliot's affinity with the metaphysicals" (p. 3). Divided into four main chapters: (1) Donne and the Metaphysical Tradition, (2) Dissociation of Sensibility and the Decline of the Metaphysical Tradition, (3) Romantic Assumptions and Practice, (4) T. S. Eliot and the Revival of the Metaphysical Tradition. Selected bibliography.

◄§ 1185. Shawcross, John T. "Donne's 'A Nocturnall Upon S. Lucies Day.'" Expl, 23:Item 56.

Suggests that the woman in the poem is Anne More and argues that the poem was probably written on or about December 12, 1617. Brief explication.

◄§ 1186. Simpson, Evelyn M. "Two Notes on Donne." RES, n.s., 16: 140–50.

(1) Donne and the Serpent—discusses Donne's use of the image of the serpent in the sermons, "The Litanie," his seal, and the motto on the frontispiece of the LXXX Sermons. (2) Donne the Seafarer—discusses Donne's use of nautical images in poems, essays, and sermons.

◄§ 1187. Sloan, Thomas O. "The Persona as Rhetor: An Interpretation of Donne's Satyre III." QJS, 51:14–27.

Proposes that Satyre III be seen more as an oration than as a soliloquy. By applying the traditional principles of dispositio to the poem, the author shows the rhetorical function of each part, the central thesis, and the intended audience. Suggests the conclusion of the poem can be best understood if the structure is seen as four parts, with the best arguments placed first and last.

১§ 1188. Smith, A. J. *John Donne: The Songs and Sonets.* Studies in English Literature, No. 17. London: Edward Arnold; Great Neck, N. Y.: Barron's Educational Series, Inc. 72 p.

Reprinted, 1966.

General critical evaluation of the *Songs and Sonets* designed for sixth-form and university students. Analyzes several poems in terms of invention, movement, form, love, and wit. Selected bibliography.

১§ 1189. ———. "Phoenix and the Urn." *TLS*, 13 May, p. 376.

In part, a reply to Horst S. Meller, *TLS*, 22 April, p. 320. Agrees with Meller that Donne may have had in mind the woodcut and sonnet found in the Giolitine editions of Petrarch when he wrote "The Canonization," but points out the essential differences between Giolito's woodcut and sonnet and Donne's poem.

১§ 1190. ———. "Theory and Practice in Renaissance Poetry: Two Kinds of Imitation." *BJRL*, 47:212–43.

Discusses Renaissance theories of imitation and locates Donne within the tradition of Petrarchan imitation. Shows that to see Donne within such a tradition is not to diminish his success as a poet. Comments in particular on "The Extasie" and "Aire and Angels." Relates the latter to Speroni's *Dialogo di Amore.* Relates *The first Anniversary* to late Renaissance conventions of the mannerist funeral elegy.

১§ 1191. Sparrow, John. "Donne's Books in Oxford." *TLS*, 25 November, p. 1060.

Describes a signed copy of Sebastian Munster's *Cosmographia* (1578) found in the Bodleian Library. Suggests it was given by Donne to Edward Parvyshe (or Parvish). Records two more books from Donne's library that had been discovered recently: (1) Antonius Clarus Sylvius' *Commentarius ad leges ... Romani iuris antiqui* (1603), and (2) Iacobus Pamelius' *Missale SS. Patrum Latinorum,* 2 vols. (1609) found in the Pembroke College Library. See also Leonard Forster, *TLS*, 9 December, p. 1159, and I. A. Shapiro, *TLS*, 20 January 1966, p. 48.

১§ 1192. Wagner, Linda Welshimer. "Donne's Secular and Religious Poetry." *LHR*, No. 7:13–22.

Close reading of Herbert's "The Flower," Vaughan's "The Flower," and Donne's "The Blossome" and "Holy Sonnet II" to show the relationship between Donne's poetry and that of Herbert and of Vaughan.

১§ 1193. Whitlock, Baird W. "A Note on Two Donne Manuscripts." *RN*, 18:9–11.

Calls attention to undiscovered manuscript copies of two Donne poems, "An hymne to the Saints, and to Marquesse Hamylton" and

"Elegie IV," which help explain the editorial decisions of Grierson. The manuscript of the latter poem sheds light on the reading of the elisions.

◄§ 1194. WOODHOUSE, A. S. P. "The Sevententh Century: Donne and His Successors," in *The Poet and His Faith: Religion and Poetry in England from Spenser to Eliot and Auden*, pp. 42–89. Chicago and London: The University of Chicago Press.

Discusses the general conditions in English religion and poetry that made the seventeenth century such an important period in religious verse. Discusses Donne's religious experience and sensibility chiefly as these are reflected in his poetry. Comments that the chief mark of Donne's sacred poems "is that they end with the resolution of tension, which, if it is the outcome of his faith, is also the achievement of his poetry. For in such poetry the religious and the aesthetic experience unite and afford each other mutual support" (p. 66). Comments on Donne's successors and compares Donne and Herbert in particular.

1966

◄§ 1195. ALLISON, C. F. *The Rise of Moralism: The Proclamation of the Gospel from Hooker to Baxter*. New York: Seabury Press, Inc. xii, 250 p.

Brief discussion of Donne's beliefs concerning the doctrines of justification and righteousness and the nature of sin (pp. 24–27). Appreciative comments on Donne's theology, with further discussion of the above topics (pp. 210–12).

◄§ 1196. ARMITAGE, C. M. "Donne's Poems in Huntington Manuscript 198:New Light on 'The Funerall.'" *SP*, 63:697–707

Describes the format and history of the manuscript, shows its relationship to the other manuscripts of Donne's poems, and discusses some of the more important variants, in particular the seemingly unique version of "The Funerall." The epistle to the Countess of Bedford, which is usually printed as a prologue to "Epitaph on Himself," stands as a prologue to "The Funerall," a positioning the author finds meaningful.

◄§ 1197. BENNETT, J. A. W. "Donne's 'Elegy,' XVI, 31." *N&Q*, n.s., 13:254.

Glosses line 31 of the poem. Reference is to a common proverb found in Erasmus and other Renaissance writers. Erasmus says: "*An ape, is an ape, be she clothed in purpre*, so a woman is a woman (that is to saie) a foole, what so euer parte she plie" (Chaloner's translation, *EETS*, 1965, p. 24, l. 13).

⊷§ 1198. Boorman, S. C. "Some Elizabethan Notes." *Trivium*, 1:184–87.

Suggests that in "A Tale of a Citizen and his Wife" (ll. 64–65), Donne may be alluding to the story of "Avarice her tragedy," which appears in Chapter 7 of *The Famous & renowned History of Morindos a King of Spaine* (1609).

⊷§ 1199. Bross, Addison C. "Alexander Pope's Revisions of John Donne's *Satyres*." *XUS*, 5:133–52.

Comments on the basic principles behind the changes that Pope made in the *Satyres*: "His propensity to set Donne's material in patterns of climactic sequence, his tendency to arrange material in order of abstract rule and particular instance, his placing metaphors and similies of similar content in close conjunction, and his untangling of complex grammatical structure" (p. 134).

⊷§ 1200. Chambers, A. B. "The Fly in Donne's 'Canonization.'" *JEGP*, 65:252–59.

Discusses the complex use of the fly image in the poem (l. 20) and claims that it functions in at least three ways. "As an object of monumental insignificance, it marks a specific turning point in the logic of Donne's argument: 'Call us what you will'—even a fly. As a creation of unnatural science, it closely corresponds to the hermaphroditic and resurrectable nature of Donne's love. As an image of audacious paradox, it serves to define the tone and technique and meaning of the poem at large" (p. 258).

⊷§ 1201. Clive, Mary. *Jack and the Doctor*. London: Macmillan; New York: St. Martin's Press, Inc. 216 p.

Popular biography of Donne. 39 illustrations. Three appendices: (1) What Happened Afterwards, (2) Francis Wolley (1583–1609) and Pyrford, (3) The Rise of Buckingham and the Fall of Somerset. Three genealogies: (1) The Family of John Donne, (2) The More Family, (3) The Three Marriages of Sir Thomas Egerton.

⊷§ 1202. Colie, Rosalie L. *Paradoxia Epidemica: The Renaissance Tradition of Paradox*. Princeton: Princeton University Press. xx, 553 p.

Examines the ways in which several writers made conscious use of the tradition of the paradox. Chapter 3, "John Donne and the Paradox of Incarnation," deals with the function and effects of paradox in Donne's secular and sacred poetry and in *Paradoxes and Problemes*. Discusses the *Anniversaries* and the paradoxes of epistemology (pp. 413–29). Also comments on Donne's paradoxical images and treatment of suicide and death, especially in *Biathanatos* (pp. 496–507).

❧§ 1203. COLLMER, ROBERT G. "The Function of Death in Certain Metaphysical Poems." *Brno Studies in English* (Brünn), 6:147–56. First appeared in *McNR*, 16 (1965):25–32.

❧§ 1204. CRUTTWELL, PATRICK. *The English Sonnet*. Writers and Their Work, No. 191. London: Longmans, Greene & Co., Ltd. 56 p.
In this brief history of the development of the sonnet in England, there is a cursory discussion of Donne's *Holy Sonnets* (pp. 27–29).

❧§ 1205. DANIEL, E. RANDOLPH. "Reconciliation, Covenant and Election: A Study in the Theology of John Donne." *Anglican Theological Review*, 48:14–30.
Discusses Donne's views on the doctrine of salvation or reconciliation. Argues that "the core of Donne's theology is his doctrine of reconciliation in which he united a covenant theology—which was influenced by the Scotist and Reformed traditions of covenant theology and which was certainly related to the Nominalist theology—with the classical Protestant doctrine of salvation by faith alone, by showing that this doctrine of reconciliation draws together as to a nucleus many facets of Donne's theological system" (pp. 29–30).

❧§ 1206. DONNE, JOHN. *John Donne's Poetry: Authoritative Texts, Criticism.* Selected and Edited by A. L. Clements. Norton Critical Editions. New York: W. W. Norton & Co., Inc. xii, 273 p.
Selections from the poetry (pp. 1–95) with textual notes (pp. 96–100). Collection of previously published items. In addition to selections from the criticism of Jonson, Carew, Dryden, Johnson, and Coleridge, twentieth-century items include: (1) Selections from introduction of Sir Herbert Grierson's *Metaphysical Lyrics & Poems of the Seventeenth Century* (Oxford, 1921), pp. xiii–xxviii; (2) T. S. Eliot, "The Metaphysical Poets," from *Selected Essays* (New York, 1932); (3) J. B. Leishman from *The Monarch of Wit* (London, 1951), pp. 91–94; (4) Joseph Anthony Mazzeo, "A Critique of Some Modern Theories of Metaphysical Poetry," *MP*, 50 (1952):88–96; (5) C. S. Lewis, "Donne and Love Poetry in the Seventeenth Century," from *Seventeenth-Century Studies Presented to Sir Herbert Grierson* (Oxford, 1938), pp. 64–84; (6) Joan Bennett, "The Love Poetry of John Donne: A Reply to Mr. C. S. Lewis," from *Seventeenth-Century Studies Presented to Sir Herbert Grierson* (Oxford, 1938), pp. 85–104; (7) Cleanth Brooks, "The Language of Paradox," abridged from "The Language of Paradox," in *The Well Wrought Urn* (New York, 1947; London, 1949), pp. 3, 9–21; (8) Clay Hunt, "Elegy 19: 'To His Mistress Going to Bed,'" from *Donne's Poetry: Essays in Literary Analysis* (New Haven, 1954; London, 1954), pp. 18–31, 207–14; (9) Selections from introduction to Theodore Redpath's *The Songs and Sonnets of John Donne* (London, 1956), pp. xv–xvi, xxvii–

xxxix; (10) R. A. Durr, "Donne's 'The Primrose,'" *JEGP*, 59 (1960): 218–22; (11) Selections from Helen Gardner's *John Donne: The Divine Poems* (Oxford, 1952), pp. xxix–xxxv, l–lv; (12) Selection from Louis Martz's *The Poetry of Meditation* (New Haven, 1954), pp. 43–56; (13) Stanley Archer, "Meditation and the Structure of Donne's 'Holy Sonnets,'" *ELH*, 28 (1961):137–47; (14) Selection from J. C. Levenson, "Donne's *Holy Sonnets, XIV*," *Expl*, 11 (1953):Item 31; (15) Selection from George Herman, "Donne's *Holy Sonnets, XVI*," *Expl*, 12 (1953)· Item 18; (16) Selection from J. C. Levenson, "Donne's 'Holy Sonnets,' XIV," *Expl*, 12 (1954):Item 36; (17) Selection from George Knox, "Donne's 'Holy Sonnets,' XIV," *Expl*, 15 (1956):Item 2; (18) Selection from A. L. Clements, "Donne's Holy Sonnet XIV," *MLN*, 76 (1961):484–89; (19) Selection from John E. Parish, "No. 14 of Donne's *Holy Sonnets*," *CE*, 24 (1963):299–302; (20) Selection from Frank Manley, *John Donne: The Anniversaries* (Baltimore, 1963), pp. 6–10, 16–20, 40–50. Selected bibliography.

⋙ 1207. EMPSON, WILLIAM. "Donne in the New Edition." *CritQ*, 8: 255–80.
Review of Helen Gardner's *The Elegies and the Songs and Sonnets of John Donne* (Oxford: The Clarendon Press, 1965). For replies, see Helen Gardner, *CritQ*, 8:374–77 and W. P. H. Merchant, *CritQ*, 8:377–80. See also Empson, *CritQ*, 9 (1967):89.

⋙ 1208. FIELD, GEORGE C. "Donne and Hooker." *Anglican Theological Review*, 48:307–9.
Points out that a 1603 tract in the Harvard College Library by William Covel entitled *A Just and Temperate Defence of the Five Books of Ecclesiastical Policie: written by M. Richard Hooker* (STC 5881) contains a Latin epigram in Donne's handwriting, which suggests that Donne was acquainted with Hooker's work and shared "a wide spectrum of agreement in matters of 'ecclesiastical policie'" (p. 309).

⋙ 1209. FORSTER, LEONARD. "Donne's Books." *TLS*, 27 January, p. 68.
In part, a reply to John Sparrow, *TLS*, 6 January, p. 9. Suggests that Donne may have known German; the evidence is inconclusive.

⋙ 1210. GAUGER, HILDEGARD. "John Donne und seine Hörer," in *Literatur-Kultur-Gesellschaft in England und Amerika: Aspekte und Forschungsbeitrage. Friedrich Schubel zum 60. Geburtstag*, ed. Gerhard Müller-Schwefe and Konrad Tuzinski, pp. 157–78. Frankfurt: Moritz Diesterweg.
Discusses how Donne could accommodate himself to the level of his parishioners in the sermons. Contends that the audience brought out the best in Donne. At St. Paul's, where there was a cross section of the

London populace, including women and the poor, whom he did not face elsewhere, his speaking abilities bloomed to the fullest. His poetic gifts helped him reach the audience. Preoccupation with death finds its expression in his sermons, but more important is his admonishment to his hearers to overcome the fear of death through religious belief.

⊷§ 1211. GERALDINE, SISTER M. "Donne's *Notitia*: The Evidence of the Satires." *UTQ*, 36:24–36.

Shows how the early verse satires reflect Donne's thorough preoccupation with religious ideas. Discusses in particular the notion that Donne in his sermons calls *notitia cum laude*, that is, the literal observance of God's manipulating hand in the affairs of men.

⊷§ 1212. GIFFORD, WILLIAM. "A Donne Allusion." *N&Q*, n.s., 13:14.

Points out that Thomas Gataker in *Discours Apologetical* (1654) mentions having heard one of Donne's sermons.

⊷§ 1213. ———. "John Donne's Sermons on the 'Grand Days.'" *HLQ*, 29:235–44.

Argues from internal evidence that at least three of Donne's Candlemas sermons, which Potter and Simpson assign to St. Paul's, were given at Lincoln's Inn, where Candlemas was a major festival.

⊷§ 1214. GORDON, IAN A. "The Seventeenth Century II: 'Loose and free' and the Baroque," in *The Movement of English Prose*, pp. 113–19. Bloomington and London: Indiana University Press.

Brief discussion of "baroque" elements in Donne's prose style. Compares Donne to Browne and Taylor.

⊷§ 1215. GUSS, DONALD L. *John Donne, Petrarchist: Italianate Conceits and Love Theory in The Songs and Sonets*. Detroit: Wayne State University Press. 230 p.

Shows how much in Donne can best be accounted for by seeing his art in the light of the Petrarchan tradition. By placing Donne as the last and possibly the greatest of the Petrarchists, the author hopes to demonstrate more precisely what is truly original about Donne's art. Discusses the history of the Petrarchan tradition and shows how Donne fits into it. Suggests that Donne belongs to the school of "witty Petrarchism," but distinguishes Donne from the Italian wits and his English predecessors by pointing out that, although Donne frequently adopts their pretenses and polite exaggerations, he rejects their merely polite intentions: "Through their sophisticated pose, he reveals a sophisticated awareness" (p. 62). Suggests that the poems be read in the light of gesture: (1) occasion, (2) attitude, and (3) relationship between what is said and what the poems do (the function of the argument). Two chapters survey Renaissance theories of love in general and Donne's philosophy of love in particular. One of Donne's greatest achievements is that he fused "amorous exaltation with realism, common sense, and a broad, sophisticated awareness" (p. 138).

➡§ 1216. HARRINGTON, DAVID V. "Donne's 'The Relique.'" *Expl*, 25: Item 22.
Argues that the poem celebrates a human love relationship "which is exclusively spiritual, indeed, in a playful sense, miraculously so."

➡§ 1217. HARRISON, ROBERT. " 'To the Countess of Huntingdon' ('Man to Gods image . . .')." *Expl*, 25:Item 33.
Argues that the poem consists of "an interlocking sequence of syllogistic analogies" and is a pseudological "defense of the paradox that woman is an inferior copy of man and at the same time a paragon of virtues." Claims that the poem is essentially "a scholastic amplification, in which a premise is expanded and twisted into apparent validity, a deceptively convincing analogy is then drawn, and truth is made to vanish and reappear like a magician's bunny."

➡§ 1218. JOHNSON, CAROL. "John Donne: Reason's Double Agent," in *Reason's Double Agents*, pp. 40–54. Chapel Hill: University of North Carolina Press.
Briefly discusses the ratiocinative nature of Donne's verse.

➡§ 1219. KEYNES, GEOFFREY. "Donne's Books." *TLS*, 13 January, p. 25.
Two books belonging to Donne: (1) Paolo Beni's *Qua tandem ratione dirimi possit controversia quae in praesens de efficaci Dei auxilio et libero arbitrio inter nonnullos Catholicos agitatur* (Padua, 1603), and (2) Sir Philip Sidney's *Peplus. Illustrissimi viri D. Philippi Sidnaei supremis honoribus dicatus* (Oxford, 1587). 204 known books in Donne's library.

➡§ 1220. LABRANCHE, A. " 'Blanda Elegeia': The Background to Donne's 'Elegies.'" *MLR*, 61:357–68.
Shows that Donne derived much of his style from the classical love elegy, particularly in the use of the dramatic speaker. Discusses the relationship of the epigram and love–epistle to the elegy and the effect of this relationship on the amatory and satiric attitudes of the *Elegies*. Analyzes the conventions governing the drama and rhetoric of the elegy: self-awareness, role of *praeceptor amoris*, intimate recrimination, and the resting point or final state of equilibrium.

➡§ 1221. LOVE, HAROLD. "The Argument of Donne's *First Anniversary*." *MP*, 64:125–31.
Challenges Martz's criticism of the lack of integration between the meditation and eulogy sections of the poem. Reviews previous scholar-

ship. Sees Elizabeth Drury as both soul and heart of the world and considers the eulogies as recapitulations of both images. Discusses features of the classical *oratio iudicalis* (*narratio, refutatio, probatio*) and sees this structure reflected in the poem. Donne argues that the world is corrupt, and the crucial part of the *probatio* is the fact that Elizabeth Drury, the most perfect thing in the world, has had to endure corruption and death.

≈§ 1222. McCANLES, MICHAEL. "Distinguish in Order to Unite: Donne's 'The Extasie.'" *SEL*, 6:59–75.

Shows that the vehicle of the poem is based on the Neoplatonic doctrine of ecstasy while the tenor is Thomistic. Donne essentially affirms the union-amid-separation of the body—soul composite that is characteristic of Thomistic thinking, even though the fiction of the ecstasy allows him to show the body and soul as temporarily separated.

≈§ 1223. ———. "Paradox in Donne." *SRen*, 13:266–87.

Traces the conceptualist tradition that assumes "as the criterion for true knowledge a correspondence between the modes and structures of mental concepts and material objects" (p. 268). Notes the "place logic" of Agricola and Ramus and the light this throws on Donne's poems of paradox. Analyzes the arguments in "A Defence of Womens Inconstancy," "Confined Love," "The Flea," "Communitie," and "The Paradox" as examples of Ramistic "place logic."

≈§ 1224. MARTZ, LOUIS L. *The Poem of the Mind: Essays on Poetry, English and American*. New York: Oxford University Press, Inc. xiii, 231 p.

Contains three essays on Donne. (1) "John Donne: The Meditative Voice" (pp. 3–20). Reprinted from *MR*, 1 (1960):326–42. (2) "John Donne: A Valediction" (pp. 21–32). Originally entitled "Donne and the Meditative Tradition," *Thought*, 34 (1959):269–78. (3) "Meditative Action and 'The Metaphysick Style'" (pp. 33–53). Originally, in much shorter form, the introduction to *The Meditative Poem: An Anthology of Seventeenth-Century Verse* (New York, 1963). This essay also incorporates materials from an essay on "Hymne to God my God, in my sicknesse" written for *Master Poems of the English Language*, ed. Oscar Williams (New York, 1966).

≈§ 1225. MILGATE, W. "A Difficult Allusion in Donne and Spenser." *N&Q*, n.s., 13:12–14.

Comments on the legend of mice destroying elephants mentioned in *The Progresse of the Soule* (ll. 388–95). Suggests that the story derives from Garcias de Orta's *Aromatum, et simplicium aliquot medicamentorum apud indos nascentium Historia* (Antwerp, 1567).

1226. MILLER, CLARENCE H. "Donne's 'A Nocturnall upon S. Lucies Day' and the Nocturns of Matins." *SEL*, 6:77–86.

Discusses the way in which the poem draws upon the nocturns of the canonical hour of matins in both structure and content. "The quintal, trinal, and antiphonal form of these nocturns provided an allegorical pattern—what might be called nowadays a mythic scheme—of recreation and regeneration which Donne adapted in a 'ritual' lyric which traces with great subtlety and power the recreation of the mind destroyed by grief, the arduous course from utter desolation to expectant resignation" (p. 86).

1227. MORILLO, MARVIN. "Donne's Compasses: Circles and Right Lines." *ELN*, 3:173–76.

Argues that lines 32 and 36 both refer to the closing of the compasses in "A Valediction: forbidding mourning." Supports this position by referring to Platonic doctrine and to "The Extasie."

1228. PAFFORD, J. H. P. "An Early Donne Reference." *N&Q*, n.s., 13:377.

Points out that a copy of Martial's *Epigrams* printed at Leyden in 1661 contains two notes on Donne. Suggests that either Sir James Astry (1653–1709) or his son James (1675–1716) wrote the notes.

1229. POTTER, MABEL. "A Note on Donne." *N&Q*, n.s., 13:376–77.

In 1912, Grierson suggested changing the title of "Lovers Infiniteness" to "Loves Infiniteness." Points out that Dr. William Balam, who owned the Dobell MS. in the latter part of the seventeenth century, made such a change in the manuscript. Grierson, however, had no opportunity to see the manuscript.

1230. RAIZIS, M. BYRON. "The Epithalamion Tradition and John Donne." *Wichita State U. Bull.*, 62, No. 4:3–15.

Comments briefly on the epithalamion tradition in Greek (Sappho) and English (Spenser) and points out how Donne in his three epithalamia is original in his uses of the genre.

1231. RASPA, ANTHONY. "Distinctions in Poetry." *Cambridge Review*, 99:64–66.

Maintains that the critic must distinguish between the philosophy of poetry held by the poet and the particular techniques he uses to convey his ideas. Uses Donne and Sidney as examples. Argues that both poets shared some similar views on the nature of sacred poetry but differed in technique and aesthetics.

❧ 1232. RICKEY, MARY ELLEN. *Utmost Art: Complexity in the Verse of George Herbert*. Lexington: University of Kentucky Press. xv, 200 p.

Contains a list of Donne's classical allusions (pp. 185–87).

❧ 1233. RICKS, DON M. "The Westmoreland Manuscript and the Order of Donne's 'Holy Sonnets.'" *SP*, 63:187–95.

Maintains that the order of the *Holy Sonnets* as they appear in the Westmoreland MS. is preferable to the ordering suggested by Grierson and Gardner in their editions. Suggests that the poems are more closely related to structural techniques of the Elizabethan sonnet sequence than to the Ignatian meditation.

❧ 1234. ROBERTS, MARK. "If It Were Done When 'Tis Done . . . ." *EIC*, 16:309–29.

Review of *John Donne: The Elegies and the Songs and Sonnets*, ed. Helen Gardner (1965). For a reply by Alan MacColl, *EIC*, 17 (1967): 258–63, and a reply by Roberts, see *EIC*, 17 (1967):263–77.

❧ 1235. RUOTOLO, LUCIO P. "The Trinitarian Framework of Donne's Holy Sonnet XIV." *JHI*, 27:445–46.

Points out that the trinitarian perspective of the poem may be influenced by Thomas Aquinas' comments on the Trinity and on the nature of sanctifying grace.

❧ 1236. SERRANO PONCELA, SEGUNDO. "John Donne o la sensualidad." *Insula*, 21:1, 12.

General discussion of Donne's temperament and personality. Characterizes him as an apostate and sensualist. Comments on the elements of sensuality in the poetry and prose.

❧ 1237. SHAPIRO, I. A. "Donne's Books." *TLS*, 20 January, p. 48.

Reply to Leonard Forster, *TLS*, 9 December 1965, p. 1159.

Discusses Donne's acquaintance with Edward Parvish, to whom Donne gave a copy of Sebastian Munster's *Cosmographey*. Suggests that evidence is not strong enough to indicate that Donne knew German. See also John Sparrow, *TLS*, 25 November 1965, p. 1060.

❧ 1238. ———. "Donne, The Parvishes, and Munster's *Cosmographey*." *N&Q*, n.s., 13:243–48.

Traces the history of the Parvish family and comments on Donne's acquaintance with Edward Parvish, to whom Donne gave a copy of Munster's *Cosmographey*. Comments on Donne's references to Munster in several of his works. Suggests that there is reason to suppose that Donne went to Germany during his early travels.

◄§ 1239. SPARROW, JOHN. "Donne's Books." *TLS*, 6 January, p. 9.

In part, a reply to Leonard Forster, *TLS*, 9 December 1965, p. 1159. Also a reply to Clifford Dobb, *TLS*, 30 December 1965, p. 1213. Questions Donne's knowledge of German. Records another discovery of a book belonging to Donne: Girolamo Menghi's *Compendio dell' Arte Essorcistica* (Venice, 1599 and 1601). For a reply by Leonard Forster, see *TLS*, 27 January, p. 68.

◄§ 1240. ZIVLEY, SHERRY. "Imagery in John Donne's *Satyres*." *SEL*, 6: 87–95.

Discusses how the imagery of the *Satyres* differs from that of the *Songs and Sonets*. "In the Songs and Sonets Donne uses a technique which might be called centrifugal; that is the central image, or images which are closely knit together, creates imaginative forces that extend further and further from the center. In the *Satyres* Donne's technique is centripetal; the images are used to throw more and more emphasis in toward the thematic center, about which the images revolve" (pp. 89–90). Points out that the imagery of the *Satyres* "is drawn from a wide variety of experience, is used in many variations, contains an image within an image, and occasionally is used with anticlimax" (p. 91).

◄§ 1241. ZUBERI, ITRAT-HUSAIN. "John Donne's Concept of Toleration in Church and State." *UWR*, 1:147–58.

Considers Donne's theological position on tolerance "in relation to his concept of Reason, its relation to Faith, the limits of authority in the Church, and the attitude of the Church to indifferent things, things which were not necessary to salvation" (p. 147). Donne takes the position of the Christian humanist and argues for toleration on all nonfundamental issues in religion while affirming the necessity of preserving fundamental doctrines. Donne allows for schism but repudiates heresy; he allows for political differences but rejects treason.

1967

◄§ 1242. ANON. "Ill Donne. Well Donne." *TLS*, 6 April, pp. 277–80.

Review of *The Anniversaries*, ed. Frank Manley (1962), *John Donne's Lyrics*, Arnold Stein (1963), and *The Elegies and the Songs and Sonnets*, ed. Helen Gardner (1965). Deplores the present state of English studies and cites Manley and Stein as examples of parascholarship. Considers Helen Gardner's edition as an example of genuine scholarship but disagrees with many of her conclusions. See the following letters concerning the general topic of scholarship: John Holloway, *TLS*, 13 April 1967, p. 309; Edward LeComte, *TLS*, 11 May 1967, p. 399; L. P. Curtis, Jr., *TLS*, 18 May 1967, p. 424; Reviewer, *TLS*, 25 May 1967, p. 467; Helen Gardner, *TLS*, 8 June 1967, p. 509; Reviewer, *TLS*, 8 June 1967, p. 509; Helen

Gardner, *TLS*, 24 August 1967, p. 772; Reviewer, *TLS*, 24 August 1967, p. 772; Mark Roberts, *TLS*, 7 September 1967, p. 804.

⋖§ 1243. ALPHONSE, SISTER MARY. "Donne's 'Loves Growth.'" *Expl*, 25:Item 43.
Suggests that a consideration of the poem "reveals a symphony in the poem's form and matter: formally, through use of musical constituents; materially, through use of the image of the elements in harmony with the universe."

⋖§ 1244. ANDREASEN, N. J. C. *John Donne: Conservative Revolutionary*. Princeton: Princeton University Press. ix, 249 p.
Shows that Donne was revolutionary only in style but was conventional in his use of genres and in his ideas on love. Divides the *Elegies* and the *Songs and Sonets* into three groups: Ovidian, Petrarchan, and Christian Platonic. Traces and defines each and explicates a number of poems to show Donne's philosophy of love. Sees Ovidian love, with its emphasis on sex, and Petrarchan love, with its excessive idealism, as negative moral *exempla*. Christian Platonic love is the positive example of true love and complements or answers the other two. In Chapter III, "The Science of Lust," "Loves Alchymie," "Farewell to love," and other poems are treated as Ovidian examples condemning the misuse of sex. Chapter IV, "Idolatry and Sorrow," consists of explications of "A nocturnall upon S. Lucies day," "The Canonization," "The Extasie," and other poems and places them at the other extreme of the Ovidian group. Chapter V, "The Ideal on Earth," contains a discussion of "A Valediction: forbidding mourning," "The good-morrow," "Aire and Angels," and other poems as examples of the positive aspects of love. Concludes that Donne "gradually grew less conventional as a poet while he simultaneously intensified his understanding of the need for love which drives man and began to express a rather derivative vision of the way that need could be fulfilled" (p. 192).

⋖§ 1245. BLOCK, HASKELL M. "The Alleged Parallel of Metaphysical and Symbolist Poetry." *CLS*, 4:145–59.
Denies a basic parallel between metaphysical and symbolist poetry. Tries to account for the alleged likeness by reviewing T. S. Eliot, Cleanth Brooks, and others. Discusses those who deny the likeness and suggests properties of both kinds of poetry that prove them to be unlike. Uses Donne's "The Dreame" and Mallarmé's "Apparition" to show that Donne was not a symbolist and that Mallarmé was not a metaphysical.

◄§ 1246. BROICH, ULRICH. "Form und Bedeutung der Paradoxie im Werk John Donnes." *GRM*, n.s., 17:231–48.

Analyzes Donne's work from the standpoint of the different types of paradox that he employed. Distinguishes between (1) paradox for its own sake—formal paradox, (2) paradox in the love poetry—love paradox, and (3) paradox in the religious poetry—religious paradox. Donne's poetry is comparable in some respects to the work of modern poets and writers, for instance, to the drama of the absurd. Yet, through his paradoxes, Donne wants to portray a deeper meaning in life, whereas modern writers depict the absurdity of life.

◄§ 1247. COOK, RAYMOND A. "Is Donne's Metaphysical Poetry Really 'Metaphysical'?" in *Popular Fallacies in Chaucer and Donne: Two Essays* by Raymond A. Cook and Robert Hays. *Georgia State College School of Arts and Sciences Research Papers*, No. 16:7–9.

Considers the various definitions of metaphysical poetry proposed by Johnson, Eliot, Ransom, Tate, Brooks. Analyzes "A Valediction: forbidding mourning" and concludes that the term *metaphysical*, which frequently suggests excessiveness, is more properly applied to Donne's imitators than to Donne himself.

◄§ 1248. DICKER, HAROLD. "The Bell of John Donne." *Centennial Review*, 11:53–64.

Original poem that mentions Donne.

◄§ 1249. DOEBLER, BETTIE A. "Donne's Debt to the Great Tradition: Old and New in His Treatment of Death." *Anglia*, 85: 15–33

Examines Donne's sermon on the death of King James to separate the traditional elements in it from Donne's unique talent for symbol, imagery, structure, and "personal scrutiny of experience" (p. 32).

◄§ 1250. DONNE, JOHN. *John Donne: The Satires, Epigrams and Verse Letters.* Edited, with introduction and commentary, by W. Milgate. Oxford: The Clarendon Press. lxxvii, 296 p.

General introduction (pp. xvii–xl): I. Donne as Satirist (pp. xvii–xxv), II. *The Progress of the Soul* (pp. xxv–xxxiii), III. Donne as Moralist—The Verse Letters (pp. xxxiii–xl). Textual introduction (pp. xli–lxxiv). List of sigla (pp. lxxv–lxxvii). The Text (pp. 1–113). Commentary (pp. 114–280). Appendix A: Verbal Alterations in the *Satires, Epigrams,* and *Verse Letters* in the edition of 1635 (pp. 281–87). Appendix B: The Crux in "Satire II," ll. 71–72 (pp. 288–89). Appendix C: "Satire III," ll. 79–82 (pp. 290–92). Appendix D: The Authorship of "To the Countess of Huntington" (pp. 293–94). Index of first lines (pp. 295–96).

✑§ 1251. ELLRODT, ROBERT. "Nouvelle Édition de Donne." EA, 20:282–
89.
Review of John Donne: The Elegies and the Songs and Sonnets, ed.
Helen Gardner (1965).

✑§ 1252. EMPSON, WILLIAM. "Donne." CritQ, 9:89.
Short addenda to his review in CritQ, 8 (1966):255–80, of John Donne:
The Elegies and the Songs and Sonnets, ed. Helen Gardner (1965).

✑§ 1253. FRENCH, A. L. "Dr. Gardner's Dating of the Songs and Sonnets." EIC, 17:115–20.
Argues that Helen Gardner's dating of the Songs and Sonets in John
Donne: The Elegies and the Songs and Sonnets (1965) remains uncon-
vincing.

✑§ 1254. GAMBERINI, SPARTACO. Saggio su John Donne. Genova: Isti-
tuto di lingua e letteratura inglese e anglo-americana dell' Uni-
versità di Genova. 157 p.
General critical survey of Donne's poetry and prose. Appendices: (1)
Sulla datazione dei Songs and Sonets, (2) John Donne e noi, and (3)
Avvertenza bibliografica.

✑§ 1255. GARDNER, HELEN. "The Titles of Donne's Poems," in Friendship's Garland: Essays Presented to Mario Praz on His Seventieth
Birthday, ed. Vittorio Gabrielli, pp. 189–207. Vol. I. Roma: Ed-
izioni di Storia e Letteratura.
Points out that many of the titles of Donne's poems were supplied by
the early editors. Concludes that it is uncertain whether any of the titles
are his own and cautions critics who use them in interpreting the poems.

✑§ 1256. GIBBS, A. M. "A Davenant Imitation of Donne." RES, 18:45–
48.
Reports the discovery of a previously unpublished poem, assigned in
Ashmole's hand to Davenant, which is based on "Goe, and catche a
falling starre."

✑§ 1257. GIFFORD, WILLIAM. "Time and Place in Donne's Sermons."
PMLA, 82:388–98.
Shows that a consideration of time and place is relevant in many of
Donne's sermons. Examines the nature of the composition and publica-
tion of the sermons and the bearing that these have on their meaning.
Concludes that only a few changes from spoken to written word alter
the meaning. Many of the changes show greater tact, suggesting that
Donne had publication in mind. Examines two sermons for contemporary
references and the manner in which Donne dealt with them.

❧ 1258. HEATHERINGTON, MADELON E. "'Decency' and 'Zeal' in the
  Sermons of John Donne." *TSLL*, 9:307–16.
Analyzes Donne's uses of the words *decency* and *zeal* and their syn-
onyms and antonyms in the sermons. Concludes that Donne admired a
rightly applied religious zeal balanced by moderation, a position that
places him "slightly left of center of the conservative Anglican *via media*"
(p. 315).

❧ 1259. HUGHES, RICHARD E. "The Woman in Donne's *Anniversaries*."
  ELH, 34:307–26.
Sees the *Anniversaries* as a fruition of much of Donne's work. Suggests
that the poems were allowed to be published as memorials to Elizabeth
Drury, but they had been conceived and written as private meditations.
The woman in the poems is an archetype symbolized for Donne by Saint
Lucy, who represents rebirth.

❧ 1260. KAWASAKI, TOSHIHIKO. *The World of John Donne*. Tokyo:
  Kenkyusha. 274 p.
Chapter 1 explains how Donne was made mysterious by various critics
and scholars of the nineteenth and twentieth centuries, especially commenting on Eliot's criticism. Chapter 2 is a survey of various critical approaches and myths that have been used to describe Donne from his
own time to the twentieth century. Chapter 3 contains comments on
Donne's love philosophy, his idealism and cynicism, and in particular
deals with Empson's "Donne the Spaceman," *KR*, 19 (1957):337–99.
Chapter 4 is a survey of the nature of Donne's imagery and his uses of
metaphor, particularly the macrocosm–microcosm. Chapter 4 is a discussion of the macrocosm–microcosm images and includes a comparison of
Donne and Jonson as private and public poets. Chapter 5 is concerned
with Donne in the context of seventeenth-century intellectual milieu.
Chapter 6 contains comments on Donne's marriage, the occasion and
theme of the *Anniversaries*, and his general outlook in the early years of
the seventeenth century. Chapters 7 and 8 are a review of Donne's religious sensibility and a discussion of his life as a preacher.

❧ 1261. KOCH, WALTER A. "Linguistic Analysis of a Satire." *Linguis-
  tics*, 33:68–81.
Detailed linguistic analysis of *Satyre II*.

❧ 1262. LOVE, HAROLD. "Donne's 'To His Mistris Going to Bed,' 45."
  Expl, 26:Item 33.
Suggests that in lines 45–46 of "Elegie XIX," Donne is alluding to the
white sheet of penance worn by whores and adulterers who were sentenced
by the ecclesiastical courts to do penance.

1263. MacColl, Alan, and Mark Roberts. "The New Edition of Donne's Love Poems." *EIC*, 17:258–78.

Discusses editing questions that arise in *John Donne: The Elegies and the Songs and Sonnets*, ed. Helen Gardner (1965). The first essay (pp. 258–63) is a reply to Mark Roberts, *EIC*, 16 (1966):309–29. The second (pp. 263–77) is a reply by Roberts.

1264. Machett, William H. "Donne's 'Peece of Chronicle.' " *RES*, n.s., 18:290–92.

Explicates line 31 of "The Canonization." Suggests that the word *peece* may be a triple pun—masterpiece, fragment, fortress.

1265. Mueller, Janel M. "A Borrowing of Donne's Christmas Sermon of 1621." *HLQ*, 30:207–16.

Points out through a close comparison of texts that John Cosin borrowed extensively in his own Christmas sermon of 1651 from Donne's sermon of 1621.

1266. Nomachi, Susumu. "John Donne: Struggle Behind the Mask of Sarcasm." *Critical Studies* (Gakushin U., Tokyo).

This item was unavailable.

1267. Pagnini, Marcello. "Sulle funzioni semilogische della poesia di John Donne." *Lingua e Stile*, 2:159–78.

Stylistic study of Donne's poetry. Comments on the symmetrical, phonological, lexical, and syntactic patterns in the poems and proposes that the often noted roughness of the metrics and the contorted syntax may well be due to Donne's desire to create symmetry at the semeiological level rather than to produce a "low" or proselike style. With the aid of texts on poetic theory from Donne's contemporaries (mainly Tesauro's *Il Cannocchiale aristotelico*) shows how the conception of the importance of form for its own sake was central to baroque poetic theory. Finds that in Donne, however, the semeiological level of meaning has two functions: (1) at times it dissociates itself from the signifié and seems to exist only for the joy found in its elaboration, and (2) at other times it puts itself at the service of the significant and assumes an important expressive role.

1268. Peterson, Douglas L. *The English Lyric from Wyatt to Donne: A History of the Plain and Eloquent Styles.* Princeton: Princeton University Press. vi, 391 p.

Traces the development of the sixteenth-century lyric, stressing the medieval origins of the plain and eloquent style, and accounting for the changes and the relative position of importance of both. Chapter VIII,

"John Donne," places the poet in the plain tradition with respect to manner and attitude and shows his indebtedness to the courtly tradition only for themes and conventions. Describes his poetic characteristics as a representative of the cultural center of the Inns of Court. Discusses the *Songs and Sonets* as serious poems, not just witty exercises, stressing Donne's Aristotelian view of the relation of body and soul and seeing some of his conceits as ways to vindicate the interdependence of the two. Examines his anti-Platonism as "alarums to truth." Discusses Donne's rejection of the dichotomy between sacred and profane love. Discusses the *Holy Sonnets* as "poetry of self-expression" written in the plain style and comments on Donne's use of the meditational mode. Agrees with Helen Gardner's sequential ordering of the *Holy Sonnets* and discusses in detail the meaning of this sequence as an effort to arrive at the feeling of contrition.

&§ 1269. ROSCELLI, WILLIAM JOHN. "The Metaphysical Milton (1625–1631)." *TSLL*, 8:463–84.

Cites three major areas of difference between Donne and Milton: (1) purpose of imagery, (2) treatment of ideas, and (3) language and versification. Limits possible metaphysical influence on Milton to the years 1625–1631 and concludes that (1) Milton was not influenced by Donne specifically; (2) in only six poems does he employ metaphysical images, and these are restricted to the subject of death; and (3) some of these images parallel Herbert, but the likenesses are not strong enough to suggest a direct influence.

&§ 1270. SACKTON, ALEXANDER. "Donne and the Privacy of Verse." *SEL*, 7:67–82.

Examination of Donne's verse letters to a few friends of similar background that shows Donne expressed "a sense of the privacy of poetry as a method of self-exploration and of intimate communication. In being set and sung to music, the poem is in a sense violated, publicized, and destroyed . . . poetry was used by friends as a private language" (p. 80).

&§ 1271. SCHWARTZ, ELIAS. "Donne's 'Holy Sonnets,' XIV." *Expl*, 26: Item 27.

Disagrees with those critics who find the doctrine of the Trinity as the controlling idea of the sonnet. Shows how the three major metaphors of the poem—the tinker of the first quatrain, the beseiged town of the second, and the nuptial metaphor of the third—"promote by their very nature our awareness of the dramatic-spiritual progression in the speaker."

✒ 1272. SHAPIRO, I. A. "Donne in 1605–06." *TLS*, 26 January, p. 76.

Presents evidence to show that Donne went abroad with Sir Walter Chute in 1605–1606. During this period his wife moved from Pyrford to Peckham. Suggests an estrangement between Donne and Sir Francis Wolley, his wife's cousin.

✒ 1273. SHAWCROSS, JOHN T. "John Donne and Drummond's Manuscripts." *AN&Q*, 5:104–5.

Points out several previously unnoticed matters concerning Donne in the Hawthornden MSS. of William Drummond.

✒ 1274. STANDAERT, ERICH. "Ik schrijf je neder op papier: Hugo Claus in het teken van 'Een Vrouw.'" *Ons Erfdeel*, 11:28–47.

Discusses Claus and his poem, "Een Vrouw," including a translation of the poem into French. Some general remarks about Donne with special reference to "Elegie XIX: Going to Bed." Maintains that the physical description in Claus's poem is not erotic or at any rate not more so than Donne's. Suggests that the two poets represent two phases of love poetry in western Europe. Both seem to have written to express the same basic experience, which makes them spiritual comrades despite their different nationalities and the centuries separating them.

✒ 1275. STANWOOD, G. P. "A Donne Discovery." *TLS*, October 19, p. 984.

Reports the discovery of a Latin epigram by Donne found in the Hunter manuscript collection in the Cathedral Library of Durham. The poem satirizes the canonization of Saint Ignatius Loyola. Reproduces the epigram, gives a prose translation, and comments on the poem. See also an article by Carlo Dionisotti in *TLS*, November 2, 1967.

✒ 1276. VIZIOLI, PAULO. "A poesia latina de Donne." *ESPSL*, 4:n.p.

Explains why Donne's Latin poems have been generally neglected and analyzes several of them. Suggests that Donne's English poetry influenced his Latin verse, not vice versa. Finds in the Latin poems the kind of subtlety and wit that characterize the English pieces. Argues that if Donne had written more Latin verse, he might have been the most important representative of baroque Latin poetry.

✒ 1277. WARNKE, F. J. "Baroque Poetry and the Experience of Contradiction." *Colloquia Germanica*, 1:38–48.

Discusses the theme of contradition as it is related to both metaphysical and high baroque poetry. Suggests that both manners, while distinctive in some ways, are rooted in the same habit of mind and same conception of art. Shows how Donne's particular version of the baroque manner is exemplified in "Lovers infinitenesse" and the closing lines of

"Batter my heart." Unlike the high baroque poets, Donne does not approach the subject "through a phantasmagoric world of sensory experience but through a rigorously intellectual concentration on paradox" (p. 44).

❧§ 1278. WHITLOCK, BAIRD W. "From the Counter-Renaissance to the Baroque." *BuR*, 15:46–60.

Discusses the differences between sixteenth- and seventeenth-century art forms. Points out examples of some of the baroque characteristics in Donne's poetry.

❧§ 1279. WILLIAMSON, GEORGE. *Six Metaphysical Poets: A Reader's Guide*. New York: Farrar, Straus and Giroux. 274 p.

General introduction to Donne with short paraphrases of 39 poems.

❧§ 1280. WOLFE, RALPH HAVEN, AND EDGAR F. DANIELS. "Rime and Idea in Donne's Holy Sonnet X." *AN&Q*, 5:116–17.

Shows that not only the imagery but also the rhyme scheme of "Holy Sonnet X" maintains the delicate tension between its major and minor themes.

Author Index

Subject Index

(The following is an index of subjects mentioned in the annotations in this bibliography. The reader is advised to check all general studies related to a specific topic.)

Index of Donne's Works
Mentioned in Annotations

About the Author

John R. Roberts is a Professor of English at the University of Missouri —Columbia. He received his B.A. (1955) from Indiana State University, and his M.A. (1957) and Ph.D. (1962) from the University of Illinois.

Professor Roberts edited A *Critical Anthology of English Recusant Devotional Prose, 1558–1603*, which was published in 1966 by the Duquesne University Press, Pittsburgh, Pennsylvania. His writings have also appeared in *Journal of English and Germanic Philology, Comparative Literature Studies, College Language Association Journal, The Month*, and *Studies in Burke and His Time*.